Problem
Management

a guide for producers and players

Problem Management

a guide for producers and players

Jim Bryant
Sheffield City Polytechnic

JOHN WILEY & SONS

Chichester · New York · Brisbane · Toronto · Singapore

Other Wiley Editorial Offices

John Wiley & Sons, Inc., 605 Third Avenue,
New York, NY 10158-0012, USA

Jacaranda Wiley Ltd, G.P.O. Box 859, Brisbane,
Queensland 4001, Australia

John Wiley & Sons (Canada) Ltd, 22 Worcester Road,
Rexdale, Ontario M9W 1L1, Canada

John Wiley & Sons (SEA) Pte Ltd, 37 Jalan Pemimpin   05-04,
Block B, Union Industrial Building, Singapore 2057

Library of Congress Cataloging-in-Publication Data:

Bryant, Jim W.
   Problem management: a guide for producers and players.
      p.   cm.
   Bibliography: p.
   Includes indexes.
   ISBN 0-471-91792-3
   1. Problem solving.   I. Title.
HD30.29.B79   1989   89-9050
658.4′03—dc20   CIP

British Library Cataloguing in Publication Data

Bryant, Jim
   Problem management: a guide for producers and players.
   1. Man. Problem solving
   I. Title
   153.4′3
   ISBN 0-471-91792-3

Typeset by APS, Salisbury, Wiltshire
Printed and bound in Great Britain by Courier International Ltd, Tiptree, Essex

Contents

Acknowledgements   xi

Introduction   1

    User's Guide   2

PART ONE: PROBLEMS

CHAPTER ONE: Where are problems?   7

    Problem ownership   11
    The search for meaning   14
    Accessing individual meanings   15
    Understanding problem spotters   16
    Social meanings   19
    Personal meanings   24
    The individual construction of reality   26
    Tailpiece   27

CHAPTER TWO: Experiencing problems   29

    Interpreting experience   30
    Discrepant evidence   32
    The construal of anomalies   35
    Retreat from fantasy   39
    Juggling concerns   41
    Social interaction   46
    Tailpiece   49

PART TWO: HANDLING PROBLEMS

CHAPTER THREE: Treating problems in practice and theory   53

    Alarms and excursions   54
    Customary repetitions   56
    Square pegs, round holes   59

Unfamiliar territory   61
Thinking problems through   63
Thinking about thinking   64
Critique of pure reason   69
Tailpiece   72

CHAPTER FOUR: Sharing our confusions   75

Clearing up problems   79
Perils of the mess   81
No man an island   84
Presenting problems   85
Inveiglemanship   91
The ramified model   93
Commonwealth   94
Tailpiece   98

PART THREE: HELP WITH PROBLEMS

CHAPTER FIVE: Supporting roles   103

Problem labelling   104
Nominating helpers   105
Passing the buck   107
Consulting the sage   109
Inviting systematic enquiry   111
Canvassing opinion   113
Asking for ideas   114
The leaky paradigm   114
Subversive colleagues   116
Tame morphologists   118
Band leaders   119
Managers of debate   119
Tailpiece   120

CHAPTER SIX: Interaction in organizational interventions   123

Negotiating the situation   124
Casting the intervention   126
Moderating involvement   128
Contracting to work together   132
Effecting intervention   134
Roles around interventions   135
Parts in interventions   139
Patterns of interaction   142
Assessing an intervention   144
Finishing off   148
Tailpiece   150

PART FOUR: PRACTISING PROBLEM MANAGEMENT

CHAPTER SEVEN: Frameworks for problem consultation 155

The archaeology of operational research 156
Loss of nerve 158
Contending imaginations 159
The purpose of intervention 161
Guiding frameworks 163
Help through problems: a topography 165
Classifying approaches 170
Tailpiece 171

CHAPTER EIGHT: Problem management in performance 173

Intervention as theatre 175
Dramatis personae 176
Audience 179
Mise en scène 180
    Time – the present 181
    Costume 182
    Set design 183
    Lighting and effects 188
    Properties 188
    Refreshments 192
Actually performing 193
    Backstage 193
    Pace 195
    Timing 197
    Critique 198
Capturing expressions 200
    Structuring debate 200
    Gathering evidence 202
    Patterning meanings 204
Becoming a problem manager 206
Tailpiece 208

PART FIVE: LET'S DO IT!

LDI for Introduction 213
LDI for Chapter One 215
LDI for Chapter Two 225
LDI for Chapter Three 237
LDI for Chapter Four 253
LDI for Chapter Five 273

LDI for Chapter Six   279

LDI for Chapter Seven   297

LDI for Chapter Eight   301

CODA: Reader's digest   311

References   317

Permissions   327

Author Index   333

Subject Index   337

To Abigail

*who appeared
during Chapter Four*

Acknowledgements

I have lived with this book for many years now, though only recently has it taken tangible form. It has been a largely private affair – until this moment – and one that, like most relationships, has had its times both of intense satisfaction and of intense exasperation. Over this same period, others have encountered us, sometimes directly, sometimes quite unknowingly, and helped to fashion what went on between us, usually for the better.

The beginnings owe much to the congenial environment created by Pat Rivett at Sussex, and to the exciting opportunities which I subseq ently encountered in Sheffield, where Peter Long has been an invaluable source of support and encouragement. In Sheffield too I have been patiently assisted by successive cohorts of long-suffering students (and staff), who have taken part in problem management exercises and made helpfully irreverent comments about them. Most recently I have had the benefit of Graham Jones's thoughtful comments for which I am most grateful. No less significant has been the support of others in the wider context of Operational Research (OR), who have done much to create a climate in which the ideas presented here can be advanced: to Jonathan Rosenhead, George Mitchell, Colin Thunhurst and Dick Martin I owe special thanks. However, my greatest indebtedness must be to that crowd of irregulars with whom I have shared some of the most stimulating and worthwhile intellectual explorations (and some of the most unbalanced meals and varied lodgings) during the past five years: namely Peter Bennett, Ken Bowen, Steve Cropper, Colin Eden, John Friend, Allen Hickling, Chris Huxham, Sue Jones and Bill Mayon-White. Without them this book could not have been written.

No book is just a matter of words: it is always the outcome of a lengthy production process. In the present case this has been pulled along (screaming quietly at times) by Diane Taylor at Wileys, who has exercised a calm but persistently persuasive influence upon me to complete the manuscript. Along the way the process has been prompted (not to say jarred) – and I believe the content much improved – by the publisher's anonymous reviewers as well as by kind friends and colleagues who have offered comments on earlier drafts. And nearest to home of all – indeed at home — I have found support of another kind from Hazel, who has provided not only sympathy, but also the gallons of tea and quantities of cakes which are essential to such an undertaking.

Thanks to all of you for shaping this story.

JIM BRYANT

Sheffield,
December 1988

Introduction

'NICOLA: "Write something new, Philip. You should write something else."
MARLOW: "Oh? Like what?"
NICOLA: "Like *this* – what has happened to you. Like real things."
MARLOW: "Pooh."
NICOLA: "*Use* your talent, Philip."
MARLOW: "Bugger that!"
NICOLA: "Write about real things in a realistic way – real people, real joys, real pains – Not these silly detective stories. Something more relevant."
MARLOW: (*With contempt*) "Solutions."
NICOLA: "What —?"
MARLOW: "All solutions, and no clues. That's what the dumb-heads want. That's the bloody Novel – He said, she said, and descriptions of the sky – I'd rather it was the other way around. All clues. No solutions. That's the way things are. Plenty of clues. No solutions."'

Dennis Potter—*The Singing Detective*

You are faced with problems: we all are. This book offers no solutions. It is neither a manual for trouble shooting nor a field guide for observers. Instead I have set out an itinerary which begins from the matter-of-fact character of problems and which leads through to the hazardous arena of problem management. Along the way, I have sought to show how you can use new conceptual frameworks to orchestrate some individual or social processes and generate a dialectic that will help in your own journey on this tricky path. You need this book then, in the everyday business of handling the complex problems presented by both professional and private life.

My intention has been to write a text that will have wide appeal. Nevertheless, it should be of special interest to those who operate (or who, as students, aspire to operate) as problem-helpers in organizational settings. In particular those whose aim is to support the process of decision in small autonomous groups of any kind – whether these clients be a board of directors, a middle management working party, a project team, or the committee of a social association – should find something of value to them here. In formal organizations those who work under such labels as corporate planning, management services, operational research, systems design, organizational development or personnel training, may find ideas in this book to help them in their roles. Elsewhere, I hope that this text will reach those who are grappling with problems beyond the reach of such consultancy support, but who wish nevertheless to address their disquiet in a systematic and structured manner. In summary, it is directed both at those who are producers and at those who are players in the drama of problem management.

User's Guide

It would be outrageous of me to suggest how you should use this book. In any case you have probably flicked through its pages and seen something of its content, so you will have formed your own opinions already. However, it may help you to decide what strategy to adopt if I explain how I have structured it, and say a little about some of the notation which I have used.

The main body of text is essentially in two sections, though you will not immediately see this reflected in the Contents. The first section, which contains Chapters One to Four, is about the day-to-day business of facing and handling problems. The second section, which contains Chapters Five to Eight, is about assisted problem management: that is, about working through problems with expert support. This overall structure is shown in Figure 0.1.

Within each of the major sections there are two parts, and these in turn each consist of two chapters: they are shown in Figure 0.1. Part 1 addresses the nature of problems and comes to the conclusion that as idiosyncratic visions they can only be fully understood through the eyes of the person who identifies them. In Part 2, attention shifts to consider how people usually deal with problems whether alone or with others, and highlights some of the dangerous simplifications that are made. The second section opens with a review, in Part 3, of the supporting roles which are available to those who seek to assist others with problems. This leads into the fuller consideration, in Part 4, of a dialectical role for a problem-helper, and a detailed examination of each aspect of the problem management intervention which such an individual might help to shape.

I have used a variety of devices to illuminate the material. First, you will notice that the text is punctuated by occasional extracts, like the one which heads this Introduction. These are intended to cut through the more serious narrative and to throw a fresh light on the subject under discussion. If they irritate you or you cannot see their relevance, just ignore them. Second, you will notice that occasionally symbols like this appear in the text:

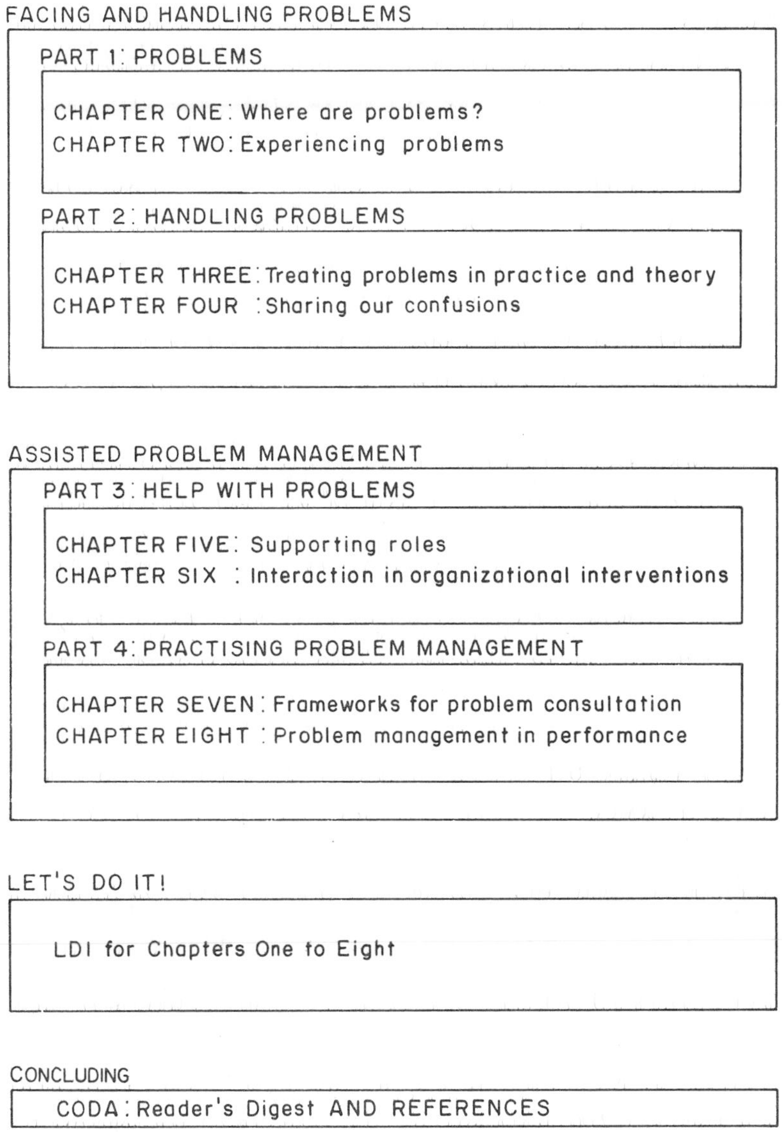

FACING AND HANDLING PROBLEMS

PART 1: PROBLEMS

CHAPTER ONE: Where are problems?
CHAPTER TWO: Experiencing problems

PART 2: HANDLING PROBLEMS

CHAPTER THREE: Treating problems in practice and theory
CHAPTER FOUR : Sharing our confusions

ASSISTED PROBLEM MANAGEMENT

PART 3: HELP WITH PROBLEMS

CHAPTER FIVE: Supporting roles
CHAPTER SIX : Interaction in organizational interventions

PART 4: PRACTISING PROBLEM MANAGEMENT

CHAPTER SEVEN: Frameworks for problem consultation
CHAPTER EIGHT : Problem management in performance

LET'S DO IT!

LDI for Chapters One to Eight

CONCLUDING

CODA: Reader's Digest AND REFERENCES

Figure 0.1. Structure of this book

These are pointers to a substantial section of practical materials which follow the main exposition. For obvious reasons, I have called them 'Let's Do It's. Each time you come to one of these symbols, you may find it interesting to refer to the appropriate **LDI** at the back. Try this now with the one indicated above. . . . As you can see though, the LDIs cal also be skipped if you would prefer just to read through the main narrative: the choice is yours. The third feature which you will notice may be found at the end of each chapter (including this one). These so-called ideographs provide a concluding visual summary of the chapter.

Finally, there is a Coda at the back of the book which gives an abstract of its whole argument, and a References section in which all materials cited elsewhere in the book are given in full.

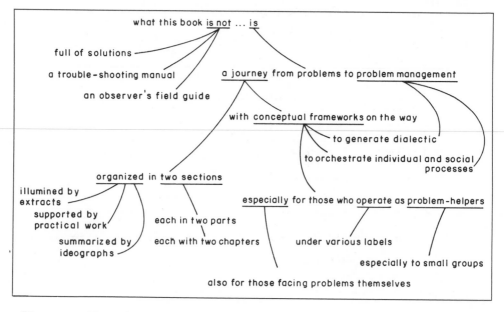

Diagram 0.1. Ideograph zero

PART ONE:

Problems

CHAPTER ONE

Where are problems?

It has become commonplace to label certain sorts of situation as 'problems'. This is a comparatively recent phenomenon, for the tag has only become fashionable during the past few decades: previous generations might have talked of a difficulty, a misfortune or a vexation.

> In her last, and perhaps least successful novel, Agatha Christie, then in her late eighties, spoke through the mouth of one of her elderly charac ters about this modern habit:
> 'Who introduced problems? Really it's Elizabeth. The cleaning help we had before Beatrice. She was always coming to me and saying, "Oh madam, could I speak to you a minute? You see I've got a problem," and then Beatrice began coming on Thursdays and she must have caught it, I suppose. So she has problems too. It's just a way of saying something–but you always call it a problem.'
>
> Agatha Christie   *Postern of Fate*

Like many commonplace words, 'problem' is an elusive term to pin down for examination. Reference to any serious dictionary will yield half-a-dozen earnestly obscurantist definitions. Most of these suggest that problems are confined to those ivory towers in which it is still economically viable to pose questions for academic or philosophical discussion. Some authorities, affecting a more wordly manner, say that a problem is something to be solved; but in the cross-reference state with tautological unhelpfulness that a solution is an answer to a problem, thereby closing the lexicographical circle. Neither explanation would attract much acclaim from a layman, for whom the word "problem" artlessly attaches to those situations where circumstances confound action and doubt clouds decision.

1.1

Looking elsewhere, a promising lead might appear to lie in the field of cognitive science, where the process of problem solving has come into vogue for intense research activity by psychologists, computer scientists and others. In this discipline, a problem has typically been characterized (Mayer, 1983) as a situation in which a gap or discrepancy between some initial state and a goal state needs to be bridged.

Such a definition owes much to the pioneering work of Newell and Simon (Newell, Shaw and Simon, 1958) and their attempts to develop a general theory of human problem solving. This was conceived initially in the context of such well-defined problems as those encountered in the game of chess. The cognitive science perspective has suggested various taxonomies of problems: for instance, Reitman (1965) has proposed a categorization based upon how well specified each of the two terminal

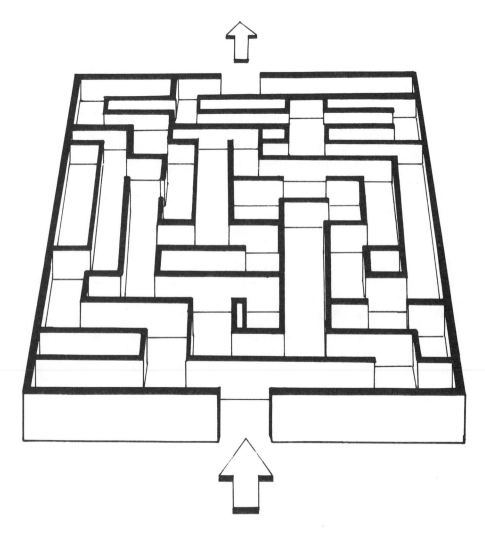

states is in any particular situation. Unfortunately, this sort of definition, with its targeting emphasis – an emphasis well characterized by Simon's (1985) view that 'a human being is confronted with a problem when he has accepted a task but does not know how to carry it out' – tends to provoke a design engineering response, rather than stimulating any more fundamental questions about the 'given'ness of the problem. Eventually, taking problems as 'accepted tasks' leads us into a cul-de-sac inhabited only by those abstract, logical, linguistic or mathematical problems which can survive in a contextual vacuum.

Information processing theories of problem management appear to be of value if we wish to investigate well-structured problems, for which the main issue is the identification of a solution or of a solution heuristic (Cohen, 1983). However, they appear to be of limited usefulness in approaching less clearly structured situations. Since we are concerned in this book with the management of those problems with which people are confronted in their everyday lives, well-structured puzzles [or 'exercises' as Ackoff and Emery (1972) have termed such conundrums] are usually of restricted interest, except in so far as we can draw upon the analytical skills which we may develop in solving them, or use them to learn about cognitive processes in laboratory settings. In order to clarify the distinction which I am making here between different types of problem, it may be useful to adopt two terms coined by Rittel and Webber (1973) in their influential treatise on policy planning: the concepts of 'tame' and 'wicked' problems. Briefly, tame problems are those which can be unambiguously stated and exhaustively formulated and which can be meaningfully isolated from their environment. By contrast, for wicked problems there is an irresoluble uncertainty over the appropriate level of description, no possibility of achieving a definitive formulation, and an absence of criteria for bounding the situation in either time or space. Employing these terms, our interest can be restated as being with the management of wicked problems, a matter for which, as we have seen, we shall need to look beyond the confines of current computer models of human thinking.

Beginning afresh in considering the nature of 'real' problems, we can obtain a more practically revealing insight by asking a group of people to indicate the connotations which the word 'problem' has for them. A rich portfolio of associations will probably be generated. I have shown the results of one particular exercise of this sort in Figure 1.1, which portrays the intuitive links which the central 'problem' label has with other concepts.

Usually there will be explicit mention of such notions as 'obstacles', 'objectives' and 'solutions', and implicit reference to the concepts of 'change', 'choice' and 'uncertainty'. 'Problem' is obviously what Humpty Dumpty would call a 'portmanteau' word, and one of some distinction; it carries within it a host of meanings, some of which as we shall see later are dangerously unhelpful.

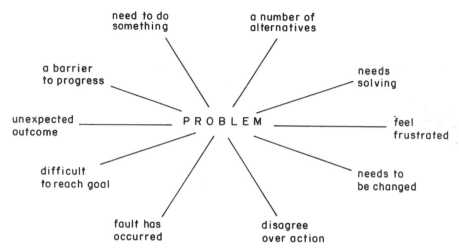

Figure 1.1. Some connotations of the label 'problem'

Since Mr Dumpty appears to be paying the word problem so much money that it is simply laden with meanings, it is not obvious how to pursue this line of investigation. Instead, I shall attempt to wriggle out of the definitional mire by means of a trick which will at the same time serve the purpose of alerting you to the philosophical stance that informs the whole of this book. Rather than concentrating upon the nature of problems, as though they were an element of mental flora or fauna to be characterized by some neo-Linnean nomenclature, I shall instead begin focusing upon the related (but somewhat simpler!) matter of considering the conditions under which a problem is said to exist. This investigative volte-face also stresses my readiness to concentrate upon the mental processes of observers, rather than upon the denizens of some external world of reality, a position which will be further justified and developed shortly.

Problem Ownership

Problems do have an uncanny knack of appearing and disappearing in the most disconcerting manner. How can this be? The reason for this slippery behaviour stems from their very nature: for problems have their genesis, not in the world 'out there', but rather within each one of us. *I am a Camera* was the title of a famous 1950s film: in a very real sense we are all cameras which encounter, frame and capture scenes from our experiences – some of these we term 'problems'.

No situation is *per se* a problem. Faced with a non-functioning motor-car engine on a cold, damp, winter's day, I may talk about a problem, where a motor mechanic may see a challenge, and a new car salesman may see an opportunity. At a common-sense level, we would all claim to be addressing the 'same' situation, but we would each view what was going on from our individual perspectives, and so would characterize it differently.

with apologies to Charles Schulz

On some occasions, the difference in perspective may be so sharp that those elements which for one party constitute a problem, are not even recognized, still less construed as a problem by others. Walking upon the Lakeland Fells I may not have the experience or the perspicacity to recognize in the sky above me the seeds of an impending storm, signs which are clearly apparent to a shepherd whom I pass: he sees me as foolhardy, yet I am so lacking in vision that such a judgement is unduly harsh. Our polarity of viewpoints simply provides wildly contrasting denominations of experience.

'Take a settlement house in a lower-class slum district trying to wean away teenagers from the publicly disapproved activities of a juvenile gang. The frame of reference within which social workers and police officers define the "problems" of this situation is constituted by the world of middle-class, respectable, publicly approved values. It is a "problem" if teenagers drive around in stolen automobiles, and it is a "solution" if instead they will play group games in the settlement house. But if one changes the frame of reference and looks at the situation from the viewpoint of the leaders of the juvenile gang, the "problems" are defined in reverse order. It is a "problem" for the solidarity of the gang if its members are seduced away from those activities that lend prestige to the gang within its own social world, and it would be a "solution" if the social workers went away to hell back uptown where they came from. What is a "problem" to one social system is the normal routine of things to the other system, and vice versa. Loyalty and disloyalty, solidarity and deviance, are defined in contradictory terms by representatives of the two systems.'

Peter Beger   *Invitation to Sociology*

Even when two people do agree that a situation is in some way problematic, it does not, of course, mean that they have identified the same problem. You and I may agree that there is a chronic problem of unemployment, but on deeper discussion we may find that we each mean quite different things by this term: for me the problem is about a lack of jobs, for you about an archaic notion of work; further compounding our differences, we may consequentially define and measure "unemployment" in contrasting ways. Because of the contrast in our perceptual filtering of circumstances and in our interpretation of events, we have recognized and shaped the salience of different features.

Manifestly, it is impossible to separate a description of a problem from the person who provides it: problems belong to people. The term 'problem-owner' will be used here to indicate the individual who has this sense of 'problem' about a situation. A problem-owner's unique conception of a situation and attribution to it of the label 'problem' are, by this definition, unchallengeable. Thus all problems have the complete legitimacy which their creation confers. [I would take issue here with Mason and Mitroff (1981) who suggest that the two classic observational errors of omission and of commission can occur in problem identification: this is logically impossible if we take the view that problems are artefacts which the problem-owner creates.] A further corollary of the definition is that the problem-owner must at some point have been aware of the problem. [I here differ from Checkland (1981) who envisages that an external 'analyst' might assign the role of problem-owner to someone who does not himself recognize his ownership of a problem: while we might colloquially say, 'Well, that's his problem', in talking of a situation, what we mean is that we identify a problematic situation to which someone else must attend – but it is no less a problem of *our* creation and ownership.] In other words, we cannot own problems unbeknownst to ourselves. Problem-owners create problems and are central to their understanding.

So far then we have determined that problems are said to exist when individuals choose to say that they do! For all its apparent triteness, the preceding discussion will have limned out some of the non-obvious implications of this stance, and shown its practical relevance: an individual can shout 'Problem!' whenever or wherever he wishes. We now need to consider why anyone should do so.

The Search for Meaning

I begin from the proposition that the concept of a 'problem' is a fundamental expression of the human experience. That is, it is a manifestation of our individual attempts to make sense of 'what is going on' for us.

Evidence for our need to rationalize experience appears in many places. In 1386 a pig, formally dressed in jacket and breeches, was publicly hanged before a crowd in the market square of Falaise in Normandy. The wretched creature had caused the death of a child, but only after judicial deliberation and an argued defence was the verdict, guilty of murder, reached, and sentence of execution passed. The trial was by no means unusual. Animals were frequently brought to European courts right up to the ninteenth century, accused of crimes ranging from murder to theft, sacrilege and obscenity, and resulting in sentences of hanging, maiming and ecclesiastical excommunication. As Humphrey suggests in his introduction to the re-issue of the classic text in this subject (Evans, 1986), what appears to lie behind this apparently strange phenomenon was not the motivation of punishment, revenge or deterrence, but instead the need to explain the social meaning of the 'criminal' behaviour: to provide a rationale for what had happened. It was the role of the medieval courts to attach meaning to events so that society might establish cognitive control: to set order upon an otherwise random and irrational world. Today perhaps we do not live as close to the edge of explanatory darkness and need less reassurance that not everything is possible at the hands of God the dice man. Nevertheless, any approach to problem management which fails to recognize the human yearning for explanation and search for causes, does not have the advantage of historical support.

The organization and classification of experienced reality is a fundamental human characteristic. By imposing order upon the flood of incoming experience we create for ourselves the artifactual worlds in which we live (Vickers, 1970). Problem identification is but one way in which we individually categorize or label certain sorts of experience. We tend to use the 'problem' label at those times when we are uncomfortable with the way things appear to be and when we are unsure how to handle these feelings. The grouping together of diverse situations in this manner is apparently essential if we are to cope with the richness of experience which life throws in our direction, although, as we shall see later, there are hazards in such a practice.

We must conclude that the incidence of problems has to be approached as one aspect of a wider search for the personal meaning of individual experience. Such an approach is well in keeping with our times: as Checkland (1981) has suggested, the concept of 'meaning' appears to be a pivot in the history of ideas that will lead us through into the next millenium, and that will affect both the nature of the world and the way we perceive it.

Accessing Individual Meanings

A concern with the subjective meanings of deliberate individual actions has been a keynote of twentieth-century thought. It comes to us through two distinct but related traditions which deserve a brief introduction.

The Weberian tradition of academic sociology centres upon the social action of individuals, and superficially contrasts with the objective study and explanation of social facts at the level of the group, which is associated with the school of Max Weber's contemporary, Emile Durkheim. People act, Weber believed, with deliberate intention to affect the behaviour of others. It is the meanings which these social actions have for individuals that provide the material of Weberian study: the knee-jerk observational theories offered by behaviouralists are, in this view, simply inappropriate for explaining social life. Weber's insight was that through placing oneself in the position of those individuals involved in a situation and recognizing the personal meanings which they attach to their experiences – the so-called method of *Verstehen* – one could begin to analyse, interpret and explain social action. This stance is therefore concerned with subjective experience rather than with objective data.

The second tradition to be mentioned here can be traced back to the works of Lambert and Hegel in the eighteenth and nineteenth centuries, but is now particularly associated with Edmund Husserl: it is the approach of phenomenology (Spiegelberg, 1982). Husserl's central focus was upon our thinking about the world, rather than upon the taken-for-granted 'external' reality, with which the contrasting positivist tradition was obsessed. For Husserl, attention was therefore directed to the *Lebenswelt* (Lewin, 1951) – the fullness of the individual's sensory, affective and cognitive experience – and he proposed the process of phenomenological reduction as a way of accessing and examining this experience. Essentially, the process is for the investigator to 'bracket' – that is self-consciously to insulate and suspend – the subject's *Lebenswelt* and to be open to it in a way which takes nothing for granted and which makes no prior assumptions. Recently, Massarik (1983) has proposed an extension of this approach in the creation of a 'double-bracketed' framework: in this the investigator first brackets his own *Lebenswelt* before attempting to experience the essence of the subject's world. Applied phenomenology therefore provides a rationale for unfolding the unique meanings of individual experience.

These two socio-philosophical streams are remarkably paralleled and reconciled in hermeneutics, the craft of interpreting the artefacts of human consciousness, perhaps most closely associated with Dilthey. The fundamental methodology of hermeneutics is expressed in the idea of the 'hermeneutic circle', a continuous process through which we engage in a dialogue with the world of our experiences. Essentially this suggests that we approach situations bearing on our backs the full weight of our history, with all its created attitudes, beliefs, expectations and values, yet at the same time we are open and receptive to the otherness of the reality which we confront. By means of the resulting interaction, we simultaneously recognize our projections upon the material of our hermeneutic enquiry, and yet also refine our perceptions of the social reality encountered. Through an ongoing cycle of learning and self-discovery, we thereby strip away successive distorting layers of prejudice and come to understand both ourselves and the subject of our enquiry. In summary, the essence of the hermeneutic position is to respect the primacy of the social world which we create through continuous negotiation with the world of everyday experience, and to seek to understand this world by focusing upon the artefacts of the human mind, rather than upon the collusive fiction of 'reality'.

If we now take the hermeneutic perspective in trying to comprehend the act of problem identification, we see that our enquiry must start from a consideration of the mental processes of the problem-holder, rather than with a pseudo-scientific study of some objective data. Indeed such data would inevitably be tainted by the meanings which have brought them into being.

> ' . . . a fact is like a sack – it won't stand up if it's empty. To make it stand up, first you have to put in it all the reasons and feelings that caused it in the first place.'
>
> Luigi Pirandello   *Six Characters in Search of an Author*

In other words, coming to grips with problems is not something to be attempted using the hypothetico-deductive reasoning of the positivist natural sciences, but instead requires the sensitivity to intentionality implicit in the social sciences.

Understanding Problem Spotters

The *Lebenswelt* of the problem-owner is central in any reflection, whether self- or externally-orchestrated, about an identified problem. Thus, to take a superficial example (or rather, a profound example superficially), it is only as I learn of Ophelia's relationship with Hamlet, of Hamlet's suspicion of Claudius and of Claudius's coupling with Hamlet's mother that I begin to understand the hero's predicament. Taking the *Lebenswelt* seriously means taking it seriously in all its dimensions: that is, as embracing sensory, affective and cognitive experience, and as representing the product of individual, interpersonal, group, organizational and societal factors.

How does this unique mix of an individual's existential experience, which we have termed the *Lebenswelt*, translate into and inform action? We can do worse than to make use of Checkland's (1981) concept of the *Weltanschauung* – the singular 'view of life' by which we convert data into information – as the mediating agency. From this stance, the attribution of meaning to events is achieved by relating them to a personal mental image which both filters and reshapes perception. Our *Weltanschauung* is this unquestioned model of the world which makes sense of the things that we encounter. Checkland uses as a vivid example of the way in which a *Weltanschauung* dominates thinking, the Ptolemaic cosmological model, which survived the threat of successive astronomical discoveries until the successive accretion of epicycles became absurd and a paradigm shift to the simpler Copernican model became scientifically desirable and theologically acceptable. It is in his ability to achieve a shift in *Weltanschauung* or to choose from a range of different views, Checkland suggests, that man differs from other animals. However, this still begs the question as to from whence these mental operators come.

What are the forces which shape meaning for an individual? The study of the structures with which we codify experienced reality has been the focus of the modern intellectual movement known as structuralism which, as Bradbury (1984) has facetiously put it 'has had an international impact in fields as various as history, linguistics, anthropology, psycho-analysis, literary criticism and the *nouvelle cuisine*'. Historically, the thrust of structuralism owes much to the twentieth-century development of the physical sciences with its emphasis on relationship rather than on substantiality, and with its recognition that an observer cannot but contribute to what is observed. Structuralist thinking shares with the contemporaneous systems movement the view that an element of a situation can only be perceived within the context of a wider whole in which its significance is determined by its relationship to other elements. The 'grail' of structuralism is an understanding of the mental structures which form and give meaning to the world of our individual experience.

ceci n'est pas un problème
d'une seule pipe

with apologies to Rene Magritte

One of the more helpful concepts which has been introduced within the structuralist current of thought has been the idea of a 'frame'. Goffman (1974) has contended that in making sense of events we employ one or more schemata of interpretation (or frameworks). That is, we perceive any arbitrary slice cut from the stream of ongoing activity in terms of the premises, or rules of some organizing structures. Thus, if we see a flock of starlings swirling in the evening air we can accommodate this in our

EVEN BEFORE THEY'D
TOUCHED THE CANAPÉS
CUNNINGHAM REALIZED
THIS WOULDN'T BE JUST
ANOTHER EMBROIDERY CLASS

with apologies to Glen Baxter

repertory of natural events; if we see one person exchange with another a number of embossed metal discs for a cardboard packet, we can provide an interpretation using the framework of purchasing, a social activity. Such primary frameworks are by definition used routinely and unconsciously in our daily lives: indeed an individual may find it hard, if asked, to provide a specification of any schemata employed.

Not always, however, are we able so easily to frame experiences. If a flock of vultures, or worse still of sheep, appears to be circling overhead, or if the exchange between individuals concerns the clothes which they are wearing, then we may find it hard to encode what is happening. In general, our sense of what is going on is frequently, though less strikingly, susceptible to the need for rereading, perhaps as a dream, a joke, a deception, or a theatrical performance. Context is usually a vital element in assisting and enabling us to make sense of the situations which we encounter. It is only through making assumptions about the setting in which actions are taken or words are spoken that we can attach any meaning to such events.

At base then, if we are seeking to comprehend how individuals construct, experience and handle the raw data of their lives, we need to understand how the frameworks which they use are constructed. This question has been the subject of sober and scholarly examination as the self-appointed task of various sects of social scientists, though their particular predilections have tended to lead to a focusing upon one aspect or another of the phenomenon, with a consequent fragmentation of perception and insight. Thus the sociologists have looked through one end of the telescope and have studied the changing patterns which constitute human society; the psychologists have looked through the other end and peered into the mind of the individual; the organization scientists have borrowed from both and contributed a further perspective. All offer ways of understanding the individual experience of reality.

We shall begin here by considering the ways in which the social setting shapes and is shaped by the individual experience of reality, before moving on to examine how this experience itself influences and colours the way in which the experience is experienced.

Social Meanings

Sociologists have long had to grapple with the seeming contradiction of Durkheim's injunction to 'consider social facts as things' and Weber's focus upon 'the subjective meaning-complex of action'. As Berger and Luckmann (1967) have pointed out these two views are not necessarily in conflict: 'Society does indeed possess objective facticity [as a human product rather than as a reification]. And society is indeed built up by activity that expresses subjective meaning.' They continue, 'It is precisely the dual character of society . . . that makes its "reality *sui generis*"', and they go on to develop a picture of the way in which this reality is constructed. Essentially Berger and Luckmann portray this as a dialectical process involving three moments: externalization (social order is produced by human activity); objectivation (the created institutionalized world becomes objective reality); and internalization (the 'real' social world impacts upon the individual). Thus 'Society is a human product. Society is an objective reality. Man is a social product': the triptych is complete and indissoluble.

There is, it has been widely argued (Berger and Luckmann, 1967), an anthropological necessity for externalization. Essentially, the sheer undirected, undifferentiated and unspecialized nature of human drives, appear to make it imperative that man provides himself with a stable environment for his activities. It is only necessary, for instance, to reflect for a moment upon the immense plasticity of the sexual drive and its varied channelling in different cultures to realize the flexibility of the untrammelled human organism. Through processes, first of habituation and subsequently of institutionaliza-tion, such activities become stereotyped and mutually accepted. For example, the repetition of the activity of preparing breakfast enables us, in time, to do so with economy of both physical and mental effort; if the activity thus habituated is routinely performed by a particular actor – 'Dad always cooks breakfast on Sundays' – then an institution has been created as a result of this history. Further, those who accept this categorization of actions are consequentially tied together by the bonds of social understanding: in short, they have established a nascent social order.

History transforms custom into practice. The transmission of habituated social order beyond its genesis in place or time objectivates it, making it real for new audiences. For example, it becomes 'normal' in a society to refrain from eating pigs; to govern through an elected autocracy; or to drive cars on the left side of a road. With oily smoothness, the new institutions acquire a tangibility that is hard to challenge: in fact, challenges may be proscribed or limited by coercive sanctions. Fresh individuals encounter these legitimized institutions as social facts, as persistent constraints on behaviour. A whole edifice of constructed institutions towers over each new generation providing them with a much-needed context, yet also apparently delimiting the world of endeavour.

Meaning resides in social institutions (Silverman, 1970): that is, the way in which meaning is ascribed to situations is a culturally determined process. Indeed, in an important sense, a culture is defined by the way in which it provides for the encoding of experience. To take an example, Western societies tend to look to science to provide what mythology has offered to other cultures: a way of knowing, encoding and coping with reality. However, like myth, the language of science is an active force in defining and creating the world of experience, not a passive mediator in interpreting events. Levi-Strauss (1972) has pointed out how the tribal shaman – the priest-doctor – pro-vides a means of expressing and understanding sickness in terms of a tension between

with apologies to Posy Simmonds

tutelary and malevolent spirits, thereby rendering intelligible an otherwise arbitrary experience, and, with a degree of success, addressing and resolving the physiological symptoms. In the same way, Western societies frequently call upon scientists or other 'experts' to furnish a 'rational' justification for such diverse phenomena as flying saucers, traffic accidents, miracles and clairvoyance. The consensual acceptance of such explanations at the same time structures and constrains a culture.

The institution of language is one of the most potent in shaping the meaning of the social world, yet it too is merely one outward realization of the human consensus in a particular place at a particular time. Thus, the relation of the English to their animals is evidenced in their attitudes to, treatment of, and linguistic categorization of domestic pets, farm animals, wild animals, game and vermin, and contrasts with those of, for example, the French or Chinese, whose eating of frogs, dogs or snails is seen through many English eyes as beastly, barbaric or bizarre. More generally then, human societies, or indeed social or political subgroups within a society, are huge collaborative conspiracies for stating and structuring the continuum of experience, conspiracies which are constantly being renegotiated and reconstructed.

'CHILDERS: "The trouble with you Marxists is that you're modern
                Calvinists: all sheep and goats."
FLORA: "Whereas to you liberals, of course goats are just sheep
                from broken homes." '

Malcolm Bradbury   *The After Dinner Game*

A consequence is that this collaborative view habituates us to a man-made world that is perceived as natural and given: the more paranoid may even see this as the intention of their manipulative persecutors! In any event, to attempt to talk of 'objective' experience of a 'real' world is manifestly futile: as Hawkes (1977) has said 'we encode our experience of the world in order that we *may* experience it'; and this encoding is a social act, though one to which we each bring our individuality.

Once established, the reality of the many intersubjective worlds which we each inhabit is maintained through social relationships with others. Thus the everyday situations which we share are reaffirmed as subjective reality by the actions and utterances of those whom we encounter. Confirmation of the common-sense world of consciousness is provided by the conduct of fellow-travellers on the underground, by the ritual of purchasing a paper at the news kiosk, by the greeting of a colleague on arrival at work. More significant others – wife, children, friends – provide underpinning support to sustain the products of earlier socialization and to confirm individual identity.

Even more powerfully, the institutions will confer upon each of us social roles to play, so that we come to define ourselves in terms of them, and similarly to define others through the framework which thereby is provided. We are prepared to be so defined, Parsons (1951) suggests, because of a willingness to conform to the shared values of a society, values which we internalize as part of the 'package deal' of societal membership. Institutionalized pressures – including modern equivalents of the age-old penalty of outlawry – may also exist to dissuade anyone from defecting from his or her given role.

In this way we develop expectations of others – we expect policemen to be honest for example, and we don't expect firemen to be arsonists – which provide us with a frame of reference to apply to our experiences. Concomitantly, we are enabled in interpreting the actions of others, and so can attribute some meaning to them through this rationale.

1.5

with apologies to Steve Bell

However, the process of internalization, which we have been touching on here, is more than a simple donning of roles. As Goffman (1974) has said, 'The individual comes to doings as someone of a particular biographical identity even while he appears in the trappings of a particular social role. The manner in which the role is performed will allow for some "expression" of personal identity, of matters that can be attributed to something that is more embracing and enduring than the current role performance and even the role itself, something, in short, that is characteristic not of the role but of the person—his personality.' This now needs to be considered in relation to our search to understand the meaning of individual experience.

Personal Meanings

> ' "Well," says Howard, "it's a very interesting story".
> "The trouble is," says Flora, "I'm not sure it is. Isn't a story usually a tale with causes and motives? All I've told you is what happened."
> "Perhaps it's a very modern story," says Howard, "a chapter of accidents".
> "The trouble with our profession is, we still believe in motives and causes. We tell old-fashioned stories."
> "But aren't there times when what happened is just what happened?" asks Howard. "I mean, didn't Henry just have an accident?"
> "Oh Howard," says Flora, "what is this thing called an accident?"
> "An accident is a happening," says Howard, "a chance or contingent event. Nobody has imposed meaning or purpose on it. It arises out of a set of unpredictable features coming into interaction."
> "Oh, I see," says Flora, "Like your parties. And you think Henry had one of those?"
> "That's what you said," says Howard, "a Henry and a window came into chance collision".
> "That's not what I said at all," says Flora.
> "You said he went into the guest bedroom, fell, and cut himself."
> "That's interesting," says Flora, "because I didn't say that. I portrayed a consciousness, with an unconscious. He went into the bedroom. His arm went through the window, and he was cut. That's what I said." '
>
> Malcolm Bradbury   *The History Man*

Just as accidents seem to happen to some people, so events appear to conspire against others to cause them continually to be immersed in a sea of problems. All of us know at least one person for whom life is just one long-running problem, and one which they evidently feel is of some considerable interest to all of their acquaintance. We could pursue Howard's argument that some people somehow manage to collude with misfortune to create their unhappy circumstances, but more reasonably we would probably agree with Flora that this denies people's psychological rights and that other motivations are usually at work.

That individuals vary greatly in temperament and mental make-up is a commonplace, and during the present century psychologists have attempted first to categorize and then to explain the roots of the observed differences. Freud (1962), for example, calls the mental organization which is interpolated between needs and action the *ego*, and described it as a kind of facade for a deeper and more extensive apparatus, the *id*: further, there is an agency which becomes differentiated within the ego, which he names the *super ego*, that is the depository of the artefacts of redirected psychic energy. The mind is portrayed by Freud as the battleground of primal forces: the uncoordinated instinctual desires of the id run up against the harsh strictures of the moralizing super ego – internalized social values – in a conflict mediated by the realistically placatory ego. Within this framework, our individual historicity provides the parameters for, and represents the trajectory of the evolving dynamic balance. These ideas have been popularized by Berne (1964) whose technique of transactional analysis seeks to make evident the three Freudian components of personality (termed by him the Parent, Adult and Child) and to establish communication between them in psychotherapeutic practice.

An alternative model of the human psyche was developed by Jung (1923). A graphic analogy for portraying this model would be a picture of a sea-girt volcanic island: the visible land represents the centre of consciousness, the ego; the vast subaquatic realm is the unconscious, part personal, part cultural; while the energy which makes the ground move is the libido, a tension between opposites. Jung's image of the ego is expressed in his work on psychological types (Jung, 1923) which sets out a distinction between so-called introverted and extraverted attitudes to life, attitudes which are expressed through four variously developed functions: sensation, thinking, feeling and intuition. The personal unconscious in Jung's framework is a repository for repressed conscious thoughts, but also contains primordial images which well up from the collective unconscious to enrich conscious experience. The theories of Freud, Jung and their successors offer a rich vein of concepts with which the development of individual personality can be described, as well as a number of observational typologies, and we shall return to them later. However, they do so in large measure in the terms of a diagnostic clinician, the individual being treated as so much red meat on the butcher's slab of psychiatric medicine, rather than as a self-invented and self-interpreted being with integrity, continuity and individuality.

The over-used but under-focused term 'personality' is usually reserved to describe character traits made apparent through observed behaviour and subsequently pigeon-holed by the flaccid typologies of 'coffee-table' psychology. Here I shall adopt a more productive and holistic definition of personality as the individual framing of personal experience: as 'our way of construing and experimenting with our personal world' (Bannister and Fransella, 1980). It is with personality in this wider sense – with the concept of a person as a process rather than as a warring dualism – that we must be concerned if we are to understand the individual act of problem identification.

The Individual Construction of Reality

There is a theory of personality called the theory of personal constructs (Kelly, 1955) which fits precisely with the hermeneutic stance that we have adopted. Kelly's theory is founded on a philosophical position which he calls 'constructive alternativism': the idea that there are many workable alternative ways in which an individual can construe his world. He thus recognizes that the evidence which we accumulate through ongoing experience is continually susceptible to reorganization and recasting as we attribute new meanings to it.

The theory starts from the assumption that human behaviour is anticipatory rather than reactive, and that opportunities open to an individual as he reconstrues the course of events surrounding him. The process of construal is unique to the individual and, Kelly suggests, is best conceived of as being achieved through the framework of a hierarchically organized system of personal constructs, each of which encapsulates a bipolar contrast of perceptions. Each of these constructs, which are the basic elements of a person's construction system, is based upon the simultaneous perception of likeness (and so therefore of difference) among the objects of its context: in sociological terms, they derive from our observation and typification of repeated themes in our lives. Kelly's theory is completed by the suggestion that 'if people are in business to anticipate events and if they do this by developing personal construct systems, then they will move in those directions which seem to them to make the most sense, that is in directions which seem to elaborate their construct systems' (Bannister and Fransella, 1980). In this view then, a personal construct system is a working theory which is changed through a continual dialogue with experience, and which at the same time shapes and mediates that experience.

Embracing Kelly's theory of personality gives us leverage on the problem of understanding how individuals structure their reality, and therefore of how they attribute personal meaning to experience. It also implies a stance on the issue of problem identification with which we began the present excursion into the mental world of the individual. Firstly, from the standpoint of personal construct psychology, the individual is not 'a lump of matter shaped by happenings of the past' nor yet 'merely the product of his culture' (Kelly, 1955), but both personal history and social setting influence the nature of the personal construct system used by an individual in the present, and so for this reason they are relevant and legitimate topics for investigation. Secondly, personal construct theory suggests that we should be concerned with the system of constructs which are being used by a person to understand the 'here and now.' Thus constructs which have fallen out of memory and into disuse for some reason — call it repression or whatever — have ceased to be imbued with meaning and therefore with utility; they do not live some covert existence triggering responses from their underground lair. Thirdly, the individual's construct system is seen as elaborating continuously through time by redefinition or extension: Kelly himself portrayed this in his picture of 'man the scientist' engaged in an ongoing experiment with his reality. The corollary is that we should interpret people's actions in terms of such elaboration. Finally, the personal construct view implies that in seeking to understand individuals and their problems we must do so in terms of their own construct systems, rather than our own: we must, in other words, work *with* them as people rather than *on* them as objects.

Tailpiece

This chapter began with the deceptively simple question: 'What is a problem?' At its close we see that we should have been asking a different question: 'What is *the* problem?' Further we realize that the answer to this latter question will depend upon whom we ask. The resonse that they give will be shaped by the individual ascription of meaning to their subjectively experienced worlds, itself influenced in turn by their social context and personal history. Through the theory of personal constructs we can begin to understand a problem and its author. However, a phenomenological analysis of problem construal is needed if we are to appreciate the everyday process of problem authorship: this is the subject of the next chapter.

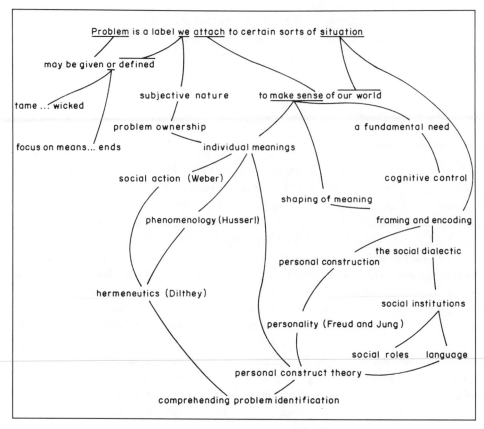

Diagram 1.1. Ideograph one

CHAPTER TWO

Experiencing problems

I have taken the view that we each live in a self-created world in which we are engaged upon a search for personal meanings, and that in the course of this quest we will find it helpful to describe certain situations as problematic. I have further made use of the concepts of the *Weltanschauung* and of the construct system to refer to the personal frameworks which we use to create this reality and have said something about the factors which make these different for everyone. We now need to examine how such frameworks interact with the raw data of experience to form our world and its significances.

Each individual is confronted by what James (1890) termed 'the blooming, buzzing confusion of sensation *sans* organization'. At any time, in addition to the sounds, sights, smells and tastes of our external environment, and the tactile messages which we receive from it, data from internal body monitors contribute to a sensory barrage. Fortunately, for our competence to handle such data is limited, we are normally unaware of this clamour. Instead, the selective focusing of awareness enables us to handle stimuli within a chosen field of concern, while largely ignoring peripheral events: this property of perception is generally termed attention.

The notion of attention invites questions about the process by which we focus preferentially upon certain data. The most influential ideas about this stem from the work of Broadbent (1958) who suggested that the incoming streams of sensory information arrive at a selective filter from which only a single channel leads forward to higher level information processing centres. This certainly seems to explain phenomena like the 'cocktail party problem' – our ability to tune in to a particular conversation amid a babble of competing voices – and there has been considerable experimental support for some form of filter theory. Since Broadbent's initial work, a number of modifications to the simple model have been proposed (Treisman, 1960) which suggest that rejected sensory data are not necessarily cast into total oblivion, but may survive in attenuated form to influence later processes. However, it is still a matter for controversy as to what cognitive constraint makes filtering necessary in the first place.

The rationale by which selective filtering operates is perhaps even more germane to our general concern with problem identification. From a large number of psychological studies (Dember and Warm, 1979), it appears that prime determinants of attention are the intensity and the novelty of the stimuli which we encounter. Thus, for instance, our visual attention is preferentially directed to those objects which are large, bright or moving and by patterns or pictures which exhibit unusual, incongruous or surprising features. Additionally, there is good evidence to support the hypothesis (Deutsch and Deutsch, 1963) that we attend to data according to their semantic content. Accordingly, signals which appear to be highly salient in the terms of our current mental set will form a more highly charged nucleus for attention than less 'relevant' data.

These characteristics of events which hold people's attention have been observed frequently to be associated with a specific physiological reaction set (physical orientation towards the stimulus, inhibition of ongoing activity, increased muscle tone, slower heart rate, pupillary dilation, vasoconstriction in the limbs and vasodilation in the head) known as the orientation response. This response is of some interest to us here because related research (Lynn, 1966) supports the theory that the response is triggered when experienced events fail adequately to match our mental models of the world. The corollaries are: first, a confirmation that the unexpected is a key determinant of attention; and second, an endorsement of the idea that we are continually trying to construct the meaning of events in order to handle the mass of sensory experience — which as a position fits snugly with our earlier discussions of the *Weltanschauung*.

Once again then it is the search for meaning that stands centre stage. Here we see how it causes our butterfly attention to land instantaneously upon a particular constellation of sensations within the *Lebenswelt*. As Popper (1963) has said, observation is always selective, always prejudiced: it is an activity which is guided by the desire to find, identify or confirm some conjectured regularity in experience. It is in this sense that we can understand Kelly's (1955) choice corollary: man's continual striving to act so as to extend and define his construction system.

Interpreting Experience

As Bannister and Fransella (1980) say, 'people interpret and re-interpret themselves and their situation' so that in relation to a time-line the individual changes from moment to moment in the light of experience. Human development is, in other words, a continuing process, not one specifically associated with chronological age or environmental circumstance, but rather relating to the evolution of a personal construct system in lively interaction with the *Lebenswelt*. According to the opportunities which are presented to us in our personal histories, so our construction systems will be stretched and refined in one direction or another and the resulting 'range of convenience' (to use Kelly's succinct term) of the frameworks which we hold at any time will vary accordingly, in turn limiting and shaping our experience of the present and our view of the future. This is not to say, however, that generalizations cannot be made about the development process, nor that similar patterns of evolution will not occur across individuals in a particular social setting.

> 'And now they were 30. He, an upstanding Wall Street lawyer chafing to work for the public good. She, a diverted case, a lover of politics and veteran of campaigns, but a mother, a clipper of part-time want ads. They had married at 25. And for several years they seemed to be typically eager people enjoying the new experience of a typical marriage within the professional class. I knew them as friends, but nothing about the quality of the threads that bound them as a couple. Except to sense that by now they had their tangles like the rest of us.'
>
> Gail Sheehy—*Passages: predictable crises of adult life*

Nevertheless, beyond the grossest level of abstraction, it is dangerous to impute any necessary commonality between individuals however similar their biographies may appear.

2.2

Many of the data which traverse the attentional filter are unproblematically encoded and assimilated by our construct systems. Making use of the psychology of personal constructs, we can assume that such unequivocal data are interpreted by means of the pre-existing systems which an individual has developed; indeed its compliance will help further to validate such systems. Sometimes the experience will be recognized and encoded as what would colloquially be called a problem: that is, as one of the class of situations which are likely to require some adjustment on our part, either through action or through conceptual adaptation. For instance, on the basis of similar situations in the past a spate of customer complaints about product quality will probably be greeted with a feeling of some apprehension by a production manager, who has come to learn that this often presages a need for tedious and confrontational trouble-shooting investigations. This labelling of the situation as a problem at a superordinate level of the construct system will be accompanied by other labellings at other, subordinate, levels of the construct hierarchy; for instance, in terms of 'complaints about Widgets', 'Widget production on Machine A last week', and so on. An array of impacts upon the construct system will occur as it is exposed to the grapeshot of happenings.

It is tempting to suggest that the individual problem experience should be correlated with psychological make-up. One might suggest, for instance, that extravert individuals dominated by the Jungian functions of sensation and thinking should be particularly sensitive to external environmental disturbances and so would feel problems directly 'out there'. By contrast, introverted intuitives, who tend to be preoccupied with the framing of inner perceptions, might more strongly sense the internal tensions resulting from external change as problem statements. However, the foregoing discussion should have raised awareness of the dangers of imputing similar *Weltanschauungen* to different individuals, no matter how alike their histories and character may appear.

Returning to the more general registration of problems, there might appear to be no more to discuss as far as unambiguously nasty data are concerned. However, an important dimension has been neglected: time. Data arrive in an ordered stream. One experience follows another, and importantly, is moderated by the previous experience. That this is so is simply to re-affirm that the construct system has a continuous dynamic, and is constantly being re-evaluated. The corollary is that the order in which data are presented is significant in shaping meaning.

This idea of contingent understanding has been confirmed in numerous pieces of experimental work in cognitive psychology, which have demonstrated the sequential patterning of incoming information that takes place. De Bono (1971), who terms such incremental cognitive processes 'vertical thinking', goes as far as to claim that 'An idea can never be the best arrangement of available information': that, it is always possible, and indeed necessary, to restructure cumulated information as each piece of new evidence arrives, if we are to make best use of our experiences. Albeit that this is a counsel of perfection, the underlying point is a valid one. It is thus perfectly possible for an individual to cast a situation as problematic or unproblematic according to the order in which he receives data and so builds up his mental picture of what is going on, quite independently of the content of the actual data arriving; equally, it is quite possible for a reshaping of this information to result in the dissolution of the perceived problem.

Discrepant Evidence

Popper (1976) has suggested that 'practical problems arise because something has gone wrong, because of some unexpected event'. This appears to me to blur the distinction between two distinct eventualities, for while we have already considered situations in which we have detected something as clearly going wrong, we must separately attend to another class of events which give rise to problem identification. By contrast with the situations which we have so far considered, when some data arrive they may pose immediate problems of encoding: the experience does not conform to any of the pre-existing structures held in the individual's construct system: a snarling response from a normally friendly dog would be unmanageable in this way. A person in this situation will probably experience a sense of anxiety, of fear or of disquiet, all feelings which stem from an encounter with the expected. Suddenly, maybe with imperceptible slyness, a chasm has opened up for the individual between the apparently solid ground of experiential wisdom and the perception of present reality, or between the certainty of the 'here and now' and the indeterminacy and uncertainty of the future. Framing the experience in other words, is problematic.

Recall the Woozle hunting exploits of Winnie-the-Pooh (Milne, 1926) in which Pooh, at first alone and then accompanied by Piglet, is tracking the strange spoors of a solitary creature in the snow near a big beech tree. Following the mysterious tracks for some minutes, the two companions are disconcerted to find that the first animal has apparently been joined by a second, as there are now two tracks ahead. Hoping that their fears that these could be Hostile Animals are groundless, Pooh and Piglet continue the hunt.

'Suddenly Winnie-the-Pooh stopped, and pointed excitedly in front of him. "*Look!*"

"*What?*" said Piglet, with a jump. And then, to show that he hadn't been frightened, he jumped up and down once or twice in an exercising sort of way.

"The tracks!" said Pooh. "*A third animal has joined the other two!*" '

Anxiously, having diagnosed that indeed there are three animals – probably two Woozles and one Wizzle – ahead of them now, the intrepid pair proceed warily. Unfortunately it is not long before the three pairs of tracks are joined by a fourth! This is enough to prompt Piglet's recollection of some other tasks needing urgent attention, and making his excuses he rushes off. Only Pooh is therefore present when Christopher Robin descends from the tree around which the two animals had been walking in circles to explain . . . .

Not all fears are so easily allayed by being exposed as resulting from a misreading. More generally we can follow the precepts of personal construct psychology (Kelly, 1955), to interpret such feelings as signalling that the capabilities of our construct systems to construe the events which we have encountered are being stretched too far: possibly the evidence which we have attempted unsuccessfully to frame is in danger of invalidating part of our conceptual structure or even of overwhelming it completely. At any rate, our world is not meshing well with our expectations of it and a problem is flagged.

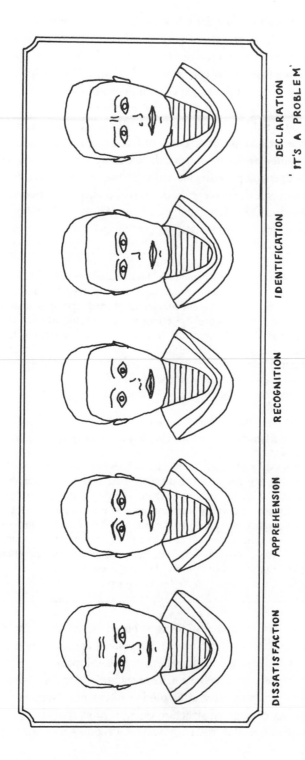

DISSATISFACTION   APPREHENSION   RECOGNITION   IDENTIFICATION   DECLARATION
                                                                   'IT'S A PROBLEM'

with apologies to Fry's Chocolate

Only when the vague signals of misgiving have raised themselves above the level of background noise can they be recognized (and only when they have been given linguistic form can they be shared with others). A sensitivity to threatening circumstances is a mixed blessing: to take a fictional example, the unfortunate Laputans in *Gulliver's Travels* were described as 'under continual disquietudes, never enjoying a minute's peace of mind', as they continually fretted about the possibility of the sun ceasing to shine, of the earth being destroyed by a comet, and of other celestial calamities. However, an alertness to the rumblings of imminent potential change can also be a strength. It has been said (Minzberg and Waters, 1983) that effective managers are those who are particularly capable at scanning the business environment and recognizing significant change: at the process that Lewin (1951) called 'unfreezing' from the current perceptual set. There are probably innate differences between people in their skill at environmental scanning. Certainly there are differences between species in their receptivity to signals of natural change: witness the observations of animal behaviour in China which have given prior warning of several earthquakes. It seems plausible that such abilities will also vary between people.

To summarize, there are thus two distinct sorts of problem experience. The first occurs when a situation is framed and recognized as potentially troublesome; in the second, a problem is logged if a situation is difficult or impossible to frame. Before proceeding to consider this latter circumstance more fully, it is worth while reflecting briefly upon a potential difficulty which stems from the implicit definition of the term 'problem' being used here. Essentially we may fall into the trap illustrated by the famous logical paradox of the Cretan poet and prophet Epimenides who asserted that 'All Cretans are liars'. In an analogous way we are saying that 'All problems are experiences that are either frameable as problematic or problematically unframeable'. However, by so labelling them as problems, we have framed them and so overcome their necessary unframeability! We must therefore interpret 'unframeable' in the second sense as meaning 'unframeable, beyond saying that it is a problem'. This is not, perhaps, a definition to satisfy the purist, but its sense, I take it, is apparent to the reader.

The Construal of Anomalies

A personal construct system is an organizing device: it therefore feeds on disorganization and strangeness.

> 'Q: "Does Ben print newspapers?"
> A: (*very forcefully, as if to a fool*): "Yes – The Gazette."
> Q: "What else does he print?"
> A: "Almanacs . . . Poor Richard's . . . Poor Richard's Almanac."
> Q: "What else is Ben interested in? Just books and newspapers?"
> A: (*loud derisive laughter*)
> Q: "Why, what are you laughing at, Tom?"

A: "Ben says, 'Fish and company stink in three days.' "
Q: "But is he interested in anything else?"
A: "Ben's . . . interested in everything . . . kites . . . and stoves . . . and
   ladies." '

In this extract from *Encounters with the Past* (Moss, 1979) it is claimed
that an elderly Philadelphian, who was once apprenticed as a printer
to Benjamin Franklin, is talking in 1972 to the hypnotist Joe Keaton
through the mouth of a 50-year-old teacher from Washington. It is
one of a huge number of recorded regressions in which hypnotized
subjects have thrown off their own personalities and assumed the
character of someone from the past, painting vividly authentic word
portraits of a bygone age. Are such memories genuine or are they
simply elaborate frauds? Is this evidence of reincarnation? Can there
really be a collective conscious which can be drawn upon or transmitted genetically?

The subject of parapsychology is concerned with the investigation of anomalies.
How can information be transmitted through apparent barriers between one organism
and another as in telepathy? How can messages be sent from an organism to its
environment as in psychokinesis? Investigators of such psychic phenomena find
themselves preoccupied with a questioning of sensory evidence and with a study of the
attachment of meaning to individual circumstance. Can there be a physiological
explanation for certain visionary experiences? Is precognition merely the result of a
sensitizing of perception to predicted patterns of behaviour? Is a doing simply a trick or
a deception? Yet such concerns are not unique to this discipline of psychical
investigation: the recognition and understanding of anomalies is one of the key
managerial skills. More pertinently, anomalies provide challenges to our construct
systems and so force us into a choice between its elaboration or the summary rejection
of our experiences.

Anomalous data force a search for a possible interpretation of events. Given that our
Weltanschauung is unable precisely to construct a meaning for the presented evidence,
the least incommoding response is to seek out a perspective which comes closest to
accommodating the experience. We may think of this being achieved by attempts to fit
the situation to one of a number of alternative schemata, each of which may represent a
plausible though inexact framework for comprehending what is happening.

'11. INT. ALLARDYCES' SITTING ROOM. DAY
*Prosperously furnished. The most prominent object in the room is an early
television set, screen about nine inches wide, in a large walnut console. On
top of it is a bowl of bananas. MRS ALLARDYCE, a fleshy and masterful
middle-aged woman, is in the act of lifting her skirt to undo her suspender,
turning away from GILBERT slightly in order to do so.*
MRS ALLARDYCE: "You're younger than I'd been led to expect.
   However."
(GILBERT doesn't say anything)

"Mrs Lockwood says she's a new woman."
GILBERT: "Have you any newspaper, Mrs Allardyce? This is a good carpet."
MRS ALLARDYCE: "Wholesale from Halifax, of course it is." '

Alan Bennett   *A Private Function*

Taken out of context, we might easily suggest a number of schemata for this extract. The unlikelihood that any of these correspond to the actual circumstances of the episode – a visit to a new patient by a timid chiropodist – is a demonstration of the author's mastery of the comically ambigious.

The process of construing has acquired considerable recent significance in the field of artificial intelligence, where the interpretation of the world of experience is a live issue. Minsky (1975) has suggested that a hierarchy of epistemological representations (or frames) are used in domains such as the visual, problem-solving and semantic contexts. An important outcome of this work has been the recognition that frames may be considered to consist not just of a collective of questions to be asked about a situation, but also of default answers to those questions and some routines for handling unexpected information including, for instance, as suggested above, rereading using an alternative frame. We may reasonably conclude that an individual will go to considerable lengths to find a suitable interpretative framework before giving up and facing the less palatable alternatives.

It may be impossible for an individual, finding no appropriate schema for construing an experience, to accept the evidence of the information which he is receiving. Consequently, it is either summarily rejected or else new data are sought, in preference to the need to make any adjustment in a fundamental belief or theory. The *Weltanschauung* therefore actively filters the *Lebenswelt* (Berresford and Dando, 1978) in the interest of its own self-preservation.

A number of famous military breakthroughs have depended on the rejection or misinterpretation of intelligence data. For instance, as Pearson and Doerga (1978) point out, the Nazi invasion of the Netherlands in May 1940 was preceded by numerous direct warnings from impeccable sources of an impending German attack. Hitler changed his mind about the attack at least twenty-nine times and so the credibility of the warnings was incidentally undermined. Although the level of tension grew following the German invasion of Czechoslovakia in 1939, it never seemed likely to the Netherlands Government that the stalement on the Western front would be broken, and a conflict confined to naval of air skirmishes, or in a theatre 'elsewhere' seemed most probable . 'Even on the night of the attack, after direct intelligence warning, as the ministers and secretaries met at the foreign minister's home and as German planes flew overhead, those present estimated the chance of attack at roughly 75 per cent.'

Quite possibly, evidence which supports the currently held view is anxiously sought in order to validate retention of an entrenched position. Recent studies (Nisbett and Ross, 1980) have shown how people contrive to engineer the selection of information which confirms espoused opinions, and values. Selective filtering of incoming sensory data, informed by the resident construct system, also helps to sustain such a conservative position. This is quite an active process (Greenwald, 1980) with prior opinion not only working as a preferential filter on incoming messages, but additionally influencing in a similar way retrieval of supportive information from memory. This process is also the basis of many everyday wish fulfilment 'illusions': for instance, the commonplace scene described by Reed (1972) in which we 'recognize' and rush across to greet a total stranger, while excitedly awaiting a friend in a busy airport arrivals area.

There may be an overweening inertia which manages to smother all but the most vibrantly viable nascent problems from ever seeing the light of day. On occasion, advantage may be taken of this resistance to new constructions of events by those who seek to mislead: again wartime offers numerous examples.

In his fascinating book *Deception in World War II*, Cruickshank (1979) describes some highly inventive ploys. To take an example, the build-up of the Eighth Army's supplies for the decisive North African battle of El Alamein was covered by a number of deceptions. The most complex, codenamed 'Munassib' involved the digging of gunpits and the installations of dummy guns well to the south of the sector on the front line from which the main attack was to come. These were left without movements for a week in order to convince the Germans that they were dummies: then one night real guns were substituted. Later, when the battle began in the North, the German forces in the South were attacked by guns which they had thought to be dummies. This then reinforced the Germans' (mistaken) belief that the South would indeed be the main focus of attack.

Only the most naive can believe that such deceptions are confined to the dastardly world of the military. The detection of problems is therefore susceptible to all sorts of malign and benign influences, deliberately induced and otherwise.

In some settings, by contrast with the examples which we have been considering, there may be considerable efforts to extort validational evidence to support a new view of the world.

> 'But no one else in the world of physics had yet spotted what she recorded in one sentence of that paper in describing how much greater were the activities of pitchblende and chacolite compared with uranium itself. She wrote, "the fact is very remarkable, and leads to the belief that these minerals may contain an element which is more active than uranium". The realisation that she might have stumbled across a new *element* raised her to an excitement that she never before experienced. She, the mistress of understatement, later recalled how she felt, "a passionate desire to verify this hypothesis as rapidly as possible". . . . What they were not then to know was that what they were searching for was present in the minerals in such minute quantities, that it would be truly hard physical labour. On April 14th 1898, ridiculously optimisic, they weighed out a one hundred gram sample of pitchblende and ground it with pestle and mortar. It was the first step of their long haul. Eventually they would work in tons.'
>
> Robert Reid *Marie Curie*

An heroic leap of vision has often provided the motivation for experiments which have underpinned the process of scientific discovery. Commonly this has been energized by an act of faith building upon observation of some anomalous event, and the subsequent development of a hypothesis intended to explain the abnormality. To cite Popper (1976) once more, 'science begins with problems, and ends with problems': from some event, inexplicable in terms of current theory, a tentative theory is advanced and tested, eventually to spawn a new generation of scientific queries. Invariably, the courage required to switch to a new paradigm is considerable. No wonder then that people go to such lengths to retain their cherished beliefs, even to cling to the driftwood of their scuppered creeds long after the water has closed over their heads.

Retreat from Fantasy

We have now seen how, often against considerable odds, a problem is experienced. The complexity of this individual act of construal is fascinating. So fascinating that it is easy to become lost in the academic world of cognitive modelling, and to lose sight of some of the key features of problem recognition. It is simply not enough to have sketched out the way in which a person confronts experience and from that encounter develops the feeling of a problem (a feeling which can presumably, subsequently, be addressed through some intentional doing). This is not how it is: or, at least, not all of how it is.

Consider some individuals faced with situations of the sort which we have been discussing. Suppose, for example, that our first subject is the brand manager for a market-leading dentifrice: the most recent consumer audit report has just landed on her desk and shows an unexpected collapse in brand share in the Midlands area. Our second subject is a commuter, travelling home from work along a busy motorway: a news flash interrupts the afternoon chat-show to warn of an accident on the carriageway a few miles ahead. A third subject is parent of two children attending a state primary school: she has just opened the local evening newspaper to see headlines stating that the school is to be closed at the end of the current term. We might quite properly imagine that each of these individuals would register a problem and then proceed to instigate some appropriate activity. We might also expect that we could come closer to understanding how these individual acts of interpretation and construction took place, by trying to achieve an empathetic insight into the mind of the respective problem-owners, although we might not expect to have to delve too deeply into the psychoanalytic morass for scenarios of the sort which have been described. I have no argument with such reasoning.

Problem Owner: *Gabrielle Coulane is brand manager for 'Medicleen' toothpaste: 'YOU deserve GREAT teeth'. She drives a sleek grey company BMW convertible on her journey home from the office along the M4 motorway. She has two children, Dominic and Tamsin, who attend the cosy village school under the tutelage of motherly Mrs Bramson.*

Reflect for a moment that our three imaginary subjects might not be three different people after all: the same individual could simultaneously be facing all three problems. Reflect further that our single problem-owner is not encountering these situations in a social and organizational vacuum, but is meeting them in a setting which is replete with other actors, all of whom will be forging their own meanings of events. Is it still reasonable to persist in claiming that we have fully explored the process of problem identification?

We have encountered what I shall term here 'The Two Simplifications' (not to be confused with Chairman Mao's Four Modernizations!). The vast majority of writing about problems and their management assumes that individuals are only concerned with construing a single problem, and that they do this alone in a contextual vacuum. This is hardly a surprising perspective, since much of the work in the field has been carried out in laboratory settings where conditions can be engineered to make these assumptions appear less ridiculous.

> 'Any experimental psychologist who has ever done a study of, say, memory, has watched his/her stubborn subjects continue to cognize, emote, perceive, sense and so on, even though the experiment called upon them only to remember.'
>
> Bannister and Fransella   *Inquiring Man*

The laboratory of life is still less well approximated to by the picture of the solo, single-problem-owner. Not only do people face multiple simultaneous problems, but they do so in politically charged and socially structured situations. All of this has an impact on problem definition.

Juggling Concerns

Acknowledging that individuals tend to be enveloped in a confusion of problems (to coin a suitable collective noun!) most of the time, how does this affect the process of problem identification which we have been tracing? This question can be answered by suggesting that interaction occurs between problems both in terms of process and content; and that this interaction takes place because any identified problem simultaneously provides the context for, and lies within the context of all the others for an individual. To elaborate, this means that the process of problem recognition in one arena modifies that in others; that the shaped content of a problem in one area influences the content of problems in others; and that process and content interfere with each other across fields of experience in a complex and messy manner. These issues will be discussed in greater detail below.

There is still disagreement as to whether human cognition can be faithfully represented by a serial information processing model (Simon, 1985), or whether important features can only be accommodated within a framework which assumes a degree of parallel processing (de Beaugrande, 1985). Whichever view we take, limitations on cognitive capacity imply that there must be shifting of mental resources within the *Lebenswelt* from one field to another, and within a field from one level of attack to another. Following contemporary views (de Beaugrande, 1985), we may consider these switching activities to be constrained in such a way that there are thresholds which both determine the initiation and termination of processing activities in an area, and which also determine the basic level of resource to be provided at any time to each of the multiplicity of issues present for consideration. It appears then, that just as we earlier used the concept of attention to explore the handling of simultaneous sensory input, so at this next level of problem construal we must adopt a similar process model in order to explain the transfer of interest within a confusion of competing problems.

The switching of focus from one problem to another is an experience which is familiar to all of us. While puzzling over concerns in one area, worries elsewhere temporarily drop out of our field of vision. For instance, my apprehensions about the completion of the manuscript of this book by the contractual date periodically obliterate worries about my managerial duties as leader of an academic OR group and more personal anxieties about the imminent birth of our first child. As I walk into work each morning, these different issues will swim into and out of relief, interspersed with more mundanely immediate concerns, such as negotiating the crossing of busy roads and buying a morning newspaper. We evidently need to review the ground rules which inform the management of a portfolio of disparate problems.

A confusion of problems may sometimes produce feelings of stress (Janis, 1971) like those experienced in situations where we are faced by physical or psychological dangers: similar reactions are elicted. Thus an individual may exhibit panic behaviour, acting in an apparently random and irrational manner and switching rapidly and haphazardly between a number of problems which clamour for notice. At other times we may just withdraw from all of our concerns, perhaps taking refuge in drink, physical activity or a mind-numbing work of fiction. It is hard to elucidate any heuristics which might consistently predict such inconsistent behaviour.

In calmer moments, when the pressure of problems is felt less keenly, more deliberate organization of attention to competing arenas of concern may be achieved by a number of devices. One obvious way in which we can cope with a multiplicity of problems facing us is by determining that some are more important than others. Thus we prioritize our concerns in accordance with some internal value set, itself informed by our construct system. We might then offer our time and energy to the problems of which we are aware in some relation to this scheme of importance. Returning to our earlier example, Gabrielle may feel that the motorway blockage problem is unimportant compared with the slump in her brand's sales. Instead of trying to handle the delay in her return home by navigating at night round unfamiliar and twisting country roads, Gabrielle may be content to sit in a traffic jam and use the opportunity to muse over possible market strategies. On the other hand, if the delay means that the children will have been put to bed by the nanny before Gabrielle gets home, she may prefer to take on the former problem and to postpone consideration of the latter.

Appealing though the importance-driven model of prioritization is, practical studies suggest that it is somewhat idealistic. People prioritize right enough, but are as likely to do so in terms of ease of handling as in terms of any rational measure of importance (such as systemic impact). Thus, Kolb (1983) found that clearly defined tasks will be tackled first; next we address well-defined prolems; unstructured problems are treated next; and finally, those open opportunities in which both means and ends are unclear will be considered. Such a 'natural' approach biases us towards short-term survival and away from longer term strategic issues, which tend to be shelved. So maybe in our example Gabrielle will address the 'driving home problem' in preference to the more intractable 'brandshare problem' after all!

The notion of prioritization implies that a hierarchy of problems is created from which one is drawn for treatment. In some situations this hierarchy may itself be restricted in length, especially if a problem-owner is feeling stressed and unable to cope with the idea of a large number of simultaneous concerns. A neat analogy for this process is to consider that the problem-owner is working with a finite, prioritized queue of problems, a queue in which those waiting can become rowdy and unpleasant as they stand in line, occasionally jostling for position, shouting at the server, or jeering at newcomers who force their way to the front. The most extreme version of prioritization is 'tunnel vision' (Mitchell, 1981) wherein an individual focuses upon a single problem to the absolute exclusion of all others; unsurprisingly this is a common feature of those intense crises which may also elicit the panic responses we discussed above.

As a result of creating a hierarchical ranking of problems, some will continually be pushed aside. They will simply never get the mental resources devoted to them even to be clearly articulated, still less treated. Setting problems aside, of course, creates further difficulties: psychiatrists derive their livelihoods from such behaviour. It is mundane to make the observation that the problems which are suppressed in this way are by no means necessarily the least important for long-term well-being; but then the criteria used implicitly to rank problems are themselves usually an ill-assorted medley of the rational and the irrational. Often it is precisely because of the enormity of certain problems that they are pushed aside, sometimes indefinitely, sometimes until the problem-owner has mustered the mental resources to face them.

When it comes to working on problems, a simple practical step for handling a collection of problems is systematically to isolate them for separate attention. This process can be facilitated by administrative arrangements or delegation. Thus, returning again to our earlier illustration, Gabrielle is able to devote herself to single-minded consideration of 'Medicleen' market performance partly because of Mrs Bramson's ministrations as child minder. She is able to modify her route home to avoid the blockage because she is not preoccupied with toothpaste sales. She can mobilize grass-root opposition to the school closure despite (and also paradoxically because of) her managerial duties. Gabrielle can effectively divide her attention between her diverse spheres of action and between the problems which arise in each of them. However, such clerical division does not lead to mental separation of the diverse arenas. Further, as Cohen, March and Olsen (1976) point out, 'every entrance is an exit somewhere else': by opting to spend time and energy in one arena we are by default determining to spend less in the others in which we have an interest. Some nice choices thus have to be made about the allocation of attention.

The determinants of the distribution of attention between competing problems can usefully be discussed in terms of three themes suggested by March and Olsen (1976b): rationality, symbolic significance and obligation. On the grounds of rationality we might expect to find that people will tend to choose to be involved in those arenas wherein they feel that their participation will make a difference, and in those arenas where things are going on which matter to them. On the grounds of symbolic significance, we might expect to find individuals involved in those arenas in which the right to participate is of intrinsic importance to those involved; in which such intangibles as status, goodwill and influence are attached to the arena itself. On the grounds of obligation, we might expect to find someone becoming involved in arenas which out of duty, routine or organizational position are those in which it is held to be proper for him to be concerned. Needless to say, these three claims on an individual's attention usually pull in different directions, as can easily be confirmed by a moment's reflection in the subject of our earlier illustrations. The result is either a compromise that neither satisfies the person nor his colleagues, or else a choice that is seen and felt to be narrowly selfish to one particular claim.

2.8

So far we have concentrated upon what, in computer analogy, might be called the operating systems which we use for processing confusions of problems. As I suggested earlier there is also inevitably interpenetration between the content of the distinct problems constructed by an individual. Preoccupations in one area will affect construal in another in at least two important ways. Firstly, there may be a carry-over of conceptual set from one area to another. Secondly, emotions roused by experiences in one area may carry across to others. We shall consider briefly these two effects in turn.

The term 'conceptual set' refers to a particular perspective that we may use in looking at a situation: it may be as precise as a frame or schema, or far looser, perhaps best expressed in terms of a role view. Such perspectives may be the result of past experience with apparently similar situations, or more pertinent to our development here, the result of ongoing attempts to manage concurrent problems. Thus, a recent episode involving the successful framing of a problem in one arena may suggest a repetition of its application in another, possibly quite inappropriate context. For instance, if in our example Gabrielle were to envision the conflict over the school closure in the same terms as the inter-brand conflict which she daily experiences in her job as manager for 'Medicleen', she would most probably perceive and structure the former issue in a way which would be unhelpfully and competitively confrontational. At other times, however, frames can beneficially be carried across problem arenas, leading to genuinely fresh and creative structuring of problems.

The emotional charge which problems carry can drastically interfere with their construction, and with the construction of problems in other areas of preoccupation. This is readily demonstrated in the 'bad day at the office routine' wherein the irritable executive comes home with a lowered threshold of anger and is easily aroused by events that in other circumstances would have been overlooked or joked about. More seriously it points to the dangers of attempting to ignore private or organizationally illegitimate aspects of personal construal when dealing with problem-owners. These and other interactions between 'separate' problems serve to emphasize that we cannot surgically segment the problem-owner for ease of analysis, without doing irredeemable violence to the phenomena which we are trying to understand.

Social Interaction

As social actors, men modify each other's meanings.

'She wants him to want her
He wants her to want him

To get him to want her
   she pretends she wants him

To get her to want him
   he pretends he wants her

Jack wants   Jill wants
   Jill's want of Jack   Jack's want of Jill
     so   so
Jack tells Jill   Jill tells Jack
   Jack wants Jill   Jill wants Jack
           a perfect contract'

R. D. Laing   *Knots*

The opening statement can be taken at a number of levels. At its simplest we can suppose that for individuals 'the meanings of particular events, situations, things and experiences arise out of the observed behaviour of significant others towards them' (Mangham, 1978), these meanings being moderated by our uniquely personal interpretative process. More penetratingly, we can follow the sociality corollary of personal construct psychology and acknowledge that our individual interpretations of others' behaviour requires an empathetic understanding of them, and impacts reflexively upon our own construction systems and so upon our attribution of meaning: that is, there is concurrent adjustment in the construct systems of those involved in a social transaction. Such considerations are crucially germane to a discussion of problem identification, since we are concerned in this book with problems in the public domain of social interaction.

I shall follow Mangham (1978) in regarding social interaction to consist in each of us, as individual performers in a social process 'forging temporary working agreements with other actors as to the nature of the situation and the appropriateness of the various performances open to them'. Within this dramaturgical context, it is apparent that the parts which we assume in each of the specific interactions in which we engage – and we take parts upon many stages – will strongly shape our perceptions of events and our consequent labelling of problems. Once again it is helpful to consider both the processual and content-related aspects of problem identification, though they turn out to be quite intimately entangled.

To begin by pursuing what has become a well-rehearsed theme in this chapter, the most obvious way in which others affect our framing of situations as problems is by diverting or re-orienting our attention so that we become either more or less cognizant of particular features within the *Lebenswelt*. The hackneyed archetype of the evil *femme fatale*, who distracts for an instant the morally unblemished hero of one-hundred-and-one spy movies, crudely illustrates this simple device. More seriously, and perhaps quite innocently, others may redirect our attention by carrying us along with their own predilections and enthusiasms; or conversely, by their sheer lack of interest and inattention they may cause us to look more closely at the features that they are so transparently overlooking.

The channelling of attention may frequently be organizationally formalized. This may be achieved by the casting of individuals in specialized roles which give them responsibilities for attending to certain features of the environment, and implicitly with-holding permission, if not actively discouraging them from, looking at others: the company accountant will not need to concern himself unduly with the effect of high manufacturing temperatures upon dye flow in a textile printing process; the production manager will not be concerned with the impact of new fiscal legislation on export arrangements to overseas franchise holders. Dearborn and Simon (1958) found evidence for role focusing in their study of Castengo Steel: asked about the most important problems facing the company, sales executives cited sales problems, production managers mentioned operational problems, and other decision-makers also tended to concentrate on their own particular sections. An alternative mechanism for channelling attention is to impose a segmentation between individuals on the basis of rank within a hierarchical framework: the bank teller does not need to concern herself with the adjustment of interest rates on the money market, although this will affect the volume of trade which she handles; the financial managers of the bank do not concern themselves with the handling of individual clients, though in aggregate this will affect the profitability of the enterprise. There are, of course, a few organizations in which choices and actions are collectively determined: these exhibit what March and Olsen

(1976b) have termed unsegmented attention patterns, and energies are apportioned to the various live problems as much under the influence of environmental factors or as a result of who happens to become active in them as on account of their inherent characteristics.

The direction of attention can cause individuals to be 'blind' to catastrophic changes simply because they are occurring in an area which lies beyond their own immediate field of responsibility: this has regrettably been demonstrated by numerous man-made tragedies in the recent past (Bignell, Peters and Pym, 1977). Segmentation of attention is evidenced in organizations of any but the smallest kind, and its effects are usually deliberately ameliorated by various schemes designed to increase information flow and participation across the structures involved. The consequences of segmentation can be quite disconcerting at the level of the individual, since she may experience a situation in a variety of ways dependent upon the part which she is given to play. Thus an off-duty airline pilot will experience a flight quite differently from a passenger seat than from the cockpit. Whenever we are issued a part we are also given a way of seeing.

Interaction with others affects the salience of experiences: that is, it affects the highlights of their content. The home security products salesman from whom we decline to make a purchase but who leaves us feeling more vulnerable and unprotected than we did before; the fanatical philatelist who in showing us his collection points out some minute flaw in what had appeared to be a perfect set of commemorative stamps; the kindly adult who first points out 'the man in the moon' to a child; all these irreversibly modify our perception of a situation. In these, and in more subtle ways, the social context of a problem-owner modifies his construction system and hence his understanding of what is going on.

There are further social pressures on problem identification. For instance, in certain organizational settings, 'groupthink' (Janis, 1972) may set in and bound the perception of individuals in a group thereby restricting the potential to recognize problems. Some organizational cultures may actively encourage this development so as to encourage compliance with corporate aims: for instance, religious and military organizations demand of members adherence to a catechism of beliefs or a code of behaviour which rigidly delimits outlook by providing members with perceptual goggles. In such an environment it may be well nigh impossible for any individuality of thought, and it will take great courage to allow an unconventional view to surface.

These then are some aspects of the social process which is played out around an individual, and which contribute to that tickle in the throat which triggers the cry of 'Problem!' This process plays an even more significant role in our handling of problems as we shall discover shortly. Taken together with the recognition that there is a confusion of problems facing each of us at any time, these additional factors indicate the real complexity of the problem experience; a complexity which is too easily lost in the emaciated conventions of academic discourse.

Tailpiece

The concept of attention lies close to the core of any understanding of the personal experience of problems: attention as a sensory filter, attention as a semantic differential, attention as a pragmatic simplifier of life's confusion. Moreover, the idea of a personal construct system operationalizes the possibility of directing an intelligent and active attention upon our individually experienced worlds, and so helps us to appreciate the process of problem identification. However, when we consider the internal and external context within which specific problems are conceived, we realize the limitations of models which fail to recognize the full complexity of this everyday process. It is particularly difficult to discuss the experience of problems without making reference to the way in which people customarily deal with them, and this forms the subject of the next chapter.

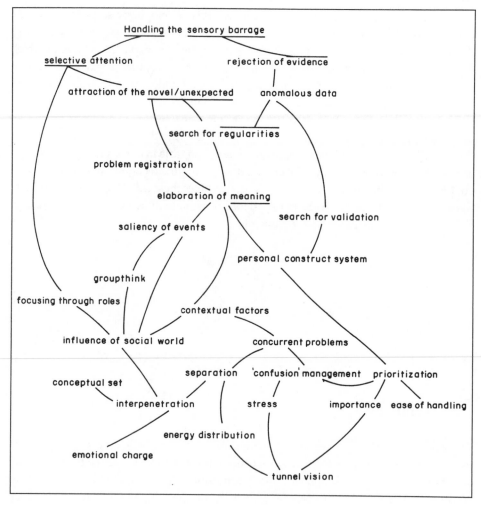

Diagram 2.1. Ideograph two

PART TWO:

Handling problems

CHAPTER THREE

Treating problems in Practice and theory

'The way never acts yet nothing is left undone
Should lords and princes be able to hold fast to it,
The myriad creatures will be transformed of their own accord.
After they are transformed, should desire raise its head,
I shall press it down with the weight of the nameless uncarved block.
The nameless uncarved block
Is but freedom from desire,
And if I cease to desire and remain still,
The empire will be at peace of its own accord.'

Lao Tzu   *Tao te Ching*

The modern notion of problem handling is considerably at odds with that of a more acquiescent age. The principle of *wu-wei* – of swimming with the tide, of going with the grain – has unhappily been displaced by an aggressive resistance to events. Those who attempt to engineer their circumstances in this way often pay a high price for their right to self-determination in terms of personal stress and emotional well-being.

3.1

In the past, the problems which an individual faced were often seen as being an aspect of his personal relationship with the world: as being a manifestation of his fate. Recall, for instance, the concept of a man's doom as portrayed so graphically in the heroic world of the Icelandic sagas. There, in tales peopled with heroes who are 'lucky', with others who are 'ill-starred' or 'accursed' the narrative unwinds inexorably, carrying each man to his fate; in the most famous saga of all, the eponymous hero Njal dimly sees what lies ahead and makes brave attempts to avoid it, yet is carried forward to meet his tragic destiny. By contrast, a more recent character, Scrooge in Dickens's *Christmas Carol*, exemplifies a successful proto-modern attempt to intervene in the course of events and alter what fate offers. Today, although the spirit of *qismet* survives in the East, in Western societies, the emphasis is very much upon taking action in order to resolve the inner tension that we feel between what apparently is or will be, and what we feel should or might be. Destiny is what we make it, not as we take it.

As a result of our protesting and non-acquiescent orientation, we tend to manage our feelings of a problem by a move to some external action, rather than by some inner psychic adjustment, although, as often as not, we have little clear idea initially as to what that action should be.

> 'Mr Podsnap settled that whatever he put behind him he put out of existence . . .
> Mr Podsnap had even acquired a peculiar flourish of his right arm in often clearing the world of its most difficult problems by sweeping them behind him.'
>
> Charles Dickens   *Our Mutual Friend*

In other words, our non-contemplative culture encourages us to see a predominant role for action – even if only of a symbolic kind – in the face of problems. Our search for cognitive control therefore often begins with a search for physical control of our encountered world, and for an indication of the corresponding changes which need to be made in order to ameliorate our circumstances. Before we even start to put together an approach to handle unfamiliar situations, it is therefore quite likely that we have foreclosed that whole range of possibilities for handling the situation centred upon the passive rather than the active mood.

Alarms and Excursions

A problem-owner is not always suffused with the contemplative calm of a Zen master. Before we go on to examine action scenarios, it is worth reflecting upon the frame of mind with which we may sometimes confront problems. Faced with the financial debris of a recent crash in stockmarket prices, with the prospect of a terrifying journey through a hostile jungle, or with presence of an unwelcome house guest, few people retain their equanimity. Instead, blind panic, fear or anger overwhelm and paralyse their minds so that an appropriate response is lost. The wise counsel us that a separation of the events and the reaction elicited permits a more worthwhile approach. By staying firmly in the 'here and now', rather than engaging in recriminations about a finished past, in worries about an unwritten future, or in judgements about a neutral present, a detachment can be cultivated which frees both physical and psychic resources for adroit and appropriate action. Nevertheless, such calmness is exceptional and most of us wear an air of some agitation as we face our difficulties.

At times our fears may quite obliterate any possibility of intentional action. Such fears arise because part of our world, possibly a major part, has become meaningless and unpredictable, and our construct systems may seem to be threatened. It may be that even the acknowledgement of a problem, still less the consideration of some appropriate action, is more than can be countenanced.

> 'Of all things, nothing is so strange as human intercourse, she thought, because of its changes, its extraordinary irrationality, her dislike being now nothing short of the most intense and rapturous love, but directly the word "love" occurred to her, she rejected it, thinking again how obscure the mind was, with its few words for all these astonishing perceptions, these alternations of pain and pleasure. For how did one name this? This is what she felt now, the withdrawal of human affection, Serle's disappearance, and the instant need that they were both under to cover up what was so desolating and degrading to human nature that everyone tried to bury it decently from sight – this withdrawal, this violation of trust, and, seeking some decent acknowledged and accepted burial form, she said:
> "Of course, whatever they may do, they can't spoil Canterbury."
> He smiled; he accepted it; he crossed his knees the other way about. She did her part; he did his. So things came to an end.'
>
> Virginia Woolf   *Together and Apart*

In such circumstances, a problem is momentarily recognized, but is then rapidly consigned to the depths of some mental black hole, never to be encountered again, or at least not in the same form.

When the pressure of events is less serious, more considered responses may be elicited. The immediate situation is then reviewed through the perceptual goggles which are provided by our developed construct systems, and a performance is set in train which is felt appropriate to the circumstances and which in the light of previous experience is felt to have some chance of effecting an improvement by ameliorating the problem. In order to do this, a number of secondary activities may need to be initiated, for instance, involving the gathering of additional information about features of the situation, or regarding other uncertainties which have been disclosed. The prevading mood of such an approach to events can best be summarized by the word 'deliberate': the problem-owner calmly and methodically sets about understanding the situation and determining how best to deal with it.

There is a further frame of mind which may well describe a problem-owner's attitude in the face of an acknowledged problem: complacency. It is by no means unusual for an individual to determine that no action needs to be taken in respect of a problem. Perhaps it is thought that the situation will 'go away' or that the problem will clear itself up. Alternatively, it may be judged that the matter is of so little importance that, although it has initially been logged as a problem, it is not worthy of the mental resources needed for its resolution. Naturally, catastrophic errors of judgement can be made here: witness, for example, the initial inaction in the wake of the Chernobyl diaster, followed too sluggishly by a realization that the problem of radioactive fallout was one which required widespread safety measures to be taken. Thus inaction may signal not that no problem was seen, but that what was seen was trivial.

This spectrum of emotional reactions to problems has coincidentally been neatly summarized by Janis (1972) in a related discussion of the human response to threat. Faced with a strong threat, individuals tend to become 'jittery' responding nervously to minor disturbances, over-reacting to scare rumours, and generally demonstrating impaired mental efficiency. When they encounter only a moderate threat, people behave more deliberately, setting out to collect specific data about the situation in order to develop considered plans for action. A weak threat is frequently denied, and little or no precautionary measures are taken as a result. It would appear that this scheme can also be applied to categorize accurately the individual response to problematic situations. While the following discussion will tend to focus upon the middle of this range of dispositions, it must be borne in mind that this is not to imply that problem-owners are necessarily diffused by a cool and rational equanimity.

Customary Repetitions

How do people generally deal with problems? Faced with situations which are not to our liking we usually scan our memories to recall similar experiences. Then, for all the world like pre-programmed robots, we proceed to put into action some well-worn formula which seems to have worked before.

> During the preparation of this manuscript I have been faced upon numerous occasions with a reprographic machine which has refused to operate.

My usual response has been the same: to open the equipment casing; to lift the feed mechanism; to clear the paper path; to close the machine; and finally to reset the monitor switch.

This has normally been a successful strategy.

However, on occasion I have swung mechanically into my customary routine, only to find that it has not worked. Sometimes I had been too hasty in reaching a diagnosis: I had jumped to the conclusion that the paper path was blocked, without noticing that the machine had simply run out of copy paper.

On other occasions, although the correct symptom had been identified, the remedy was unsuccessful: removal of the offending material did not suffice to put the machine back into operation, and a skilled maintenance engineer had to be called.

Off-the-cuff reactive tactics save a problem-owner from excessive mental exertion every time that a problem is faced, and serve as a first stage in selecting out for more considered scrutiny those few occasions when they are unsuccessful.

Good reasons for the choice of a familiar remedy as the initial response to an acknowledged problem have already been hinted at. The mental effort involved in an automatic re-running of a previously successful ploy is slight: indeed what effort is needed is not required so much for the execution of the solution as for the monitoring of its effects. A similar inertia to retain the trusty recipes of the past is apparent in organizational planning; Cyert and March (1963) have pointed out that in very few cases are management willing to discard their investment in abilities, technologies and processes in the face of change, and that the whole managerial ethos which is built up around historical strategies favours modification rather than rejection of tested routines. Further, it is unlikely that if a successful strategy exists for dealing with a problem, any search will be initiated to see if this approach can be bettered. The penalties for failure are frequently so severe in contemporary business, that management are, perhaps unknowingly, prepared to sub-optimize drastically rather than to risk innovative methods; a neurotic fear of 'throwing out the baby with the bathwater'. Stock reactions are easy, familiar and (hopefully) safe.

Fortunately, as Weick (1983) has pointed out, organizational outcomes are frequently so overdetermined that thought may have little effect indeed on outcomes, which are instead shaped by luck, misjudgements, inattention, inheritance and other apparently random or arbitrary events or circumstances. The belief that deliberate action actually leads to desired outcomes has also been partly exploded by March and Olsen (1976a), who remind us that a less self-centred view would perhaps see a problem-owner acting in a way which objectively owes little to the environment, and which has little impact upon external events – despite a firm conviction on the part of the individual concerned that his acts *are* significant, a belief encouraged by the anxious collection of appropriate validational evidence. An individual may therefore succeed by re-running old routines, despite, rather than because of, any real understanding of what is going on, and in so doing may build up an internal model of his world that is beautifully consistent and apparently predictive, yet which is liable to be overturned as soon as a step change occurs which transforms the nature of the events. We may thus conservatively apply a 'cure' in a situation because we do not realize that it is ineffective or damaging, and because the circumstances in which we are acting are so robust that we have the good fortune to succeed, and to go on succeeding, in the use of this habitual response in cases where we have blantantly misread the situation. It should not come as a surprise therefore, if people seem almost invariably to offer stock reactions to encountered problems: as the saying is, they simply act in character.

> 'Since everyday life is dominated by the pragmatic motive, recipe knowledge, that is, knowledge limited to pragmatic competence in routine performances, occupies a prominent place in the social stock of knowledge. For example, I use the telephone every day for specific pragmatic purposes of my own. I know how to do this. I also know what to do if my telephone fails to function – which does not mean that I know how to repair it, but that I know whom to call on for assistance. My knowledge of the telephone system also includes broader information on the system of telephonic communication – for instance, I know that some people have unlisted numbers, that under special circumstances I can get a simultaneous hook-up with two long-distance parties, that I must figure on the time difference if I want to call up somebody in Hong Kong, and so on. All of this telephonic lore is recipe knowledge since it does not concern anything except what I have to know for my present and possible future pragmatic purposes.'
>
> Peter Berger and Thomas Luckmann
> *The Social Construction of Reality*

Some problems are prematurely labelled as 'insoluble': this is a special case of putting into action an off-the-shelf response to a problem, and is much favoured by some people. If a situation bears a dreary similarity to one that has been encountered many times before, and to which no appropriate response has been developed, then such a reaction is perfectly understandable. However, it may also be a view that is produced when a problem-owner declines, for whatever reason, to become involved in further treating a problem and wishes simply to push it aside for the time being. An over-rapid move to so label a situation may cause a problem-owner to overlook novel features in the current situation, which make it more tractable. In either event, it need not be assumed that the abandonment of such problems spells the end of work upon them. We are all probably familiar with the 'insight' experience by means of which an approach to a problem which we had earlier set aside, wells up to our consciousness while we are otherwise engaged. Neglected problems may thus be inexplicably solved through the exercise of no apparent mental effort, and without drawing upon our repertoire of standard responses.

'Knee-jerk' responses are less likely to succeed or to be attempted when situations clearly display the appearance of novelty. However, sometimes we may still be able to get away with a suitably tailored version of a previously discovered solution. I may never have had to remove the skin from a kiwi-fruit before, but my experience with apples may be adapted to help me to prepare a fruit salad. The degree of similarity to a previous situation, and so the probable extent of any reshaping of earlier prescriptions, may be one measure of the ease with which we handle a situation. Thus, when Mae West commanded, 'Beulah, peel me a grape!', prior peelings of tomatoes or peaches would have been valuable qualifications, whereas if Beulah had only worked on oranges or bananas before she would have found grapes more troublesome. The difficulty of a situation will also depend upon our individual expertise in the general field concerned: to pursue the earlier illustration, a chef should be more readily able to draw on appropriate strategies to make use of an exotic fruit in preparing a dessert than would a professional footballer engaged in the same task. Recent research (Buchanan, 1982) in the development of expert systems has corroborated these suggestions by identifying domain-specific knowledge and specialized problem-solving procedures as the twin resources which an expert offers.

This is another way of saying that the more highly developed are our construct systems in the field of concern, the more easily are we able to relate a variety of present circumstances to past experience.

Square Pegs, Round Holes

Encountering apparently novel circumstances, however, other possibly more hazardous procedures are possible. Rather than remodelling a tried and tested solution, we may instead try to redefine our present experiences in more familiarly manageable terms: to massage or prune it into a happier form. In other words, an analogy may be forced by a potentially falsifying simplification of a situation. Thus, to take a striking example, the French experience of the value of a line of military defences strengthened by forts was reinforced in the Franco-Prussian War and later during the Battle of the Somme: used again, in the very different setting of the Second World War, the concept proved disastrous as the enemy simply circumvented the defensive Maginot line. Effortless solutions are achieved in this way but at the loss of practical relevance.

The forces towards taking a simplified view of an acknowledgedly complex issue are considerable, yet perfectly understandable. In short, an individual may feel pressured both by internal and external influences. Firstly, there may be a need to handle a confusion of concurrent problems, possibly under severe time constraints. Secondly, the problem context may be such as to affect the degree of detail employed in the individual problem construction. Because of their pernicious effects, these factors need to be examined a little further.

It cannot be denied that by defining and addressing complex situations as if they are really simple we are freed to take action rapidly. This is a position that has overwhelming attractions if, for example, someone is about to blast our brains out, or we are otherwise immediately threatened. We can perceive here a basic biological survival mechanism at work. Less dramatically, if we face a cluster of problems and want to pick them off quickly one at a time, it makes sense to treat them in this way. Mental resources can be used more frugally if small, tidy problems are conceptualized. More generally, the principle of Ockham's Razor – that we should adopt the simplest possible explanation of events that is consistent with the evidence – is, in any case, a most valuable one to adopt. The dangers lie in the cutting away of significant evidence in the interests of expediency.

The social and organizational pressures upon the individual to simplify are much in evidence today. On the national and international scene, the seductive attraction of simplifying away the complexity of the modern world has gained many adherents: witness the growth of fundamentalism in all its guises. A contemporary politician who advocates a crudely direct frontal attack on a rising crime rate by the imposition of dire penalties on offenders, is likely to gain more immediate public acclaim than one who insists that deeper social causes need to be addressed by more subtle reforms: and the former may well have some success in the short term, and to have left the political stage before the full consequences of his policy come home to roost. For similar reasons, complex global issues like human population growth, deforestation and environmental pollution, have tended to be addressed singly and weakly instead of being perceived and handled as related through complex systemic interactions. The pressure to pare down complexity can be found within other organizational contexts. I can think of more than one firm for whom I have recently consulted, where the managing director's simple-minded characterization of a competitive situation has been adopted, despite clear signs that there were massive changes afoot in the product market concerned. While this narrowness of view may occasionally be traced back (Jongeward, 1976) to the personality of a charismatic founder, it is more easily seen as constituting the texture of the overall bureaucratic fabric; as part of the organization's whole *modus vivendi*. All around us then, we are being persuaded that a simple picture is sufficient; that to go beyond this is an academic indulgence.

Simplication offers smart, straightforward prescriptions for coping with difficult questions and provides sure, rapid-fire answers to the uncertainties of everyday life. Contrast this with the emotional turmoil that faces a more open-minded approach and the attractions are apparent . However, in less pressing and more contextually relaxed circumstances, we can usually benefit from some opportunity for reflection on our best course of action through attempting to make sense of the full richness of what is going on. This more challenging alternative to re-using old scripts involves recognizing the unfamiliar elements in our predicament and seeking a genuinely fresh approach to deal with them. Since this is a far more demanding orientation to problems, it is less frequently chosen.

Unfamiliar Territory

Encountering a problem for which no routinized response has been developed, and which appears, no matter how much we try to make it not so, to lie outside the scope of Procrustean surgery, we are apparently faced with the unknown. And yet, as individuals, with a wealth of experience in a thousand-and-one spheres of activity from breast feeding onwards, it is almost inconceivable that there is not some corner of our minds which holds within it the germ of a possible strategy for addressing our present circumstances. It is equally improbable that we could dream up *ab initio* some totally new and original strategy that lies somehow outside all of this previous knowledge. In practice, as Berger and Luckmann (1967) have suggested, what we seem to do is to integrate the new situation with its embedded problems into the hoard of individual memorabilia; to link it into the expanding network of our worldly wisdom; or as Kelly (1955) would surely put it, to elaborate our personal construct systems!

'In the early years of the last war when armaments of all kinds were in short supply, the British, I am told, made use of a venerable field piece that had come down to them from previous generations. The honorable past of this light artillery stretched back, in fact, to the Boer War. In the days of uncertainty after the fall of France, these guns, hitched to trucks, served as useful mobile units in the coast defence. But it was felt that the rapidity of fire could be increased. A time–motion expert was, therefore, called in to suggest ways to simplify firing procedures. He watched one of the gun crews of five men at practice in the field for some time. Puzzled by certain aspects of the procedure, he took some slow motion pictures of the soldiers performing the loading, aiming and firing routines.

When he ran these pictures over once or twice, he noticed something that appeared odd to him. A moment before firing, two members of the gun crew ceased all activity and came to attention for a three-second interval extending through the discharge of the gun. He summoned an old colonel of the artillery, showed him the pictures, and pointed out the strange behaviour. What, he asked the colonel, did it mean. The colonel too, was puzzled. He asked to see the pictures again. "Ah", he said when the performance was over, "I have it. They are holding the horses." '

E.E. Morrison   *Men, Machines and Modern Times*

The tendency to retain elements of historical performances in new situations runs deeply through all of us. So too with problems, the impulse to hold on to the known, already noted above in its most obvious guises of refashioning solutions or tailoring problems, is very strong. Faced with the shock of the new, we may therefore carry over elements of earlier scripts, though using them within a freshly bespoke framework; or we may carry over the form of previously used frameworks, but set them with new dramatic elements.

The rudiments of the tactics of improvisation, as we may term our impromptu problem-handling compositions, have already been indicated. Necessarily they depend upon a degree of skill or expert knowledge in successfully categorizing the new experience, or in recognizing within it the nuances of some earlier related happening. This provides a metaphorical piton by which we may affix ourselves to the rockface of experience: a sort of conceptual placenta which can feed us ideas and sustain us as we venture into the unknown. Improvisation also appears to depend upon the individual's particular facility for coping with novel situations: this ability for devising creative approaches to unfamiliar problems is something which it is claimed can be cultivated (de Bono, 1978) and for which a large range of methods has been proposed.

Nevertheless, the features which make some people manifestly so much more able at handling tricky situations than others have still not been satisfactorily explained.

Today's improvisation becomes tomorrow's tradition. Weiss (1980) has noted how moves that are made spontaneously in response to events, become precedents which are cited when vaguely similar events subsequently occur. In time and with refinement and adjustment they are hardened into operating rules and policies, which duly become an integral part of general procedures. Once again it must be pointed out that this can be a method for fossilizing inappropriate or inefficient actions as easily as for generating productive ones. The social process of institutionalization, of which this is an example, and which was discussed earlier, is no arbiter of such matters.

Beyond the concept of improvisation, how much further can we proceed in attempting to describe how individuals deal with problems? Is it possible to create a sequential model (Sanderson, 1979) which describes how people customarily handle such situations? Do individuals take time out to use some logical process of experiential learning (Kolb, 1983) by means of which to tackle problems? I incline to concur with Weick (1983) who suggests that to the contrary in the context of managerial performance at least, problem solving is an integral part of executive action, rather than a discrete and separate activity. In this view, thinking – and by implication what we have termed problem handling – is folded imperceptibly into action: it is the stream of calls, actions, memos and meetings that constitutes executive problem management. There is much to support this position to which we shall return later. Meantime, however, it is worth while casting our minds back over our observational review of the individual response to problems, to see if any light can be cast by theory upon the practical processes apparently involved.

Thinking Problems Through

'It takes thirty minutes to go on foot to Mazar, and it is five times faster by bicycle. How long will it take a cyclist to get there?'
'You say a bicycle goes five times faster? Then the journey will be one-fifth as long, so it will take just six minutes to get to Mazar by bicycle.'

The school problems of our childhood present us with a goal or question, and give us the task of reaching it using logical reasoning under specified conditions from information provided. The way in which people solve problems of this type has been much studied as a proxy for the investigation of the vastly richer subject of thinking, and so has had a slightly malign influence upon cognitive psychology by offering an attractively manageable but resolutely academic field of research. However, it is precisely the extent of experimentation on problem solving in this sense of the term that makes this an appropriate starting point for a examination of the theory of problem handling.

Although it may later appear unduly naive to do so, we can at least begin by thinking of our handling of problems as involving two tasks: first, sizing up the situation with which we are faced; second, deciding what to do about it. Needless to say these two activities are usually carried out intuitively and unselfconsciously, in a fluid manner which leads our energies from one mode to the other in a continuous iterative way until eventually the problem is somehow 'finished' and we can turn our attentions elsewhere. Sizing up situations is a process which requires us to make sense of what is going on, and as we have seen, we will make reference to developed mental frameworks in order to pattern the evidence of our experiences. Deciding what to do is a process which necessitates a generation of, and selection between, alternatives and an eventual commitment to some package of appropriate measures, and so involves the use both of cognitive models to produce imaginative constructions of potential and intended actions and also of some referent evaluative function to help in the act of choice. In each of these aspects of problem handling both inductive and deductive reasoning plays a part: the former, for instance in attempting to establish the rationale for what we think is occurring and therefore what might occur; the latter in anticipating the development of events and so of actions. It is therefore fitting that we should examine briefly contemporary understanding of these two key mental tasks as a prelude to a wider examination of problem handling.

Thinking about Thinking

'Here Legrand, having re-heated the parchment, submitted it to my inspection. The following characters were rudely traced, in a red tint, between the death's head and the goat:

53++∧305))6*;4826)4+.)4+);806*;48∧8!60))85;1+(;:+
(;:+*8∧83(88)5*∧;46(;88*96*?;8)*+(;485);5*∧2:*+(;4956*2
(5*−4)8!8*;4069285);)6∧84++;1(+9;48081;8:8+1;48∧
85;4)485∧528806*81(+9;48;(88;4(+?34;48)4+;161;:188;+?;

"But," said I, returning him the slip, "I am as much in the dark as ever. Were all the jewels of Golconda awaiting me upon the solution of this enigma, I am quite sure that I should be unable to earn them."

"And yet,"said Legrand, "the solution is by no means so difficult as you might be led to imagine from the first hasty inspection of the characters. These characters, as anyone might readily guess, form a cipher – that is to say, they convey a meaning; but then from what is known of Kidd, I could not suppose him capable of constructing any of the more abstruse cryptographs" . . .

"In the present case . . . the first question regards the *language* of the cipher . . . In general there is no alternative but experiment, . . . but with the cipher now before us all the difficulty was removed by the signature. The pun upon the word 'Kidd' is appreciable in no other language than the English." . . . .

"There being no division [between words], my first step was to ascertain the predominant letters, as well as the least frequent. Counting all, I constructed a table . . . Now in English the letter which most frequently occurs is e. Afterward, the succession runs thus: a,o,i,d,h,n,r,s,t,u,y,c,f,g,l,m,w,b,k,q,x,z." . . .

"Here, then, we have in the very beginning, the groundwork for something more than a mere guess." '

Edgar Allan Poe   *The Gold Bug*

Thorndike's cats are among the most famous in the history of modern psychology. In experiments carried out in the closing years of the last century, Thorndike (1898) demonstrated that the random behaviour of these animals when placed in a puzzle box was gradually replaced by a systematic response leading to their escape, as they became more accustomed to the experimental situation through a number of trials. From these and similar studies stems the associationist view of thinking, whose antecedents can be found in Hobbes and Locke and traced back to Aristotle; an approach essentially based upon the idea that subjects elucidate the 'rules' of their world through trial-and-error experimentation, and thereby build up an ordered repertoire of appropriate learned responses.

Later work has appeared to confirm the general validity of this model for certain types of thinking, though refining it in a number of ways. For instance, the notion that as a result of experiences an individual is effectively reordering a hierarchy of potential responses has been retained in some theories, but with two glosses: first, that the response hierarchy is itself selected as being appropriate to the specific situation, from a wide set of alternative available hierarchies (Maltzman, 1955); second, that the content of the hierarchies offered is affected by past experience (Mayzner and Tresselt, 1959), or frozen by *Einstellung* – habituation – (Luchins, 1942). An alternative development of the associationist model, which has been supported in some experiments, suggests that at any time only one, most-favoured response is elicited by circumstances. This is equivalent to the idea (Restle and Greeno, 1970) of sampling from a pool of alternative hypotheses which are available for trial at any time. In this modified view, it is suggested that people retain one dominant hypothesis or rule with which they operate exclusively until experience indicates that it should be replaced by an alternative. Experimental evidence supports this 'win stay, lose switch' approach.

The theme of associationism is that individuals are effectively continually engaged in testing hypotheses about their world. Now this should not seem a particularly novel idea in the light of our previously espoused theory of personal constructs and its corollaries. Indeed, if we re-examine the associationalist propositions above from the perspective of personal construct psychology, we shall not find obvious dissonance, but instead considerable accord. However, there is a crucial feature missing in associationalism: the centrality of personal meanings. As Bannister and Fransella (1980) have pointed out, 'No one ever yet responded to a stimulus. They respond to *what they interpret the stimulus to be* and this in turn is a function of the kinds of construction the person has imposed upon the universe.' Whatever we may choose to infer from observation of experimental subjects, their deliberate actions derive from the elaboration of meanings in their personal construct systems, and may or may not happen to correspond to some externally perceived distinction which an experimenter chooses to focus upon. With this shortcoming very much in mind we shall draw later upon the ideas of associationalism to consider people's confrontation with problems.

It is appropriate to turn now to the second major strand in the historical development of the psychology of thinking. The Gestalt school, which also has ancient precursors, considered that individuals attempt to obtain understanding of their world by reorganizing and patterning their experience, making use of mappings on to earlier experiences in so doing. Like associationalism, these ideas also stem from animal experiments, and were specifically introduced in order to attempt to explain the curious phenomenon of 'insight' in solving laboratory problems.

Many recent studies have provided corroborative evidence for Gestalt theory. In particular, support has been found for the concept of assimilation to schema (Bartlett, 1932) as a key element in interpreting events. Thus, it has been demonstrated that people appear to cope better with situations for which they can find an appropriate setting or context: the experiences become more meaningful. Once again, a number of factors have been found to intrude upon this process. For instance, studies (Duncker, 1945) have shown that the past experience can impose an unduly restricted apprehension of a situation, with elements being seen narrowly in stereotypical roles, rather than as having a potential variety of functions in problem resolution. Other work (Kohler, 1969) has suggested that the way in which a problem is first represented or envisioned can have a strong effect on the way in which an individual assimilates it, notably in respect of the ease with which it can be related to the personal archive of experience. More fundamentally, the critical process of recentring or restructuring, upon which Gestalt thinking relies to explain the 'eureka' experience, has been quite widely studied (Hayes, 1965) and modelled in terms of a sequential addressing of subproblems created by an analytical reformulation of the original problem. All of this experimental evidence lends credence to the Gestalt view.

If the theory of associationalism is that people are playing the scientist, then that of Gestalt theory is that they are engaged in a continued quest for meaning: another idea totally consistent with personal construct psychology. Adopting Kelly's theory, we would expect the observed effects of prior experience to affect problem-handling behaviour in the way that the experiments suggest, because of the framing properties of our personal construct systems. The search of memory for a similar problem is similarly catered for by construct theory, which relies upon the perception of similarity and differences in experience, to explain the growth of the hierarchical system itself.

'I find from my notebook that it was in January 1903, just after the conclusion of the Boer War, that I had my visit from Mr James M. Dodd, a big, fresh, sunburned, upstanding Briton. The good Watson had at that time deserted me for a wife, the only selfish action which I can recall in our association. I was alone.

It is my habit to sit with my back to the window and to place my visitors in the opposite chair, where the light falls full upon them. Mr James M. Dodd seemed somewhat at a loss how to begin the interview. I did not attempt to help him, for his silence gave me more time for observation. I have found it wise to impress clients with a sense of power, and so I gave him some of my conclusions.

"From South Africa, sir, I perceive."

"Yes, sir," he answered, with some surprise.

"Imperial yeomanry, I fancy."

"Exactly."

"Middlesex Corps, no doubt."

"That is so. Mr Holmes, you are a wizard."

I smiled at his bewildered expression.

"When a gentleman of virile appearance enters my room with such a tan upon his face as an English sun could never give, and with his handkerchief in his sleeve instead of his pocket, it is not difficult to place him. You wear a short beard, which shows that you were not a regular. You have the cut of a riding-man. As to Middlesex, your card

has already shown me that you are a stockbroker from Throgmorton
Street. What other regiment would you join?"
  "You see everything."
  "I see no more than you, but I have trained myself to notice what I
see." '

Arthur Conan Doyle   *The Case Book of Sherlock Holmes*

Induction, which we have examined above, is the process of creating and developing
frameworks for anticipating events: deduction, which we shall now turn to, is the
process of using these frameworks. More narrowly, we may regard deduction as
describing the way in which we interpret information and use it to draw conclusions
about our world. The study of deduction, like that of induction, has a long and
distinguished history rooted in the disciplines of philosophy and logic. For obvious
reason it has attracted interest in recent years, because of its significance for computer
information processing.

Perhaps the most telling icon of deductive reasoning is the syllogism: that system of
premises and conclusion which for many psychologists has been taken as the
elementary unit of human rationality. A large number of studies have been carried out
to investigate human performance in syllogistic tasks (Wason and Johnson-Laird,
1972). These have suggested that human and formal logic coincide surprisingly often,
and that when 'errors' of logic do occur, they tend to emerge from difficulties in
encoding premises rather than in the later processing activities. Misinterpretation often
appears to relate to ambiguity or looseness in the linguistic expression of conditions, or
in subjects' casual construction of information.

When the deductive task is clearly stated, there may still remain opportunities for
mistake if the solution search is across an extensive problem space: that is, if there is a
high degree of complexity in the mental manipulations required for finding a solution.
This is clearly illustrated by work in another area of experimental psychology: that on
so-called MOVE problems (Newell and Simon, 1972) which involve producing a given
goal state for a system from a given initial state by means of a sequence of simple
operations. When a large number of alternative routes is possible, success depends
upon an individual's mastery of efficient search heuristics or algorithms. Similarly,
successful deduction depends upon the ability to marshal large quantities of information and to use effective methods of squeezing from it sound conclusions.

3.10

Induction and deduction 'are the prototypical tasks that are at the core of human intellectual life' (Mayer, 1983). However, it would be foolish to pretend that they are any more than two supremely important functions which can be identified in human problem solving. Equally significant must be the overarching 'operating system' (to re-use the convenient computing analogy) which determines how an individual moves between these two modes of cognition to compose those passages of thought by which problems are addressed. An effective way of putting together the elements of thinking which we have encountered is provided by personal construct psychology. Kelly (1955) suggested that individuals move through a cycle involving circumspection, pre-emption and control – the C–P–C cycle – in preparing themselves to take definitive action.

Overall, the C–P–C cycle portrays a person as scanning and reviewing the phenomena of concern; as preferentially selecting certain issues as crucial, thereby giving one construct pre-eminence, and so deciding what sort of situation is faced; and finally, as making a commitment to some specific choice. The personal construct system shapes each of these stages. First of all, it informs the initial process of circumspection by offering frameworks (or schemata in Gestalt terminology) within which events may be viewed. This task necessitates comparison and matching with established constructs and so leads into the pre-emption phase. Secondly, the construct system, itself based upon similarity and difference, provides an efficient skeleton for locating the experienced situation. Possibly a number of construction subsystems (like the associationalist hypotheses) will be tried in order to find a good explanation. In the third stage, the construct system's categorization will highlight a range of actions for consideration. These will be such as to provide the greatest opportunity for elaborating the system itself: for augmenting its deductive power. Within this context, strategies for coping with problematic situations will be based upon the fund of wordly-wise knowledge which the system itself represents.

Critique of Pure Reason

We turned earlier from an account of the way in which people customarily deal with problems to the immediately preceding discussion of ideas in the psychology of cognition. It is now necessary to examine the extent to which the latter may serve as a model of practical problem solving, and to identify where, if any, discrepancies appear to exist.

The developed theory of human problem solving has grown as a result of extensive experimental research during the present century. In fact, as Greene (1975) has pointed out, there has been a concentration upon problem solving among cognitive psychologists because it is, of all mental activities, the easiest to externalize, manipulate and control: further, an experimenter can set his subjects clearly defined tasks and have some assurance in his interpretation of what happens as a result. Both behaviourist and cognitive schools have provided plausible explanations for observational data, and most recently this has been supplemented by information processing theories of thinking which have contributed much to our understanding of reasoning. We have seen above how these various theoretical positions can also be aligned with the principles of personal construct psychology and so appear to be consistent with our adopted stance on problem construction. However, despite the success of theory in illuminating the elements of thinking there is a generally acknowledged failure to explain crucial systemic features of the normal business of dealing with problems: the integration of past, present and future; the determinants of individual performance and competence; the movement between convergent and divergent thinking; and so on. More critically for present purposes, the experimental situations themselves are scarcely remotely congruent with everyday problem-handling contexts.

> 'What experience and history teach is this – that people and governments never have learned anything from history, or acted on principles deduced from it.'
>
> G.W.F. Hegel

One of the central ideas in classical behavioural theory is that of learning appropriate responses through repeated experimentation: action leads to outcome leads to interpretation leads to rules leads to improved action. The application of empirically proven routines as a reaction to superficially familiar problems apparently illustrates one aspect of this process. Yet the prevalence of recurrent misjudgements, misreadings and mistakes casts doubt upon the effectiveness of the presumed learning process, as superficially straightforward events are seemingly eliciting the wrong responses. The development of superstitions, myths and fictions by organizations as well as by individuals illustrates another aspect of this phenomenon, wherein a cue produces a systematic but peculiarly inappropriate response to an apparently random world. Feldman (1986) has appraised the evidence for and against the view that people learn from experience, and has concluded that we do indeed learn, but in a way that is strongly shaped both by the environment in which experiences occur and by our own specific expertise and motivation. Although Feldman does not use the term, he indicates that the key to learning is the personal construct system: this provides us with a framework for categorizing experiences and therefore for detecting those inconsistencies which lead to discoveries; it shapes the content of what we learn by providing schemata which influence the salience of events; and it provides a baseline for the testing of fresh hypotheses stemming from newly encoded knowledge. Learning thus depends upon the pre-existing cognitive structures, and relative to this, the type of task encountered and the nature of feedback received: in short, learning occurs when events contradict expectations and when new patterns are discerned.

The notion of learning from experience is even more problematic in the organizational settings in which many problem-owners operate than the above discussion

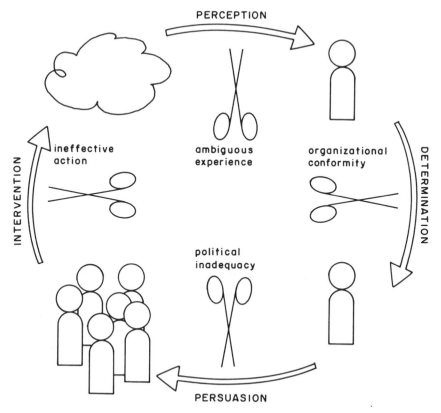

Figure 3.1. Breakpoints in learning

suggests. March and Olsen (1976c) have pointed to four potential breakpoints in the classical learning cycle (see Figure 3.1).

Firstly, an individual may be inhibited in the modification of his espoused theories by factors in the organizational context: a new marketing manager may believe that a particular advertising medium is ineffective, but be reluctant to fly in the face of accepted practice and abandon its use. Secondly, although actions may produce no effect the individual may act as though they do: a personnel director may institute a stress clinic for managers and interpret changes in morale as resulting from it, although the clinic in fact has had no effect. Thirdly, the individual learns, but fails to influence organizational action, and so foregoes the opportunity to test out his developed hypotheses: a company accountant is frustrated in his attempts to persuade the board that a loss-making subsidiary should be sold, and so can never establish if his recommendations are sound. Fourthly, the individual's experience is itself ambiguous or difficult to understand, so learning is imperfect: a R & D manager makes speculative changes in the specification of a new product which failed to live up to its promise, but has only weak market information on which to base his new design. Consequently, although associationalist theory may have some broad relevance in describing the aggregate behaviour of individuals – for instance, as consumers (Amstutz, 1967) – or in predicting the results of skills training, it is less immediately useful as a descriptor of the way in which particular people handle 'real' problems, especially in 'real' organizations.

Gestalt ideas are predominantly concerned with the handling of novel situations by so-called productive thinking, rather than with the management of familiar situations using reproductive thinking that is the central focus of associationalist ideas. Consequently, the empirical evidence which we must seek to corroborate Gestalt theory is less easily obtained than supportive data for behavioural notions. Nevertheless, at a superficial level Gestaltism sits easily within the context of accounts of everyday problem solving: this is probably as much because the ideas themselves are comparatively loose and so more difficult to invalidate, as because of any more-than-commonsense agreement. The importance of insight – historically the initial Gestalt research focus – as a way of finding a path through seemingly impenetrable problems has earlier been noted as a feature of practical problem handling. Unfortunately, it is a feature which many organizational cultures succeed in smothering beneath a blanket of rationality and serious-mindedness. Consequently, there is less opportunity for us to see Gestalt ideas in action in many problem-solving settings. Nevertheless, such evidence as there is supports the centrality of the human search for meaning in events and confirms the situational and experimental influences on problem reorganization.

More dubious by far is the carry-over of the idealisms of deductive reasoning. Apart from the fact that few people are so fortunate as to possess the completeness of reliable information that is needed for sound conclusions to be drawn from unambiguous evidence, the exigencies of problem-handling settings rarely permit an individual the time or resources for a comprehensive analytical approach. Isenberg (1986) has suggested that managerial reasoning is based upon a principle of plausibility, rather than upon one of strict logic: that is, upon the idea that people work from premises that are likely or plausible, rather than accurate or certain, and that they often use informed or inspired guesswork as the basis of action, rather than being able to rely upon rigorous evaluation. Weick (1983) goes further in challenging the widely held view that managerial problem solving can be considered (and improved) as a sequential process akin to scientific research. It is, he says, more usually experienced as an immediate and holistic activity, in which, given a body of evidence, the required completion of the problematic situation is simply 'there'. These and other writers on managerial thought have highlighted the idealizations implicit in the simple application of cognitive theory to the practice of dealing with problems.

Tailpiece

There is an obvious and anticipated gap between any account of what people actually do when confronted with problems, and the explanations which can be provided by a core of theory that is based in the main upon limited laboratory experiments. Despite this, useful insights into certain sorts of problem-handling activity can be obtained. Nevertheless, if we are to build a practically useful approach to problem management, the everyday complexities of dealing with problems must be acknowledged and made explicit so that ways of working with them can be developed. This enrichment of our picture of the process is the subject of the following chapter.

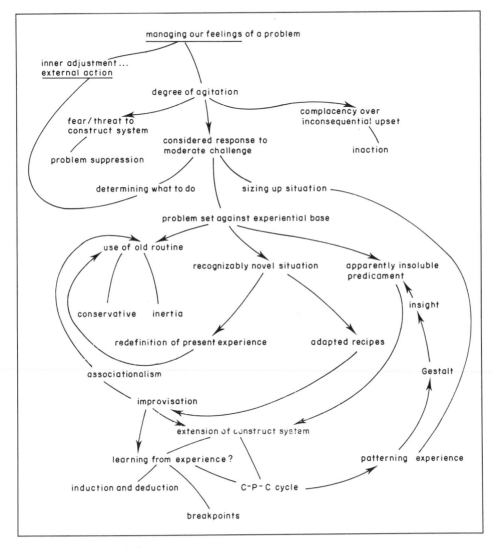

Diagram 3.1. Ideograph three

CHAPTER FOUR

Sharing our confusions

It is doubtful if, as he carried out his famous studies, Thorndike was particularly alive to the varied concerns if his experimental cats: for instance, their irritation by fleas, their distaste for the odours of the laboratory, their lingering memories of attempts to scratch their gaoler. Like most psychologists Thorndike felt able to assume that the escapological problem which he had set was the one in which his subjects would be most interested. Similarly he believed, probably quite rightly, that the behaviour of his trapped cats would not be affected by peripheral features: for example, that a caged tom would not 'play up' to an attractive female held in a neighbouring box. It is hard to believe, however, that human subjects would be as single minded or would retain as focused a perspective as the dedicated experimental animal! In any case, outside a tightly controlled experimental situation, there is no limit upon the number of a subject's simultaneous concerns, nor any restriction on the influence of environmental factors upon problem-handling performance. Consequently, success in dealing with real problems will depend crucially upon these parameters. The main tool which is used to manipulate these practical complexities is the same as that with which we handle the identificaton of problems: selective attention.

In Chapter Two we made explicit recognition of two features that are frequently simplified away in portraying individual apprehension of problems: that people are simultaneously concerned with a multiplicity of variously related problems; and that they encounter these confusing situations in a social context. It is equally important to recognize the impact of these two factors upon the process of problem handling and we shall now consider then in turn.

4.1

For the individual faced with a confusion of problems, there are clear decisions to be made at two levels: first, to which problems should attention be directed; second, what should be done to deal with each of these concerns. Just as with the apprehension of problems, we can conceptualize the former process as being informed by some sort of prioritization of the concurrent problems, with a hierarchical ordering determined according to a rationale of importance, messiness or whatever. The way in which the selected problem is subsequently handled naturally depends upon the way in which it is shaped, and may be affected by carry-over influences from other current spheres of concern. However, it should not be assumed that this whole two-level process is managed with extreme rationality. For example, an individual may be attracted to and decide to work upon one specific problem to the exclusion of others, because of its intrinsic interest rather than because of any widely considered appraisal of its merits relative to other current concerns: further, these interests will themselves be in a constant state of flux. Similarly, it would be false to pretend that each problem is handled to completeness in a single episode. It would probably be more accurate to depict the treatment of a specific problem situation as consisting of a number of forays, varying in direction and productivity, and possibly taking very different forms, leading unpredictably to a reshaping of the initial concern or its summary extinction. For instance, a number of fruitless attempts to remove a persistent vegetable stain from a tablecloth may unexpectedly be crowned with success when I recall an ancient remedy that I was once told as a child. This corresponds to one of the nicer features of handling real problems: the delightful possibility that a problem may just go away of its own accord. This never happens with laboratory problems, but fortunately for our sanity, happens often enough in the real world.

An individual's ability to handle a confusion of difficulties depends not simply upon conceptual abilities or subject expertise, but also upon personal capacity to cope with the stresses imposed. Today, perhaps more than in the recent historical past, individuals are being forced to address a hugely diverse span of issues. The self-service society forces us all to become mildly expert across a wide range of previously separate specialisms: thus I need to have some knowledge of mechanics, plumbing, carpentry, gardening, cookery, child-care, driving, the law, medicine and a hundred-and-one other minor skills, in addition to the deeper knowledge I require in relation to my career and the technical expertise I must possess in relation to my hobbies, if I am to have any credibility as a competent member of late twentieth-century society. Each of these arenas of activity can throw up problems for attention: indeed, our extended knowledge can of itself generate fears and concerns in areas to which we would heretofore have been oblivious. People's ability to cope with these pressures varies widely: for some, the strain becomes too much and stress-related diseases take over; others seem able to handle their feelings by setting problems in perspective.

The methods advocated by stress counsellors and occupational psychologists – lifestyle appraisal, assertiveness training, relaxation – have the general effect of causing problems to be seen from new angles and so provide coping strategies which modify both the portfolio of problems facing an individual, and the content of these problems.

While the whole purpose of the laboratory format is to isolate problems, real problems are encountered in real contexts , and it is to these that we must now turn. We saw in Chapter Two how context can shape the perception of problems; similarly it will modify their treatment, both in terms of which problems we address and also in terms of how we address them.

'"It takes thirty minutes walk to village X, and it is five times faster on a bicycle. How long will it take on a bicycle?"

"My brother in Dzhizak has a bicycle, and he goes much faster than a horse or person."

The problem is repeated

"Five times faster . . . If you go on foot, you will get there in thirty minutes, but if you go by bicycle, you will get there much faster, of course, probably in one or two minutes."

. . .

"And if you figure it exactly?"

"I couldn't say exactly, only approximately; I myself never went! People who did could tell you . . . so I'm telling you approximately." '

A.R. Luria   *Cognitive Development*

People who are unused to the concepts of academic problem solving, for instance, are frequently unable to accept the conditions of the problems which they are given, especially when they contradict experience, and may decline to deal with them further as a result. This intuitively understandable refusal to work within a closed logical system of rules, and the desire to operate on a purely practical level is familiar to all teachers, but is far more widespread than the classroom. The implication is that the way we think about problems requires either a clearly stated and accepted context or else the ability to bracket the experience and see it in more abstract terms. However, difficulties may arise in the latter case if the connection between our constructed abstraction and the 'real' world situation is severed and cannot be re-established effectively. As we shall see in later chapters, this 'relevance gap' is an issue of some importance for those who seek to help others with problems.

A further aspect of context, personal role, also has a strong bearing upon the individual's handling of a problem. Roles create specific expectations of people. So, for example, on a trans-polar expedition, the team will turn to the meteorologist for advice on weather conditions, to the geologist for comment on mineral prospects, to the veterinarian for guidance on looking after the huskies; correspondingly, it is probable that individuals will suppress their own relevant knowledge in areas which are not their designated responsibility. Sometimes the constraints imposed by role are even stronger, and the right to participate in a problem is limited to certain individuals. Thus, only individuals of a certain caste, or with certain abilities may be allowed to work on problems within a society: the 'closed shops' operated in the United Kingdom by the medical and legal professions are obvious examples.

Context will also affect what we decide to do about problems, since the opinions and beliefs of others will usually modify our choice. For instance, external action may attract critical comment from others, comment which will by association be attached to the agent who is seen as having caused it: thus, we may moderate our immediate desire to beat a naughty child because people are watching. In order to avoid such reproaches an individual may decide not to act: that it is preferable to live with the discomfort of an unresolved problem. Not surprisingly, people who adopt such strategies, often seem to take only a short time thereafter to persuade themselves that the problem never really mattered anyhow. Contrariwise, context may elucidate an exaggeration of intended actions: thus, knowing that he has an admiring female audience, an adolescent boy may be spurred to feats of reckless daring in a situation where a more muted performance would be quite adequate to the problem. The social context of problem handling is thus a crucial determinant in constructing action.

It must not be thought that problem handling context is wholly external to the problem-owner. A vital component of the context within which we each attempt to deal with problems lies inside us, and can be personified using Berne's (1964) model as the Parent, Adult and Child egostates. These three elements of individual personality shape and constrain what we permit ourselves to think about a problem and its treatment. For example, we may feel that certain sorts of solution are 'not in good taste', or are 'unexciting', and so censor them without any serious consideration taking place as to whether they might actually be appropriate. Thus, because of these hidden imperatives or prohibitions, an individual will tend only to draw upon a limited repertoire of approaches, which eventually become the hallmark of his problem-handling style, and are seen by others as an outward expression of his personality.

Contrasting ways of managing a problem portfolio and contrasting attitudes to problem context relate to contrasting aims in handling problems, and these must now be examined.

Clearing up Problems

Ackoff and Emery (1972) have proposed a typology to characterize the three principal ways in which we deal with problems: solution, resolution and dissolution. Problem solving they define as being the search for a way of achieving a goal which will remove our personal feelings of dissatisfaction. Problem-solvers accept the conditions which produce the problem. Their solutions often simply shift the focus of a problem or effectively offload it on to someone else. For example, I may be fed up with the litter of old (and largely unread) newspapers which I have accumulated. I could solve this problem by burning the papers, much to the annoyance of my neighbours, whose sunbathing would be spoiled as they became enveloped in clouds of smoke, and whose washing would be besmirched by ashen deposits. The second approach, problem resolution, also involves achieving satisfaction through goal seeking, but in a way which recognizes and responds to the plurality of viewpoints usually implicated; essentially it is a socially sensitive process involving compromise and negotiation to achieve a settlement, though the core of the problem is seldom defused. I could resolve my 'newspaper problem', by burning the papers at night. More adventurously, I could take the offending items to a skip at the local hospital, so that they might be recycled and thereby be used to raise money for much needed medical equipment: my neighbours would like this too. Problem dissolution is the third approach identified by Ackoff and Emery, and has the effect of totally removing a problem. Here the conditions which produce the problem are changed, so that it no longer occurs; alternatively, a new perspective is adopted from which the circumstances experienced are no longer regarded as problematic. In order to dissolve the newspaper problem I could simply re-assess my need to purchase the papers in the first place: could I not reduce or even cancel my daily order, especially as I hardly ever seem to have time to read the papers anyway? Or, to take a rather more bizarre attitude, why should I worry about the piles of papers, as I have plenty of storage space? Needless to say, in practice dissolution is exceptional and resolution uncommon; despite the alternatives, most of the time people attempt simply to solve problems.

During the preparation of this book I overheard the following half of a telephone conversation (or something very like it) one Sunday morning in the dining room of an hotel where I was staying in Cambridge:

Waiter: 'Good morning. T**** Restaurant.'
....
Waiter: 'For today, sir? No, I'm afraid that we're fully booked.'
....

Waiter: 'I'm sorry sir, but we haven't any tables at all for luncheon.'

....

Waiter: 'Unfortunately we would still be unable to accommodate you at that time: it appears to be an exceptionally busy weekend in town.'

....

Waiter: 'Certainly sir. If you wouldn't mind holding for a moment I shall fetch him to speak to you.'

Waiter rests the telephone receiver on the desk and walks across the room to intercept the Head Waiter as he completes serving at a table. They engage in a short conversation, and the Head Waiter crosses to the phone

Head Waiter: 'Head Waiter, T**** Restaurant. Can I help you sir?'

....

Head Waiter: 'That is correct sir. We are fully booked for luncheon today.'

....

Head Waiter: 'Indeed sir? You are very kind. I'm sure that I should recollect the event.'

....

Head Waiter: 'We should be only to happy to oblige you on another occasion sir, but I'm sorry that we are unable to help you today. We have a large number of residents dining in on account of the unseasonable weather.'

....

Head Waiter: 'It may seem unlikely sir, but we should be unable to cater for even such a small luncheon party.'

....

Head Waiter: 'Knew him at school you say sir? I'm sure he would be pleased to hear from you. Would you like me to put you through to speak to him?'

....

Head Waiter: 'Regrettably that is the position sir. Perhaps I might venture to suggest that you try the W*** Hotel Restaurant sir. I believe that they provide an adequate luncheon on Sundays and they would be unlikely to be fully booked.'

....

Head Waiter: 'Good morning to you sir. We shall look forward to welcoming you at another time.'

Sometimes people go to extraordinary lengths in attempting to extort a solution from a situation. Occasionally this may even extend to the specific form of the solution desired, though more usually it simply relates to the desire to have a problem solved.

A fixation on solution – a sort of 'anti-problem' which when combined with a problem causes both to disappear in a puff of smoke (quite literally in the case of that global solution to ideological differences, nuclear weapons!) – is a regrettable feature of our culture, and one which is encouraged and perpetuated through the educational system. As Eden (1986) has pointed out, it relates to the comfortable feelings which we have about completion, end points and rightness, and to the approbation with which we reward those who can provide such conclusions to problems of whatever sort. This predilection runs wholly counter to a more reflective understanding of many problems, particularly those with strong social or political, rather than purely logical, dimensions, which we recognize as not amenable to simplistic 'answers'. Nevertheless, we feel psychologically at ease if we believe that someone or other knows what to do about them.

> 'No problem is insoluble, given a big enough plastic bag.'
>
> Tom Stoppard   *Jumpers*

> 'There's always an easy solution to every human problem – neat, plausible and wrong.'
>
> H.L. Mencken

Perils of the Mess

Earlier I made use of Rittel and Webber's (1973) concept of 'wickedness' which encapsulates those characteristics of 'real world' situations that render them intractable using routine approaches. To the characteristics already mentioned may be added: the impossibility of formulating a wicked problem independently of stating its solution; the lack of closure through solution, and the absence of criteria with which effectively to test the validity of proposed answers; and the uniqueness of each situation and its irreversible destruction by the solution process. These awkward properties, which suffice to invalidate the naive idea of problem solving, deserve fuller consideration.

> 'If we can really understand the problem, the answer will come out of it, because the answer is not separate from the problem.'
>
> Krishnamurti   *The Penguin Krishnamurti Reader*

Popper (1976) has written 'the first theories – that is, the first tentative solutions of problems – and the first problems must somehow have arisen together'. Whereas tame problems can be exhaustively formulated and expressed in a manner which in no way need predetermine a solution, the formulation of a wicked problem corresponds to a statement of its solution. Consider, for example, a contemporary problem such as the apparent prejudice of some employers against job applicants from certain ethnic groups. In order to explore and address this complex and contentious issue it would seem necessary to record the views, attitudes and experiences of employees and employers. Such a data collection exercise would itself need to be informed by an operational definition of racial prejudice and by some provisional hypotheses about the underlying processes, both of which would be more easily generated after rather than before the study. Further, as an understanding of the various positions emerged, so potential ways of ameliorating or modifying the situation would also appear. These would, however, probably be hopelessly entangled in a web of contrary argument: each apparent solution would, in other words, probably issue from the untangling mess of the problem 'hand in hand' with its antithesis. Thus, the results of such a study would almost certainly be a better understanding as to *why* the stated problem was a problem, but not necessarily any corresponding suggestions as to *what* to do about it.

> 'Whan o dowte is determyned and kut away, ther wexen oother dowtes with-owte nowmbyr right as the heuedes wexen of ydre the serpent þat Ercules slowh.'
>
> Geoffrey Chaucer   *Boethius*

Wicked problems are indeed like a hydra. Since there is no stopping rule (Mason and Mitroff, 1981), it is never possible to say that a problem has been dealt with; the consequences of a problem are played out indefinitely. For instance, it has been claimed that large-scale food production schemes, modelled upon those of industrialized nations, can help African countries to break free from the poverty trap. However, for all their superficial economic benefits, such schemes have often pauperized local communities, created industries which are technologically inappropriate to their settings, and encouraged dependence upon a narrow product base in volatile and globally determined markets. Shanty urbanization, bureaucratic corruption and debt crises appear in later 'rounds' of the problem solving process. To misquote the old adage, old problems never die, they only change shape.

4.5

There is never more than a single opportunity to tackle a wicked problem, and there is no antecedent history to which we can closely refer in doing so. Consider, for example, the situation facing Richard Beeching, when as Chairman of the British Railways Board, he launched major studies for the reshaping and development of the nation's rail system. The survey produced startling statistics: one-third of the route miles carried only 1 per cent of the passenger traffic; one-half of the stations generated less than 2 per cent of passenger receipts; some 2000 main-line coaches were used on average less than ten times per year. The result was a drastic pruning of the railway network and curtailment of rural services. Yet the changes hardly affected the railway's trading deficit. Discussion still rages in railway circles today as to whether Beeching's remedy was right. Concurrent developments in road freight, the expansion of the motorway network and of car ownership, altered fuel prices and wage levels: all of these affected the competitive position of the railways in ways which make a *a posteriori* appraisal of the Beeching Report almost impossible. It has been argued that the structural changes led to the removal of those very branch lines from which the network derived its life-blood; that these 'inefficient' veins were needed to drain the catchment area: yet now that the system has been irreparably altered, how can we ever be sure what might have been?

"Now?" inquired Deep Thought.

"Yes! Now ..."

"Alright," said the computer and settled into silence again. The two men fidgeted. The tension was unbearable.

"You're really not going to like it," observed Deep Thought.

"Tell us!"

"Alright," said Deep Thought. "The Answer to the Great Question ..."

"Yes ...!"

"Of Life, the Universe and Everything ..." said Deep Thought.

"Yes ...!"

"Is ..." said Deep Thought, and paused.

"Yes ...!"

"Is ..."

"Yes ...!!! ...?"

"Forty-two," said Deep Thought, with infinite majesty and calm.

It was a long time before anyone spoke.

Out of the corner of his eye Phouchg could see the sea of tense expectant faces down in the square outside.

"We're going to get lynched aren't we?" he whispered.

"It was a tough assignment," said Deep Thought mildly.

"Forty-two!" yelled Loonquawl. "Is that all you've got to show for seven and a half million years' work?"

"I checked it very thoroughly," said the computer, "and that quite definitely is the answer. I think the problem, to be quite honest with you, is that you've never actually known what the question is."

"But it was the Great Question! The Ultimate Question of Life, the Universe and Everything," howled Loonquawl.

"Yes," said Deep Thought with the air of one who suffers fools gladly, "but what actually *is* it?"

Douglas Adams   *The Hitchhikers Guide to the Galaxy*

The wickedness of practical problems represents a serious complexification of our earlier artless considerations of problem handling. It is not enough to recognize, as we have already done, the plurality of problems facing an individual, nor the fact that they are confronted in a social context: we must also remember that they may be insoluble in any straightforward sense, and that we are probably being over-optimistic if we even think that we can clearly state what they are, still less that we can confidently suggest what should be done about them. Consequently, our focus of interest must be not on the solution of problems, but upon their formulation: we must ask not 'What is the solution?' but 'What is the problem?'

No Man an Island

There is a second twist to be added to the braid of problem handling, beyond recognizing the muddlesome complexity of problem content: it is the human art of working on problems, of engaging in conjoint processes with others. We have already admitted that we attend to problems in a social context, which determines in part the objects of our attention, which may moderate our actions, and which in any case provides us with a fund of experience upon which we may draw implicitly, if not explicitly, in tackling situations. We must now acknowledge that it is a rare individual who works as a solo operator through a problem to its conclusion; others are usually drawn into the process at some stage, for instance, to provide alternative perspectives, to act as sounding boards for ideas, or to become involved in implementing a solution. Even when no one else is apparently consulted, internalized others may be important in helping us to think through a situation.

'Suddenly Gollum sat down and began to weep, a whistling and gurgling sound horrible to listen to. Bilbo halted and flattened himself against the tunnel-wall. After a while Gollum stopped weeping and began to talk. He seemed to be having an argument with himself.

"It's no good going back there to search, no. We doesn't remember all the places we've visited. And it's no use. The Baggins has got it in its pocketses; the nasty noser has found it we says."

"We guesses, precious, only guesses. We can't know till we find the nassty creature and squeezes it. But it doesn't know what the present can do, does it? It'll just keep it in its pocketses. It doesn't know, and it can't go far. It's lost itself, the nasty nosey thing. It doesn't know the way out. It said so."

"It said so, yes; but it's tricksy. It doesn't say what it means. It won't say what it's got in its pocketses. It knows. It knows a way in, it must know a way out, yes. It's off to the back-door. To the back door, that's it." '

J.R.R. Tolkien   *The Hobbit*

Presenting Problems

Problem description is the interface which provides a window into another's world and its embedded problems. I use the word window here in a considered way, since it connotes the artful engineering of a suitably proportioned framework, which bounds a subtly chosen view and which serves to separate the viewer from the scene, much as a proscenium arch distances an audience from the action in a play. This is important, for conceding that we have a problem, even admitting it to ourselves, is not always easy. The consulting rooms of Europe are littered with people seeking exorcism for their problems; problems which are too painful or too deeply set for them to reach unaided. It may be even more unacceptable publicly to admit to owning a problem; tantamount in some circles to confessing some lamentable weakness of character. Such fine considerations inevitably affect the way in which we portray our dilemma to others.

At the same time it would be unfair to suggest that people invariably use Machiavellian artfulness in describing the situations which they face. Quite frequently the sheer confusion and apparent complexity of a perceived situation can be overwhelming. There is a compelling need to share concerns; perhaps also to obtain reassurance or sympathy.

' "You a friend of Pinkie's?" Ida Arnold asked.

"Christ, no," Cubitt said and took some more whisky.

A vague memory of the Bible, where it lay in the cupboard next the Board, the Warwick Deeping, *The Good Companions*, stirred in Ida Arnold's memory. "I've seen you with him," she lied: a court-yard, a sewing wench beside the fire, the cock crowing.

"I'm no friend of Pinkie's."

"It's not safe being friends with Pinkie," Ida Arnold said. Cubitt stared into his glass like a diviner into his soul, reading the dooms of strangers. "Fred was a friend of Pinkie's," she said.

"What do you know about Fred?"

"People talk," Ida Arnold said. "People talk all the time."

"You're right," Cubitt said. The stained eyeballs lifted: they gazed at comfort, understanding. He wasn't good enough for Colleoni: he had broken with Pinkie. Behind her head through the window of the lounge darkness and retreating sea. "Christ," he said, "You're right." He had an enormous urge to confession, but the facts were confused. He only knew that these were times when a man needed a woman's understanding. "I've never held with it," he told her. "Carving's different." '

Graham Greene   *Brighton Rock*

The language with which we tend to articulate problems is usually messy and often illogical. It may be difficult to know where to begin, and once started, a description can be prey to all sorts of digressions and embroidery as we attempt to capture the richness of our dilemma. Theories become interwoven with evidence, and solutions overlain with fear of the incomprehensible. Sometimes the very act of setting out a problem forces us to relive the emotions and experiences which we are transmitting and itself distorts and influences the resulting picture. People vary in the skill with which they can communicate their situation to others and with which they can thereby enlist support and assistance.

Mitroff (1983) has identified the three main ingredients of storytelling as narrative, characters and plot. From the narrative we learn what is happening: from the characters we learn who is involved: from the plot we learn why this is happening to them. Thus, when we are recounting a problem, we give a listener a tale which outlines the historical development that we have seen leading up to problem identification; we also indicate the actors or agencies which appear to us to be involved; and we usually provide some causal theories to explain the events that have happened. It is worth dwelling briefly here on these three elements in turn.

It is common for a description of a problem to be prefaced with a little history. To 'put you in the picture' we sketch what we propose as the relevant background or antecedents for a situation. Although this provides valuable context, it would be realistic to recognize that frequently it is also offered to give covert justification for our viewpoint and solutions. It serves to disarm potential criticism, and may help to demonstrate that the unhappy situation faced has developed almost inescapably. The problem-owner beguiles the listener (and probably himself), and at the same time constructs legitimacy as a necessary figleaf for his actions. For all their apparent confusions, people tend to pre-package problems with studied care so as to accentuate their plausibility.

Essentially we can regard the narrative of a story as consisting of a coherent succession of themes (Abelson, 1973) or interactive episodes between actors – Abelson provides a taxonomy that includes the themes of devotion, appreciation, cooperation, love, alienation, betrayal, victory, dominance, rebellion, antagonism, oppression and conflict – which can be put together in various ways. For instance, the 'worm turns' story involves successively dominance (of A by B), rebellion (of A against B), conflict (between A and B), victory (of A over B), and finally dominance (of B by A). Although themes may exhibit some universality, stereotypical stories vary across cultures and between individuals. To the extent to which a scripted story in this sense is part of the shared heritage of both problem-owner and the person who is being regaled with the sorry tale, an appreciation of the dynamics of the characters is transmitted. If this mutual understanding exists, then far more than a mere sequence of events is transmitted: each scripted scene carries within it its own argumentation, its own moral points, its own mood and atmosphere. Thus, if I share with a workmate an episode in which I have been unjustly criticized by an unsympathetic foreman, but in which through quick thinking I have somehow emerged to advantage, then I am regenerating in his mind all the feelings of outrage and of self-congratulation that go with this story, as well as signalling the operation of the conventional reasons which made things turn out as they did. Thus the mechanisms of causation are integral to the elemental scene, and if the scene as a whole is accepted, then little effort has to go into justifying the causal links.

4.7

The roll-call of characters whom we see as implicated in a problem provides a very powerful shaping for our tale. Apart from causing a focusing on certain actors (and a corresponding diversion of attention away from others) the cast list which we produce is often overlaid with a covert mapping of these characters upon the classic archetypes of storytelling. Thus the roles of the Aggressor, the Magician, the Fool, the Victim and many others may be consciously or subconsciously sought out and attributed to the participants whom the problem-owner sees as significant in a situation. Needless to say such labelling of actors inhibits a rounded presentation of their part in unfolding events, and tends strongly to dictate how events are to be seen and what they may become.

> 'The fairytale holds us and moves us because it expresses so vividly the hope that however much of a nobody we are, we will be somebody, some day. But in its contemporary retellings, Cinderella only becomes that somebody by accepting the hierarchy of wealth and power, and she only secures her own exaltation when she excites the desire of the Prince, and is chosen by him. She needs the mirror of the Prince's approval to find her new self. Only in the glass of his love does she come into her own. . . .
>
> No one used to question this. But today woman ask the question that shatters the fairytale: "What happened afterwards?" . . .
>
> Brought up to be Cinderellas, we fear that our daughters will be, too. We don't want that, we want them to walk away from the fairytale, off into another one, where they will choose for themselves and speak their minds, where they will come to terms with the wicked stepmother and the ugly sisters, laugh at the father, doubt the Prince, eat the cake and break the glass.'
>
> Marina Warner *The Cinderella Story*

Further, there may be significant others (Mead, 1966) who, although important to the storyteller, may be *persona non grata* to mention in the context of problem presentation. An individual's private life, for example, is conventionally distanced from his professional existence, and although perturbing factors may be secretly acknowledged and possibly made allowance for, the impact of the players from that drama upon events in a separate stage of existence can rarely be publicly dicussed.

'Joan ushered Mr Campbell-Lewiston in. He was wearing a light-weight grey suit and carried a fawn German raincoat. When he smiled Reggie noticed that his teeth were yellow.

"How are things going in Germany?" said Reggie.

"It's tough," said Mr Campbell-Lewiston. "Jerry's very conserva-tive. He doesn't go in for convenience foods as much as we do."

"Good for him."

"Yes, I suppose so, but I mean it makes our job more difficult."

. . .

Suddenly the penny dropped.

"Good God," said Reggie. "Campbell-Lewiston. I thought the name was familiar. Campbell-Lewiston, E.L. Ruttingstagg. The small bore rifle team."

"Of course. Goofy Per . . . R.I. Perrin."

They shook hands.

"'You're doing pretty well for yourself," said Reggie.

"You too," said E.L. Campbell-Lewiston.

"You were a nauseous little squirt in those days," said Reggie.

E.L. Campbell-Lewiston drew in his breath sharply.

"Thank heavens for small bores, for small bores grow bigger every day," said Reggie.

"What?"

"I really must congratulate you on the work you're doing in Germany," said Reggie. "Do you remember the time you bit me in the changing room?"

"I don't remember that."

"I think you've done amazingly well with those flans in Schleswig-Holstein," said Reggie. "And now what I'd like you to do is pave the way for our new range of exotic ices. There are three flavours – mango delight, cumquat surprise and strawberry and lychee ripple."

"I can't believe it. I've never bitten anyone." '

David Nobbs   *The Death of Reginald Perrin*

The casting of others reflects back upon the narrator of a problem by providing a complementary role for him. In Goffman's terms (Goffman, 1959) this is part of the presentation of self and communicates to the listener, not only who else is perceived to be involved in a problematic situation and the parts that they are to be seen as playing, but also indicates the way in which the storyteller wishes to be seen in the interaction. Thus, for example, by elaborating a situation in which we are set among a prestigious cast of fellow-actors, we can add glory to our own position and to the whole heroic episode in which we are bound up : a shabby or routine sales campaign can be made to sound like the storming of the Winter Palace (or more likely, the St Valentine's Day massacre!). As Mangham (1978) explains, an individual brings into life a script with parts for himself and others, and presents this script as an account of what is going on.

There is more to a script than characters, although as has been suggested some archetypal characters carry within them a powerful indication as to what is likely to happen in a tale in which they are involved: the Bully will threaten others, the Wise Man will offer sage advice, the Prodigy will surprise everyone. Development occurs through the interaction of these actors and an explanation or prediction of the consequent changes requires an articulated theory of causation.

It is the plot, which ties together scraps of action into a coherent whole, that enables someone to make sense of what is going on. When people present their version of the plot that underlies happenings, they probably reveal themselves even more than they do when sketching a narrative or providing a cast list of characters, since their belief systems directly inform the argument given. To take an example given by Holsti (1976), following President Kennedy's assassination in Dallas, many Texans feared that the killing was part of a communist plot to undermine the US government, while many liberals, associating Texas with extreme conservatism, assumed that radical right-wing groups had been responsible. In other words, in retailing the plot surrounding a problem, we draw strongly upon our internalized theories about the way the world is, and about the ways in which particular individuals and groups may be expected to interact. For obvious reasons therefore, we may doctor the presentation of plot to others in order to conceal aspects of our thinking and beliefs.

Not all situations are seen as offering a simple and compelling plot. Frequently, the apparent causality is complexly confusing: it is then that we may feel our greatest urge to share problems, but when unfortunately we also have our greatest difficulty in expressing them. What tend to emerge as a result are fragments of argumentation that link together disparate aspects of the discomfiting scene; fragments which stand as isolated and unrelated statements of belief. Sometimes the mere recounting of a tale may help us to perceive connections and to allow the elements to gel together, but as often this does not occur; indeed contradictions and inconsistencies between the separate elements may not even be realized.

Problem stories are often told to preface an account of our intentions. They are simply background to lead into an indication of what needs to be done: they allow us to suggest action – exit routes from a situation – rather than to invite a discussion of circumstances and feelings. Indeed it is uncommon for a problem-owner to claim complete ignorance of potential remedies, and a problem may often be first stated in terms of solutions: 'the problem is that our product needs to be available in metric sizes'; 'the problem is that we require more beds in the geriatric wards'; 'the problem is that I can't wash the clothes until the machine is repaired'. Consequently, as related, our actions carry an air of inevitability and our solutions are thoroughly justified. Not surprisingly, it is difficult for someone else to see matters differently after such an indoctrination.

"Why Don't You – Yes But" occupies a special place in game analysis, because it was the original stimulus for the concept of games. . . .

White: "My husband always insists on doing our own repairs, and he never builds anything right."
Black: "Why doesn't he take a course in carpentry?"
White: "Yes, but he doesn't have time."
Blue: "Why don't you buy him some good tools?"
White: "Yes, but he doesn't know how to use them."
Red: "Why don't you have your building done by a carpenter?"
White: "Yes, but that would cost too much."
Brown: "Why don't you just accept what he does the way he does it?"
White: "Yes, but the whole thing might fall down."

Such an exchange is typically followed by a silence. It is eventually broken by Green who may say something like, "That's men for you, always trying to show how efficient they are." '

Eric Berne   *Games People Play*

Carried to pathological excess, the practice of storytelling can develop from a single transaction, perhaps soliciting reassurance or suggestion, into a ritual game such as 'Ain't it awful' or 'See what you made me do' (Berne, 1964). Of course, if the other person is prepared to join in, ulterior motives on both sides may be satisfied, and the game completed to mutual benefit.

Inveiglemanship

There may be straightforward reasons for disclosing a problem to someone else: for example, we may genuinely want advice, help or suggestions as to what should be done. However, the support which we want is not necessarily always forthcoming, the problem not necessarily resolved, the joint experience not necessarily a happy one. The process of activating others is most easily understood at a theoretical level by means of Weiner's (1976) version of Cohen, March and Olsen's (1976) model of organizational choice, whereby participants in joint processes dump problems and solutions into a 'garbage can' from which *inter alia* decisions and choices emerge. We can consider a problem-owner (or carrier in Weiner's terminology) as bringing a problem along to such an arena. Possibly, the owner will be unable to interest others in the problem and will decide to take it to different arenas, in search of attention; possibly, in conjunction with others, the owner will succeed in matching up the problem with a solution or a choice and so effectively deal with it; possibly, the problem-owner will be persuaded by others to ignore the problem, which is subsequently ejected from the arena; and possibly the owner, having interested others in the problem, will allow them to adopt it, and himself leave the arena.

The first task for the problem-owner arriving in an arena with a problem package is to generate some interest in it among those present. In order to capture their interest in our problem we need to provide a suitable bait to attract and motivate others to devote their time and mental resources to our concerns. Thus, to fascinate and captivate our audience, a problem may be elaborated in those directions which are known to appeal to our listeners. For example, few ardent do-it-yourself enthusiasts can resist the temptation to fix a dripping tap or a creaking door: the blatancy of the trap appears to be of little consequence in such situations. Indeed, there is even the occasional danger that sheer zestful single mindedness will lead to a new problem being constructed around a person and pinned to him by one of these zealots.

It is Christmas Eve at the JACKSONS' and some people have been invited for drinks. While GEOFFREY chats to SIDNEY and JANE HOPCROFT who have arrived first, EVA is in the untidy kitchen devising a suicide note and planning to do away with herself. JANE comes quietly into the otherwise empty room where EVA is now kneeling, her head inside the dirty oven, but she doesn't see her at first. Crossing furtively to the sink JANE

> *begins to rinse two glasses, but as she does so EVA, trying to get comfortable, throws an oven tray on to the floor with a clatter. 'JANE, startled, takes a step back and gives a little squeak. EVA, equally startled, tries to sit up in the oven and hits her head with a clang on the remaining top shelf.*
>
> JANE: "Mrs Jackson, are you all right? You shouldn't be on the cold floor in your condition you know. You should be in bed. Surely? Here . . ."
>
> *She helps EVA to her feet and steers her back to the table.*
>
> "Now you sit down here. Don't worry about that oven now. That oven can wait. You clean it later. No point in damaging your health for an oven is there? Mind you, I know just what you feel like, though. You suddenly get that urge don't you? You say, I must clean that oven if it kills me. I shan't sleep, I shan't eat till I've cleaned that oven. It haunts you. I know just that feeling. I'll tell you what I'll do. Never say I'm not a good neighbour – shall I have a go at it for you? How would that be? Would you mind? I mean, it's no trouble for me. I quite enjoy it, actually – and you'd do the same for me wouldn't you. Right. That's settled. No point in wasting time, let's get down to it. Now then, what are we going to need? Bowl of water, got any oven cleaner, have you? Never mind, we'll find it – I hope you're not getting cold, you look very peaky." '
>
> Alan Ayckbourn *Absurd Person Singular*

More normally, the task of the problem-owner is to provide an opportunity for the other person to develop some stake in the presented problem: to construct a problem of his own, the treatment of which will coincidentally remove the original problem. To re-use the dramaturgical perspective which was earlier suggested, what we are doing in such a situation is inviting others to take parts in a script which we are offering. It is quite possible that we may either audition a number of people for the part, or offer a number of alternative scripts to our intended collaborator.

If casting proves impossible, then the problem-owner may determine to take his problem elsewhere. Some problems may be hawked round a number of arenas: so much so that people may eventually mutter grimly 'Here comes X with his problem' when X appears in view! To some extent this also explains why individuals seem always to be working on the same problem: apart from their innate predisposition to construct problems of a certain type, some problems may simply be part of the backpack carried by the person from place to place. These ideas are supported by Cohen, March and Olsen (1976), who note that decision-makers always feel that they are attacking the same problems in different contexts with the same (lack of) results, and that problems correspondingly always seem to bump up against the same people! If a problem-owner cannot eventually find someone with whom to discuss or tackle his problem, then he may resign himself to doing so alone.

Once a captive audience has been obtained, the problem is inevitably subtly transformed. No longer is its treatment a matter of satisfying the original problem-owner alone: now the aspirations of all those others who are implicated must be fulfilled. This may be of little consequence if all that is sought of the others is an opinion about a proposed solution, or some advice on implementation, but may be quite significant if there are more direct payoffs for the collaborators. Quite possibly, for instance, a participant may have a strong vested interest that a solution which he has tossed into the garbage can should be paired up with the problem concerned. Thus, a computer-naive businessman who consults a software house about his information technology requirements, does so with the very real danger that a specific system will be foisted upon him: it is a predatory solution in search of a submissive problem. Alternatively, the others involved may turn out to have opinions about the situation in which their interest has been awakened, which are wholly or partly in conflict with the original problem-owner, and so their views will now need to be accommodated within any eventual solution.

The result of consultation with others may be quite different from straightforward or moderated problem solving. Possibly, the problem-owner will come to see the situation in a new light, or from a new angle. It simply ceases to be a problem and is transformed from something to worry about into somthing to laugh at or to ignore. This is problem dissolution in its purest form. Alternatively, the problem-owner may determine to abandon her problem to others, who elect or are constrained to handle it for her. This may be achieved in formal organizations through an appeal to authority. Consider a mail-order firm: the manager saunters into the packaging section and after a few prefatory remarks to the superintendent, mentions that she has had relayed to her a number of customer complaints about insecure parcels; 'look into it and make sure it doesn't happen again!' A problem can thus be passed on to others in a situation in which one-way traffic is enforced: the problem is fed up or down the hierarchy to the level at which it must be attended. In this situation we can equally conceive of the problem-owner abandoning the problem in an arena which she subsequently leaves; or of the problem being booted into a new arena for attention. In more informal settings the same result can be achieved with the awful prefatory phrase, 'I thought you ought to know that . . .'

The Ramified Model

We have noted then two complicating factors to superimpose upon the model of problem management with which we began in the last chapter.

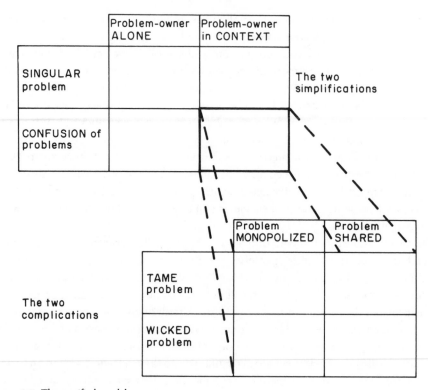

Figure 4.1. The ramified model

First, we stripped away the two assumptions conventionally made in laboratory-derived theory, that problems occur singly and are dealt with by individuals who are mysteriously abstracted from any real context. Now we have recognized that practical problem handling involves working on wicked problems, and that we usually do so with other people. These developments are shown schematically in Figure 4.1. We must now proceed towards a consideration of the practice of problem management in this new and complex setting.

Commonwealth

Mangham (1978) suggests that 'society can only be realized, that microscopic and episodic action can only occur, and that individual purposes can only be achieved through the sharing of meaning about particular events, situations and relationships and that such sharing is realized symbolically, rhetorically and dramatically'. For the individual, a commitment to acting jointly with others offers an opportunity to reduce the uncertainty of their world but from within a scipted organizational framework that by defining role expectations, simultaneously limits the reflected risks and may proscribe genuinely fresh opportunities. However, a cooperative venture may also have the potential for the instigation of a more powerful action than a single person may accomplish. Casual observation suggests that despite little prior reflection, joint actions may often be embarked upon quite fluently, and on such occasions we can consider those involved to be following some implicitly contracted script; on other occasions, no convenient script is to hand and the actors are forced to adapt or develop one to suit the negotiated situation. In either case, within the safety harness of dramatic convention, individuals can feel their way through rehearsal and reciprocal manoeuvring towards a mutually acceptable performance.

All problems stem from individual acts of interpretation. Nevertheless, in the sense of conjoint enterprise and experience suggested above, there is a sense in which we can usefully think of groups of individuals owning a problem. This is especially important in the case of formal organizations — collectivities originally established to serve certain purposes and characterized by a strong patterning of relationships (Silverman, 1970) — in which there may be a clear and pervasive feeling of 'problem' in relation to the achievement of legitimized institutional goals. However, it is also true for more informal groupings. Nevertheless, we must at the same time remember that organizations are dynamic coalitions of individuals in which there is no necessary consensus beyond that imposed by social pressures and within which each person will be seeking to re-orient the common purpose to align more closely with his or her individual expectations. The individual is, in other words, seeking to express himself and to validate his meanings through experiences within and outside the organizational setting. This is organizational politics in action: the management of meaning (Pettigrew, 1983).

If an individual's presentation of his problems is itself problematically suggestive, how much more difficult matters become when a number of people come together to discuss a situation in which they all recognize some interest.

'An upstairs room in an English public house. The room is heavily decorated in a rather vulgar style but overlain by the dull saffron staining of nicotine. It is mid-evening, and a group of a dozen-or-so mainly middle-aged people are sitting on uncomfortable wooden stools around a table on which their respective drinks are set before them.
The Annual Meeting of a small amateur dramatic society is being held, and the conversation has turned to the future of the group. CLIFFORD is in the chair.

CLIFFORD: "The problem of attracting new members is timing. Our season has to begin before many people have returned from their holidays."

SUE: "When we last advertised for new members we didn't get the right sort of people."

CLIFFORD: "Of course, we need to be sure that present members come along if we have an open evening for recruits."

JANE: "Shouldn't we be trying to bring back people whose membership has lapsed? Of course we may not have their addresses . . ."

ANNE: "New people need more encouragement when they do come along."

SUE: "We've got to be clear with newcomers, of course, that they can't expect to be cast in the first play that they read for. Young people especially have things too easily these days. They expect instant success, but won't put in the necessary effort."

BILL: "But we do need more young people. Our casting in some recent productions must have pushed the audience's credibility to its limits by distorting the ages of parts."

CLIFFORD: "I'm not sure that people really notice age as much as all that as long as there is at least one young person in the cast. But I do agree with Bill that we need more youngsters; we've got to regenerate this group, and that means new blood and, just as important, new audiences."

ANNE: "If we had just a few new people, things would probably 'Snowball' when they brought their friends along to productions."

JANE: "So how should we set about advertising then?"

BILL: "It bothers me that even if new people come along, there isn't anything for them to do once a play is cast until the actual week of production."

ANNE: "We could all get together for a general discussion of the rehearsal at the end of the evening."

And so the discussion continues as the glasses are refilled and new prejudices and ideas are aired . . . .'

Apart from the obvious variety of perceptions, of labellings and of motivations involved, it is by no means the rule that people within such a group will even 'hear' each other. Exceptionally, there is a genuine exchange of views and a renegotiation of individual understandings which may lead to personal redefinitions of the 'real problem', and of its associated solutions. More often, there is a stubborn adherence to a single viewpoint, and continued attempts to persuade, cajole, coax and otherwise manipulate others into accepting its rightness. The exercising of power , whether it has been institutionally conferred or stems from an individual's natural endowments, is a crucial element in these exchanges, as theories are advanced and refuted, kites are flown and shot down, answers are explored and discarded. Eventually these games may be played out and, through sheer exhaustion, a mutually bland target agreed, and action taken. Alternatively, the whole process may itself simply be a vehicle for the airing of views, for the flexing of political muscle, for the establishing of alliances, or the staking of claims; that is, for bargaining rather than problem solving.

4.11

Eden (1986) has convincingly presented a four-phase description of what he calls the social business of working on problems. This is shown schematically in Figure 4.2.

Eden's model suggests that a group will often start from a portfolio of proffered solutions. Arguments will then be advanced by those present as to why one or other particular solution seems to be right: this process is one of constructing the problem in such a way as to justify the variously preferred solutions. The airing of views may modify individual perceptions, and will feed into a separate reflection upon the

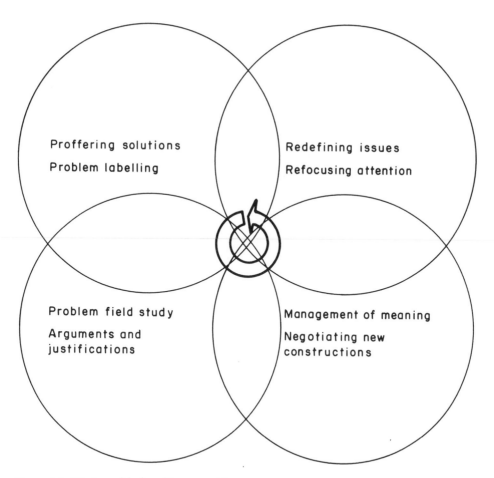

Figure 4.2. Eden's model of working on problems

exchanges; making sense of what has been said. Renewed attempts will then be made to define the issue afresh: and so the dialogue continues.

Eden's model is valuable as a general framework, and when overlain with the real variability of interest, motivation, purpose, concern and intention within a group, it serves as a reliable guide to what may actually go on in a group context.

Tailpiece

When there is genuine commitment to a group and to tackling in an open and considered way the problems which its members severally or individually face, then appeals to precedent or reliance on flashes of inspiration; application of academic analysis or of intuitive judgement; instigation of games or assumption of poses; recourse to flattery or reliance on coercion; none of these in isolation is likely to be appropriate or workable, or singly is likely to be sufficient or necessary. Instead, the situation requires collective exploration and elaboration by those involved, but in a context that recognizes and supports the individual in coming to terms with his own problematic world. Such an approach requires expert orchestration if it is to be worthwhile for the participants. The next chapter sets out some of the implications of mobilizing such assistance with problems, and indicates some of the directions from which such help can come.

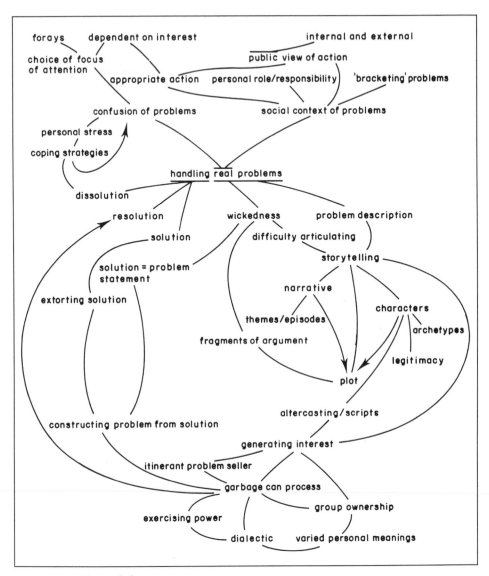

Diagram 4.1. Ideograph four

PART THREE:

Help with problems

CHAPTER FIVE

Supporting roles

Although there are undoubtedly some predatory consultants who make a living by generating synthetic problems for unwitting clients, the initiative for using support in handling problems usually comes from the problem-owner.

"'Count Rouvaloff has given me an introduction to you," said Lord Arthur, bowing, "and I am anxious to have a short interview with you on a matter of business. My name is Smith, Mr Robert Smith, and I want you to supply me with an explosive clock."

"Charmed to meet you, Lord Arthur," said the genial little German, laughing. "Don't look so alarmed, it is my duty to know everybody . . ."

" . . . If you want one [an explosive clock] for home use" [said Herr Winckelkopf], "I can supply you with an excellent article and guarantee that you will be satisfied with the result. May I ask for whom it is intended? If it is for the police, . . . I am afraid that I cannot do anything for you. The English detectives are really our best friends, and I have always found that by relying on their stupidity, we can do exactly what we like. I could not spare one of them."

"I assure you," said Lord Arthur, "that it has nothing to do with the police at all. In fact the clock is intended for the Dean of Chichester."

"Dear me! I had no idea that you felt so strongly about religion, Lord Arthur. Few young men do nowadays."

"I am afraid that you overrate me, Herr Winckelkopf," said Lord Arthur blushing. "The fact is, I really know nothing about theology."

"It is a purely private matter then?"

"Purely private." '

Oscar Wilde   *Lord Arthur Savile's Crime*

During the course of an average week each of us consults a considerable number of different people for help with problems which we are facing. These interactions range from the most perfunctory – perhaps asking someone in the street for directions – through more protracted consultation – for instance, deciding the format of a sales promotion – to the continual joint monitoring and handling of a chronic problem – as in the medical treatment of an illness. Few people reflect greatly about these exchanges because they are so much an integral part of everyday life; yet they have a crucial impact upon the ease with which we cope in all aspects of our lives.

Sometimes it appears obvious to us to whom we should turn when facing a problem: for a leaking tap we call a plumber; for an emergency delivery we use a courier; for a view of the future we consult an astrologer. At other times it is by no means apparent whom to approach, and we may either ask a number of people or else determine an adequate if not ideal choice. The process of selection assumes a prior categorization both of the problem and of the potential helpers.

Problem Labelling

By the time that we get to the point of seeking outside advice, we have usually conceptualized our problem to a considerable degree. Indeed, the result may sometimes be little more than a neatly stylized caricature of the richly messy world we face. Quite possibly this process of preliminary reflection and clarification of ideas will have been carried out in concert with others; indeed such discussions may have been crucial in determining the current 'shape' of the problem, and therefore the way in which we might subsequently classify it. Further, the problem will have been given a cloak of legitimacy (Eden, Jones and Sims, 1983) in order that it may fit snugly into its social and organizational context, and this will have caused certain features to be emphasized and others correspondingly to be de-emphasized. These and other related forces will be influential not only in the presentation of the problem to others, but also more subtly and insidiously, in how we ourselves come to see the situation which we face: we are, in others words, susceptible to be taken in by our own distortions and misrepresentations. Thus, an individual may be persuaded that he has a personal assertiveness problem; a manager may convince himself that his problem is a stingy directorate; a government minister may fervently believe that there is a law-and-order problem. In summary, the problem-owner's picture of the problem in hand is a pragmatically constructed artefact.

Not surprisingly, the location of our current predicament in our personal taxonomy of problems is usually equivocal and also inconsistent through time.

Depending upon how we look at any realistically complex situation, we shall find a variety of distinct issues to tackle, each of which may call for a different kind of help. For example, a problem in goods inventory management may be looked at in terms of storage space allocation, capital utilization, product range rationalization, just-in-time manufacturing, and so on. Within the adopted framework of personal construct psychology we can see this as a choice between alternative candidate groupings and levels within the construct hierarchy.

Additionally, as our appreciation develops and changes, both through reflection on the situation and through discussions with other people, our view as to what the problem is will also shift (Eden and Sims, 1979). In this way, for instance, what started out as a problem of factory operative slackness may turn first into a problem of workforce morale and subsequently be viewed as concerning labour force uncertainty about overall company prospects. In personal construct terminology we can understand this as expressing the restructuring of the classificatory construct system through the dynamics of the *Lebenswelt*, with a consequent relocation of the contained problems.

Nominating Helpers

Just as we may have strong ideas about the appropriate way of 'solving' a problem, so we may also have a clear view as to the sort of assistance which would help us to tackle it. This is implicitly based upon a matching of problems to helpers. In certain complex situations we may analyse the problem into a number of separate elements and use a categorization of helpers to seek the counsel and expert support of a number of specialists. Thus, when buying a house, we may effectively draw together a back-up 'team' consisting of a solicitor to handle the conveyance, a surveyor to inspect the property, and a banker to advise on loan facilities, as well as others to fulfil specific additional tasks. Whether a single helper or a support team is required, the process of nominating such assistance takes place at two levels: what general type of support is needed? and, who specifically should be called upon?

We are influenced, when it comes to the selection of an appropriate source of help with a problem, by our perception of what is offered by potential consultants, and therefore of what it would be proper to discuss with them. As we shall see shortly, there are a number of roles which a helper can fulfil for a problem-owner, and different professions will be seen as offering distinctive blends of knowledge, skill and experience. However, in practice, people are frequently ill-informed. Sometimes this is a result of the misleading public image of a profession. To take an example from close to home, 'Operational Research has been equated by managers to mathematical masturbation and to the absence of any substantive knowledge or understanding of organizations, institutions or their management' (Ackoff, 1979). This particular misconception has been challenged (Mitchell, 1980) but is still alive today. Nevertheless, the external image of virtually any occupational group is usually seen by its practitioners as something of a parody of what they are about and what they do, and is something which, protesting awhile, they have to live with.

Sometimes, when we seek aid, we may be quite unaware that there exist persons trained to help us. Until we are informed of it, how many of us realize that firms exist which will encapsulate and remove asbestos from buildings, which provide a fitting service for artificial limbs, or which give training in welding technology? This is a reflection of the differential evolution of the construct systems which we each employ to think about people's jobs, for to follow the examples just cited, it is likely that a builder, a nurse or an engineer, respectively, would be familiar with such specialist occupations. We tend to have richly developed systems of constructs relating to potential helpers in the fields of our own job, hobbies, interests or worries, and weakly developed ones elsewhere.

Given that we have decided what specialism we wish to call upon to help us in a problem, we still have to find an individual with the requisite background. There is a variety of routes by which such persons are normally identified, this depending too on the organizational and social context in which the problem-owner is set.

Within formal organizations, specialist helpers may be provided precisely in order that they may offer an internal consultancy service, and it will then be the expectation that they should be used wherever their expertise might appear appropriate. In such contexts these internal consultants will tend, through case history over time, to define and redefine their professed specialisms (Conway, 1977), so that through this and other means potential clients know on whose door to knock. Frequently, the specialist helping function will in addition sell itself internally in a purely entrepreneurial manner so as to expand its range of activities. The reputation or self-professed expertise of a helping group for certain types of work will tend to lead to further work of a similar sort, either with the same or with new clients, thereby hardening their focus and at the same time possibly limiting opportunities elsewhere. A side-effect of this image building is the categorizing of individuals by their flag under which they sail: this can blind us to idiosyncratic talents (e.g. a carpenter may also be an expert on medieval pottery or skilled at first-aid, yet because of his labelling we would not think of calling upon him in the corresponding circumstances). On the other hand, as relationships between problem-owners and helpers develop over time, the latter may become the first 'safe' source of opinion across a widening span of problem content. This, of course, happens on a personal level: for example, the family solicitor may be consulted if legal difficulties are faced in any arena.

When there is no provision for appropriate help within the organizational framework, and external consultation is necessary, many of the same considerations may still apply. For instance, a helper may have links of a personal or professional nature with either the problem-owner or with someone else in his organization, and through this contact establish his qualifications as a possible source of assistance. Less directly, a helper may be known by reputation or advertisement: Schein (1969), who works as a process consultant, mentions that many of his clients come to him after hearing him talk, after reading his books, or after completing one of his training courses. Anecdotal evidence confirms that this form of introduction is very common among external consultants: indeed it is the whole *raison d'etre* of many professional courses and publications, which set out to raise awareness of the possible improvements that could be achieved through the use of the helper's peculiar skills.

In the absence of any such immediate contacts, we may seek the advice of friends or colleagues as to whom we should approach for help with our problem. This is more likely if we need guidance in some unfamiliar field of activity: unprompted, few of us can probably call to mind the name of a reliable local sorcerer. A good example of such assistance is that provided by a variety of centralized agencies which help small businesses to obtain one-off technical support. Others occur where potential helpers are deeply embedded within a large and unfriendly bureaucracy: this explains the existence of services which provide guides to the topography of complex systems such as that for welfare benefits in the United Kingdom.

Otherwise, in the absence of any other information, we may, in the last resort, simply select at random from a published list of appropriate specialists; and hope for the best!

Passing the Buck

We may call upon others to help us through a problem because they appear to fulfil any of a range of possible roles. This extreme position is one in which we totally abnegate liability.

The hero of classical (and not so classical) stories is usually called upon to act in a situation on behalf of a problem-owner. Thus modern wish-fulfilment figures like Superman and Captain America follow in the steps of Hercules to defeat evil or to right wrongs. In this capacity they are usually given a completely free rein to use their initiative and imagination in dealing as they think fit with villainy and misdemeanour. Indeed a problem-owner only tends to feature incidentally in their doings, either as a catalyst for their action or as a victim-object in their avenging adventures. The problem is thus taken over by the superhero who uses his own superlative skills to put matters to rights.

> 'There was nothing mystical about the Superman of history. As we enter the 1980s, the movie *Superman* is quite a different matter. First of all, it is no accident that he should have an onerous father . . ., or that his father should impart to the child about the leave for Earth a Knowledge of which we know nothing. . . . Or that he should give his son a highly trinitarian viaticum, put him in a spacecraft in the form of a cradle, which navigates through space like the comet of the Magi.

> Or that the adult Superman, possessed by ill-tempered voices like a Joan of Arc in skirts, should have problems worthy of the Mount of Olives and Tabor-like visions. He is the Son of Man.
>
> . . .
>
> The reincarnation of Superman would seem to be the pop version of a series of more complex and profound phenomena that apparently reveal a trend: the return to religious thought.
>
> . . .
>
> Man somehow feels he is infinite, or rather that he is capable of desiring in an unlimited fashion; he desires everything, we might say. But he realises that he is incapable of achieving what he desires, and therefore he must prefigure an Other (who possesses to an optimum degree what he most desires), to whom he delegates the job of bridging the gap between what is desired and what can be done.'
>
> Umberto Eco   *Travels in Hyperreality*

The superhero mode of support is not confined to comic fiction. Some professional consultants may encourage the idea that they provide this sort of 'action-packaged' service (the term 'superconsultant' has certainly been reflexively used), and some of their clients may actively seek such help. An obvious benefit for the problem-owner is the removal with the problem of the related mental stress. More craftily, the problem-owner can distance himself a little from any untoward fallout from the superhero's solutions. Doubtless the superhero also gets a reaffirming, macho 'kick' out of rescuing such 'damsels in distress'.

It would be incorrect invariably to criticize either party involved in such an arrangement. In those cases where the helper can offer specialist knowledge or abilities and can fully appreciate the difficulties facing the client, such support can be invaluable. A good example is the use of a professional fund raiser by an institution seeking to find its way through the maze of EEC legislation in search of Community funding for a research project. More mundanely, superheroes may offer services such as clearing drains or repairing clocks.

However, sometimes the motives involved on either side are less than pure. The consultant may have a vested interest in forcing a particular outcome: for instance, in selling an insurance policy as a way of handling an investment problem. The client may covertly wish to abrogate responsibility for decision or action: for example, for terminating a relationship as a way of handling a marital dispute. In cases like these a degree of hidden duress or game playing may be taking place, which makes the relationship between problem-owner and helper less than honest, though the symbiosis may nevertheless be mutually convenient. This style of consultancy support has aptly been termed 'coercive' by Eden, Jones and Sims (1983) and can lead, as they point out, to helpers using, by intention or through collusion, 'some of their power to tell the client what problem they think the client ought to have' – which is a distinctly inappropriate stance in many problem settings. It is apparent that coercion operates in the reverse direction too.

We can gain an insight into the performance and accomplishments of a superhero, by following any of a number of management authors – for example, Friend and Hickling (1987) – in considering the process of working on problems to involve a number of foci, as shown in Figure 5.1.

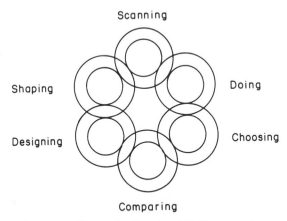

Figure 5.1. Foci in working on problems (after Friend and Hickling, 1987)

Thus from initial awareness of a complex problem a problem-owner may proceed first to clarify and structure the issues involved. This helps to initiate thinking about the design of possible ways of dealing with the situation. Necessarily there is then a need to compare alternative coping strategies. Making use of some suitable criteria, an appropriate package of commitments to action for subsequent implementation can then be determined. Seen within this framework, we can recognize that the superhero effectively shoulders the whole process following the raising of awareness. The key to his effective use, of course, is that he understands what his client wants at the start, or things can go disastrously (or comically) wrong.

Consulting the Sage

Another favourite consultant from the world of folk myth is the wise old man. This archetype differs from the superhero in a number of ways, the most significant of which is that he tends not to dirty his knarled old hands with involvement in action, taking instead a more passive role in affairs. Thus wise old men from Merlin to Machiavelli and beyond have given their sage guidance to kings and princes. Here the problem-owner is responsible for putting into practice the advice proffered, though with a considerable degree of confidence that it will be successful: the wise old man does all the thinking.

The wise old man is alive and well in contemporary society, although seldom are modern versions able to offer such a catholic range of expertise as their legendary counterparts. Instead they have limited domains of wisdom: baby care, computer graphics, antique porcelain, investment management, fire safety, and so on. For the wise old man of today is the 'expert' who offers instant opinions and advice on the arcane subject of his specialism. The problem-owner is provided with guidance for action based upon a framing and diagnosis of the presented problem. Provided that the appropriate expert has been called in to help and that disinterested advice is forthcoming, such support may be most useful in handling those problems whose content is technically complex. The problem-owner is not shifting responsibility to the helper as decisively as when the superhero is called in, since he carries the final task of putting the advice into practice: in some cases, he may decline to do so, or else may seek a number of expert opinions and then devise a forward strategy based on one or a combination of these.

The role of the wise old man is today being taken over in some fields by computer-based expert systems, which can carry out a superficially similar classification of evidence and provide relevant prescriptions for action. Unfortunately with these systems, as with other more traditional experts, the weight of their magisterial opinions may be treated with excessive deference by problem-owners anxiously seeking psychological support, or simply overawed by the accumulated knowledge which they represent; this is a pitfall which can be deliberately exploited – or at least not clearly exposed – by the wise old man, who will wish to wear an air of omniscience and perhaps of some mystery.

'TEACUPS, reading the leaves

The right way to test out the fortune of the leaves is . . . given below:
    Drink the contents of the cup, leaving about a teaspoonful at the bottom as dregs. That done, take the cup in the left hand – this is important – and turn it three times to the left, so as to make the few drops remaining in the cup swing round and round. Then turn the cup upside down in the saucer, doing it gently so that the leaves may fall naturally into their places. Leave for a few minutes to allow it to drain. Then lift and examine the leaves.
    All readings should begin at the left side of the handle and travel round the cup.
    Those leaves which lie high up the side of the cup near the rim tell what is going to happen quickly. Those half-way down denote what will happen shortly, those at the bottom concern the far future.
    Do not be disheartened if at first nothing can be made out of what is seen. Gradually, after concentration, one figure after another will emerge, and each attempt at reading will be more easy than the last.'

Laurie's Household Encyclopaedia

Two further archetypes possess a subset of the features of the superhero: the mystic and the genie. Like the wise old man, both of these are specifically content experts: that is, they are involved because of their knowledge about the substantive content of the problem-owner's difficulties, rather than, for instance, because they are particularly talented at working through the problem with a client.

The mystic may be called upon by a problem-owner to provide an interpretation of experiences, and possibly to suggest an appropriate response: thus a plague of locusts may be read as a portent of ill-fortune which can be averted by a suitable animal sacrifice. The mystic specializes in giving form to the shapeless muddle facing the problem-owner. Modern-day mystics tend to occupy such roles as economic or weather forecasters, or to be seers in more respectable professions, and their advice is prudently sought by problem-owners who wish better to understand events and to safeguard their decisions against environmental perturbations.

The genie is called upon to effect some transformation which the problem-owner wishes to see, but which he has not the resources to bring about unaided. He thus complements either the wise old man or the mystic, who disdains such activity. Real genies tend to be more limited in their capabilities (and more expensive) than those summoned by rubbing dusty oil lamps. The work of a football team manager springs immediately to mind as a good example of such a role: the directors recruit a suitable individual to reinvigorate their hapless club, the person being selected for his very special talent, let us say, for building up the players' defensive skills. Other genies are recruited because of their power to make things happen, perhaps because of their connections or influence.

Inviting Systematic Enquiry

'A motorcycle may be divided for purposes of classical rational analysis by means of its component assemblies and by means of its functions.

If divided by means of its component assemblies, its most basic division is into a power assembly and a running assembly.

The power assembly may be divided into the engine and the power-delivery system. . . . The engine consists of a housing containing a power train, a fuel–air system, an ignition system, a feedback system and a lubrication system.

. . .

And so on.

. . .

It sounds like something from a beginning textbook on the subject. . . . What is unusual about it is seen when it ceases to be a mode of discourse and becomes an object of discourse. Then certain things can be pointed to.

The first thing is . . . [that] it is just duller than ditchwater. . . .

If you can hold down that most obvious observation, some other things can be noticed . . .

The first is that the motorcycle, so described, is almost impossible to understand unless you already know how one works. . . .

> The second is that the observer is missing. . . . "You" aren't
> anywhere in the picture. . . .
>   The third is that the words "*good*" and "*bad*" and all their
> synonyms are completely absent. . . .
>   The fourth is that there is a knife moving here. . . . You get the
> illusion that the parts are just there and are being named as they exist.
> But they can be named quite differently . . . depending on how the
> knife moves.'
>
> Robert Pirsig   *Zen and the Art of Motorcycle Maintenance*

There is another role for a helper, which has historically been of great importance in dealing with problems: that of the scientific analyst. From the problem as given by the problem-owner, the analyst sets out on a tightly structured solution process. This proceeds through an interweaving of inductive and deductive reasoning and an alternation between the observable world and the analyst's constructed mental models of the logic of this world. The problem statement suggests hypotheses which are set up and tested; the results confirm theories and inform action. The analyst is primarily concerned, in terms of our previous characterization of work on problems, with the elucidation and confirmation of hidden problem structures and with the manipulation of these in search of potential routes towards solution. The problem-owner takes up, if he so chooses, the analyst's recommendations and executes the implied action.

The analyst's skills are much revered in Westernized societies, and in organizational contexts a plethora of analytically based occupations have sprung up: management accountancy, operational research, systems analysis, market modelling, computer auditing, information engineering, and so on. This range of specialisms is dictated by the need for a depth of expertise in managing tiny sectors of modern business systems. However, the assistance of an analyst is a two-edged sword: while it may help a problem-owner to cut through the Gordian knot of some perplexing situation, it may conceal alternative ways of untangling the mess, and it may work in a way that is mysterious and technically incomprehensible. The helper may thus be in a position of 'blinding' the problem-owner with science, and so, as with the wise old man, of generating unchallengeable outcomes through an opaque procedure. However, as Eden (1982) has pointed out there can be strong motivations on both sides for a retention of this position: the helper may be encouraged to indulge in arcane analysis by his peers or paymasters, or may simply enjoy its intellectual thrill (Eilon, 1975); the problem-owner may demand a 'clever' analysis in order to provide a smokescreen against others for his controversial decisions, or to aggrandize the demands of his responsibilities. Unfortunately this arrangement may rebound upon both parties: the helper paints himself into a purely technical role, while the problem-owner does not fully understand the basis from which he is arguing.

Jones (1988b) has pointed out a related role which he terms 'the doctor'. This helper, like the scientist, has both content knowledge and an explicit process of enquiry. In addition, however, he may be involved in implementing solutions, and to a certain

extent in problem diagnosis. The 'doctor' label clearly points out the obvious example
of this sort, but individuals working in arenas other than medicine – notably with
organizational problems – also adopt this guise.

Canvassing Opinion

Even more limited in respect of involvement in the total problem-handling process is
the role which Eilon (1975) has called 'the chronicler'. The function of the chronicler is
to record for posterity a fair and objective picture of events or behaviours. This record
may subsequently be interpreted and used by problem-owners as part of the evidence
upon which strategies for dealing with problems may be based. Although chroniclers
may frequently be portrayed as impartial – a stance which most will go to some pains
to emphasize – in practice they necessarily make a value-laden selection of data to
record, data which their mere presence can in any case distort. While it is easy for us to
see biases at work in such obviously political documents as the *Anglo-Saxon Chronicle*,
it may be less easy to detect them in 'scientific' studies.

Present-day chroniclers come packaged in a variety of forms. Most obvious are
investigation agencies ranging from private detectives through to market research and
auditing organizations. These will work to a client's commission in seeking specific
information, using their contacts and networks to find out what is required. This sort of
assistance can be vital in dealing with situations in which some of the uncertainty
surrounding an issue can be dispelled, and choices clarified by the garnering of suitable
data. However, unless the problem-owner is skilled at the interpretation of the
intelligence material, such help can sometimes only exacerbate indecision as to what
should be done.

A variant on the helper working in a purely observational capacity is the role of the
critic: a chronicler with teeth! The critic is invited into a problem by the owner in order
to provide an opinion about what is going on: this can, of course, include helping to
distinguish problems. Critics are frequently expert in the subject content of the problem
and so may be selected on similar lines to wise old men for their acknowledged
experience and knowledge of problem content. Alternatively, they may be able to
bring a particular critical approach to bear on the situation: for instance, work study
practitioners do this without requiring any technical knowledge of the processes which
they investigate. Critics are not usually expected to do more than to highlight the
weaknesses or strengths in what they encounter, leaving any remedial steps to the
problem-owner: taking a facile example, a theatre critic is not expected to improve the
performance upon which she comments, but merely to provide a chastening stimulus
should it be appropriate.

There may be a variety of motivations for calling upon the services of a critic to look
at a problematic situation. The most obvious of these is to obtain an assessment of a
situation relative either to other similar situations with which the critic is familiar or to
qualities of performance in other arenas. The critic thus provides a yardstick to gauge
the problem-owner's narrow experiences against the wider world outside in which

other people have dealt with apparently similar situations: to enable the situation to be seen in historical perspective and sensible proportion. Less straightforwardly, though not necessarily less commonly, the critic may be invited in to a problem so as to say things which cannot be said from within established organizational positions: later he may also provide a convenient scapegoat upon whom unpopular changes can be blamed. In an equally devious manner, some critics may be called in so as to confirm the obvious in a situation, providing variously reassurance, influential support or a source of smug self-satisfaction for the problem-owner. Familiarly, critics occupy posts such as those of inspector in formal organizations, positions from which they discharge their responsibilities with some authority.

Asking for Ideas

What the critic provides is a view of events from a fresh perspective. Sometimes a more positive output is called for, and the helper is also expected to make some suggestions as to what might be done in a situation, though not to the extent of recommending a single specific policy. This role falls through into the stage of the problem-working framework which we called designing, and is that of the inventor: the Leonardo function. Once more, content-related expertise is a common qualification for such helpers, though as de Bono (1971) has pointed out creative input is often as readily obtained from people whose interests lie outside a problem area, as from those who are heavily submerged in its orthodoxies.

Both critic and inventor bring a breath of fresh air into a problem arena. They often do so as invited intruders, a position which is not without its hazards (Baum, 1982). Alternatively, their position may be an institutionally legitimized one.

The use of such free-standing minds is not uncommon in industry or government, where 'task forces', 'think tanks', 'commissions' and 'research centres' have been created specifically to provide a safe haven for such originality to flourish. That sanctuary is necessary, is a measure of the customary strength of opposition to new opinions or ideas in most organizations. However, while such protection allows fresh concepts to germinate, the barrier frequently proves to create or imply a cloistered atmosphere which can cause the suggestions of such helpers to be treated as idealistic and impractical. It is all too common for contributions from such helpers to be greeted by the response that those concerned are ignorant of the practicalities of day-to-day operations, or of the social and political forces at play in a problem; a shortcoming often quite fairly laid at the door of the more 'academic' groups.

The Leaky Paradigm

All of the roles which we have so far discussed are ones in which the helper effectively takes over from the problem-owner a subset of those stages of problem handling indicated earlier. This is illustrated in Figure 5.2.

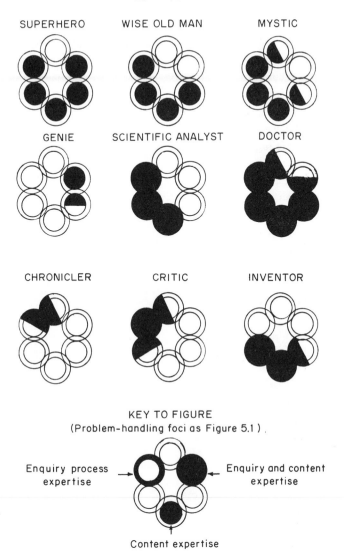

SUPERHERO WISE OLD MAN MYSTIC

GENIE SCIENTIFIC ANALYST DOCTOR

CHRONICLER CRITIC INVENTOR

KEY TO FIGURE
(Problem-handling foci as Figure 5.1)

Enquiry process expertise → ← Enquiry and content expertise

Content expertise

Figure 5.2. Problem-helpers' prime contribution for various possible roles adopted

In each of these cases the consultant's services are being purchased for part of the work on the problem.

As Schein (1969) has explained, a successful conclusion to such consultation depends critically upon a number of factors: a 'correct' diagnosis of the problem; unambiguous communication of the problem to the helper; accurate assessment of the consultant's capabilities; and a willingness to face the consequences, both of the consultant's involvement and of implementing any recommendations. The alternative paradigm of traditional consulting, which Schein (1969) terms the doctor–patient model, also covers some aspects of the roles which we have been considering. For this mode of working to succeed, there must be a high degree of trust between problem-owner and helper, and a preparedness to accept the prescription offered. In view of the demanding pre-requisites for success in either of these sorts of consultation, the observation that they are frequently less than satisfactory comes as little surprise. An alternative approach is offered by a distinct set of alternative roles for problem-helpers which involve working through some part or parts of the problem-handling process in collaboration with the problem-owner. These are discussed below.

Subversive Colleagues

Across the critical divide between working on a problem *for* a problem-owner and working on a problem *with* a problem-owner, there is a further set of roles which a helper may fulfil.

> 'FOOL: "If thou wert my fool, nuncle, I'd have thee beaten for being
>   old before thy time."
> LEAR: "How's that?"
> FOOL: "Thou should'st not have been old till thou had'st been wise."'
>
>   Shakespeare   *King Lear*

The first of these roles, and one to which we shall return, is that of the fool or jester. At the medieval court the fool occupied a position that was essentially outside the normal social hierarchy, and he was licensed, nay required, to speak to his lord freely – indeed even with studied impertinence or discourtesy – without fear of retribution. It was expected of him to challenge and question authority, either in a purely mischievous way or as a more deliberate devil's advocate. The fool offered an alternative, heretical view of what was going on, and also injected a jarring, provoking dislocation into the smooth continuity of discussion or reflection. He thus attacked not only the substantive content of the perceived situation, but also the process through which its meanings were being explored and negotiated.

The iconoclastic role of the fool has been identified by Eilon (1975) as one of the essential facets of the action researcher's task in the field of modern managerial decision making. His special skill is to provide a new outlook on events, and he may do this either from the basis of his own specialized knowledge of the problem area, or by means of generalized techniques or approaches which encourage laterality in thinking. In other words, he may be an expert either on problem content or on the process of enquiry itself. However, as Jones (1988a) has indicated, the fool may also minister to other needs: notably, he may be an inspirational – and possibly an entertaining – shaper of the social process within the problem-owning client group. For clarity, perhaps we should label this latter role 'the jester'. In terms of our earlier characterization of aid through the problem-handling process (Figure 5.1 above), the fool/jester may be collaboratively involved at any or all stages, though he can also inject his own idiosyncratic views at any point. In his practice, the fool tends to find himself working as a (key) member of a multi-function, problem-handling team. Here his role can usually be seen in a positive light, since the demolition of cherished beliefs can lead to refreshing new theories to inform action. However, in some hands, there may be too much satisfaction in the more destructive side of the role, especially if the individual concerned does not remain non-partisan and seeks instead to further sectarian ends.

Across different organizations, the fool's formal designation will vary greatly: it may be as a non-executive member of a board of directors – in itself an intriguing role (Eilon, 1980) – or else at a lower level in the hierarchy, as a designer, planner or internal consultant. In order for the latter positions to be effective, the fool must, like his antecedent at court, at least have some security against powerful opponents of his provocations: for instance, as an early text insisted 'The OR man must report to someone who is sympathetic to what he is trying to do. He must be so securely located that if this man moves on elsewhere he will not find himself out on a limb. He must have access to the top management of the company and he must have ready access to all the information of the company' (Rivett and Ackoff, 1963). Such internal niches are not always easy to find today, hence the prevalence of external consultants in the fool's motley.

Mann (1981) has affirmed that organizations will always need bright people to perform the fool's work – notably at the interistices between functions – and to provide a creative and systematic spur in management and planning. However, even the abilities to offer and to generate novel perspectives on a situation and to conduct social interactions in a skilful manner, are not usually enough for anyone except the most academically distinguished, the most politically influential, or the most venerably patrician to retain an organizational position of any permanence. Indeed, Smith (1978) has less kindly referred to the role of the 'professed fool' as one aspect of a wider function which he christens the 'organizational tinker', which picks up and handles in a more-or-less effective way all the odd jobs for which it would not be worthwhile hiring a full-time specialist. There is some truth in this characterization. Most professionals concerned with aiding management decision making have other strings to their bows, which provide them with more robust credentials. Foremost among these is an expertise which Bennett and Cropper (1986) have described as a facility for 'setting the problem in some structured framework': the role of an expert conceptualizer.

Tame Morphologists

We each encounter our experienced world through the frame of our own constructions. What the expert conceptualizer claims to offer a problem-owner is a special 'framework of inquiry' (Bryant, 1988a); a framework that has been tempered in the laboratory of practice, and which is believed to have a broader relevance than the impromptu researching of the layman. As Cropper (1984) has put it 'the consultant acts as a therapist here, asking pertinent, searching questions of the client although engaging in the substance of the problem only in the abstract, as a professional, intellectual conceptualiser and facilitator of a process of substantive enquiry'. The crucial feature is that the helper's frame is both intellectually coherent and practically viable. That is, he asks 'a systematic set of questions ... the answers to which help one to think about problems of a certain type. The layman might well have asked some of these questions, but not as a system. ... it's the ability to see how they fit together, and hence do something with the answers, that is the real skill' (Eden, Bennett and Huxham, 1986). Any such patterned inquisitions rely for their coherence upon a specific, clearly articulated perspective.

Perhaps the most influential conceptual structures for enquiry have been provided by the world's religions, which over the years have provided professionals – be they priests, Brahmans, rabbis, gurus or imams – with systems of questions that can be put to those searching for meaning in their lives or seeking to understand experiences and determine outcomes. Modern inheritors of this tradition include psychiatrists, social workers and educators. In formal organizations, jobs are provided for such people in management science, decision analysis, and organizational audit functions. As Phillips (1984) has so clearly expressed it, their support operates through the specialists contributing the form of the model while the problem-owners provide content; the specialists also assist in encoding the content to be compatible with the form.

The great strength of the conceptualizer function is that through the emphasis on joint reflection and on active diagnostic collaboration, the client with consultancy support builds up an understanding of the situation which he fully owns, and is enabled to develop his personal resources to cope with his predicament. Through time, and with repeated beneficial consultation, the client may come to adopt the stance of a particular framework for himself, and subsequently act as a champion of its application elsewhere. Most of us have probably witnessed this sort of support in relation to unorthodox medical methods: and also seen the ensuing fights between champions! Difficulties can arise if the helper strays too far into the role of content expert – for instance by adopting the owner's problem for himself and then indicating preferred responses – creating a harmful dependency in the relationship, and possibly leading to suspicions of partiality or advocacy, if not by the client then by others in the organization. However, the pressures from some problem-owners for their helper to step into an advisory role and tell them what to do may be considerable. A further ever-present hazard is that even if the helper retains a neutrality over the problem content, others external to the enquiry process may be culturally unaccustomed to the apparent closeness of the client–consultant relationship and find it conspiratorial and threatening.

Band Leaders

In those most common cases where a situation is exercising not just one but a group of individuals, a further role is apparent: that of the facilitator of a social process of problem management. Like the other roles examined above, this too is an ancient function, whose modern inheritors include those involved in counselling and mediation, as well as in more general activities such as acting as a chairman, go-between or amanuensis. The facilitator acts so as to encourage interchange and mutual understanding within a group most notably for our present concerns in respect of 'the management of communication and negotiation within the group as to the nature of "the problem"' (Bennett and Cropper, 1986). This may be achieved by acting as an active listener and recorder of the dialogue within a group, using any of a range of media or formal languages to capture ideas, opinions and expression, for public or private confirmation, feedback or reflection. More actively, the facilitator may intervene in the process, through being delegated the power by a group to structure their use of time and resources, or more strongly still to mediate between them over disputed issues.

The facilitator, like the conceptualizer, need have no specialized knowledge of the content of the problem confronted. Nevertheless, it is likely that through experience in acting in such a role, an individual will develop an approach to working with groups that make use of specific techniques or models for capturing subjective information and for handling the process of enquiry. These may be made explicit as, for instance, Fisher and Ury (1982) have done for the art of negotiation, as Delbecq, van de Ven and Gustafson (1975) have done for programme planning, or as Shaw *et al.* (1980) have done for human relations skills. A skilled facilitator can help a group to surface unstated beliefs and theories, and to share private hopes and aspirations in a way which not only leads to an effective treatment of any problems, but which also has a catalytic effect on the social dynamics and cohesion of the group. For some facilitators, this latter effect is indeed the more significant, and the one which they seek on behalf of their clients to influence. However, there can sometimes be a small step in the exercising of such fluent group process management skills to the active manipulation of group members, and unless the processes initiated are quite transparent to those participating, the shadow of suspicion may hang over even the most benignly self-abasing helper.

Managers of Debate

There exists a further role which to some extent straddles the three archetypes which we have discussed above: the fool/jester, conceptualizer and facilitator. This role is that of the dialectician. Mason and Mitroff (1981) have described dialectics and argumentation as methods of systematizing doubt, and have suggested that they involve the exposure of assumptions; the raising of equivocal issues; the construction of arguments; and the reconciliation of contradictions in a transcendent view. The dialectician sets out to take his problem-owners through a process which encourages them to use this principle of Yin–Yang – of the unification of opposites – first to challenge, then to build upon the perceived experience. Accordingly the dialectician is part jester in stimulating or eliciting polarities of view; part conceptualizer in providing a framework which will accept the content of a problem; and part facilitator in helping the client group through a process of exploration and learning about each other and each other's concerns, from which they can build commitment to joint action. As we shall see, dialectical ideas, hitherto largely the preserve of the philosopher, pervade much of the current thinking about effective problem management. They are energized in contemporary organizations by a new breed of helpers: 'the future consultant' (Eden, 1985b) in embryonic form.

Tailpiece

When faced with a problem we often feel the need to call upon others for help. Sometimes we hand over the ticking parcel for them to defuse, or ask them for instructions or advice on how we might proceed. Elsewhen we work with them to unwrap the layers, and they keep our spirits up with their clear vision and bonhomie. Our focus here is upon the latter, cooperative roles for the problem-helper. In such a context, there is a need for a clear understanding of the parts which they and others will play in the unfolding drama. This forms the subject of the next chapter.

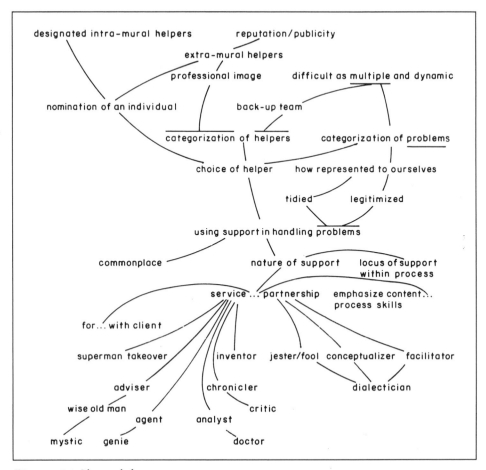

Diagram 5.1. Ideograph five

CHAPTER SIX

Interaction in organizational interventions

'More damp and snowy officers were gathered below, among them Tommy Blackhouse. No one took any notice of Guy, except Tommy, who said:

"Hello, Guy. What on earth brings you here?"

There was a very slight difference between the Tommy whom he had known for twelve years and Tommy the commanding officer, which made Guy say: "I've orders to report to you, Colonel."

"Well, it's the first I've heard about it. I looked for you when we were forming, but that ass Job said you'd gone to Cornwall or somewhere. Anyway, we're losing chaps so fast that there's room for anyone. Bertie, have we had any bumf about this Applejack – Guy Crouchback?"

"May be in the last bag, Colonel. I haven't opened it yet."

"Well for Christ's sake do."

He turned again to Guy. "Any idea what you're supposed to be here for?"

"Attached for training."

"For you to train us, or for us to train you?"

"Oh, for you to train me."

"Thank God for that. The last little contribution from HOOHQ came to train us. And that reminds me, Bertie, Kong must go."'

Evelyn Waugh   *Officers and Gentlemen*

We may arrive upon the set of a problem-handling performance – or in a fresh garbage can, to use Cohen, March and Olsen's (1976) happy phrase – as a result of a variety of chance or intentional events. Possibly we have been called upon to help a problem-owner; possibly we are a problem-owner entering an arena and hoping to find some assistance there; possibly we are simply present at a pre-arranged event or meeting at which we anticipate that a variety of problems, solutions, decisions and

123

choices will be introduced. We may be aware or ignorant of the sorts of issues which are likely to be explored, and we may be unclear as to the contribution which we may be able or expected to make to the occasion. The stage – to pursue the dramaturgical analogy, which will be used extensively here – is bare, though possibly suggestive, and awaits a melodrama, thriller or farce to be enacted.

Negotiating the Situation

I have sketched in the last chapter a number of parts that are open to the potential helper of a problem-owner. The availability of such parts depends upon the willing complicity of the problem-owner in accommodating such roles within his own perception of the performance which he wishes to see orchestrated around the problem. In turn, the desire to assume such roles on the part of the helper depends upon his enthusiasm for the script which he is offered. In other words, a process of negotiation between the problem-owner and helper over the drama in which they are to engage must accompany any joint action, and will be an ever-present aspect of such cooperative activity as long as a relationship between the parties persists.

> 'GUILDENSTERN: "But for God's sake what are we supposed to do!"
> PLAYER: "Relax. Respond. That's what people do. You can't go through life questioning your situation at every turn."
> GUILDENSTERN: "But we don't know what's going on, or what to do with ourselves. We don't know how to *act*."
> PLAYER: "Act natural. You know why you're here at least."
> GUILDENSTERN: "We only know what we're told, and that's little enough. And for all we know it isn't even true."
> PLAYER: "For all anyone knows, nothing is. Everything has to be taken on trust; truth is only that which is taken to be true. It's the currency of living. There may be nothing behind it, but it doesn't make any difference so long as it is honoured. One acts on assumptions. What do you assume?"
> ROSENCRANTZ: "Hamlet is not himself, outside or in. We have to glean what afflicts him."
> GUILDENSTERN: "He doesn't give much away."
> PLAYER: "Who does, nowadays?"'
>
> Tom Stoppard   *Rosencrantz and Guildenstern are Dead*

An individual projects a definition upon any social situation which he enters, and attempts to influence the definitions of it held by others whom he encounters there. Using the dramaturgical model, these definitions embrace the theatrical identities of the individuals concerned. As we come on to stage, momentarily dazzled by the illumination of the set, we take a few moments to size up the others whom we find there, also in varying states of preparedness. In those few moments, our impressions are shaped by the way in which our fellow artistes present themselves, a process which is in every case artfully prepared. In Mangham's (1978) words, A's presentation says, 'This is who I wish to be taken for in this interaction.' It also says, 'And this is who I take you to be': a process termed altercasting. We seek to influence others largely by suitably moderating their impression of our performance, encouraging them to react in a way which is consistent with our intended definition.

Goffmann (1959) has shown that we each make use of a surprising range of subtle techniques to control the expression which we give and give off to others in the interests of achieving this end. The success of these techniques is determined by the way in which they modify others' mental rehearsals of the performances with which they decide to reciprocate in the interaction. If the definitions of the situation and the resulting intentions of all concerned mesh sufficiently closely, then a working consensus is achieved: 'not so much a real agreement as to what exists but rather a real agreement as to whose claims concerning what issues will be temporarily honoured' (Goffmann, 1959). It is this consensus which provides the base for cooperative action.

6.1

Returning to the dyadic interaction between problem-owner and helper, we must now see how the drama sketched above in theoretical terms is likely to unfold in practice. We are talking here about what may be called an exploratory meeting, which will lead to some form of initial contract between the parties. A problem-owner may come to such an encounter with a potential helper bearing a script that self-designates him as an employer, a patron, a puppetmaster, a sponsor, a supplicant, a petitioner, a prisoner, a layman, a novice, or a dunce. The same script will include a part for the helper which provides the correct dramatic counterpoint to this role: the knight in armour is matched to the damsel in distress; the wise man to the *ingénue*; the master to the servant. Provided that this script is not too inconsistent with that anticipated by the helper, then a working relationship may be initiated. This is not to say that the consequent interaction is necessarily deeply fulfilling or longlasting – it may consist of a brief ritual or a shallow and boring game – but it must still be based upon mutual accommodation and understanding.

The conditions under which a working consensus is struck up are not simple. There are usually numerous considerations relating both to the negotiated script and to the wider working environment which make it more or less likely that a problem-owner and helper will be prepared to cohabit. These must now be considered.

Casting the Intervention

Within the script, the roles offered must be sufficiently close to the self-image of those involved, for them to be able both to play their parts credibly and to live with the implications. Thus, a technical consultant, hired for his expertise at computer modelling of automated manufacturing systems, is likely to balk if asked to take part in an organizational performance which requires him to mediate in a dispute between management and shop-floor over the impact of those very systems which he is evaluating for installation. Such reluctance to act the part stems not only from a self-assessed and possibly self-confessed lack of the requisite skills, but also because the role is not consistent with the 'front' (Goffmann, 1959) which this consultant wishes to maintain as a scientific analyst of mechanical systems rather than as an expert on human relations. In contrast, a process consultant will usually resist firmly any attempt to trap him into playing the part of a content expert (French and Bell, 1984) because this would negate his intentions of helping the client to become self-sufficient through thoughtful and open exploration of a problem, and instead hoodwink him into being a provider of evidence, arguments or reassurance. At a more fundamental level, a helper will not normally be willing to be inveigled into a role which appears to undermine the constructed impression (or possibly the actuality) of his competence or integrity: for instance, a consultant may not be prepared to take part in a process of public competitive bidding for a contract in case he is made to appear ineffective compared with other contenders, or to act for unscrupulous clients because he may fear being tainted by association with the latter's dubious reputation. For their part, problem-owners may not be prepared to take parts which undermine their credibility in wider roles: for example, a manager will be reluctant to call upon the services of an adviser if he feels that by doing so his own professional competence is likely to be questioned, or if by so doing the dignity or authority which attaches to his office might be undermined.

> 'He was giving me a careful once-over. "Tell me a little about yourself, Mr Marlowe. That is, if you don't find the request objectionable."
>
> "What sort of thing? I'm a licensed private investigator and have been for quite a while. I'm a lone wolf, unmarried, getting middle-aged and not rich. I've been in jail more than once and I don't do divorce business. I like liquor and women and chess and a few other things. The cops don't like me too well, but I know a couple I get along with. I'm a native son, born in Santa Rosa, both parents dead, no brothers or sisters, and when I get knocked off in a dark alley sometime, if it happens, as it could to anyone in my business, and to plenty of people in any business or no business at all these days, nobody will feel that the bottom has fallen out of his or her life."
>
> "I see," he said. "But all that doesn't exactly tell me what I want to know."

I finished the gin and orange. I didn't like it. I grinned at him. "I left out one item, Mr Spencer. I have a portrait of Madison in my pocket."

"A portrait of Madison? I'm afraid I don't—"

"A five thousand dollar bill," I said. "Always carry it. My lucky piece."

"Good God," he said in a hushed voice. "Isn't that terribly dangerous?"

"Who was it said that beyond a certain point all dangers are equal?"

"I think it was Walter Bagehot. He was talking about a steeplejack." Then he grinned. "Sorry but I *am* a publisher. You're all right, Marlowe. I'll take a chance on you. If I didn't you would tell *me* to go to hell. Right?"

I grinned back at him. He called the waiter and ordered another pair of drinks.'

Raymond Chandler   *The Long Good-Bye*

'A good detective doesn't go by the book. No sir. But he has to have a few rules to help him chew the cup cake. First off, never trust your client.'

Dennis Potter   *The Singing Detective*

Beyond the self-centred appraisal of role in terms of personal repertoire lurk the dangers of the masque: each partner, both problem-owner and helper, has to size up the concealed other. This may be comparatively unproblematic where both parties have formally designated roles which set them up as natural partners in problem handling – as, for instance, where a production function seeks scientific advice from a technical support unit – but is more difficult where one or both sides are unused to such collaborative work, or unaccustomed to dealing with persons of the other's sort. These problems are most vividly illustrated when the cultural divide between the participants is greatest, as, for example, in the work of 'professionals' with community groups: Jones and Eden (1981) emphasize the fear of a loss of control over problem construction to meddlesome, 'clever' do-gooders which such clients may feel in such an intervention. However, suspicions may dog other, less awkward relationships: for instance, Sims and Smithin (1982) point out the habitual caution with which academics may be treated by clients, who may think that they are simply providing research fodder rather than being taken seriously. Such doubts may, of course, be wholly justified, as both problem-owner and helper may be expected to have hidden agendas, and these can easily have pernicious effects upon the outcome of a performance. And, after all, the service relationship *is* a strange one: as Goffmann (1961) points out, the server offers to take an intense temporary interest in his client, from their own point of view and in their own best interests, yet he has publicly taken a kind of secular vow of chastity by apparently disavowing the normal personal, ideological or contractual reasons for providing help. The crucial requirement is that even despite, yet in the awareness of, these unstated motivations, the partners will be prepared to trust each other enough to take each other on, at least as far as the task in hand is concerned.

A wariness on both sides may quite properly lead to a prudent researching of the potential companion. Thus, for example, some process consultants go to considerable lengths (Cropper, 1984; Bryant, 1988a) in finding out about their clients, so as to anticipate how power is likely to be exercised in a client group during the course of an interaction. Elsewhere, and more mundanely, helpers may conduct pragmatic investigations to assess their prospects of a client fulfilling his obligations to pay them for their work. Similarly, a problem-owner may seek the experience of others who have made use of a particular helper to establish his credentials; to be assured, for instance, that discretion, promptness or reliability will be delivered. Some helpers may even be covertly 'tested' by cautious or suspicious clients. Such investigations lie behind the definition of the scene, but provide essential information for the mental simulation of anticipated action by self and others, which must precede any commitment to joint participation in a performance.

Moderating Involvement

Moving outside the immediate context of an encounter, all parties will have interests in other arenas upon which an interaction will impinge, most obviously at the basic level of re-apportioning resources: recall Cohen, March and Olsen's (1976) dictum, 'every entrance is an exit somewhere else'. Involvement in a process of problem handling will necessitate the expenditure of time and energy, which will consequently not be available for competing claims on either a problem-owner's or a helper's attention. These outgoings will relate to the role of the participants in any interaction: for example, working conjointly will usually involve a greater commitment of resources by the problem-owner than when a helper is simply commissioned to go away and deliver a solution. There are thus delicate choices to be made as to the parts which a problem-owner decides to play in each of the several problems with which he is troubled at any time, and as to the issues best delegated to a helper for investigation. The helper has a similar set of choices to make, requiring him to decide between alternative requests for his services in a variety of roles. Each opportunity will involve a commitment of his limited time, and will make different technical and logistic demands, so that a careful process of project portfolio management must be continuously maintained.

The planning of the activities of an interventionist consultant includes considerations other than those with direct resource implications. There are choices to be made both about the clients for whom work is to be done, and about the nature of the work to be done for these clients. Within broad limits, helpers will select between opportunities to produce a portfolio of activity that appears likely to serve them best in pursuing their own ends. It is plausible to assume that additional considerations will come into play for helpers who float freely between organizations, as opposed to those who are retained within an organization to provide help with its problems.

Conway (1987) has proposed a useful model of the process whence the mix of projects handled by an OR group derives: this is shown diagrammatically in Figure 6.1 and explained more fully below. Similar considerations probably apply for other professionals who help with organizational problems.

For an established group, one of the most common sources of work is a previous client, who may be courted through a succession of varied projects. In this so-called closed-linkage process, a fruitful symbiosis develops between client and helper which permits them to reach a working consensus more and more readily. Alternatively, a helper's reputation may travel more or less widely around an organization (external or internal linkage processes) and lead to new commissions. Norman (1988) has confirmed the importance of this sort of introduction, notably in the case when a consultant specializes in specific types of work with a mix of clients. Naturally, over the course of time, the substantive content of the project portfolio which a consultant undertakes will cumulatively impact upon his expertise and reputation, causing it to become focused in one area or another: this can either be a handicap or a strength. Typically these linkage processes of project generation account for 80 per cent (Conway, 1987) of an internal consultancy group's work. The remainder derives from problem-owner initiated enquiries, or from the deliberate selling of the helping service to likely customers, the latter including speculative problem solving in cases where no client is immediately in view. Conventional wisdom (Houlden, 1979) suggests that internal consultants should aim to maintain entries right across the business, to strike a balance between tactical and strategic studies, and to attack clearly defined, technically manageable subjects. However, this view is challenged by the apparent success of groups working from a diametrically opposed position (Hemmer, 1983): selecting 'messy', high-risk, high-level jobs. The reconciling truth is that there is no one 'right' answer: as Conway (1987) clearly demonstrates, the balance of a group's work will be related to the stage it has reached in its own evolution, with both new and dying groups characterized by a smaller proportion of linkage-generated projects.

For external consultants similar sources of work can be identified and similar portfolio balancing considerations apply, though there may be additional self-imposed constraints and objectives. Thus they may believe that their sort of assistance is most

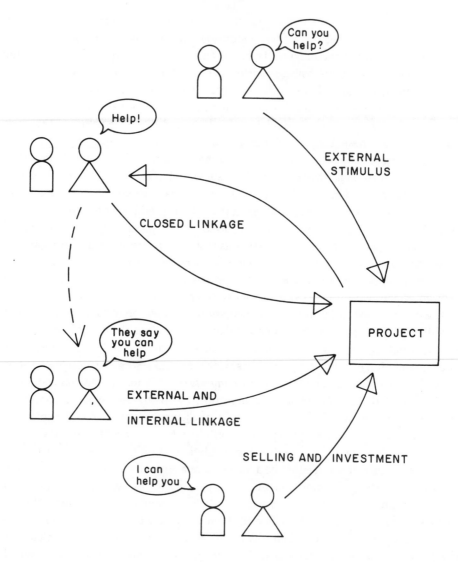

Figure 6.1. The project process (after Conway, 1987)

effective with organizations of a particular size (Mercer, 1981) or culture. They may also seek to work for clients who appear to offer greater potential for future studies, or whose prestige or influence will be a potent advertisement for future self-marketing. Linkage processes are vital for external consultants, but they can never afford to allow the other more aggressive modes of project generation to be ignored.

Outwith the more routine management of a consultancy portfolio lie a number of overarching factors which will modify the whole direction of work undertaken by a helper. First among these are the moral and ethical judgements (Ackoff, 1974a) which a consultant has to make every time he contemplates working with or for a client: is the nature of the work consistent with his own personal code? This is an issue which is especially prominent, for instance, in the application of methods of conflict analysis (Bennett and Huxham, 1982) but which is ever present in less overtly divisive studies. Second, the helper must decide whether the social and political stance of the opportunity for intervention (Rosenhead and Thunhurst, 1982) is one that he is prepared to work with: will his work simply serve to exacerbate inequalities of opportunity or to limit the power of the disadvantaged? The position adopted here opens as well as closes doors in terms of the work which may be undertaken: Rosenhead (1986) has shown how a radical perspective on the practice of OR leads to a new range of opportunities for client support. And third, the helper will wish to assess the potential consultation in purely personal terms: will it be enjoyable, fulfilling and intellectually satisfying? Schein (1969) mentions that one of his principal tasks at an exploratory meeting with a client is to determine whether the problem is going to be of interest to him. Similarly, in planning the forward loading for a consultancy team, where there is a wish systematically to develop more junior members, the educational worth of projects may be a criterion for selection.

Such ideals set broad limits on the field of activity, but can be strongly challenged: in order to keep body and soul together most consultants have routinely to consider whether they can afford not to carry out work. Nevertheless, they will still seek an adequate return in the very literal sense of meeting financial requirements. As with the selling of any other type of service, the helper's own skills and preferences are naturally influenced by commercial considerations, but as Goffmann (1961) has stressed 'a fee is not a price'. In a sense, as Goffmann claims, 'a fee is anything other than what the service is worth to the client': a server may restrict his fee if his client's need is extreme; he may forgo it or charge exhorbitantly if a trivial service has been rendered; he may make no charge for a service to impoverished clients. Setting an appropriate fee can help the server to maintain a degree of detachment, which well suits the tinker's role.

Problem-owners also have their motivations for seeking out particular bedfellows in consultancy interventions (including, of course, the obverse of the reasons rehearsed above – a problem-owner may not wish to be over-dependent on one particular helper, or may desire to call in whoever is the 'best in the business' on each occasion). Carlisle (1985) has entertainingly described some of the reasons why 'external' consultants may be called upon: a desire to get an 'outside' view free from the effects of internal machinations; the prestige attaching to the use of a consultant, and the implication that one's problems are important enough to warrant this; the wish to demonstrate a determination to make radical organizational changes; the pleasure of being able to share one's intimate managerial problems with a stranger; or simply a need to hire in specialist expertise for a one-off task, because internal help is unavailable or inadequate. At the next level of decision, a problem-owner will be able to express preferences between different types of 'external' helper: full-time consultants or moonlighting academics, for example. And lastly, within these categories, there will be a favouring of certain individuals by virtue, perhaps, of their personal style, their personality, their interests or their physical appearance. Once again, such predispositions operate on both sides of the contract too: I know of at least one consultant for whom a shared interest in sailing on the part of a potential client is a significant factor in his keenness to work with him. The linking of problem-owner and helper is almost as complex a process as getting married, and one that need be no more rational.

Contracting to Work Together

The initial sparring tells all those who find themselves lined up for a problem-handling performance – and it must be recalled that although we have talked above as though this consisted of an owner–helper dyad, there will usually be many others involved, and a plethora of problems swilling around – much about what could happen and what part they each might play in unfolding events. They will have developed views about the extent to which they might be able to manipulate others into accepting their definitions of what is going on, and will probably have attempted to do so. They will have struck up relationships with others, and tested them to probe beneath the veneer provided by occupation or position; in dramaturgical terms, to see what motives and values lie beneath the costume and make-up. In short, they will have seen if they can work together.

If the explorations seem promising, then these opening interactions represent the beginning or renewal of a relationship which will develop through the work on the problem which follows. In order to summarize the shared understanding of the intended intervention, it is usual for the parties to generate a form of contract which sets down for future reference their understanding of what is to be done. Formally this may be expressed in a project proposal, which will usually contain a working definition of the problem and identification of its owner, an outline of the main stages of the planned intervention and its phasing through time, a confirmation of the proposed financial arrangements, and a procedure whereby the process may be terminated. Behind this may lie operating documents structured in a variety of ways: for example, Checkland (1981) has set down a useful 'workbook' for a helper embarking on a systems-based study, which includes a checklist relating to what he terms the 'problem-content system' and 'the problem-solving system'.

The formal terms of reference have both an enabling and a disabling function. They enable in the sense of providing a passport which the helper can use to gain access to people and information in the prosecution of his work, and in conferring upon him the delegated right to order and manage processes involving others whose witness may be relevant to the problem in hand. They disable by setting barriers and boundaries upon the work, helping to keep skeletons tightly locked away in closets and firmly steering the helper away from certain areas of controversy. Delimited frankness is not consistent with all modes of problem handling, and is more likely where the helper is performing a technical function for the problem-owner rather than where they are working through a problem in concert. Further, Eden (1982) has warned of the strength of terms of reference in shaping the content of the work undertaken as well as the process by which it is carried out, notably in relation to the implicit emphasis on problem solving rather than problem exploration, and on a static definition rather than upon an evolving one.

Shadowing the formal terms of reference is the 'psychological contract' (Schein, 1969): what the client and consultant each expect to gain from the relationship. These expectations, because they are not usually written down, can be an easy source of misunderstanding. Thus, Schein (1969), for example, takes trouble to state clearly at the outset what he is and is not prepared to do in an intervention; to explain that he will view not just the contact person or the person of highest rank but the entire organization as his client; to demand that he shall find a willingness to diagnose and explore problems and a commitment to the project across all those he works with; and to disabuse his client that he might provide expert advice on content issues, or support for predetermined decisions. This is done so that the client shall not be disappointed should he subsequently make inappropriate demands upon the consultant. Not all consultants are so clear in setting out their position, but the ambiguities of role and expectation which then arise (Cropper and Bennett, 1985), and the consequent likelihood of failure in an intervention suggest that this is misguided. A lack of candour on the part of problem-owners is if anything probably more common, perhaps because they have may have more to lose: after all they may already have made themselves vulnerable by admitting to a problem. The key lies in establishing an open relationship, for this will make clear from whence each player starts and enable later difficulties to be acknowledged and faced together.

Effecting Intervention

Argyris (1970) says that 'to intervene is to enter into an ongoing system of relationship, to come between or among persons, groups or objects for the purpose of helping them'. Taken literally, such a definition of the process which I have already loosely referred to as intervention is at the same time too narrow and too broad to describe the activity to which our imaginary problem-owner and helper, meeting on the stage of an unplayed drama, have now committed themselves. As Argyris himself is at pains to point out, the simple definition is too narrow in denying the collaborative and participatory nature of the consultant–client relationship, and in neglecting the development and exercising of effective autonomy by the problem-owner. As French and Bell (1984) have indicated, the definition is too broad in failing to signify that formal problem handling is concerned specifically with structured interventions, and with structured interventions moreover in which a working group engages in a managed process. It is with these glosses that the term will be used in what follows.

The eventual outcome of an intervention is a commitment to responsible action (Carter *et al.*, 1984): that is, action taken after a conscientious effort to understand a situation, and for all the consequences of which the problem-owner accepts full responsibility. Given our starting point, the implication is that the interpolated process must be one which generates valid and useful information that helps a problem-owner to grapple with the complexity, uncertainty, partiality and discontinuity of his perceived world, and which ensures that he is better able to make free, considered, committed choices in both the present and the future. The question is therefore, how do those involved work together to achieve this, and what parts do those in the arena take in realizing this dream? We shall first consider this question at the level of the infrastructure which shapes working practice, leaving until a later chapter the more intimate details of frameworks which lend form to the interaction.

'Pride seized Henry by the arm and hurried him out through a back door into a long corridor. At the end of the corridor were some large double doors, and on the doors was a large notice, which said *Serious Damage: Production Office*. Pride pushed Henry through the doors, and inside he saw a room, filled with activity. About fifty desks were in it, some with moveable screens round them, some with telexes or wordprocessors on them, some stacked with television monitors. People sat at the desks, creative-looking people in creative-looking clothes. Some of them typed. Some of them were making small models of rooms. Some of them read books. Some of them drew maps. Some of them held up photographs. Most of them were drinking tea or coffee from plastic cups. Nearly all of them were on the telephone.

"That's the team," said Pride proudly. "Those over there are design, those are costume and props, those are production and co-ordination, those are transport, those are casting, those are locations, those are finance. They're brilliant people, brilliant. Lord Mellow has hired them for enormous sums. They could be in Hollywood. They could be in Rome. They could be in London. They're the cream of television talent. And all they're doing is sitting around on their high-priced butts drinking tea, just because they haven't had your scripts."

"My word," said Henry.'

Malcolm Bradbury   *Cuts*

We have explored at some length the casting and altercasting which take place in the first episode of an intervention. Once the action begins it becomes necessary to move from a consideration of roles *for* an intervention to roles *around* an intervention and roles *in* an intervention.

Roles around Interventions

The problem-handling arena will contain a miscellany of people, some with little interest in or understanding of what is going on, others with a keen concern for how matters are treated and for the eventual outcome of the intervention. Most obviously significant among these are the problem-owner whose unease about a situation has triggered off the whole process, and the helper or agent whose support as problem-solver, adviser, facilitator or whatever has been sought to get some constructive action going. However, there are a number of other important roles which are germane to the management of the problem. These are shown schematically in relation to each other in Figure 6.2 and will now be examined in turn.

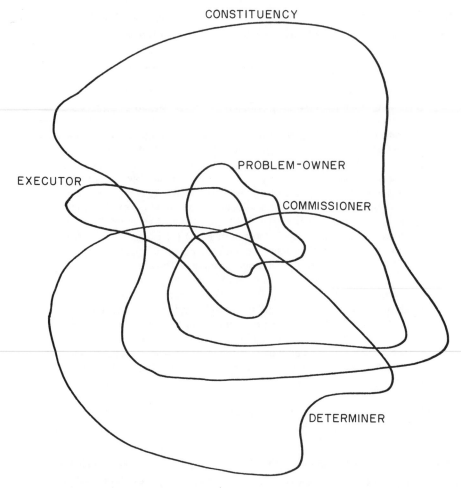

Figure 6.2. Roles around an intervention

The helper becomes involved in a problem through a summons or call for aid. I shall refer to the author of this call as the 'commissioner' of the intervention. In many cases it will be the problem-owner who acts as the commissioner – and possibly also as the paymaster or sponsor – for the helper's services. However, there can be instances where a third party is involved, who is in effect making the help available to a problem-owner, and who may do so only under specified conditions. Thus, for example, legal aid in the United Kingdom is available provided that a person is financially handicapped. The commissioner is important precisely because of the conditions which he or she may impose upon a problem-owner/helper linkage, since they can influence profoundly the shaping and handling of a problem. Elsewhere, (Carter *et al.*, 1984; Checkland, 1981) the commissioner has, confusingly, been referred to as 'the client'.

The second role around an intervention to be considered is that of decision participant or 'determiner': he who decides what is to be done. We may take as a guide here the spirit of Checkland's (1981) definition of a 'decision-taker' as he who is in a position to alter the content of the problem situation. That is, the determiner has the authority, influence or resources to effect change. Sometimes the problem-owner will also be the determiner, but more usually he will need to refer elsewhere to sanction or implement policies. In other cases the commissioner will be the determiner, causing the intervention to occur so as to inform a subsequent decision. In either event, the role is frequently one occupied by a collectivity of people who are capable of, or responsible for, bringing about change, rather than being occupied by a single individual. They may formally constitute what Friend and Hickling (1987) call an 'accountable group" – for instance, a board of directors, a council of elected politicians or the members of a workers' cooperative – who ultimately 'carry the can' for any actions taken; or they may form a managerial group at a lower level of the classical organizational hierarchy, which is concerned with a more restricted subset of choices.

Since the handling of any problem of respectable complexity will involve the taking of many related decisions in lots of distinct arenas, and since these will tend to transcend conventional organizational boundaries, decision participants will often be found dotted about the problem environment in a range of positions. Wherever they are located, a common characteristic is that such determiners will spend much time and energy engaged in 'decision-making processes' that have little to do with making decisions (March and Olsen, 1976b) and a lot to do with exchanging views, developing relationships, exercising power and simply indulging in shameless hedonism; they have their own personal concerns within the social process in which they are caught up by virtue of their membership of such a group. This means that it is possible for the heartfelt concerns of the problem-owner to be treated in a more or less casual way by the decision participants for whom the emotional commitment to the problem can be far less.

The third key role to be recognized is that of the 'executor'. Just as we distinguished earlier between the commissioner and the problem-owner in relation to the initiation of a consultancy intervention, so we must distinguish now between the executor and the problem-owner in relation to the emergent action. We saw in the last chapter that there are a number of ways in which a helper can work with a problem-owner including several in which the implementation of committed choices was delegated to the helper. It is also possible that a third party might be asked to handle this phase of the process. The executor *might* thus be the problem-owner or helper, but might equally be an individual or an agency specifically called upon to carry out the determined outcomes.

Crucial in any realistically sensitive management of problems are the many occupants of a set of other parts: collectively I shall refer to them as 'the constituency'. This comprises those individuals or groupings who have some vested interest in the problem and in the outcome of the problem-handling process. Conceptually, the constituency is similar to the notion of 'stakeholders' used by Mason and Mitroff (1981), which itself made an earlier appearance in Ackoff's work (Ackoff, 1974b), and bears a strong relation to what Churchman (1968) calls the 'customers' or 'clients' [sic]. The constituency includes all those for whom the potential change in the content of a situation is important, and its members will have views as to the merits of alternative actions or plans which may be set in train.

The participation of the constituency in the process of problem handling is usually vital if outcomes which are likely to achieve a degree of acceptance are to be produced. This means that the problem-owner role may even be defined as a subset of the constituency, drawn so as to represent the different interests which are alive in the arena. It may also be that the constituency overlaps with the decision participant group, being the only consortium which is likely to be able to implement recommendations; or else, in a more negative sense, the body which is most likely to be able to block proposals. Since the consent of the constituency may be a prerequisite for work on a problem going ahead in the first place, they may also form the commissioners of an intervention.

The constituency embraces both those who will be impacted by outcomes of the problem-handling process and those who have, or feel that they have, a right to make an input to it: any significant discrepancy between the membership of these two groups will signal all manner of political difficulties ahead unless there are correspondingly great disparities in the power which can be wielded by the two sides. Once again it is worth noting that the actual members of the constituency will usually be active in many other arenas, and so their involvement in a specific problem is subject to their attention not being required elsewhere. This comment is no less valid for groups which have been created specifically in response to a problem – for instance, a strike committee or a single-issue campaign organization – as no matter how focused their energies, they will still have other calls on their time and resources.

6.6

As has been hinted above there will normally be a considerable degree of overlap between those occupying the different roles which have been identified around an intervention. Particular individuals or groups may appear wearing a variety of hats, not only between roles, but also within a single role. The situation is further complicated by the operational linkages which necessarily occur during the course of an intervention between parts, some of which have been suggested above. Thus, the problem-owner may need to sway the decision participants' views if he wishes to see a solution implemented; the commissioner may put pressure on the problem-owner to accept an edited version of his problem; the helper may seek to involve the constituency in the intervention against the problem-owner's wishes; and so on. These forces are expressed and find their resolution in the process of intervention, and it is to the parts which are played in this that we must now turn.

Parts in Interventions

It is convenient to refer to the troupe of actors assembled on set for a problem management intervention as the 'working group' in this prototypical performance. As has been implied above, these individuals may arrive on the stage for a variety of reasons: it may be they who have identified the problem; they may be present as consultants on its content or on processes by which it may be addressed; they may be there to represent or safeguard the interests of a wider group with interests in the matter; or it may be they who are charged with the responsibility for taking whatever action is deemed necessary. Although this lineage will seldom be forgotten, once becoming part of the company of players, each individual will be called upon to take a new part in the social process which subsequently unfolds. These roles, defined within the narrower context of the drama itself, are shown schematically in Figure 6.3. They relate to three crucial but overlapping areas of the performance: content, process and context.

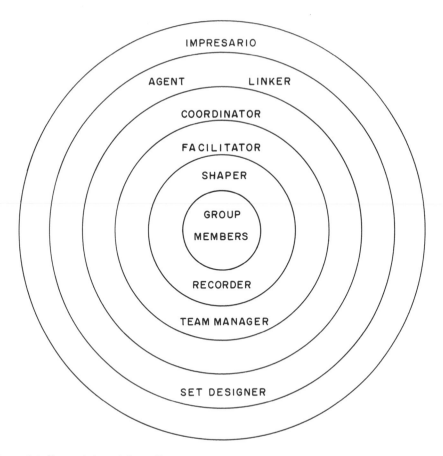

Figure 6.3. Key parts in an intervention

The roles which most immediately spring to mind as impacting upon problem management tend to be those concerned with handling the substantive content of the situation. The first of these, and the least differentiated in functional terms, is that of the ordinary 'group member'. Each participant in a group will usually have some substantive input to make to the intervention, bringing a unique perspective to bear upon the problem of shared concern. Sometimes members will actually have been selected or invited to join the group because of their specialized knowledge; at other times the depth of knowledge is less important than broader experience in a field and an ability to think laterally; on other occasions again, what is needed is a range of values or beliefs across those present. If the diverse viewpoints can be effectively captured and exchanged then the group as a whole can develop a far richer picture of the problematic situation and its possibilities than would be feasible otherwise.

It is the job of another role type to attempt to help in the construction of a shared meaning from the mass of information and ideas contributed by the group members: we shall call this role the 'shaper'. Essentially the shaper takes a mess (Ackoff, 1974b) and sorts it out. This is something that may be done away from the group, when the shaper may make use of some privileged structural framework to order the material produced by the group; this would later be fed back to the group. Alternatively, the shaper may work 'on the hoof' with the group, sharing and using his adopted structure in an interactive manner. Some shapers also indulge in 'clever' analysis of the data which they have collected, and their subsequent interpretation of the results can then become important in forming a group view.

The shaper is assisted in his part by the 'recorder' whose secretarial skills are used to keep a note of the substantive material invoked by the process. This is potentially a very powerful role, since it is usually through a record kept in this way that the transactions of the working group are both transmitted to others and documented for reference in future episodes or for posterity.

The way in which all of these content-related roles are realized on a particular occasion will be unique. Nevertheless, the familiar formal tasks of chairman and clerk can be recognized in the roles presented: the former will usually take the part of reactive shaper, the latter that of recorder. However, most capable chairmen do far more than summarize and feed back discussion; they also take the lead in determining the dynamics of the intervention as a social process, which in turn can radically affect the content of debate. This function is more accurately described by the title of 'facilitator'.

The management of internal group relations is the general task of the facilitator, this being achieved through the guidance of interactive sessions, as well as through the management of debate between and within created subgroupings of the overall working group. The facilitator need have no special knowledge of the content of the problem to be addressed, but does require the personality to work with a group which may contain people of sharply contrasting interests and concerns, and the intellectual agility to direct a process in the direction which is most likely to prove beneficial to the participants.

Subsidiary roles, often carried by the individual who acts as facilitator but sometimes usefully handled by others, are those of 'monitor' and 'finisher'. The former, by periodically stepping back from the process, reviews and assesses the progress being made during sessions and reports his appraisal to the group: the latter, is preoccupied with the attainment of any deadlines or targets set by or upon the group's work, and seeks to ensure that they may be achieved.

It is also possible to discern a further part for what might be termed a 'team manager' within the working group. This role carries the responsibility for helping the individuals to work together as a group, possibly by guiding the microscopic structuring of subgroups and their activities, possibly in a more general sense of building a spirit of collective enterprise. A more significant and distinct role is that of the 'coordinator'. There is usually a need for someone to handle the macroscopic arrangements by which individuals within the working group are brought together, perhaps during a series of meetings when different participants may be required, and this is the coordinator's job. It is often convenient for this management of continuity of group activity to be handled by what Friend and Hickling (1987) call a core group. This usually comprises a subset of the main working group, perhaps consisting of two or three individuals, who can easily get together to sketch out meeting schedules, to suggest targets and formats for working group sessions, to review general progress, to disseminate group products and, significantly, to modify the working group composition. In practice the core group may also act as a steering committee for the entire intervention, and in more formal settings typically includes a process consultant (who may simultaneously act as facilitator, recorder and shaper), a contact person from the client organization and key decision participants.

Finally, we must move on to review the roles concerned with the management of the total context of an intervention, embracing both the organizational or social environment and the physical setting in which the problem-handling activity takes place. The first, and most wide-ranging role to introduce is that of the 'impresario': the organizer, maybe the *éminence grise*, behind the whole entertainment. The impresario can sometimes be the problem-owner, but is frequently a more powerful background figure who permits or encourages the problem-handling process to run its course. It is the impresario who creates the infrastructures within which those taking part in an intervention can legitimately operate: it is he who may set out the rules by which the process proceeds and who determines what is an acceptable style for it to assume.

Operating at a lower level is a second role type, the 'agent', whose task it is to contract the participants who shall become involved in the intervention. Naturally this work meshes with that of the coordinator, but the agent is more concerned with identifying and auditioning suitable actors than with determining the needs of the process.

The third contextual role, the 'linker', is also related to earlier parts, this time to the recorder and core group. The linker serves as a communication channel between the working group and the external world, providing a means by which, for example, the feelings of the constituents can be input to the process, and a route for informing others of the outcomes of the group work.

There are further roles, often sadly underestimated and undervalued, relating to the creation of a suitable physical setting for problem management. The role of the set designer is to provide a working environment that serves the process that is to be enacted. While the set is frequently perceived, if at all, as just imposing constraints upon what takes place it may have a far more positive effect than this: accommodation which is well proportioned and laid out will contribute greatly to process dynamics and so to the value of the work undertaken. Supported by the subsidiary roles of properties manager, costume designer and catering services, as well as by the efforts of lighting and sound technicians, the whole backstage staff make a substantial impact upon the performance. Lest it be felt that this is taking the dramaturgical analogy too far, evidence and examples of the way in which these roles can be used to create effective problem management interventions will be discussed in the next chapter.

I have dwelt at length upon the parts which individuals may take in and around an intervention because of the light which this throws upon the way in which they may act, or be called upon to act, during an intervention. It is now time to consider the consequential mood of the intervention which develops with the cast settled more or less uneasily into the various roles which have been identified, and to see how this evolves and runs its course as a problem is worked upon.

Patterns of Interaction

'Visiteur: "Je veux voir M. Whitworth."
Commissionaire: "Le chairman? Fat chance. Vous avez un appointment?"
Visiteur: "Non, pas un appointment exactement."
Commissionaire: "Pas un appointment exactement. Quoi, alors? Un blind date?"
Visiteur: "Non, mais je suis expected."
Commissionaire: "Oh, vous êtes expected, hein? Il a dit: 'Pop in any time'?"
Visiteur: "Non, pas exactement, mais . . ."
Commissionaire: "Regardez. Je suis un homme très busy. Toute la journée il y a des gens qui vont et viennent. Ils disent: 'Je suis pour le

Marketing Director.' Je dis: 'Troisième étage.' Cinq minutes plus tard,
le Marketing Director vient à mon desk et dit: 'Pourqoi vous avez
laissé entrer ce nutter?' Maintenant, je détourne tout le monde."
Visiteur: "Alors, vouz pouvez téléphoner à la secrétaire du chairman."
Commissionaire: "Non."
Visiteur: "Comment, non?"
Commissionaire: "Elle est allée a lunch."
Visiteur: "Oh. Alors, on peut téléphoner au chairman?"
Commissionaire: "Charmant. Lovely. J'appelle le chairman et je dis:
'Pardon de vous interrompre, M. Whitworth, mais c'est Hodgkins au
desk ici, et il y a un jeune homme qui a l'air de quelque chose que le
chat a apporté, et peut-être, M. le chairman, vous pouvez descendre
pour lui dire bonjour.' Savez-vous ce qui'il me dirait, le chairman? Il
dirait: 'Hodgkins, vous êtes un blithering idiot!'"
Chairman: (qui sort soudain du lift) "Graham! Te voilà!"
Visiteur: "Oncle! Bonjour!"
Chairman: "Mais pourquoi tu n'est pas monté à mon bureau?"
Visiteur: "C'est le commissionaire qui m'a bloqué la route . . ."
Chairman: "Hodgkins, vous êtes un blithering idiot!'"

Miles Kington   *Let's parler franglais again!*

Mangham (1978) defines situational scripts as 'relatively predetermined and
stereotyped sequences of action which are called into play by particular and well-
recognized cues or circumstances, of which we acquire knowledge through socialization'. Even when they turn slightly awry, their sheer familiarity tends to transcend the
events and to sustain a kind of order in our lives. Now it might not be expected that
such apparently rigid and predictable interactions would be relevant to a discussion of
the handling of problems tossed into an arena occupied by the motley crowd of social
actors, whom we have been considering. However, observation (Mangham, 1978) of
interpersonal interactions demonstrates that, in business organizations and presumably
elsewhere, such activities as financial budgeting, market planning, interdepartmental
negotiation, and so on are in the main routinely and efficiently processed through the
adoption of scripts, which cumulatively constitute a manual of company lore and
culture. Even within a persisting group which over time works across a variety of
issues, there may be a strong script-based pattern of interactions despite the diverse
substantive content involved: thus, a trick of dealing with differences of opinion by
making an appeal to authority followed by sullen compliance, may be part of the
repertoire of the performances enacted. Situational scripts appear to dominate
organizational life rather than to be a minor aberration.

How are scripts performed? If a sufficient number of those in a problem arena can
reach some mutual accommodation – and this will depend upon the variety present in
terms of sheer numbers of individuals and in terms of competing *Weltanschauungen*-
– then a familiar situational script will be played through. However, this will be

overlain by the personal and strategic scripts (Schank and Abelson, 1977) of the actors present: that is, the laminations added to their parts stemming respectively from the quest for personal satisfactions and for manipulative control over others. The result is a unique dramatic event.

A situational script is played in a way more reminiscent of a piano than a pianola: that is, there is scope for interpretation by the performers. Nevertheless its adoption strongly defines the relationships between those involved, specifies the processes likely to ensue, predetermines the dénouement, and delimits the performance. Consequently, the way in which a problem is managed and, quite possibly, the very solutions reached or actions determined, are inherent in the script to which those involved attach themselves. Where individuals have most room for expression is in the attribution of meanings to what goes on, and thus in the lessons that they take away from the experience. Collectively, these individual interpretations contribute to the whole feel of the drama; its pace, tensions, mood and overall success.

Assessing an Intervention

Let us examine an intervention through the eyes of a theatre critic, though stopping short of asking for the time being what the performance is about. From this perspective we would notice both the broad sweep of its development and the contributions made to its animation by individual actors.

'Birdboot: "Simon Gascoyne. It's not him of course."
Moon: "What?"
Birdboot: "I said it's not him."
Moon: "Who is it then?"
Birdboot: "My guess is Magnus."
Moon: "In disguise, you mean?"
Birdboot: "What?"
Moon: "You think he's Magnus in disguise?"
Birdboot: "I don't think you're concentrating, Moon . . ."
Radio: "Here is another police message. Essex county police are still searching in vain for the madman who is at large in the deadly marshes of the coastal region. Inspector Hound who is masterminding the operation, is not available for comment but it is widely believed that he has a secret plan . . . Meanwhile police and volunteers are combing the swamps with loud-hailers, shouting, 'Don't be a mad-

man, give yourself up.' That is the end of the police message. . . ."
Birdboot: "The answer lies out there in the swamps."
Moon: "Oh."
Birdboot: "The skeleton in the cupboard is coming home to roost."
Moon: "Oh yes. Already in the opening stages we note the classic impact of the catalysic figure – the outsider – plunging through to the centre of an ordered world and setting up the disruptions – the shock waves – which unless I am much mistaken, will strip these comfortable people – these crustaceans in the rock pool of society – strip them of their shells and leave them exposed as the trembling raw meat which, at heart, is all of us. But there is more to it than that . . ."
Birdboot: "I agree – keep your eye on Magnus."'

Tom Stoppard   *The Real Inspector Hound*

We can totally ignore the storyline of the generic intervention and instead assess its dramatic qualities. Most apparent among these is its vector of movement; its speed and direction from curtain-up. The momentum which is attained results from the energy that the actors contrive to attach to the skeleton provided by the script. An effective facilitator can do much to engineer a good pace throughout, handling things so that there are quiet times when mental batteries can be recharged and others when an explosion of power blasts forward the thinking of the entire group. This can contribute to making the process work at a personal level so that it is both exhilarating and worthwhile.

Unfortunately, the air of excitement about an intervention can easily be dispelled by difficulties in managing the content of the problem. This may be caused by ineffective shaping, resulting in a feeling of going round and round in circles: 'whirling' (Friend, 1987). When an intervention is based upon a sequence of meetings, a dulling of the experience can also stem from poor scheduling, as participants' memories of what they were jointly engaged in and what they have jointly achieved become lost, and intervening discussions outside the group swamp the recollection of the collective products. In both cases, the facilitator may need to go to some trouble to make explicit the progress that a group has made on a problem, since the movement may not always be apparent to those who are bound up in its drama.

6.9

Problem-handling performances are invigorated by the tensions that flex the interpersonal relationships of the cast. These can be successfully harnessed by a skilled facilitator to set up a creative dialectic within the group, but in less adept hands can disrupt or even destroy an intervention. Particularly dangerous can be attempts to exercise power by individuals within the group seeking to attain personal ends, rather than being prepared to contribute to a genuinely collective resolution. Frequently similar in effect can be the development of emotional attachments within the cast of actors, which can lead to the formation of cliques and alliances that undermine group solidarity: contrastingly they can lead to fraternal and sororal cooperation and push the process to a successful outcome. The agent plays a vital part here in ensuring that personality clashes within an assembled cast are not likely to be destructive.

The real mood of a performance stems from the way in which the relationships between individuals are redrawn through time. This also informs the constant reworking of the contract between the players, a process of negotiation of meaning that underpins the whole intervention. A valuable framework for conceptualizing the nature of interaction between individuals in working settings has been proposed by Fry and Pasmore (1983) and is sketched in Figure 6.4.

Figure 6.4. Typology of working interaction (after Fry and Pasmore, 1983)

They suggest that the most basic (single-frame) form of interaction is one-way communication of one's own sense of meaning to another, with no desire to change, debate or reframe it: lectures or books work in this way. Multiple-frame interaction involves an exchange of views between a number of parties, which highlights differences and similarities in perspectives: the soliciting of specialist opinion by a manager would illustrate this sort of dialogue. At the next level is the frame-linking interaction, typically found in the work of task forces or project teams: here a group attempts to reach a mutually acceptable outcome after exchanges in which each seeks to influence the others, and in which a variety of personal experiences are used as a reference to the viability of any potential common position. Frame-sharing interactions involve making collective sense of the setting or immediate process that the parties are currently engaged in: it is seldom practically realized in work contexts, since it is primarily concerned with personal interpretation of situations rather than with completing some task, but may appear in a bastardized form in role playing or executive 'retreats'. The final level of interaction is termed frame breaking: it involves transcending the present situation to find a new perspective, an activity that requires courage and that must be supported by interaction with significant others. Frame breaking involves the discovery of one's 'theory in use' (Argyris, 1983) through others' experience of oneself, and a realization that it differs from the theory that we have espoused. This can be extremely risky in a business setting: the very reality of being one's authentic self in a process can force out organizational myths which have been foisted upon us, and even cause a basic questioning of the meaning of one's own life and its congruence with the organization's goals. From a dramaturgical perspective, frame breaking means stepping back to view the drama from the audience, and then thrusting a new and more appropriate play script into the hands of the cast.

Viewing interactions in an intervention through Fry and Pasmore's (1983) typology, it can be appreciated that very different results will emerge from interactions at different levels. Thus a performance in which actors simply talk at each other will lack the dramatic punch delivered by one in which there is an attempt to reach a joint understanding, or in which a situation may be flipped over by the dramatist to reveal a totally different way of understanding it. The achievement of any specific intervention will depend upon how the facilitator, shaper, coordinator and others combine to design the process, and upon the organizational and physical environment in which it is created.

6.10

The relationships between participants in an intervention naturally impact upon the individuals themselves, both in terms of their vision of the situation and in terms of the performance which they continue to deliver. Involvement in a problem-handling performance can be a more or less risky venture, depending upon the degree to which each person is expected to expose himself in interaction with others, and will be balanced against the motivation for continued participation. It is part of the job of a facilitator to ensure that the level of threat which is felt by individual actors is kept to a productive level, unless of course, there is a wish to drive out a member of the group, or otherwise to capitalize on such feelings of alienation or separateness.

As the interaction proceeds, each individual will find his level of commitment to the collective process fluctuating. This is frequently related to the degree of ownership which is felt for what is going on, and more specifically for the products of collective activity. It can be a crucial aspect of the shaper's work to manage the content generated by the group in such a way as to allow them to retain their proprietorial feeling for it. The interposing of unfriendly technological aids between the group members and their output, or the use of opaque analytical techniques to generate conclusions from information produced by a group, are two further hazards to be dealt with in the design of an effective process of problem handling.

A theatre critic sees the development of characters through the drama which they bring to life, and sees the way in which the framework of this drama at the same time inhibits and extends those whose deeds define it. Viewing intervention as a piece of theatre, we can see how, in a similar way, the process of working on problems with others, no matter how messy the garbage can in which the action takes place, has the potential both for changing the problematic situation and also for changing the lives of those who choose to become involved in it.

Finishing Off

At some point the performance ends, and among plaudits or catcalls the curtain falls. Just as in the theatre there would be a sense of incompleteness on the part of both audience and cast if a play were to be prematurely curtailed by a fire alarm, so there is a sense in which a problem-handling intervention must also run its course if it is to be a satisfying experience for those involved.

Our feelings about completion can be better understood through use of the concept of problem finishing. Eden (1986) has explored the nature of problem finishing in some detail and suggests that when 'a person's anticipations about the future change from being an unknown worry and become a "conscious dream"' and when 'he feels that a messy problem has become an agenda of things to do', then a problem is finished. This is the case even despite the possibility that further formal analyses or other work on the problem remain to be done. The essence of these ideas is that the process of closure 'is such that it is related not to an analysis of the situation but to the owners of the problem'.

While problem finishing is necessarily a matter which centres upon the problem-owner, the social process of completing a problem-handling intervention is something which, as we have seen, involves a wider group. The end point of such an intervention must correspondingly be defined by changes in the meanings which the situation has for all those involved. We may take it to represent the point where continued joint work on the problem is felt to be unnecessary, and where the joint interests which have held the group together are overwhelmed by their individual wishes to proceed separately.

There can be real difficulties if the issue of disengagement is not tackled responsibly by those involved. Since the helper is usually in the business of writing himself out of a job by enabling the problem-owner to become more resourceful and autonomous, there are delicate matters of dependency and self-sufficiency to be confronted in the relationship between these key players. There may also be important emotional ties to be loosened among all concerned when an intervention runs towards its close, and the business of allowing the working group to 'die' is one that has to be taken seriously. Indeed, just as French and Bell (1984) suggest in the context of organizational change, so too in the context of problem-handling interventions, a way must be found of facilitating a process of mourning for and creating a memorial to the cooperative venture.

A withdrawal from the problem-handling arena by those involved does not, of course, mean that they will not meet up again. As I have stated elsewhere (Bryant, 1988a) it is quite misleading to portray consultancy intervention in purely episodic terms, although this is unfortunately what even the most enlightened practitioners tend to do. Most usually, as was made clear when we earlier discussed the initial engagement between helper and problem-owner, the work on an individual problem can represent a further stage in a developing relationship between the parties, rather than resembling the passing of ships in the night.

Contrasting with the traditional view of organizational problem solving, we can see a 'looking-glass world' in which the problem-centred project is simply a stage on which an organizational relationship is further unfolded. This world contrasts with the conventional one with its sequence of projects that may, quite incidentally, moderate a relationship between actors. From this perspective, the work on a problem is *inter alia* simply another opportunity, albeit one legitimated in organizational terms, for furthering a relationship, and it will have personal dimensions as well as institutional significance. Thus, to take a facetious example, a piece of work by an in-house OR group for the marketing function may both cement dependencies between them and also lead to a romance between the analyst and the brand manager. In turn, these relationships at all levels will influence both the likelihood of future collaboration, and the potential inherent in these cooperative ventures. In organizational terms, the value of a problem-handling performance which has been staged is, therefore, to be read holistically, in the impact which it has on the trajectory of the whole enterprise. However, it may be far more telling to consider instead the impact which it has on the individuals involved.

By discussing earlier the changes wrought in the individuals caught up in an intervention through their participation in it, we came perilously close to the vexed question as to what the performance is all about. We might answer this in a facile manner by suggesting that it is about producing solutions to problems, but our discussions in Chapter Four cast doubt upon the value of such an orientation. A more worthwhile idea is that it is about developing insights which will enable individuals to make sense of their personal worlds so as to act more powerfully in them. This implies a view of interventions as a stage for action research and learning.

Argyris (1983) has introduced the ideas of single- and double-loop learning to distinguish between those cases when an individual achieves a match between intention and outcomes by changing actions, and when he achieves a match by changing first intentions and then actions. This is essentially adopting a restatement of the cybernetic notions of goal-seeking and purposeful systems (Ackoff, 1971) to describe human executive action. Within this conceptual framework, we can see an intervention as providing an opportunity for double-loop learning, through helping participants to reflect both on their actions and also on the 'theories in use' by which they determine these actions.

Nor would it be right to suggest that the learning process is simply one which applies to those who are involved in an intervention as problem-owners. There are lessons for all players, not least for the helper. Boothroyd (1978) has stressed the importance of reflection on consultancy practice by the operational research practitioner, as the route to strengthening methodology in later interventions. More generally, Schön (1983) has indicated what it means to reflect in action – 'to become a researcher in the practice context'. In particular, as the reflective practitioner tries to make sense of his experiences 'he also reflects on the understandings which have been implicit in his action, understandings which he surfaces, criticizes, restructures and embodies in future action'. In this sense every intervention is an opportunity for professional growth on the part of the helper who is prepared to remain sufficiently open to the experiences it offers as it presents them.

Tailpiece

Problem-handling interventions are places where individuals may be enabled to 'act thinkingly' (Weick, 1983) in their work, and which at the same time modify the whole texture of the fabric of the organizational or social world which they inhabit. We have seen in this chapter some of the issues which are raised when individuals seek help with the problems that they face through enacting such performances with others. In the next chapter we shall look at the way in which these issues have been addressed in the practice of problem management.

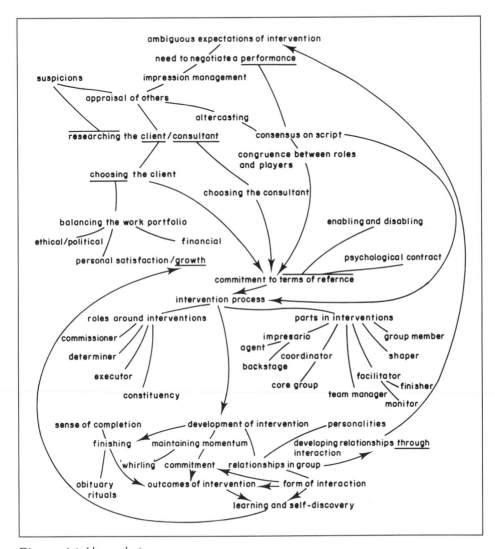

Diagram 6.1. Ideograph six

PART FOUR:

Practising problem management

CHAPTER SEVEN

Frameworks for problem consultation

The tradition of assisted problem management stretches back through time, as the archetypal roles for problem-helpers enumerated in Chapter Five indicate. Its contemporary manifestation as the domain of a miscellany of expert specialisms reflects the nature of the Western society in which it is set. This is a world in which, since the Reformation, the history of ideas has been dominated by what Schön (1966) calls the Technological Program: the notion that human progress would be achieved through the application of science for human ends. It is also a world in which, especially since the Industrial Revolution, economic and social history has been dominated by the capitalist division of labour and need for an expanding world market: the creation of a society based on the individual appropriation of wealth, power and status through the gravitational forces of 'free' exchange. Taken together these two strands have created the context for the concept of the scientific management of human enterprises, bringing the rigours of chill positivist analysis to everyday dealings between men and women and at the same time reifying and dehumanizing them.

Central to the tenets of the new management sciences, which emerged around the turn of the century, were the authoritative idea of Technical Rationality (Schön, 1983) and the appearance of a distinctive role for 'management' as a legitimate apparatus for controlling activities (Rosenhead and Thunhurst, 1982). Once these beliefs are accepted as given, the consequent spawning, first of work study and industrial engineering, subsequently of ergonomics, management accounting, market research, industrial psychology and sociology, seems inevitable. The result was the creation of a new élite of professionals whose mystic utterings were guaranteed by scientific dogma and unilaterally imposed by management upon a sceptical but voiceless majority. However, as Rivett and Ackoff (1963) point out, it was only during the preparations for the Second World War, that this approach was first directed at the executive function; that is, towards issues relating to the integration of policies and operations across the fragmented fields of management.

The Archaeology of Operational Research

The application of the 'scientific method' of observation, hypothesis construction, experimental testing and validation as a basis to inform executive action first appears clearly (Crowther and Whiddington, 1947) in the work of the (radar) operational research teams formed in Britain during the late 1930s to determine the most effective way of using this new invention during hostilities. The emphasis in these pioneering studies was firmly centred upon first-hand observation of what was going on (Stansfield, 1981) and the subsequent attempt to understand and explain these phenomena through the use of logical analysis. Unfortunately, the later development of OR has tended to overshadow this early history of live experimentation, preferring exemplars dominated by elegant mathematical analysis, so the 'fossil record' is incomplete. Nevertheless, it is clear (Easterfield, 1987) that most work was far more rustic in character then that to which a modern audience would be accustomed.

Despite the 'feet on the ground' philosophy of early OR work, there was still a potential barrier to acceptance of recommendations. This stemmed from the military's initial and very understandable doubts about the viability of the academic analyses provided by the scientists: after all, the latter had until then maintained a disdain for the world of affairs and adhered to 'a particular epistemology, a view of knowledge that fosters selective inattention to practical competence and professional artistry' (Schön, 1983). Even in Coastal Command's classic study of anti-submarine tactics, in which probabilistic analyses were used to estimate the optimal depth-charge setting to be used, it has been suggested (Rivett, 1968) that pure good fortune in the run of sinkings during trials rather than force of scientific argument was largely instrumental in swaying opinion in favour of the OR team's conclusions. Equally, at other times, work that ran counter to official mythology or popular feeling was not acceptable: Checkland (1983) cites the OR finding that a bomber crew's chance of surviving a mission did not increase with experience, as an example of a 'scientific' result which was discounted, unfortunately at some cost in lives. Consequently in this early work, great pains were taken by OR staff to work collaboratively with service personnel (Lardner, 1943), each party respecting and appreciating the other's contribution. This position was used by the OR teams to exercise to mutual benefit the right of challenging established views: as Lardner (1943) said, using a simile we have already encountered, 'the ORS enjoys the one supreme privilege of the court jester of old, namely that of saying things which would be *lèse-majesté* from anyone else'.

" . . . Look at these fellows, for instance, what are they making?"
I picked up their instruction card. The pair of men adopted expressions of injured pride and gazed distantly over our heads while Dutoit looked at their work labels, quaintly called rexes.
"Eye ointment."
"And that's some kind of paraffin wax, presumably? If that's not an old label?"

"Yes it is."

"Well d'you know much about this particular procedure?"

"Not the individual steps. I'm not sure what you're—?"

"Well look at them." Dutoit did so, and they immediately stopped work. "They keep sterilizing everything. Why don't they sterilize just once, just before they put the miracle drug in?"

"I couldn't say, offhand—"

"Offhand?" I said. "Come off it. There's no reason. The chemist did it with his two micrograms because it was no trouble and he'd just had a pause for lunch but there's no reason why these chaps should do it."

In fact, though the intelligent stranger gambit is always useful to operational researchers if they happen to be intelligent, their purpose is the application of scientific method to policy decisions. . . . I personally, being unbelievably lacking in interest in what anybody actually did in the end, always listed the true problems and provided the executives with a quantitative basis for their decisions, leaving the rest to them. Since they are fatheads virtually to a man this is less useful than it might be . . .'

Ian Jefferies *Dignity and Purity*

After the war, OR in the United Kingdom made the transition to applications first in the nationalized industries, later in the manufacturing and commercial sectors, an expansion that was broadly paralleled in other countries. However, there was a price to be paid for achieving this level of penetration across such a broad span of organizational contexts: a loss of vitality and relevance to the very issues which it had at first appeared that the new discipline would contribute most. Disappointingly quickly, OR became a narrow functional specialism directed in the main at relatively paltry tactical problems rather than at strategic issues: further, it tended to conduct analysis for, as opposed to working with, its management clientele. Accordingly, the corpus of knowledge required of its practitioners hardened around an arbitrary set of logico-mathematical techniques appropriate to solving the recurrent problems of large organizations, and in time the character and abilities of its practitioners came to reflect this bias towards the certainties of quantification (Dando and Sharp, 1978). Although most recently, over the past two decades, OR has sought to address broader policy issues as well as fuzzier problems of planning and control such as those encountered in the public sector, it has not achieved notable success. This evolutionary process has reflected back on the discipline itself, with the brashly self-confident assertiveness that accompanied the creation of the massive and refined technical apparatus, being succeeded by a crisis of conviction as these methods were seen repeatedly to founder when applied to more politically charged situations. This failure of nerve is critical to understanding the fundamental paradigm with which the subject has functioned over the years, and through this the limits to what it has to contribute as an approach to problem management.

Loss of Nerve

In a penetrating and influential paper Dando and Bennett (1981) identified the challenge to the entrenched positivist approach, which had come to dominate post-war OR, as resembling what philosopher of science Thomas Kuhn called a paradigm shift: a desire to replace the 'leaking boat' of conventional OR by a new one rather than to attempt running repairs. However, as Dando and Bennett also point out, OR is not a science, but is more exactly a technological activity, and so has no distinctive empirical paradigm in the Kuhnian sense: what was at stake was a meta-paradigm—OR's commitment to 'the scientific method' as an heraldic device describing its methodology. We shall come back shortly to examine the futures which they envisioned for the subject, but the key issue here is their view (which I share) that the dominance of the traditional approach was doomed.

What was the Achilles heel of the accretion of technologies which the OR world complacently claimed as its own? If we look carefully we can see that a modern-day Paris has a number of points of attack. The most fundamental of these flow right back to the assumptions of the supremacy of technical rationality and the legitimacy of the controlling role of management. The general faltering of confidence in science as a panacea and the consequent definition of a more realistic and restricted range of convenience for scientific ideas has cast doubt on OR's claims of impartial objectivity in its approach and of holistic comprehensiveness in its products. The wider distribution of expertise, information and power through the networks of people caught up in organizational problems had undermined OR's single viewpoint solutions and assumptions of hierarchy and, more important, of consensus. To these can be added fundamental ongoing changes in the role of the professional, and in the nature of organizations. In respect of the former, the mystique of expert knowledge is taking a severe battering (Schön, 1983) and new breeds of counterprofessionals and of citizen-experts are appearing to challenge the professional establishment, with mixed results. In respect of the latter, smaller, more agile decision-making units are appearing across the organizational spectrum operating in self-consciously designed, segmented fields, and led by teams of mobile and adaptable individuals. Viewed in this light, what is surprising is not that traditional OR wavered, but that it survived so long before doing so.

We can neatly crystallize the approach to problem management represented by traditional OR by looking at an intervention through the eyes of a practitioner from this mould. From the outset a client is perceived bearing a problem to be tackled: the OR worker has, if anything, only a very limited role in its definition. The client, moreover, is seen as a singular entity: even if a group is involved, its members are seen or treated as if they are of one mind and intent. When work on the problem begins, the practitioner anticipates making extensive observation of, and gathering of data about, some relevant systems: their relevance is determined by appeal to the logic of the situation. The OR worker would then expect to structure this information using any of several formal languages in which he is versed, and to feed back to the client his developed understanding of what seems to be going on and the implications of any intended changes. Maybe implementation of his recommendations follows. Lest I be accused of setting up a vulnerable straw man in this caricatured description, I must emphasize that such an approach can be highly effective in handling certain restricted sorts of problems. However, the limitations also shine through. They are limitations which have to be broken if the messy social business of problem management is to be effectively handled.

Contending Imaginations

I have dwelt at some length on the *Weltanschauung* of traditional OR because it neatly typifies a wider range of management science approaches which have quite under-standably gained a good foothold in the echelons of middle management. However, as I have tried to demonstrate, it is a view which is impoverished by its superstitious attachment to the scientific ideology which it espouses. To the extent that the 'theory in use' (Argyris, 1983) of this position is based upon technical wizardry and to the extent that its adherents service a monologue for a monolithic client it is restricted in application and potential. It is therefore necessary to seek other archetypes upon which more effective problem management can be based.

An initial loosening comes by addressing the partiality of scientific observation. Obviously all observation is selective, and we have reviewed earlier the everyday attentional factors which inform the choices that we make in this respect. The assembly of observational evidence in the conventional OR approach is still more strongly discriminating, being driven by working theories and conjectures about a situation, which in turn derive from a peculiar mix of the practitioner's worldly wisdom and the client's practical experiences. However, these contributing influences are seldom made explicit even within the cosy coterie of the consultant–client bipole. Covertly, for instance, the consultant may be massaging the information into a form which suits a specific modelling framework to which he has easy access, while the client may be seeking to confirm his hunches or prejudices by accredited means and so try to shape matters in such a way that the required conclusions are obtained. The corollary is that the emergent arguments bolstered by scientism will reflect a monocular vision whose vantage point may be inadequately triangulated even for those most intimately concerned.

We have already acknowledged the variety of *Weltangschauungen* around any situation: this is implicit in the adoption of the framework of personal construct psy-chology. At the same time there is a commonality of experience across individuals, which usually makes it worthwhile to talk about the taken-for-granted reality of everyday life in a way which can leave unattended, questions about its seductively self-evident facticity. However, this reality is only maintained, often with infinite subtlety, through social interaction with the others who appear in our intersubjective worlds. So, although at base 'everyday life presents itself as a reality interpreted by men and subjectively meaningful to them as as coherent world' (Berger and Luckmann, 1967), the individual act of construal creates bridges between people only through the correspondences between their meanings, which in turn stem from the society which they share. What 'scientific' approaches do is blithely to assume that the construction of common-sense reality is unproblematic: in other words, that there is unanimity as to the way in which some presumed common experience of a world 'out there' is to be interpreted and treated. It is evidently incumbent on us to devise some alternative means of embracing the multiply imagined world of a group who share vexation over some 'real' everyday situation. At the same time we must accept that assumptions of consensus, objectivity and uniqueness of comprehension cannot be sustained.

Now, at the start, it must be noted that whether or not a diversity of views is of any practical significance for the way in which problems are managed depends upon the political texture of an intervention. At one extreme, but an extreme which nevertheless represents much of current practice, the only legitimate viewpoint is taken to be that of the sponsoring organization; of the commissioner of the problem-handling effort. This is a very natural bias, and one which, for instance, in the exigencies of wartime operations, seems moderately defensible. However, it has consequences at a number of levels, as Rosenhead and Thunhurst (1982) have pointed out: most immediately, for example, 'The problems of industrial management are not the problems of the industrial worker. The problems of social service management are not the problems of the social service consumer. Indeed, many of the latter are the consequences of the former.' But at a deeper level, 'By presenting the problems of management as *the* problems, as *inter alia* [traditional] operational research does, the fundamental conflict between management (as the representative of capital) and labour, is assumed away . . . Thus both problems and their "solutions" have as a concealed presumption the continuation of the existing relations of production.' The notion of 'best' or optimal decisions, solutions or policies can thus have no meaning unless we ask 'best for whom?', 'within what context?' and 'under what assumptions?' If the locus of power with relation to actions on problems happens to correspond to the adopted viewpoint then a positivist stance may well be viable: otherwise there will be difficulties. It might be suggested that a contrasting extreme to the unilateralist position which we have just considered would be the case in which the feelings of everyone with an interest in 'the problem' could be taken into account. After all, in the majority of practical cases, the problem-owner has usually 'infected' a larger group with his worries and concerns, and there will be a wider constituency who will be affected by and have some say in any intended actions. This pluralist assembly will each have 'their own personal and organizational agendas, areas of power and responsibility' (Cropper, 1987a) and so separately and collectively they may need to be considered or even consulted. However, naively to adopt this stance is to imply, as the same author expressed it in an earlier paper (Cropper, 1983), that the problem exists as 'a single space within which any number of viewpoints may be held', and that there is some meaning in speaking about it as though it had some sort of independent existence. Our previous, lengthy consideration of the nature of problems causes us strongly to reject this idea in favour of a cognitive relativism in which 'there are as many spaces as there are viewpoints and [in which] the spaces may not be commensurable' (Cropper, 1983). It therefore appears to be impossible to move away from the original single-perspective position without losing hold of the very problem which we are seeking to address; yet it seems untenable to cling to such pseudo-objectivity in realistic organizational settings where a range of viewpoints must be acknowledged!

The Purpose of Intervention

There is an escape from the apparent impasse into which we have wandered. It is to step back and to consider afresh the purpose of the intervention. As long as we adhere to the notion that the sole aim of an intervention on the part of a helper is to provide a client group with a clearer understanding of a situation 'out there', which they face in common, then the issue of group *Weltanschauung* will arise. Perhaps individuals may be prepared to submerge personal beliefs in the interests of collective solidarity, and perhaps there can be some agreement on a joint statement of intent or even upon what appears to be amiss in a situation, but such a compromise does not necessarily imply any identity of views or intentions. In such a situation, any attempt on the part of a helper to represent or analyse a defined problem must recognize the plurality of perspectives and so either capture and integrate them or else secure them for mutual consideration and debate. However, to do this is to take the helper into a qualitatively different arena of activity in which he is more centrally, if not predominantly, concerned with the facilitation of a social process within the client group, rather than with expertly portraying their 'common' problem picture. In other words, the focus has shifted from some 'external', 'objective' situation to the 'internal', 'subjective' relationships between those in the interaction, the latter including, of course, the helper himself. The intervention must be primarily about negotiating the problematic situation, not about the less ambiguous (though not necessarily less trivial) matter of dealing with it. This is a far cry from the scientific examination of a problem where this chapter began, and is now an exercise in what we earlier termed applied phenomenology.

> *'Mervyn Lillicrap, psychiatric counsellor from the Crisis Centre, has been invited by the Director to observe the interactions within his staff team at the Medical Centre at Lowlands University. As he reports back, the mood of the group becomes even more hostile . . .*
> "How would you like a punch in the snout, Mervyn?" asked Bob Buzzard.
> Mervyn yelped. . . .
> "You realize you're confirming my tentative hypothesis?" said Mervyn in a rather squeaky voice.
> . . .
> Rose smiled sweetly.

"I'd have found Mervyn's analysis much more convincing," she said,
"if he hadn't spent the last half hour trying to look up my skirt".
"I never!" gasped Mervyn

. . .

Jock McCannon, who had been austerely silent till now, entered the
discussion with a voice that rumbled like thunder.
"Dr Lillicrap."
"Yes?"
"We all need help. We are all poor forked creatures. Even psychiatr-
ists."
"A lot of people don't realise that." gabbled Mervyn.
"Yes, yes. There's a lot of pain isn't there. Tell me, Mervyn. How does
it feel?" Jock's compassion was quite excruciating.
"Well I can't pretend it's not a strain, Dr McCannon."
"No. No. Tell me Mervyn. How does it *really* feel, *right now?*"
"T-terrible." He could hardly choke the word out.

. . .

And then the sobs came, would not be denied, lovely terrible hot
choking sobs that shook Mervyn Lillicrap's skinny little body, rocking
him to and fro. . . .
"Poor wee man," said Jock.'

Andrew Davies   *A Very Peculiar Practice*

It will be recalled that the essence of the 'pure', double-bracketed, phenomenological
transaction is a searching, in a climate of mutual trust and caring, for a shared
understanding (Massarik, 1983). There is an attempt by those involved to enter each
other's existential *Lebenswelten*, in relationships of genuine equality and with complete
commitment to the process in hand and to its outcome. Now this ideal sounds like a
Utopian fiction whose practical realization would be improbable to say the least.
However, unlike the model of scientific enquiry, it does at least appear to be
asymptotically attainable and can represent for us here a contrasting position to
explore and set against our earlier discussions.

There is a key distinction between the purpose of the intervention which we are now
considering and that implicit in the approach which we earlier examined. In the latter
we were preoccupied with activating an intellectual process with which a group might
explore a problematic situation; in the present case we are mainly concerned with
prosecuting a socio-political process within a group to support negotiation of a
common prospectus. The process we are now considering is 'about the group' rather
than 'about a problem'. Most obviously the new approach casts the helper quite firmly
into the role of facilitator, or at least indicates that this role is crucial to progress,
whereas the helper would most probably have acted primarily in the roles of jester or
conceptualizer within the earlier archetype. However, if the helper is to be a helper
rather than just an encumbrance to the group, he will need to do more than emote a
drivelling empathy for their predicament; thereby he would simply become another
problem-sharer. What he can contribute is his experience and wisdom as a reflective

practitioner; as one who has engaged in and learnt from interventions, both those that he has conducted at first hand and those carried out by others about which he has heard reports; and also as one who comes to the present situation with a developed and theoretically sound philosophy of action appropriate to such work. Such a craft base will most obviously express itself in the form of a language or framework which is offered to the group, either directly or through the subsequent intervention process.

Guiding Frameworks

There are two candidates for framing: the intervention process itself, and the substantive content of the issues which are exercising the group. A helper contributing the former is acting as an expert facilitator; the latter as an expert conceptualizer. There is a third role – the dialectician, mentioned in Chapter Five – which embraces both of these activities. Many consultants move freely between these roles. I shall later examine some specific frames that have been used to structure both process and content, but here shall focus briefly upon the main alternatives which exist. The choices centre upon the authorship of the script which underlies the intervention: that is, upon whose terms will the process be shaped, and the content be crystallized? We may contrast a situation in which the helper provides, or even attempts to enforce or impose a specific, developed framework upon his clients, with one in which he works with them to develop a framework in an organic manner as the intervention proceeds. This is an issue that has been explored more fully by Freire (1976) in his writing on education, which he similarly views as needing to be based upon a genuine dialogue (as opposed to cultural invasion) and to require the sensitive use of linguistic codes in problematizing interaction between the two parties.

Turning first to the process of the intervention, namely, what goes on between actors during the performance, the use of a prefabricated structure can be looked at in terms of Fry and Pasmore's (1983) stratified typology of individual interactions, discussed in the last chapter. Evidently, the intervention can be framed in ways which are more likely to elicit one level of interaction than any other. If we were to characterize most team-based, project-oriented problem management in these terms we should find that it was frame linking in nature: involving collaboration in the building of a model or representation of a situation, and from which a joint decision somehow awkwardly spurts. Frame-sharing or even frame-breaking work is distinctly uncommon, for reasons elaborated earlier, but can form an alternative guiding principle for process design in an intervention: an open exchange of views and collective redefinition of issues which *of itself* generates the group's vital commitment to act. Experience suggests (Fry and Pasmore, 1983) that frame linking can occur more or less spontaneously, given at least a minimum level of bonding between group members, whereas frame breaking will seldom occur by chance, except in the most intimate and highly developed relationships. Accordingly, what is offered by many of those professionals who work in and around problems as helpers is a designed approach, which is deliberately organized so as to support the achievement of frame breaking. Many of these methods depend, as we shall see shortly, upon the articulation of a dialectic within the working group.

Precisely because of the difficulty of achieving worthwhile interaction within groups other than through quite ingenious, though not necessarily complex, processes, it is the norm for helpers strongly to encourage, if not actually to force, a clear framework upon the process of an interaction; this is the main stock-in-trade of those who, for example, work as organizational development consultants. The contrasting position of the helper working, for instance, at a higher level by conducting a meta-process through which a group might design its own intervention process, is unusual and, being less predictable in terms of outcome or supposed benefits, less easy to sell to a client. It is also an approach which has its own peculiar hazards (Huxham *et al.*, 1988), since the group's attention is divided between attention to process design and its actual use. When a consultant helper does bring along a tried and tested framework to a performance it is in any case rarely totally inflexible, and may be explained to the working group before the intervention proper starts (Mason and Mitroff, 1981; Hickling and Friend, 1987; Phillips, 1987a; Checkland, 1987) – though there are some who quite consciously do *not* expose their schema in this way – and possibly be modified incrementally through group discussion and agreement as the work proceeds. In terms of the distinction made earlier therefore, it is normal, for very good reasons, for the helper to be quite directive in proffering process frameworks for an intervention.

When we turn to the framing of the substantive content of the group's predicament, there is more diversity in what helpers tend to offer. At one extreme, when a specific model is suggested as providing a suitable medium for viewing that is going on, it can strongly direct the eventual outcome. This coercive approach (Eden and Sims, 1979) depends upon the helper to sieve the data which are generated by the group and to slot the selected elements into their appropriate places within his organizing schema. Thus, it is relative to the model rather than relative to the views of those involved, that relevance or saliency is defined, and it is through the model that their individual views meet. The resulting picture, which may be owned by the participants only to the extent that they are prepared to accept its necessary distortions, can be seen, at best, as a 'highest common denominator' of their several perceptions. However, if used with care, even the most apparently rigid and forbidding mathematical formulations can provide a language for a group to explore mutual perceptions in a situation (Bryant, 1988a). 'Softer' frameworks, can be less immediately off-putting to a group, and may employ concepts drawn from everyday parlance (though defined with greater clarity) to structure content. In either case, it is usually the helper's role to build up the model for the group, since his prior experience with it will enable him to use it fluently and efficiently. As Cropper (1987a) has indicated it is at this model development stage that the clients have their main opportunity to influence the problem definition; the subsequent stages of content manipulation may be less transparent. Consequently, such work needs to have built into it a facility for recycling around the process of client input (Cropper, 1987a) so that the model can be repeatedly reformulated through debate within the client group.

There is less case history to set in contrast against the position of using the helper's vocabulary in problem shaping. Such formal approaches as do exist are based upon encouraging members of the working group to express their perceptions in their own terms, rather than through some artificial conventions. While this is most simply done by just letting everyone 'have their say', the result of such a loose process is often less than satisfactory. It is also inefficient in terms of the amount of time and 'space' which is required, and can be badly affected by the social dynamics of the group causing some people to be inhibited and others to contribute excessively. Eden, Jones and Sims (1983) have explained how such 'rambling' about a problem can cause frustrations for both helper and problem-owner even in two-person dialogues. For this reason a number of approaches have been developed that attempt to capture the essence of what problem-owners have to say on their own terms. These range from interviewing styles and techniques to graphical conventions for trapping causal, evaluative, associational or other cognitive relationships, and they vary correspondingly in the gentleness with which they handle the client's expressed beliefs and perceptions. It is claimed (Cropper, 1987a) that using such 'natural frames' tends to ensure that persons' views as a whole enter the negotiated problem definition and the simultaneous development of individual constructions of a situation, so that commitment to act is part of, rather than an awkward follow-up stage to, the content management in the intervention.

We have now seen how a helper can approach a problem-handling arena with a variety of scripts to offer to those with whom he works. These can be designed to set out the moves for a ritual dance, or more loosely to provide a quietly persuasive backdrop for an impromptu workshop. They can help to pattern ideas in some sharply defined way, or can offer a more relaxed organizing rationale for thought. A number of formal methodologies have been developed which provide a coherent guide for those engaged in interventions. These vary greatly in their underlying philosophies and implementation and will now be reviewed.

Help through Problems: a topography

In a fascinating study of the mental images which we each individually construct of the geographical space in which we live, Gould and White (1974) show how parochial and idiosyncratic are the 'maps' with which we think about places. Such mental maps are of interest, not just because of what they tell us about the topographical distortions with which people operate, but because they can also capture perceptions of the attributes of location; for instance, we can plot the invisible, mental geography of individual psychic stress in a neighbourhood on to a spatial plan. Looking back through the map we also have a window into the mind of its owner. Now this idea of mental mapping can be carried outside the confines of physical geography. Thus, in a similar way, each of us could set down mental maps of the world of ideas and concepts which we occupy. As in the case of geographical maps, we might expect that people with broadly similar backgrounds and interests would set down pictures of their cognitive worlds which bore some resemblance to each other: the differences would tell us something about contrasts in the saliency of ideas between them. It is from this subjectivist position and without ambitions of didactic generality, that I have attempted to picture below the way in which I see the relationships between ideas in the very specific area of modern thinking with which we must here be concerned: frameworks of enquiry for problem management.

I shall focus on just one slice of the history of ideas – the chronological and conceptual development of thinking about general problem management during the present century – while acknowledging the debt to earlier workers. Accordingly I shall take as input to this network of methodologies the pre-existing disciplines of philosophy, natural science, psychology, social science, and so on. I shall further take as the environment of the network's development, the concurrent changes in each of the above fields of thought, together with the social, political and economic changes which have taken place in the world of affairs. I shall, in other words, concentrate narrowly upon the formal management of interventions in organizations.

The map of problem management shown in Figure 7.1 attempts to depict both the temporal development and cross-influences within the field, and the conceptual proximities and relationships between methodologies. It may be compared with the more limited picture of the systems movement provided by Checkland (1981), and with Mayon-White's (1986) more nearly comprehensive model of change methods. As in the latter work, the directed (arrowed) links shown may be read 'influenced the development of', though there can be a variety of processes through which these influences worked: it may be either advances or difficulties in one field that spurred development in another. The remaining links are connotative in nature: the ideas are related, though there is no obvious causality. The figure also names, in a highly selective manner, the principal proponents associated with each approach. As we shall

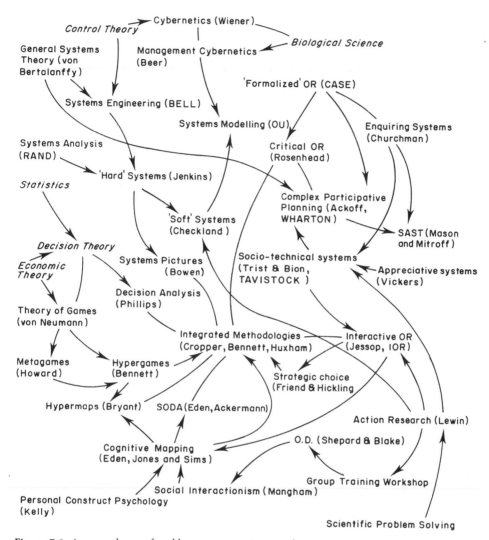

Figure 7.1. A personal map of problem management approaches

see, it is difficult and probably unhelpful to try to separate methodologies and methodological development from the agents involved.

I have already said something about the birth of the subject of operational research. Post-war development in this area was strongly underpinned in the United States by newly established academic groups, including the influential team at the Case Institute of Technology. This group, headed by Ackoff, who worked there with Churchman to establish the first academic graduate programme in OR, had a profound impact on the subsequent development of the discipline. Quite apart from its pioneering work in OR education, and the theoretical development which accompanied this, the group at Case can be seen at the origin of at least two major strands of thinking. Ackoff's approach was one: this subsequently reached maturity in the systems planning work (Ackoff,

1974b) that he promoted at the Wharton School. Churchman's studies of enquiring systems (1971), which addressed the philosophical roots of formal model building, was the other strand that led, through the notions of contingent truth and the counter-image, to the SAST methodology of Mason and Mitroff (1981). There was no obvious parallel development of distinctly articulated methodologies in the United Kingdom where practice was always more pragmatically based. Pidd and Woolley (1980) have characterized the apparent 'theory in use' of this body of working experience by the label 'the Exploration Approach' and have noted how, after an initial broad appraisal of the problematique it tends to be patterned upon the hypothetico-deductive approach of science, though with an elaborated learning and recycling mechanism. However, the growth of critical OR from about 1970, reflected in the writings of Rosenhead (1976), contributed to initiating a debate which proved to be a major spur towards contemporary 'soft' OR. A separate, but significant line of thinking towards the same end was represented in Boothroyd's (1978) writings on the nature of OR practice.

Simultaneous with the expansion of OR another new discipline, organization development (OD) was coming into being. The origins of OD can ultimately be traced back in the United States to John Dewey's (1933) seminal ideas on human problem solving which were influential in the creation of action research as an approach to the management of change that required joint effort by researcher, practitioner and client. Lewin's name appears (Gill, 1975) both in the early prosecution of this work and in the related but distinct contribution which he made through inaugurating group training workshops (later called T-groups). However, it was through the later experiments and subsequent planning of programmes for effecting system-wide change in a number of corporations, conceived by Shepard and Blake (French and Bell, 1984), that the term OD was first coined. Parallel developments in the United Kingdom largely centred upon the Tavistock Clinic and the work of Bion also linked through Trist's work on socio-technical systems (Churchman and Verhulst, 1960) back into OR, a link consolidated by Ackoff and Emery (1972). Research at the Tavistock led into other fields: Vickers's (1970) theory of appreciative systems was shaped in part by the work of the Institute; and the work of the Institute for Operational Research (Friend, Norris and Stringer, 1988), a joint venture by the Tavistock with the Operational Research Society, gave birth to the strategic choice approach (Friend and Jessop, 1969), a methodology with roots in public planning, which has recently been elaborated and extended in scope (Friend and Hickling, 1987).

The mention of systems-related studies a little earlier provides a cue for outlining the developments that had taken place there since the very earliest notions of systems engineering in Taylor's 'scientific management' at the start of this century. Following the Second World War, systems engineering, viewed as the total task of design, evaluation and implementation of a system to satisfy some stated need, had been promoted by work at Bell Telephone in the 1950s (Hall, 1962). Contemporaneously the RAND Corporation had devised a methodology that came to be known as systems analysis (Optner, 1965), and which through a costed evaluation of alternative instrumentalities based upon mathematical models, gave back-up and guidance to expert choice. Taken together these ideas fed into the 'hard' systems methodology of Jenkins (1969) and ultimately into the 'soft' systems school represented by Checkland (1981), though the latter takes pains to distance itself from its antecedents. Up to a point this disassociation is fair, since the work of Checkland and its derivatives at the Open University (Bignell and Fortune, 1984) stems from action research in the OD tradition and also owes a debt to the concepts of General Systems Theory (von Bertalanffy, 1968). The latter owed its origins to a recognition that such concepts as stability, information flow, feedback and control transcended traditional disciplinary boundaries and that their study was of interest in its own right. New subjects such as cybernetics (Wiener, 1948) and related ideas about communication (Shannon and Weaver, 1949) not only supported the subsequent development of the computer sciences, but also suggested new ways of looking at problems in organizations: Beer's novel analogical approaches (Beer, 1972) clearly derived from these roots. More directly, systems conventions for representing managed human activities were adopted in the work of Bowen (1983) on problem formulation.

As quickly as they were adopted, there was a reaction in the social sciences against the implantation of systems ideas, which were seen as deterministic, functionalist and decidedly positivist in character. An earlier, contrasting, humanistic perspective, which stressed the primacy of the individual experience, was held up as a more appropriate paradigm for work in organizational settings. Out of this dialectic came some new frameworks which may be labelled with the general title of social interactionism, because of their stress upon the interplay between people as a determiner of individual action and personal meanings. This work was most clearly expressed at the Centre for the Study of Organizational Change and Development at Bath. Here, Mangham (1978) made use of a dramaturgical model to view the performance of people in social organizations, and thereby suggested new roles for OD consultants in shaping interventions. Eden (1985a) using a framework which drew upon personal construct psychology (Kelly, 1955) and which emphasized the political forces underlying organizational life, developed a methodology, SODA, (Eden, Jones and Sims, 1979, 1983) which provided new ways of managing meaning and debate within working groups.

There is a further strand of development which can be traced back to the desire to advance economics as a science through the application of mathematical formulations and technique to the complexities of a social exchange economy. As a starting point along this ambitious path, von Neumann and Morgenstern (1944) first propounded their influential Theory of Games and Economic Behaviour. However, the practical application of these ideas to those live organizational problems to which they so obviously had relevance had to wait until much later when the metagame (Howard, 1971) and hypergame (Bennett, 1977) concepts were first floated. These subsequently came to form the basis of new decision-aiding methodologies (Radford, 1986; Bennett and Huxham, 1982, respectively). Meantime other approaches which focused quite specifically upon conflict issues had grown from experience in arbitration and international relations (Fisher and Ury, 1982). There were also further points of contact between economics and quantitative science, this time statistics, which led to the specialism of decision theory. This subsequently flowered into a more rounded methodology for organizational problems under Phillips (1982) becoming known as decision analysis.

Finally, the various integrating studies which have been carried out across methodologies by members of the Decision Management Research Group in the United Kingdom must be briefly mentioned here. These include some in which developed approaches have been used in tandem in practical studies (Huxham and Bennett, 1985; Matthews and Bennett, 1986; Bennett and Cropper, 1987), and others in which theory-based links have been proposed (Bryant, 1983). These have necessarily involved a re-examination of the bases of the various methodologies which has in turn suggested future directions for development (Bennett and Cropper, 1986).

Classifying Approaches

I have sketched out by means of a semi-temporal, semi-thematic storyline the terrain of formal intervention methods. Others, who have similarly reviewed this landscape, have made use of different conventions to organize their coverage of the material. It is worth mentioning some of these overviews here, since they suggest alternative typologies of problem management methodology to which I shall find it useful to refer later. The first is the literature review carried out by Woolley and Pidd (1981) which suggests that there are four streams of thought on the crucial activity of problem structuring: the checklist stream; the definition stream; the science research stream; and the people stream. These correspond respectively to viewing problems: as things to be diagnosed and corrected; as situations in which considered choices have to be made; as facets of some underlying reality which has to be elucidated; and as constructions placed by individuals upon their worlds. A more rigid taxonomy is offered by Jackson and Keys (1984) who use a two-way classification: this is based along one dimension upon the nature of the decision-maker (or problem-owner), and along the other upon the nature of the system (or problem setting). We have met the nominal scales which they use along these dimensions before: the decision-maker is classified as unitary or pluralist; the system as mechanical or systemic (that is, as simple or complex). In this schema, 'classical' OR and systems engineering are located by these authors in the unitary/mechanical sector; cybernetic approaches like Beer's (1966) are unitary/systemic; Mason and Mitroff's (1981) SAST methodology is pluralist/mechanical; while Checkland's (1981) 'soft systems' approach falls into the pluralist/systemic category. Jackson and Keys's organizing framework has, they claim, implications for the practitioner by providing guidance in the selection of an appropriate methodology for a specific intervention: this is a claim whose underlying assumptions will be considered later.

A third and quite different investigation across decision-aiding methodologies was carried out by Cropper (1984). This relied upon interviews with practitioners, carried out as part of a research project, in which they described their espoused theories of practice. These were set within a context in which attempts had been made using repertory grid analysis (Fransella and Bannister, 1977) to elucidate the 'theories in use' of a wide range of methodologists. Cropper's summary of this work provides valuable signposts for intending explorers in the immensity of intervention craft-lore.

Tailpiece

A variety of methodologies may be drawn upon, for theoretical underpinning or practical guidance, by those who would seek to help others through problematic situations. The approaches which they inspire may be more or less sensitive to the perspective of the problem-owner and to his intentions. Nevertheless, the actual realization of an intervention, almost irrespective of the guiding principles underlying it, cannot be predicted simply from a statement of the approach used; rather it will be a unique combination of personalities, circumstances, technology and logistics. The choices which shape an intervention form the subject of the next chapter.

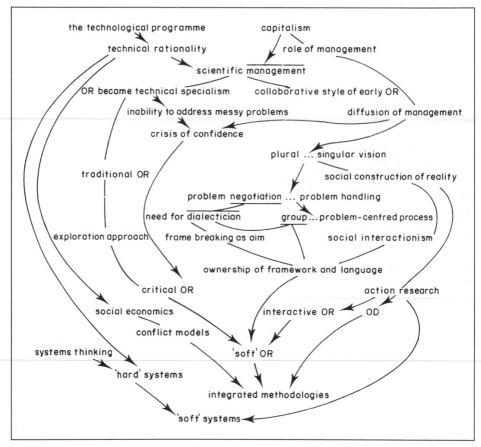

Diagram 7.1. Ideograph seven

CHAPTER EIGHT

Problem management in performance

Metaphor provides an organizing principle both for making sense of what is going on, and for deciding what to do. More specifically, different metaphors inform the theories of practice, which authentically or allegedly underlie the various approaches to problem management that have been introduced briefly in the last chapter. I shall seek to expose these metaphors here, firstly because of their intrinsic importance in framing the corresponding interventions, and secondly in order to pave the way for an examination of the way that they shape intervention management.

The range of intellectual positions which we can use to view interventions in organizations is legion. Scanning the analogies which have been employed, we find the conception of organizations as organisms; as cultures; as systems; as mechanisms for exchange; as arenas of conflict; as social controls; as interpersonal lubricants; and so on! Each of these perspectives gives rise in turn to models of the more restricted activity of problem handling in such settings.

From any one position we would focus selectively upon aspects of our experience of what is apparently going on, and thereby interpret it. The viewpoint chosen gives us a fulcrum around which the meanings of our *Lebensweld* revolve; it provides a way 'of grasping some things in terms of others' (Mangham and Overington, 1987). There is, of course, no 'best' position or metaphor for helping us to make sense of things, though in order to elucidate certain features, it might plausibly be assumed that some frameworks would be more effective than others.

Bennett (1985) has made the useful distinction between rationales of decision aiding based upon theories about the structure of the social world, and those based upon theories about decision-making processes. The former see the world through definitional conventions which stress form, and thereby provide a framework with which experiences may be organized and structured. For instance, game-theoretic approaches conceptualize the world in terms of a conflict between players, and so assume the existence of autonomous decision-making units, whose choices affect each other and which separately act in a considered manner. Taking another example, most optimization methods posit that there is a single decision-maker with clear objectives, who is faced with multiple choices between alternatives which have differing impacts upon the resources available to him. The contrasting theoretical approach to decision aiding focuses upon the process of decision, and so offers methods the use of which aids individuals to develop a commitment to act with others. For example, the social interactionist approaches are founded upon the idea that individuals try to make sense of their worlds and that they do so through the negotiation of meanings with others. The conceptual base of other approaches which set out to create a strong dialectic between participants is that the process of argumentation is the best guarantor available for systematizing doubt, and coping with uncertainty.

These differing stances in the theoretical base give rise, as Bennett (1985) points out, to differing emphases in decision-aiding practice. Thus the former, morphological approaches tend to generate 'theories in action' which concentrate upon the external world facing the problem-owner; the latter, performation approaches tend to produce 'theories in action' which underline what is going on in the interaction process itself. This is a contrast which we have encountered in the last chapter when looking at the choice of frameworks open to a problem-helper. It now appears that there is likely to be some strong correlation between the guiding rules which he adopts in relation to the several elements of interventionist management, since all will be informed by a theoretical foundation with its own unique and pervading flavour. This systemic property must be borne in mind when we proceed later to treat these aspects of intervention successively.

What then are the crucial dimensions of an intervention along which those coherent intellectual metaphors, that we refer to as methodologies, may be gauged? I shall make use of a schema based upon a double bifurcation, shown in Figure 8.1, to organize the investigation which follows here.

The first distinction to be made is between the context in which the performance takes place, and the craftwork that goes on within it. Considering these two aspects in turn we can discern a further division within each of them. Defining the context of an intervention means identifying who is involved in it (and so by implication, who is not), and saying something about the artefacts' with which they find themselves in the problem-handling arena. In turn this means, firstly, addressing the social, organizational and personal background of those entering the arena of performance; and, secondly, considering the temporal and spatial coordinates within which the interaction takes place and the material media which are employed in its fulfilment. In part, this context is something that is determined by the working group, led more or less strongly by the problem-helper; in part it is something in which they acquiesce or cooperate as taken-for-granted conditions for their activities. The second, craftwork, aspect of interventions involves considering what process goes on during an intervention and examining the mental models used by participants in rethinking their problems. In turn, these determine, firstly, how the dynamics of the relationships between actors are played out; and, secondly, how the mental gymnastics of the participants over the common ground of substantive problem content are orchestrated. The direction taken may be left very much to the problem-helper, though it will still be negotiated with the working group as the intervention unfolds. This schema with its four-fold division

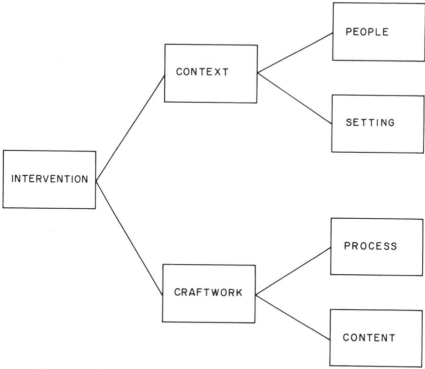

Figure 8.1. Dimensions of intervention

forms a convenient basis for analysing what goes on in interventions. However, to do so, I wish to make use of a particular conceptual framework.

Intervention as Theatre

I am much attracted to the use of the image of organizations as theatre, so persuasively advanced by Mangham and Overington (1987). They point out that this particular metaphor not only has, for good reason, a rich historical pedigree, but also permits a greater freedom in thinking about organizations and what goes on within and between them than does a model of systematic rationality. In particular, they argue that this metaphor 'offers a general framework for understanding conduct in organizations which can grasp both individual and group conduct, which can locate the situational constraints on joint action and can achieve this without resort to *ad hoc* additions from other metaphoric frameworks'. Further, they suggest that the analogy encourages an approach to organizations which supports the view that we construct their own destinies and our own within them. All of which heartens me as I proceed to apply the same metaphor to problem-consultancy interventions.

In making use of the dramaturgical metaphor I am saying that it is helpful to consider interventions *as if* they were events in theatre: that through the analogy we can gain a fuller understanding of what is going on. The metaphor thus provides a stimulus to asking certain sorts of questions about the process of problem management, and helps to organize the answers in a coherent manner. However, it must be apparent from my earlier treatment of the parts that people play in and around an intervention (Chapter Five) and from the phenomenological perspective that I adopted from near the start (Chapters One and Two), that the metaphor is one with which I have a sympathy as a model of rather wider social processes. I do not wish here to invite your critique of the use of the analogy upon this broader canvass; simply to go open-mindedly along with me as I use it within the tightly limited social world of consultancy intervention.

Drawing upon the metaphor of theatre, the four aspects of intervention identified above roughly correspond to casting the play, creating the programme and set, orchestrating the drama and interpreting the plot, respectively. These will now be examined in turn.

8.1

Dramatis Personae

The human context has already been alluded to, albeit obliquely, when I discussed in Chapter Five the roles which are to be filled around an intervention. These served as broad labels for a number of categories of individuals with some interest or involvement in what occurs during the performance. However when it comes to a specific case, particular people, not generic representatives, have to be cast in roles. A crucial aspect of any methodology must therefore be the way in which it guides the composition of the various overlapping sets of individuals who are caught up in the process. While this is principally to do with the so-called core and working groups, there is scope for narrowing or widening the membership of the other roles through judicious planning. It may be helpful to provide here some illustrations of alternative approaches to this issue. Eden's work tends to involve working with interest groups which are exercised by the need to negotiate a problem definition (Eden, Jones and Sims, 1979). Accordingly, the membership of the working group whose social process forms the focus of the intervention is critical: significant others outside this group will be relevant for establishing individual meanings, but are not directly party to the interaction. Mason and Mitroff (1981) explicitly advise on the optimal composition of the participants in a SAST process: they should 'be selected so that they represent all of the relevant perspectives on the problem and the different skills and know-how necessary to implement a solution'. This is a direct consequence of the need in this approach to develop convincing and contrasting strategies for handling the problematic situation. The strategic choice approach (Friend and Hickling, 1987) most strongly emphasizes the need for group boundaries to be permeable, so that as an intervention progresses different people can be drawn into the work. Hall (1988) says that two of the four rules for successful decision conferencing are that 'the chief decision-maker must be present' and 'all major problem-owners must attend'. Finally, in Ackoff's (1974b) idealized planning schema there is the widest possible participation by all the affected stakeholders. How rigidly and forcefully these guidelines are implemented is naturally contingent upon local circumstances, and while in some the initiative for defining groups comes from the helper, in others it comes from the problem-owners, and in yet others is a matter for negotiation.

I noted in Chapter Six that the real value of a single intervention might best be assessed within a wider view of an unfolding relationship between the people and groups who might from time to time choose to work together in this way. We see then a kaleidoscope of individuals, which is shaken first in this way, then in that, to create fresh patterns for successive problem-handling performances. Manifestly, the lives of, and relationships between, these individuals outwith the confines of an intervention will play a dominant part in setting the mood when they meet and work together. In this very fundamental sense the interpersonal context will impact upon what takes place, and so needs to be addressed by any methodological framework.

Mangham and Overington (1987) illustrate beautifully the fuzzy boundaries around an intervention in their discussion of a contrived script in which a senior manager, Tony, talks to some of his executives about objectives:

'The point about the extract is not the resolution but the fact that the interaction cannot be understood without regard to the context. Were we to be an audience to previous exchanges, we would know that Tony's objectives were influenced by both Bob and Eric working through a third party. We would know that without this influence, Tony would not have got himself organized enough to talk of strategy and objectives. . . . Furthermore, we would also know from previous exchanges that they, Bob and Eric, are aware that John has not prepared a strategy document and is hostile to the idea that he should. Bob and Eric . . . consider from what they know of Tony that he is unlikely to instruct John to prepare such a document, so they manoeuvre the present circumstances so as to place both John and Tony in a corner. Clearly, therefore, this scene has aspects which tie it back to previous scenes and previous setting while containing within it the future.'

Iain Mangham and Michael Overington   *Organizations as Theatre*

Superimposed upon this mish-mash of relationships will be the more formal organizational or social stratifications which are significant to the worlds of those involved, and which will duly moderate their interactions. Thus, as we saw in Chapter Two, individuals' designations within an organization will temper what they say and do and what is expected of them by others in an intervention. So, for instance, some participants may be looked to for specific professional knowledge, while others' opinions across a range of fields may be overvalued by virtue of their high status or the power which they wield. These factors need to be recognized in advancing any guiding principles for managing an intervention. In most formal methodologies attempts are made to uncouple such effects by deliberately concentrating upon workgroup participants as individuals rather than as occupiers of certain roles, so that within the intervention a freely participative and democratic mood can prevail. In other words, while occupational role may be a qualification for participation, the interaction is so structured or operates under such rules (van de Ven, 1974) that once work starts it becomes irrelevant. This ethos can be supported by suitable management of the physical environment of the intervention as we shall see shortly. However, the extent to which those involved can genuinely free themselves from their external labels still varies greatly from case to case.

A further lamination is provided by the particular personalities of those who are brought together 'on stage'. This can be critical in determining the success of an intervention, and clashes of temperament can be defused and submerged or exacerbated and harnessed in the service of the process which is being played out. To give just one example of how the personality variable is capitalized upon in a formal approach, we can cite the SAST methodology (Mason and Mitroff, 1981) in which one suggested method for forming the working subgroups upon which the internal dialectic is based, is in terms of Jungian psychological types, with different perspectives upon a problem being generated by internally homogeneous subgroups. However, personality clashes are not always contained beneficially, and since the more exacting forms of interaction – those involving frame breaking – necessitate a degree of self-exposure and openness which can be hampered by ill-humour in a group, they can have a serious impact upon the value of an intervention as a whole.

Continuing this theme of interpersonal tension and idiosyncratic payoffs, it must further be appreciated that an intervention may serve for some individuals as simply another stage for exercising power or reshaping relationships: that is, it may be perceived as being of little significance *per se* but as offering a not-to-be-missed opportunity to re-open old wounds, to clinch a deal, or to curry favour. In other words it may be simply a means to restructure a person's world, rather than being viewed as primarily an opportunity to address shared concerns. This is a perfectly natural situation: our concentration on deliberate, structured interventions must not, after all, blind us to the fact that these are episodes which are superimposed upon a far more extensive backcloth of ordinary, everyday interactions between many of those involved, and that for most participants the 'real business' in which they are engaged is that outside rather than within the performance framework. However, this discrepancy must concern us when the 'everyday' causes the artfully constructed process to feel false and contrived, or worse still irrelevant. To handle the potential perceived divide between 'normal life' and interventions, a number of measures have been developed, some of which set out to emphasize the gap while others attempt to bridge it. Those measures which relate primarily to the human context will be considered here leaving until later others which concern the careful management of the physical context of work.

Audience

Invoking the dramaturgical analogy once more, if the troupe of individuals caught up in an intervention are the players, where then is the audience? There is an obvious and a not-so-obvious answer to this question. The obvious answer is that the audience is those others outside the intervention – the workmates, family or compeers of those present – with whom they privately interact. The team of performers is in the business of constructing and projecting a definition of the interaction for the benefit of this audience, which at the same time cements their own solidarity. The not-so-obvious audience is found within the intervention itself. Each of those present is momentarily the audience for the others' presentation: and, as Goffmann (1959) points out, any performance involves collusion between performer and performed-for, relying upon concessions and raising expectations on either side. This internal interaction sustains the definition of what is going on in the intervention. It is the art of managing impressions before both these audiences that a helper can bring experience to bear, and it is in the manner in which this is done that approaches differ.

Goffmann (1959) shows that there are two important components of interpersonal relationships within performing teams: first, the bond of reciprocal dependence that no one will give the show away, since public disagreement would prove embarrassing; second, the bond of reciprocal familiarity through the definition of others as 'in the know', since maintenance of 'front' would undermine group performance. Formal methodologies offer special routes to enhancing these bonds, though at a general level all approaches *per se* provide those secrets – whether of process or content – for a group to share, that consequently link them in cosy conspiracy. For example, the 'activity' of Strategic Choice (Friend and Hickling, 1987) involves collectively mounting a pageant whose intimacies bind those who have lived it on the stage: the 'language' of, let us say, Decision Analysis (Phillips, 1982) both ties those who have been tutored in it through experimental work, and separates them from others who are not initiates. More directly, methodologies may be centred upon the peeling away of protective layers as those involved in an intervention come closer to appreciating each other's perspectives: this is certainly one of Eden's (1982) intentions through the cognitive mapping approach. Necessary prerequisites for such frank exchanges are a protective wall of confidentiality around what happens in the group to permit free speaking, and a protective umbrella (Bennis, 1969) which allows it the time and space to occur without disturbance from the environment. It is part of the skill of the helper to ensure that these barriers are solidly in place and that the performers believe in their substantiality. Group solidarity does, of course, have its hazards: 'groupthink' (Janis, 1972) is an obvious danger, and an impenetrable barrier around the snug coterie can create suspicion, distrust and jealousy. Partly to allay such fears, many formal approaches are structured so as to take account of these problems. This can be done by explicitly considering as part of the intervention how intended actions may be viewed by others – as, for instance, game-theoretic methods do by modelling those players in the planning arena – and how their effects may therefore be achieved in this context. Those approaches which generate output in the form of commitments to action that are wholly owned and understood by the performers also help them severally, with conviction, to justify decisions to significant others in their lives.

Performances before others within an intervention must be facilitated in such a way as to maintain the necessary dramatic distance from this internal audience, while still involving them. Most obviously this can be achieved through explicit or implicit rules, which control who a person should be taken to be at any time during the intervention. Thus, when ideas are pooled using a 'round robin' method in the Nominal Group Technique (Delbecq, van de Ven and Gustafson, 1975), everyone knows who is to contribute at any time. Different methods of structuring people's 'air time' are found in other approaches. While such rules are in force, they override or suspend any other procedures, though the performance will still usually stay within the bounds of civil etiquette. This releases people from the inhibiting effects of their external roles, as already noted, but also legitimizes 'silly' or at any rate 'unusual' behaviour. To take a slight, though significant example of such odd behaviour, we need look no further than the Strategic Choice approach (Friend and Hickling, 1987), wherein people are encouraged to make written contributions to group work by recording ideas on big sheets of paper on the wall, something that lies outside the normal experience of many of those participating in such workshops. These and other devices require the suspension of judgements about performers' actions within an intervention, and can be sustained only as long as everyone sees it as in the interests of all to see the performance through. If at any time this theatrical balance is not maintained, then an intervention can be shattered as surely as when, in the theatre, a member of the audience stands up and hurls abuse at the cast *as actors*. Generally, people will go along with the understanding which maintains the performance, consciously overlooking or suppressing events that appear to threaten it.

Overall then, the performance must be one which moves both the audiences and inspires them to actions of their own on stages within or outside the intervention: any actor knows how hard this can sometimes be to achieve.

Mise en Scène

Interventions are a 'special' sort of activity for most of those involved in them (except perhaps for the helper, for whom they are the 'bread and butter' of his professional existence). While lying outside the mainstream of events, interventions – if they are to have any relevance – are at the same time intimately part of it. The transition between the reality of everyday life and the reality of an intervention performance is marked in a number of ways, much as in the theatre the rising and falling of a curtain symbolizes the shift in meanings. Further, within the other worlds of a staged drama, different constraints may apply, new orders may be established, things may be taken for what they ordinarily are not: in short, fresh possibilities are created. Many of the signifiers and instruments of the shift are found in the logistical and physical arrangements made for an intervention, and these, with their effects, will now be considered in turn under a succession of appropriately theatrical sub-headings.

Time – the present

Like dramatic performances, problem-handling interventions are bounded in time. However, as in the theatre, the boundaries are fuzzier than they at first appear. Any performance, after all, represents the culmination of a period of arduous preparation and has its impact in future actions. Furthermore, the preparatory period will usually vary across performers: for an impresario or director it stretches back to encompass the commissioning of works, casting of actors and financial planning; for the cast it simply includes a lengthy schedule of rehearsals leading up to the first night; for the audience it just means getting to the theatre. Similarly, a problem-centred intervention stretches back to the negotiation of terms of reference or before, flows forward to disengagement and beyond, and variously involves different participants: it is a ripple in the puddle of associations.

The management of the temporal context is an essential part of what has to be done about an intervention. As I highlighted in Chapter Six, the way in which this is handled is what lends pace and momentum to the activity. A variety of devices are used to deal with this in different methodologies. At one extreme, a complete programme for an intervention may be set down. A good example of this is provided by Mason and Mitroff (1981) who suggest a comprehensive blueprint for a typical SAST workshop, complete to the specification of meal breaks and activity sequences. At the other extreme, agenda setting *ab initio* may be the first task for the group to address. Hickling and Friend (1987) would commonly do this, working from the position that the process framework must be fully owned by the participants: nevertheless they could still proffer for approval a pre-prepared outline scheme for leading the group through the Strategic Choice approach. Most methodologies employ some timetabling framework, though how strongly it is emphasized or applied will usually depend upon the dialectician involved. In 'traditional' approaches the timetable may simply consist of a promise of delivery of a final report by an agreed date. While I shall leave, until I later consider process issues, any discussion of the content of these timetables, their general parameters are of concern here.

Certain guiding principles can be discerned in the time planning of formal interventions. Most apparent is the notion of 'time out': that the work is set aside from day-to-day concerns, and demands an appropriate allocation of working hours for its execution. Often this time comes in the form of a sequence of days of concentrated effort, separated by short periods for 'normal' activities, and so also makes demands in terms of calendar time. However, some approaches require a longer concentrated 'burst' of energy: Decision Conferencing (Hall, 1988), for instance, is a ' product' specifically designed around a two-day format. The rationale for working through protracted sessions is easy to understand, for this is how the group can most effectively build the cohesion and sense of common purpose which is needed for successful theory construction and problem negotiation. Such concentration may also be required because of the need for participants to become familiar with new languages or forms of expression, and proficiency in their use may best be attained in this way. The sequencing of work through elapsed time is less consistent across approaches: while some favour using consecutive days to develop work through to completion – as in the SAST example (Mason and Mitroff, 1981) mentioned earlier – others are more flexible in scheduling meetings. Friend and Hickling (1987) see positive value in the inter-meeting intervals as an opportunity for seeded ideas to germinate and for people to adjust to the novelty of potential change. Eden (1985c), however, cautions that in his experience no more than one 'psychological week' should elapse between contacts (i.e. the longest permitted gap is between Monday of one week and Friday of the next) if energy is to be maintained.

Usually any time schedule will need to mesh with the other demands being made on participants and this can impose severe constraints upon what can be arranged; a weekly or other regular cycle is often the simplest way to handle this issue. Full participation may be achieved by more or less overt pressure being brought to bear on individuals: Mason and Mitroff (1981) advise that the highest ranking executive should 'formally invite the participants to attend and strongly encourage them to arrange their schedules so that they can be present for all sessions', but this sort of armtwisting could be inimical to the philosophy of some dialecticians. Of course, the involvement of all parties is not usually required at all stages – there may be, for example, certain 'backroom analyses' performed by the helper alone – but the engineering of the time for an intervention to occur is hardly made much simpler.

Costume

Let us switch our attention now to the costumes and manners of the players in an intervention. As Mangham and Overington (1987) explain, the dress and demeanour of an actor communicates to others and confirms for the individual who he is and what he represents. Within an intervention therefore, an apparition accoutred in pin-stripes and waistcoat, in regimentals, kimono, surplice or breeks says something about who he wishes to be taken for and what he sees his role as being. Lest this is seen as taking illustrations beyond reasonable limits, consider for a moment the 'front' which is constructed by some professionals in dramatizing, and therefore making real for their clients, elements of their performance. Since the task of a problem-helper is, within the sorts of intervention upon which we are concentrating, not seen as an activity that is equivalent to laboratory science, the donning of a white coat is inappropriate. Nevertheless, many consultants contrive to create some sartorial distance between themselves and their clients, by remaining soberly suited while the problem-owners are self-consciously informal, or by wearing the apparel of a Victorian smuggler, while their audience is in lounge suits. Such uniforms manage to convey the otherness of the helper, his peculiar genius and skill, without recourse to further emphasis, though some individuals may reinforce their image by eccentric eating habits or other adopted foibles. In contrast, other consultants go out of their way to merge into the group – to '. . . do as the Romans do' in matters of dress. They may wish thereby to de-emphasize the special nature of their role (and perhaps by association and mystique of any accompanying technology), by simply being 'useful – but quite straightforwardly normal – chaps to have around' with a reputation for helping groups to make sense of chaos. In a like manner, the members of a working group may strive for, and in some measure achieve, that degree of uniformity in informality, which means that they want to be seen as taking participation seriously, as they interact in the unfamiliar arena of collective problem handling: only the more perceptive will notice the difference in quality of the designer cardigans worn by the managing director and the shop steward. Regrettably, little has been written about the use of dress in formal interventions, and so we cannot associate particular styles with particular methodologies.

When it comes to the behaviour expected in an intervention there is a similar dearth of information, though this time not because it is felt to be irrelevant to what goes on, but because it is regarded as so fundamental a premise as not to require stating; fundamental, that is, that the individuals will behave towards each other in a civilized and decorous manner, respecting each other's views and their rights to express them within the group. This is an issue that I touched upon earlier in considering participants as mutual audience. However, a little thought reminds us that this politesse may be quite at odds with the behaviour of the group members outside the protective shell of the intervention performance. The extent to which it is achievable is a measure of the power of the helper to impose a temporary behavioural code upon those present, suspending their normal abrasive antagonisms; yet it is something which, in their adherence to the notion of democratic participation, virtually all formal problem-handling approaches seem to assume is feasible.

Set Design

The physical setting – the venue and its internal appointments and arrangement – is so determined within any given methodology as to be conductive to the form of activity that is desired to stimulate. In every case, a number of general factors must be weighed in determining a suitable venue. The first of these, and in some ways the most important, is the perceived ownership of the setting. In order that group building should be effective, it is helpful that the locale should be seen by all involved as 'neutral' ground. If meetings take place on the territory of one participant then he is immediately in a position of advantage, and others will be correspondingly inhibited in the way they use his 'space'; effectively they will be entertained on sufferance and have to create for themselves through unspoken negotiation a leasehold on a portion of the room. This can be overcome in various ways: Filley (1975) gives the example of a company which succeeded in minimizing the divisive effects of the proprietary uses of work space by providing common problem-solving rooms for everyone's use. Alternatively, hotels and other places offering private accommodation for functions are frequently used by interventionist consultants as meeting venues: the space can then be 'allocated' by the helper or else is negotiated between participants with everyone starting on the same footing. Equally, a group may meet at the consultant's own premises. This raises a second major factor for consideration: the potential availability at a venue outside 'the office' of suitable accommodation or specialist facilities, which may help better to support the kind of performance which it is wished to mount. If they are available, such locations can help to emphasize the 'away from home' nature of the activity – the third major factor to be appreciated – and may assist in releasing inhibitions associated with the customary work environment. Working out of reach of the office in this way also has the mundane benefit that participants are unlikely to be interrupted in their joint activities, and so will not be constantly reminded of their day-to-day responsibilities; nor of their hierarchical relationships to others. This is also important when the activity itself is perceived as not being 'proper work' (Friend and Hickling, 1987): how disconcerting for a group to be engaged in such apparently frivolous activity under the eyes of, or even in the same building as, their colleagues who are earnestly plying their serious trades! However, the success of the device of moving 'outside' also depends upon how seriously the experience is taken by participants: as Fry and Pasmore (1983) point out, if the intervention is seen to be similar to the annual staff weekend retreat held at a resort and accompanied by much junketing, then it may simply be viewed as a diversion with which participants will decide to cope, rather than as a learning experience in which they determine to engage, and the results will be correspondingly disappointing.

The physical environment is important in at least two other senses: it tends to predispose the atmosphere of an intervention, and it restricts what can actually be done. Naturally requirements vary greatly across methodologies.

'On the east coast of the United States, at Harvard University, and on the west coast, at Xerox's Palo Alto Research Center, high-tech rooms are in operation to facilitate the work of groups. Participants sit around a U-shaped table at positions equipped with networked micro-computers that are recessed into the table. At the front of the room, a large projection screen displays the output of any one computer, or of aggregated information. Sub-groups or individuals can move to small syndicate rooms, each equipped with micro-computers that are networked to the ones at the table, and a variety of software is available to help participants in their work.

A different approach is evident-on the other side of the Atlantic. At the London School of Economics and at International Computers Limited, group members sit around a circular table in an octagonal room (the Pod) whose walls provide conventional and self-copying whiteboards, and two screens for displaying 35mm slides, overhead transparencies, drawings and printed material, videotapes and the output from computers. Save for a single infra-red hand-controller, which enables the user to turn the displays on and off, and to adjust the levels of room and board lighting, no computers or other IT devices are evident.

These two types of room reveal fundamentally different approaches to group decision support. ... In the workbench environment, individuals interact mainly via computer models; in the Pod, computers and other media support the participants who interact directly with each other. One is computer-based, the other group-centred.'

Lawrence Phillips *Decision Analysis for Group Decision Support*

Archaeologists are familiar with the puzzle of trying to infer from the fragmentary remains of buildings the events that took place within them. The definition of spaces for interventions in the sense of the dimensions, proportions and relative positions of rooms used, in an ideal world would similarly mirror the intervention design. Hickling (1987) has, for example, given a detailed specification of a suitable environment for 'activity-based' decision management: a clear, well-lit area having plenty of un-interrupted wall space, comfortable seating, partitions and tables which can be rearranged, and multiple options for technical support. In arriving at his plan he catalogues the familiar difficulties of using 'off-the-peg' settings: difficult room shapes, excessive fenestration, inflexible furnishings, broken interior spaces, and plush surface finishes. Although Hickling has interventions of a particular kind in mind (Friend and Hickling, 1987), his critical and constructive remarks are sufficiently general to indicate the main features which are likely to be important in meeting room design. Finding such Utopian settings can be almost impossible.

'Whatever takes place at the dress rehearsal will bear absolutely no relation to what has gone before in the rehearsal period. The first thing to be discovered is that the set is completely different from the plan used in rehearsal. Probably the designer has omitted a door, so all exits and entrances go for nothing and the whole show has to be plotted again. Even if the set does have the requisite number of doors it is probable that one of them will open on to a brick wall.

. . .

The furniture will be at least four times as big as that used in rehearsal. Property mistresses must scour the junk shops of the world for the elephantine pieces they produce. Usually, when all the furniture and props are set there is no room for anything else on stage at all (and that includes the actors). Not only that, but all the doors are firmly blocked.

Anything other than simply speaking or squeezing between the furniture will at this stage be found impossible. The drink of whisky which was so important to the plot cannot be managed now, because to reach the sideboard it is necessary to climb over the sofa. The fight scene, in which originally the contestants hurled each other around like professional wrestlers, is now reduced to a crushed-in version which looks like two dancers smooching in a night club.'

Michael Green   *The Art of Coarse Acting*

There can be additional problems with hired rooms, as Eden (1985c) narrates in one case report: his request for three compact syndicate rooms materialized as three large and awkward rooms with wall lights and fixed pictures that got in the way of using on-wall flip charts; further, as he amusingly recounts, the suitable room that he had pinpointed for a later meeting with the same clients was sabotaged by a well-meaning but uncomprehending hotel management which decided to move his sessions to a 'better' room – without wall space!

Having room to manoeuvre in a meeting room is particularly important. The need for personal space is ever present. Shaw *et al.* (1980) suggest a need for between 25 and 50 square feet per participant in role playing; other authors are less definitive. Without becoming too precious about the psychological niceties, it is evident that for comfortable interaction there must be sufficient personal space (Filley, 1975) around each individual for a degree of privacy, and, as important, the freedom to define a small area of individual territory within the room where an intervention takes place. This said, the territory need not necessarily be seen as fixed in physical space. Eden (1988) has recounted how the use of a totally flexible plan, using armchairs on castors as seating, frees up an otherwise static event: indeed, the movement of participants around the room can be crucial in shaping the evolution of an intervention, through its effect on the social dynamics of a group.

Typical room layouts suggested for interventions vary greatly: some examples are shown in Figure 8.2.

Thus in using the Nominal Group Technique (Delbecq, van de Ven and Gustafson, 1975), since the focus is upon a list of ideas generated by each of a number of subgroups, a plan which contains replications of a basic U-shaped seating plan is employed (Figure 8.2(a)). Hickling's (1987) plan for an intervention using the Strategic Choice approach (Figure 8.2(b)) brings all participants in view of each other and facing an area on which group products will be developed and recorded. The workbench environment (Figure 8.2(c)) (deSanctis and Gallupe, 1986) and the Pod (Figure 8.2(d)) involve variants which are different again, the latter resembling in some ways Preedy and Bittlestone's (1985) conception of the 'boardroom for the 90s' (Figure 8.2(e)): both these prototypes assume that extensive reference will be made to external banks of information, unlike the earlier examples which are self-sufficient. For some other

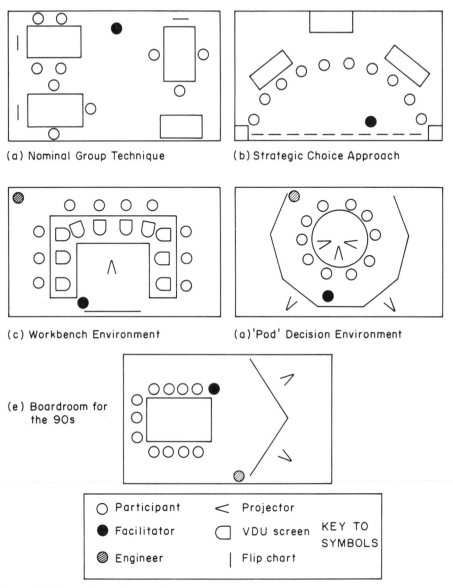

Figure 8.2. Intervention environments

approaches there is less need to be prescriptive: thus in role playing (Shaw *et al.*, 1980) as long as superfluous furniture can be removed, the exercise can proceed. Interestingly, all of the floor plans shown differ strikingly from those used, for example in operational gaming where position tends to connote role, or in conflict resolution or arbitration where spatial arrangements may reflect alliances or viewpoints: in the intervention illustrations, roles are undifferentiated and location is arbitrary. Further, the interventionist plans all seem to take account of the finding (Filley, 1975) that people seem to prefer side-by-side arrangements for cooperative activities and face-to-face arrangements for competitive ones. To summarize, the form of the physical environment should follow the function for which it is intended – but it takes a very well-organized dialectician to see that this occurs.

Lighting and Effects

Windows are a cursed blessing of twenthieth-century design. The kinds of modern building in which designed interventions tend to take place are usually over-endowed with large areas of plate glass. Not only are these distracting for participants and voyeurs alike, but they result in uncomfortable solar gain and irritating, intrusive noise. At the same time, the light which they admit provides undiscriminating illumination that overwhelms the puny forces of electrical displays; they even make unsuitable surfaces for affixing worksheets. As a disaster area, they come a close second to rooms. However, until recently few decision consultants have seriously addressed lighting, or its sister subject of acoustics, as an element in the design of interventions. Instead, people have just tended to muddle through, sometimes having to darken rooms to such an extent in order to see displays, that the participants were hidden from each other in the gloom; sometimes forcing themselves to maintain interest in proceedings despite intriguing events outside; sometimes straining to hear colleagues against background crashes and harsh local reverberations.

The contemporary interest in the sight and sound technologies, which have been used in the theatre for hundreds of years, as a means of creating mood and directing attention in organizational interventions, is shown by the development of purpose-designed environments within which such activities may take place. Although this may appear to be a wholly modern innovation, it has military antecedents in, for instance, the War Room used by the British during the Second World War. However, today the emphasis is on creating hi-tech environments intended for civil organizations, and both off-the-shelf (deSactis and Gallupe, 1986; Preedy and Bittlestone, 1985; Austin, 1985) and bespoke versions (Beer, 1975) of such meeting-room environments are available and have been used. Within such limited and defined spaces, total environmental control is possible and this can be used to augment the effectiveness of the performances which are enacted, for example by creating a focus on specific artefacts, or by drawing in images or aural material as part of the process. Such multi-media settings lead the present discussion naturally into the next area for examination.

Properties

In many ways, the material resources used during an intervention are symbolic of the process used, and so are best thought of in connection with that aspect of an intervention. However, a review of approaches reveals such a degree of overlap in the perceived requirements that it seems worthwhile considering this common inventory, and attempting to interpret the part which it plays in general in the sorts of methodologies which we are examining.

A fundamental need in interventions is a means of recording, retrieving and displaying the data generated by participants. A variety of media may be used. In the designed environments which I have just considered, projection screens, photocopying whiteboards, video facilities and other features may be installed. However, as a way of thinking about some of the qualities of these media we can do no better than to consider perhaps the most basic and familiar, and certainly the most deceptively simple of all, the flip chart.

In an intriguing footnote of OD history, French and Bell (1984) note that flip charts were invented by Lippitt and Bradford in 1946, who, having only small blackboards available to them, went down to the local newspaper and got a donation of end of press runs which they cut up for use in their training sessions. This provides the clue to the flip chart's success: it offered a way of moving beyond the small surface area represented by a fixed black or white board and a way of keeping a permanent record of proceedings. Flip charts are also technologically minimalist and can be used almost anywhere. Thus the full flow of the thinking of participants – dead-ends, repetitions, misunderstandings, and all – is preserved for later reference.

'...the full flow of thinking of participants...'

Furthermore, if flip charts are affixed to the walls of the meeting room (with re-usable adhesive like 'Blu-Tack'), rather than being displayed one at a time on an easel, their development and overall drift can be viewed, and they can be rearranged and modified to examine or support new arguments. In addition, completed charts can be stored and either used in later sessions, or photographically transcribed for subsequent reference or for circulation and feedback.

'...charts can be photographically transcribed...'

The qualities of the flip chart which I have indicated above, have strong implications for any approach which uses them. First, it assumes that the group is in the business of creating a shared and public information base: there is an openness between participants. Second, it assumes that what is recorded is meaningful to all those involved: it is not, for instance, cast in some obscure jargon: or if it is, it is a shared jargon. Third, it assumes that there is something to be gained by retaining the bulk of historical material generated: the focus of debate may cycle back to review and reconsider it. And fourth, it assumes that some rationale for intelligent editing and organization of content is available: there is no way that every detail of a group's deliberations can be captured in this medium. These four assumptions are by no means universal in the formal methodologies which have been developed, and so their use of flip charts correspondingly varies. Perhaps the most sophisticated users are those employing the Strategic Choice approach (Friend and Hickling, 1987), for whom all the above assumptions hold, and who have in addition developed the technology of 'pen and paper management' to a high degree. In this approach, considerable power attaches to the person holding the pen and recording discussion. By contrast, in Nominal Group Technique (Delbecq, van de Ven and Gustafson, 1975) the charts are just used for listing ideas in individuals' own words, so no special skills are required of the recorders. In still other approaches, such as Checkland's (1981) there are apparently no thought-through procedures indicating how flip charts may best be used to support the process.

Often there is a need in group work for the ideas of individuals to be brought together into a pool, possibly for subsequent negotiation and merging. There may also be a need for the reverse process whereby individuals comment upon or evaluate a pool of ideas which they have previously generated. While this can be done with flip charts, in the hypermap approach (Bryant, 1988b), for example, key issues raised in individual interviews may be brought to a plenary meeting written on removable self-stick notelets, subsequently being arranged and rearranged in patterns which make sense to those involved. Whether or not these elements are colour coded to identify their originator, or for other reasons, depends upon the need to retain such information in any specific case. Other methodologies (Eden, Jones and Sims, 1983; Cropper, 1987b) also encourage the shuffling of cards or labels on which ideas or concepts have been previously written. The underlying rationale throughout is that members of a group will learn much about themselves and each other by rehearsing their reasons as to why certain concepts should be seen as proximal, and by recounting their personal theories of causation and association between elements. Hence, such methods are found in approaches where the construction of individual meaning is seen as important, and are less likely to be used in those where the emphasis is on the group.

The evaluation of pooled ideas can similarly be achieved by the use of a further theatrical property: the self-adhesive sticker, which can be employed in various kinds of

'.. the self-adhesive sticker can be employed in various kinds of voting procedure..'

voting procedure that allow each member of a group to assess each of a number of alternatives being considered (Huxham *et al.*, 1988).

Such devices are a further means for ensuring equality of opportunity to approve, censure or veto group suggestions, and so will only be found within those methodologies which espouse this as a fundamental element of their philosophy.

The astute reader will have noticed that I have not referred to the use of computer-based systems for multi-media management. This is not because I regard computers as unimportant, but because the design of computer-based systems, beyond the most general specifications, relates strongly both to the process which they are intended to support and to the way in which the associated methodology attempts to organize the substantive content generated during an intervention, matters which will be dealt with later. However, it is worth noting a number of key distinctions in approach. Firstly, as Phillips (1987b) has indicated, a facility may be designed so as to form the hub of a network through which individuals interact, or it may represent the periphery with a group-centred activity going on at the core. Secondly, the computer may be directly and intelligibly accessed by participants, or its support may be mediated to them through an expert third party. Thirdly, the computer system may be designed simply to secure and re-present the materials which are fed into it, or it may be able to perform analyses upon the data and to rearrange them in various ways. And fourthly, the system may provide a link with the world outside the intervention, accessing external information or feeding ideas from the group to others for comment or confirmation. Now many of these points are really those which were made about flip charts (with an intelligent facilitator) dressed up in a new and more futuristic guise, and so the same considerations as were raised above could be restated. What appear to be new are the abilities to interact with other databases, and rapidly to carry out complex analyses within the intervention itself. The value of such possibilities naturally varies between approaches, though as I shall indicate shortly, there appears to be some room for this sort of support used with care in most methodologies. The need for caution stems from a possible distancing of data from the problem-owners and a clouding of their understanding by opaque analyses.

Refreshments

A final prop. Interactive working on problems through structured interventions is demanding and tiring: it should also be fun. Huxham *et al.*'s (1988) suggestion that an informal atmosphere should prevail and that there should be 'a copious supply of tea, coffee, biscuits, cakes and fruit' should not be taken as lightly as it reads. Friend and Hickling (1987) confirm the importance of having refreshments available in the working room so that momentum is not lost through breaks for snacks.

While attending to the inner man cannot guarantee success, it certainly seems to be prudent to ensure that he is adequately propitiated.

'..the importance of having refreshments in the working room so that momentum is not lost..'

Actually Performing

The theatrical producer has the immense advantage over the problem-manager that not only does he have the opportunity to rehearse and reinterpret the script, but when the curtain does rise he can leave the auditorium and head for a consoling drink in the bar. The problem-helper, whether conceptualizer, facilitator or dialectician cannot so distance himself from the scene of action, at least not for any protracted period, and is rather more in the grand old tradition of the actor-manager – perhaps overlain with some of the attributes of the television editor – rather than following in the footsteps of the director of amateur dramatics. Furthermore, in an intervention there is no written text, only some broad indication of the manner in which a wayward cast is likely to improvise; there is no guarantee that any or all the players will bother to remain for the duration of the performance, nor that others will not wander in from the audience or the streets; and there is no *a priori* reason to believe that anything which happens on stage will have the slightest influence on anything or anyone else. Nevertheless, for all these differences, producer and problem-manager share one thing in common: the awful finality of performance.

Faced with the challenging and explosive mixture of circumstances which a process for problem management must address, the interventionist has to make many choices. The character of the process which is eventually prosecuted, will certainly relate strongly to the purpose of the intervention but also depends upon the methodology used and the style in which it is employed.

Backstage

In those cases where the prime input of the helper is seen as being to assist in structuring the substantive content of some external problem, then it is likely that the associated process will be one which bears more than a passing and coincidental resemblance to that adopted in conventional scientific research. That is, the helper may gather together evidence and data with the support of the problem-owners, and then 'go away' to piece it together into a coherent pattern which is subsequently re-presented to them for discussion or decision. By contrast, in those cases where the helper's major role is to guide a social process within a group of people who are individually seeking to make sense of what is going on, but who need collectively to negotiate some shared commitment to action, then what transpires will be very different. The helper will usually spend a large proportion of time working interactively 'on the hoof' (Eden, 1986) with the group and the construction of a covenant will be an inseparable aspect of this work. These two extreme patterns of working can, for example, be found respectively in systems analysis (Optner, 1965) and strategic choice (Friend and Hickling, 1987). Intermediate positions along this dimension are taken by other approaches, with, for instance, visual interactive simulation modelling lying nearer the former process, and hypergame analysis (Bennett and Huxham, 1982) nearer the latter. In practice the sheer complexity of the content generated during interventions usually forces some 'time out' on the part of the helper, who can make use of his specialized skills when working in a 'backstage' mode between sessions, to bring together a diversity of evidence to stimulate new insights for a group.

Bearing in mind throughout that the notion of backstage work applies equally to the helper and the client group, it is worth looking briefly at the implications of this definition of distinct regions for activity. Most obviously, backstage work is invisible to other parties.

> 'Dirtiness is inherent in hotels and restaurants, because sound food is sacrificed to punctuality and smartness. The hotel employee is too busy getting food ready to remember that it is meant to be eaten. A meal is simply "*une commande*" to him, just as a man dying of cancer is simply "a case" to the doctor. A customer orders, for example, a piece of toast. Somebody, pressed with work in a cellar deep underground, has to prepare it. How can he stop and say to himself, "This toast must be eaten – I must make it eatable"? All he knows is that it must look right and must be ready in three minutes. Some large drops of sweat fall from his forehead on to the toast. Why should he worry? Presently the toast falls among the filthy sawdust on the floor. Why trouble to make a new piece? It is much quicker to wipe the sawdust off. On the way upstairs the toast falls again, butter side down. Another wipe is all it needs. And so with everything.'
>
> George Orwell   *Down and Out in Paris and London*

If a helper is to present what he does in this secret world to others, then he will need to dramatize what he has done in some way that will make it real for the client.

Goffmann (1959) instances the invisibility of the work carried out by undertakers, which is made concrete for customers by creating the coffin as a highly visible product. In much the same way, some management consultants place emphasis upon smart technology or presentational devices as plangent symbols for their backstage efforts: unfortunately this can backfire upon them, as their skills may be too strongly identified with the tangible hardware, with the result that their talents are undervalued. Additionally, the glossiness of the packaged product may hide some very tacky backstage manoeuvring since the invisibility of backstage activity offers the opportunity to conceal things from both audience and fellow-actors. The opportunity to cover mistakes and give an air of infallability is naturally well used by consultants. Indeed, when a helper takes away materials to work on the substantive content of a problem, it must always be an act of faith on the part of the problem-owner that when the helper returns with the results of analysis they have been correctly and rigorously determined, rather than simply being concocted and then impressively but falsely substantiated. More seriously, it is uncommon for the problem-owner to appreciate all the assumptions that are likely to have been made in technical modelling, yet these hidden inputs can strongly influence findings. This sort of opportunity for concealment is, of course, used equally by problem-owners, who may foster impressions about their off-stage responsibilities or influence which are well wide of the truth. A further corollary of the use of backstage regions is that within them, members of the group taking part in an intervention may interact with each other in ways that are distinct from the way in which they behave on stage. Thus, members of a consultancy team may indulge in 'shop talk', perhaps cruelly dissecting the conduct of other players, perhaps planning the staging of the next part of their revue, perhaps agreeing cues for subsequent collusive activity. Such opportunities may be essential for a smooth performance, especially when a professional showpiece is to be mounted, but will be less pernicious in interventions based upon the phenomenological stance where honest and open exchanges are *de rigeur*.

Pace

The scheduling of work upon a problem between interactive discussion and non-interactive investigation can have a major bearing upon the pace of development of understanding about a situation. It is part of the job of a facilitator to so organize affairs that momentum and interest are maintained, or there may be a draining of enthusiasm for the intervention and a consequent failure to reach any satisfactory end point. I have already discussed the general timetabling and logistics of various interventionist frameworks, but we need now to address the more detailed issues of people and time management within the elements of the drama.

The key element of dramatic development in an interaction comes through the successive conjunction of different groups of individual actors. This is the process that a helper as facilitator or dialectician helps to orchestrate and manage. To complement the way in which they demand the structuring of substantive problem content, some methodologies make use of quite complex procedural designs which may deliberately split members of a group into distinct subgroups, which knit them together in different ways, and which subsequently reform and redissolve the original cast list as the process develops. Some examples of this dynamic structuring are shown schematically in Figure 8.3, where the SAST process (Mason and Mitroff, 1981), the hypermap process

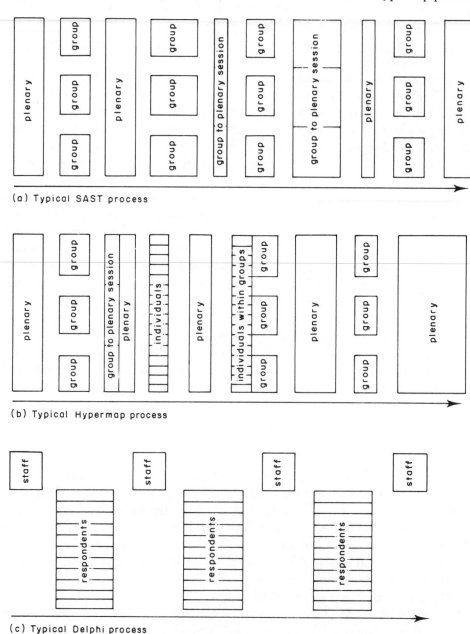

(a) Typical SAST process

(b) Typical Hypermap process

(c) Typical Delphi process

Figure 8.3. Orchestration of grouping in interventions over time

(Bryant, 1987) and the Delphi technique (Delbecq, van de Ven and Gustafson, 1975) are outlined as a weaving of the thinking of different sets of people over a time dimension (the content of these activities is considered later).

Structures of this type have also been pieced together on an *ad hoc* basis (Bennett and Cropper, 1986; Huxham *et al.*, 1988) for one-off research experiments, and are doubtless used widely in practice though seldom reported. Handling the problem-owning group in this way permits a number of ends to be achieved: first, some equity may be achieved in providing everyone with air-time to express their ideas within the small group setting; second, inhibitions which may be present in addressing the plenary group may be relaxed in a more intimate context; and third, a variety of distinct perspectives may be developed in subgroups and then brought together in productive confrontation before the whole team. Consequently, the philosophy of the various formal methodologies can often be discerned in their people-handling processes. Checkland (1981), for instance, tends to work throughout with the whole group, emphasizing their joint creation and exploration of relevant systems models; Friend and Hickling (1987) tend to work in the same way, though with a view to creating a joint commitment package. In contrast, although the cognitive mapping approach (Eden, Jones and Sims, 1983) naturally works in plenary session, since the group process is its central concern, this is preceded by individual interviews which have a paramount importance, as the management of individual meanings drives the whole methodology. The three approaches illustrated in Figure 8.3 are representative of further methodologies which are founded upon the deliberate fostering of contrary viewpoints about a situation. The authority to bring together participants in a variety of ways is a very powerful weapon in the facilitator's armoury, and one which may be conferred with some misgivings. However, even the most seemingly eccentric ideas may be tolerated if they appear to be productive.

Timing

Progress during an intervention tends to be measured against some yardstick of achievement – the area of commonality achieved in conflict resolution, the viability of solutions generated in problem solving, the extent of mutual understanding in counselling work – rather than upon the absolute scale of time. Nevertheless, time represents a limited resource in any practical exercise, and it needs to be well managed if it is to be used, and seen to be used, efficiently. Thus, participants will tend to become impatient or disenchanted with a methodology if they feel that they are 'not getting anywhere' and so this is a major issue for the facilitator to address. Some approaches self-consciously link achievement and elapsed time during phases of an intervention: for instance, in Nominal Group Technique (Delbecq, van de Ven and Gustafson, 1975) a five-minute period is specifically suggested for generating individual ideas. This focusing on time, which can be even more strongly emphasized by the use of a resettable timer that is started when an activity commences, is said to force concentration on the task in hand, as well as building a feeling that some sense of completion must be achieved by the end of the nominated period. Since this sort of pressure may be counterproductive and just lead to panic on the part of participants, a variant used by Hickling and Friend (1987) is to employ a timer, but with the understanding that this is merely being used to record how long is being spent on a task, rather than with any normative end in mind: in other words, a renegotiable, rather than a fixed interval is being marked out. As previously suggested, this idea of a constantly open agenda pervades work in Strategic Choice (Friend and Hickling, 1987), and means that although some general outline of how an intervention is likely to proceed can be offered at the start, this remains 'on the wall' so that at any time it can be returned to and modified in the light of experience. Most other methodologies approach this degree of flexibility, though they are less self-conscious about it.

Critique

Usefully, time control can be coupled with the deliberate evaluation of achievement of a process. This can be handled either purely informally, by seeking the feeling of the group, or more formally and in more detail by having participants indicate upon, say, a 5-point scale, their assessment of the session as a whole, of specific stages of activity, and also of the manner in which the process has been managed (Priestley *et al.*, 1978; Friend and Wedgwood Oppenheim, 1970). It must be noted, however, that the positivist idea of measuring the extent to which some pre-established objective has been reached has no place in these action research ratings of effectiveness, which rely instead upon a phenomenological stance. Although the more comprehensive appraisals would not sensibly be carried out frequently during a performance, they can help immensely as a way of forcing reflection upon where an intervention has reached at any time. Regular reflection upon progress can also help to highlight the so-called 'invisible products' (Friend and Hickling, 1987) of work: developing rapport between participants, mutual appreciation of pressures and constraints, and so on. This may be achieved by even more forceful process management on the part of a facilitator, who every half-hour or so forces the participants to take stock of their position. While some methodologies would encourage a facilitator to review or even summarize the position (Bowen, 1983) at such intervals, in others (Eden, Jones and Sims, 1983) this intrusion of the helper's views would be deemed improper, and instead the products of work might be scanned in a holistic manner, so that everyone would pick up a sense of what had transpired.

The whole matter of 'reflection in action' is equally important for the facilitator as for the others in the group. Schön (1983) suggests that 'when a practitioner makes sense of a situation he perceives to be unique he *sees* it as something already present in his repertoire': this, after all, is how we bring past experience to bear upon the case in point. If we accept this theory, then we can conceive of a problem-helper seeing *this* group with whom he now works, and their predicament as *that* group with whom he worked the other month, at least as an initial orientation. To the extent that this is the case, he can draw upon what happened before to create an artistic performance in the here-and-now, although wishing, of course, to make the experience seem fresh and unique for the present company (Goffmann, 1959), perhaps by unconsciously stressing the spontaneous aspects of the situation, or by skilful redirection of attention away from routinized elements by the use of a fluent patter. The reflective practitioner allows himself to be puzzled and confused (Schön, 1983) by the way in which things turn out as a result, and by investigating the sources of these surprises learns about his practice.

If one of the qualities which marks a 'good' problem-helper is an openness to learning (a use of a Model II Theory in Use as Argyris (1983) terms it) rather than a determination to extort validational support for preconceived beliefs (Model I Theory in Use), then are other qualities more contingent upon the sort of practice professed? Consider, for example, the specification given in Shaw *et al.* (1980):

The good facilitator is an 'open' rather than a 'closed' type of person and should be friendly and flexible. A good sense of orientation — which means that the trainer can see the trees *and* the forest in any problem — is highly desirable. The facilitator must know what is going on and have a keen sense of awareness of the relative importance of situations. He or she must be adroit, i.e. have the tact and sensitivity to deal with people and the capacity to straighten out complexities and entanglements. Persuasiveness and the capacity to get people to understand what is going on and to want to participate is critical. The facilitator must have good judgement and be able to assess situations and make rapid decisions of good quality. Beyond all this, the really good facilitator is sincere.

Although this is a pen-picture of an ideal facilitator for role-play work, I suggest that there would be few differences in the portrait of an effective helper for most interactive problem management. However, the critical feature which distinguishes one practitioner from another is the way in which the individual operates in creating a process *in vivo*. Cropper (1985) has dubbed this elusive property of an individual decision aider 'style', and suggested that it has a range of determinants including personality, interpersonal skills, experience, and technical, procedural and role repertoires. Elsewhere (Cropper, 1987a) has brought these ideas together with the Model II learning paradigm (Argyris, 1983) to create a dynamic picture of the interplay between practice and theory. Thus, it is in such matters as deciding when to anticipate and when to attend the client's thinking; as determining when and what to record of a group interchange; as resolving how to handle an unexpected conflict within the intervention; or as gauging just how quickly to introduce methodology-specific jargon, that helpers differ from each other. These stylistic attributes appear not to be systematically related to particular methodologies — except in so far as different methodologies appear to be espoused by people from different backgrounds or with different personalities — but to be features that mark out every interventionist's unique fingerprint of practice across the range of approaches which from time to time he may employ.

Capturing Expressions

I have talked about theatre as if it were a process which simply engaged actors and audience. It is not. More exactly it is what Lazarowicz (Mangham and Overington, 1987) terms a 'triadic collusion', involving the creation of a fictional world by actors, audience and, necessarily, an author. The work of the actors is to transform the literal expression of the author into drama which will touch the audience and thereby enrich them. However, authors speak from idiosyncratic positions in personal languages; nor is authorship any guarantor of fluency. Actors make their own expressive interpretations of a text; more or less effectively. Audiences construct their own meanings of what is going on; which might surprise both actors and author. The whole communication is precariously ambiguous.

In an organizational intervention, the participants are at the same time actors and audience and authors. The words they speak and the things they do are (in the main) of their own devising, and their reactions to others are to those others both as actors and as authors of their actions. The manager of dialectic within a problem managing group has to contrive a medium which can cope both with the ambiguities of theatrical communication, and with the simultaneous mutating presence of all parties to the triadic collusion. Since problem management is a voluntary social activity, based on the negotiated understanding between individuals that it is worth expending a certain amount of energy in order that they are severally better able to make sense of their worlds, the medium for representing problem content must at the same time both respect individual perceptions and create a usable, unequivocal, communal product. Any framework, which is offered by a problem-helper as a way of capturing the complexity of shared concerns, imposes its own fret upon this collective vision, and so creates a further artefact that must, if it is to succeed, be valid for and owned by those involved.

Structuring Debate

Although it may appear perverse to do so, I shall start by looking at the precepts of methodologically informed interventions, only later coming to the conceptual bases that may be used to achieve them. This is because we can find wide concordance about intentions across approaches, despite very diverse starting points. Such agreement relates back to my earlier conclusion that the prime aim of the interventions with which we are concerned is to develop a mutual understanding within the working group, that can serve as a basis for committed joint action. A corollary of this position is that suitable methodologies must be instrumental in shaping within-group dialectic.

The counterposing of contradictory visions and their subsequent merging in a higher, transcendent panorama which comprehends them and offers new insights is the essence of the Hegelian ideal. It is not an approach which is usually touched by traditional analytical frameworks in management science, where alternatives may well be identified and evaluated, but where the problem-owner is then left high and dry to 'get on with things' alone, or else is impelled along the route towards one particular choice by some form of multi-attribute decision modelling. By contrast, the methodologies which we shall examine set out, often in quite subtle ways, to generate discussion and debate within a group engaged in an intervention, and make use of data-structuring devices which support this intent.

The work of Eden and his co-workers (Eden, Jones and Sims, 1983) represents one extreme approach to the creation of a dialogue within the working group. This is achieved by the deceptively simple device of having them interactively create a shared qualitative model of their thinking about an agreed problem label. In the process of creating this model, divergences in view come to the fore as competing theories are aired and some working agreement reached as to what is going on. Hence, debate between the participants, whose attention is focused upon the creation of a shared mapping of beliefs, is effortlessly and shrewdly stimulated. Phillips (1987b) similarly sets out to construct 'requisite models' of the shared social reality of a client group and then examines the new meta-perspectives and insights that emerge. When the implications of the developed models become available to Phillip's clients, they are able to compare these with their own individual holistic judgements and the dialectic is driven by the perceived discrepancies. As these deviations in turn become the centre of attention so the debate moves through into new realms of appreciation, at the same time indicating possible transformations which may be practically effected. In quite a different tradition, Walton's work (Bryant, 1988a), using interactive analogue linear programming models, also employs a centring upon the building of a shared model of a situation as a device for creating a dialogue between participants, and he too engineers a progressive exploration of possibilities through model elaboration.

Other approaches also rely to a degree upon the construction of shared models as one focus of exchange between group members, but place their principal emphasis upon more explicit means of energizing debate. Thus Checkland (1985) sets out a highly structured process which will lead through to a set of conceptual models that are methodically contrasted with the 'real world', in a way that raises awkward questions about current procedures, and hints at possible alternative routes for development: the Hegelian contrasts are here the constructed models and the world of affairs. Noticing, but sidestepping, the knotty question as to whose 'real world' is to be used in the contrast, the debate that is started by Checkland leads directly through into ideas for desirable and feasible change. Many alternatives to the device of conceptual modelling exist: for example the 'wish poems' employed in charrette-based planning (Sanoff and Barbour, 1974) wherein individuals express their concerns about the *status quo* in the form of listed ideals. The core idea throughout, however, is the same: the tapping of problem-owners' diverse personal theories and values and their exploration by individuals as a means of introspective learning and by the group as a springboard for communal commitment to act.

There is an alternative approach to catalysing working group debate, which is used in another cluster of methodologies. This relies upon the participants setting out deliberately to create or explore a number of contraposed *Weltanschauungen*, perhaps representing the perspectives of different actors or agencies which are seen as being in some way caught up in the problem fabric. The most transparent of these is the method of scenario analysis (Miles, 1984) in which contrasting visions of the future (normative scenarios) or contrasting assumptions about current trends (exploratory scenarios) are used to fuel discussion about present policy. Scenarios are also used as an input to Rosenhead's robustness methodology (Rosenhead, 1980) which includes a wide-ranging review of alternative decision sequences before a robust decision set is alighted upon. Another school of work, embracing Churchman's ideas of enquiring systems (Churchman, 1971) and Ackoff's ideas of participative planning (Ackoff, 1974b), which sets out to activate discussion between contrary views, is typified by the Strategic Assumption Surfacing and Testing methodology (SAST) of Mason and Mitroff (1981). Here subgroups are deliberately set up to scrutinize in extreme detail the assumptions which underlie a range of indicative policies. A formal debate then ensues between proponents of the different stances, which is intended to lead through to the creation of common ground for joint action, and to agreement about a programme of research into areas of uncertainty.

The different story-lines of scenario analysis, and to a lesser extent the different policies used within SAST, tend to be based upon antithetical representative views of the world, rather than upon the perspective of any specific interest group or organization. However, there is a range of approaches which deliberately sets out to look at problems from the viewpoint of those actors who are apparently involved in them. Since, in most cases, these players will not be party to the intervention, then an imaginative leap has to be made by the working group to see things through the eyes of the former. This cluster of methodologies includes hypergame (Bennett and Huxham, 1982), metagame (Howard, 1987) and hypermap analysis (Bryant, 1987), and as their labels suggest is ultimately based upon the metaphor of problems as arenas of conflict. Within these approaches, the mechanism for creating the intervention dialectic is an inventive reconstruction of the choices and preferences of the cast list of significant players, and a working through of the consequences of these positions and of the opportunity for unilaterally or multilaterally agreeable outcomes. Possibly, as in hypermapping (Bryant, 1987) or role play (Shaw *et al.*, 1980), the debate may be played out through theatrical improvisation. Elsewhere, a more tightly structured gaming session may be arranged (Radford, 1984; Eden and Huxham, 1988) or the working group may engage in the situation at an even more cerebral level through discussion and analysis. Nevertheless, there is a common feature across all these approaches: the growth of a more highly developed personal appreciation of what seems to be going on, within a collective determination to construct some joint initiative.

Gathering Evidence

It is now time to step back into the intervention to see the concepts which are variously used to capture individual views, to see the rules of evidence employed, and to see the techniques by which these data are patterned for debate and consequential problem management.

Corresponding to the theoretical footings of each methodology, distinctive conceptual frameworks are used to assemble material for debate. Among these, perhaps two major concerns can be identified: agents and alternatives. There is a set of methodologies which open up an intervention by asking questions as to who is involved or affected by the concerns in the problem arena. These hominocentric approaches naturally include those with game-theoretic antecedents which are inevitably concerned with the players interacting around the problematic situation, and those, such as SAST, which make use of the concept of stakeholders as a way into policy investigation. The way in which a cast list of actors is assembled and represented, ranges from a simple listing to the Venn diagram format preferred in hypermapping (Bryant, 1987), the systems-based pictures used by Bowen (1983) in his interaction analysis and the issue-focused models of the Preliminary Problem Structuring stage of hypergame analysis (Bennett and Huxham, 1982). From this basis, these approaches proceed by assuming that each actor is able to exercise choice between a range of alternative actions, and that he will have preferences between the resulting outcomes. Analysis then continues either by investigating the implications of concurrent actions by independent players and the retaliatory measures which may be taken as a result (as in metagame or hypergame analyses), or by simply testing the impact of the exercising of unilateral choices upon the intentions of the problem-owner (as in interaction analysis or SAST).

The other principal group of methodologies take the decisions facing the working group as their starting point, and so ask questions about the choices, options and alternatives available. It would be easy to assume that, these decision-centred approaches take a more limited view than the agent-centred ones discussed above, since only the client's view is explicitly considered. However, in practice, the actions of others and their implications come in piecemeal as alternatives are inspected. Such methodologies attempt to flesh out the consequences of the choices available, recognizing the uncertainty that surrounds them. They do so in ways which place varying emphasis upon the interrelationships between decisions: in strategic choice (Friend and Hickling, 1987) these are explicitly set down at the start, whereas in other approaches such as linear programming (Bryant, 1988a) they make their presence felt only later and indirectly in the way in which potential solutions are proscribed. Subsequent analysis is then based upon a comparative evaluation of the identified feasible policies, the level of dimensionality employed again varying from one methodology to another.

If data are trawled in the ways that are described, on what basis should they be taken seriously in any interaction? In other words, what are the rules which are used to validate the evidence put forward and used as the basis for joint action? The answer to this question in the case of scientific analysis or legal arbitration has been long established and forms the basis of these disciplines, but in the helping professions it is less clear. Scanning the principal methodologies, we can discern a number of positions.

For some, the only credentials needed for a theory or opinion to be taken into consideration is the personal affirmation of one of the participants in the intervention. Thus in cognitive mapping (Eden, Jones and Sims, 1983), individual maps around a problem need no further justification: they simply represent the unique views of their owners and their authority is the authority of belief. However, in the process which is elaborated around these data, individuals are forced to question and possibly to re-evaluate and reform their beliefs as they encounter new perspectives and construct new meanings. In strategic choice (Friend and Hickling, 1987) more explicit attention is paid to the uncertainties which exist for people around the issues being discussed, and these are consciously exposed and then used to structure a major component of the final commitment package produced, in the form of agreed explorations and investigations. Decision analysis (Phillips, 1982) makes use of statistical ideas to quantify judgements about target events and then follows through the implications of these probabilities when taken in combination. Any shared uncertainties which remain in the later stages of an intervention are taken up in subsequent commissioned work. A very much more tightly structured approach to evidence is taken in the SAST methodology (Mason and Mitroff, 1981) which scrutinizes data through a critical framework suggested by Toulmin (1958). Here, as each claim is put forward with its associated data, this is accompanied by an explanation of the warrant which licenses the link between them, by a statement of the range of validity of this justification, and by an indication of the ultimate 'self-evident' assumptions which provide the backstop for the warrant. The associated argumentation analysis is a powerful tool for assessing data, and although encountered in one specific methodology, could easily be used in others.

Patterning Meanings

Finally, I shall turn to the methodological 'tools of the trade' employed across approaches, to encapsulate and record the debate and its outcome. What is set down naturally varies according to the driving concepts used, but there are still common characteristics, as well as unique twists. The most straightforward graphic device of all is the simple list, used in virtually every approach to summarize key issues or ideas, be they items on an agenda, players in metagames (Howard, 1987), stakeholders in SAST (Mason and Mitroff, 1981), ideas for defining relevant systems (Checkland, 1985), or even just 'odds and ends' [which Hickling (1987) collects in a 'Rhubarb Sack'!]. Such lists may subsequently be prioritized, edited or redistributed, by means of a variety of procedures including voting (Delbecq, van de Ven and Gustafson, 1975), counterplan-ning (Mason and Mitroff, 1981) and categorization.

It is a short step from an ordered list to one which can be recorded or spatially organized, perhaps by being written on cards or restickable notelets: this is an idea used, for instance, in hypermapping (Bryant, 1988b) and the charrette method (Cross, 1978), where the basis for reorganization might be cognitive proximity, hierarchical relationship or network clustering. In SAST (Mason and Mitroff, 1981) elements are 'plotted' in terms of the two dimensions of certainty and importance; this exemplifies the wide use of geometrical methods for arranging data. Sometimes two or more lists may be brought together and their interactions examined. This can be done through a matrix form of display which is widely used, and can even be extended beyond two dimensions by means of tree diagrams (Phillips, 1982; Friend and Hickling, 1987). Computer-based methods provide means of slicing in different ways through even more complex multi-dimensional structures. One step further forward again, in terms of formal organization, lie techniques which depend upon simple or directed graphs to relate data elements. Good examples of the former are provided by Buzan's (1982) mind maps and Bryant's (1987) ideographs, while cognitive maps (Eden, Jones and Sims, 1979) and strategic maps (Howard, 1987) illustrate the latter.

In most methodologies, these working artefacts also serve to summarize debate, and to indicate outcomes. However, mention may be made of the 'commitment package', an explicit concluding statement of intent, which is generated in the Strategic Choice approach (Friend and Hickling, 1987). As a visual summary of progress it serves to distil negotiated aims, yet it does so in a way which relates back to the original conceptual basis of the analysis, by cross-referencing each proposal for action or exploration against the decision areas which were identified: thus the methodological snake's tail is tucked into its mouth!

If an approach is to work, the resulting products must be ones which can be owned by all participants. Generally this aim is achieved by maintaining a transparency of process that keeps contact between the expression and any restatement of personal data. By using technologies which may appear crude or even backward by today's hi-tech standards, many methodologies succeed in avoiding opacity of technique, and so ensure that no distancing occurs. However, this is not to suggest that computer-based methods are inappropriate in this field. On the contrary, they may be exploited in virtually every approach as a way of rapidly processing or reorganizing materials. Thus SODA makes use of the COPE software (Eden, Jones and Sims, 1983) to present and analyse cognitive maps; metagame analysis employs a package called CONAN (Howard, 1987) to find and test viable policy options and sanctions; and other methodologies use software to assist at one or other stage of the work. However, what does appear crucial, from experience to date with these aids, is that great care has to be taken to capture people's thoughts in as close a form as possible to their original expression, and that any 'clever' analysis must be explainable, at least at an illustrative or conceptual level, outside the software. This parallels the hard-won experience in more conventional modelling.

The above review indicates some of the ways in which existing methodologies enable individuals in problem managing interventions to handle the complexity of their mental models and to renegotiate with others the meaning of events. How this wealth of ideas can be effectively exploited by the supported individual or group seeking to manage complex organizational problems is the final topic for discussion.

Becoming a Problem Manager

Something has to happen. Having seen something of the structured approaches which have been developed for handling problems, and having considered some of the issues raised in their implementation, it is time to turn to practice ourselves. An initial question for anyone finding himself or herself precipitated into a problem arena with a group of other unfortunates is, 'what now?' The answer, in so far as there is one, must ideally be approached through meta-methodology: a discourse on methodology itself.

Let us be quite frank; there is, as yet, no developed meta-methodology for problem management. All that currently exist are what Boothroyd (1978) terms 'prescriptive fragments': an eclectic set of ideas, methods and theories drawn from a variety of disciplines. A unifying conceptual framework to set these in relation to each other, thereby to create a sound basis for the future development of theory and practice, remains to be constructed. We do not know enough about the reasons for success or failure in interventions; about the fragility or robustness of organizational problems; about the relationship between practitioners' espoused theories and 'theories in use'; or about any of the other meta-level questions without answers to which we cannot claim to have understood problem management. In these circumstances, the best that can be offered are some optimistic shots in the dark.

One pragmatic probability for the would-be problem manager is to take an approach 'off the shelf'. The notion of a toolbox of methodologies, from which an appropriate one may be selected is attractively neat. However, in order to use a toolbox, one needs to know for what each tool is intended, and under what conditions it is likely to be useful. Further, one's limited experience is likely to mean that compared with a skilled mechanic one is unlikely, except by chance, to exploit the device to its potential; the result of one's work may bear little relation to that produced by an expert. These two issues stand four square in the way of this, most obvious, procedure. The sorting of tools has been addressed by Jackson and Keys (1984) who have suggested that their two-way classification of methodologies, referred to earlier, may serve to indicate appropriate approaches to be used in each of four categories of situation. However, I am sceptical that 'a problem' can be unambiguously identified, never mind labelled, in the manner which this rationale appears to require. Accordingly, all that can guide choice must be a feel for the dominant features of the mess in question, superimposed upon which will be the fortuitous experiential portfolio offered by any helpers who are available to provide input. This touches on the second issue raised above: the requirements for successful use of an approach. As I have already noted, a methodology is mediated to a problem-handling group through an individual who colours it with his own particular style. Thus, the Strategic Choice approach in my hands, will be a very different creature from that described by Friend and Hickling (1987); and Friend's practice will significantly differ from that of Hickling. Once more there are no simple answers. Some people will feel happy with some methodologies, in much the way that they feel comfortable in certain clothes: these preferences will tend to encourage the building of a repertoire of skills with a unique bias, and it is from these that a helper must draw.

The more ambitious alternative is to produce a bespoke methodology.

> 'The Word "thread" (*Faden*) was one often used by Wagner to describe the material from which he did his musical "spinning". It does not mean simply a "theme" in the sense in which other composers employ that word, but, as it were, the musical incarnation of a situation, a character, or a mood, from which all conceivable tonal and psychological mutations would follow later as a matter of course.
>
> . . .
>
> We are compelled to attach labels to these ["motives"], for otherwise we could not refer to them in our discussion of a work; but some of these labels have done considerable harm by bringing up in the listener's mind the same too literal connotation each time the motive appears. There are Wagnerian motives, of course, the meaning of which is virtually unchanging . . . but . . . the import of a motive can rarely be pinned down throughout to any particular person, object or episode. The motives are sensitive, plastic musical materials, on a par with those of the symphonist, with which the composer weaves a fabric of thought and emotion.'
>
> Ernest Newman   *Wagner Nights*

The composition of an intervention is an artistic enterprise which cannot be treated as though it were merely a capricious assembling of parts; it must have its origins in the very soul of its creator. Lest this claim be read as just so much precious nonsense, it should suffice to consider for a moment the dismal results obtained in any other walk of life where people attempt endeavours to which they have not given full emotional commitment: why should problem management be the one exception? This said, the question must arise as to whether any general guidelines of good composition can be discerned, for most of us are men of many parts without resources or inclination to aspire to methodological invention *ab initio*.

Some hints about general methodological structure have been offered by Bennett and Cropper (1986). They suggest that as time unfolds, four elemental issues must be addressed in any intervention: the way in which the problem fabric might be opened up with the client group; the choice of frameworks to be used to structure problem content; the stage at which developed models should be used with the clients; and the handling and integration of analytical fragments. In a combined approach which they set forward, an entrée is favoured based upon individual interviews, perhaps recorded using the notation of cognitive mapping. As these data are collected, they are shaped by the consultant working in a 'backroom' mode, and employing a dominant framework which relates to the apparent emphasis of the matters which have been raised, supported as necessary by other conceptual models. These 'twin tracks' of process are then brought together through interactive exploration with the client group of the developed representations. Subsequent analysis may be carried out either within the group, or by the consultants alone, depending on circumstances and content. Such an outline certainly appears to fit around the practice of some consultants and has formed the basis for experimental work involving the linking of formal approaches (Matthews and Bennett, 1986). However, under closer scrutiny what it represents is a 'toolbox within a framework' development, and the fundamental choices regarding the selection of methods at different stages remain. Unfortunately too, there is currently no evidence as to whether this structure provides a better basis for the successful prosecution of work than what may be termed the default option: an attempt to 'muddle through' picking up here or there an element drawn from one of the more familiar methodologies. Nevertheless, even this eclecticism may compare favourably with the age-old basic strategy of living on one's wits and using 'common sense', in the belief that this is problem management.

Tailpiece

Working on problems with others is ultimately not so much a matter of learning about the world, as a matter of learning about oneself. Through the processes and approaches which I have discussed lie ways of embarking upon and sustaining both the outer and the inner search. It is a search for meaning, which, if taken seriously, can help us, whether as problem-owners or problem-helpers, to grow through a reflective understanding of our uniquely individual experience.

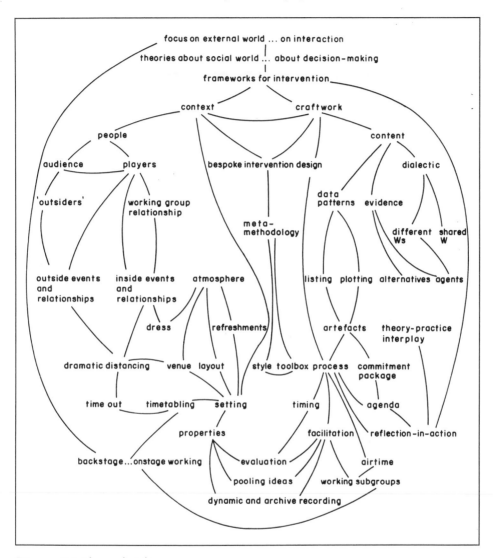

Diagram 8.1. Ideograph eight

PART FIVE:

Let's do it

LDI for Introduction

LDI 0.1

Congratulations, you've arrived safely!

The intention in these notes is to provide you with some practical experience of ideas that have been covered in the text, and to fill out the discussion given there by means of further examples, explanations or references.

I have made use of a simple set of symbols to indicate at a glance the different kinds of things which you will find in any 'Let's Do It' slot. These are as follows:

 Keywords

 Mini-Tutorial

Case Study Example

 Exercise

References

Any references will be found in full in the 'References' section at the back of the book.

Please now return to the main text.

LDI 0.2

 Ideograph

 An ideograph is a graphic device used to summarize an argument or dissertation. It resembles a 'mind map' (Buzan, 1982), but uses a more tightly structured notation and is employed in rather a different way.

The essential idea is to represent a linear argument or account into a form which organizes related concepts spatially. Since ideographs are frequently employed to keep an account of interviews or meetings, they must retain what is said verbatim. The diagram is begun as the narrative opens, and as it continues, salient phrases are noted down. As each item is recorded, it is linked, by a line, to related items already present. The lines themselves are unlabelled, although when a group discussion is being recorded, lines may be colour-coded to indicate contributors. Since some links may tie in to only one part of a previous item, the relevant part is highlighted or underlined to stress the precise nature of the relationship. When theories are being advanced, causality may be shown by use of an arrow, rather than a line, linking cause to effect, as in cognitive mapping (Eden, Jones and Sims, 1979): and as in mapping, bipolar constructs may be used for clarity in place of concepts in the diagram.

Turn back to the main text now, where you will shortly find an ideograph summarizing the Introduction.

LDI for Chapter One

LDI 1.1

Problem

What is your personal definition of the word 'problem'? Write it down on a sheet of paper and then put this into a safe place for later reference.

LDI 1.2

Problem, Concept map, Nominal Group Technique

You will probably find it interesting to see if I have presented you with a biased picture in Figure 1.1, by constructing concept maps for yourself or (better, since you've just seen my example) for your friends.

Take a large sheet of paper and write the word 'problem' in the centre. Then simply ask what connotations the word 'problem' has and write these down around the central label in whatever way you wish. Anything goes! There are no 'wrong' answers. Just set down what comes to mind. Compare the map you have produced with mine. How do they differ and in what respects are they similar?

Different people will produce very different concept maps. Try asking a number of people to carry out this exercise. Once you have done this, set the maps down beside each other and contrast them. What do the differences tell you about the people who produced them? Do you think that you would have guessed the authorship if you hadn't known who produced each one?

You may like to try this exercise in a group format. This time use flip-chart paper to set down the 'problem' label. Fix it on a wall where everyone can see it. Ask each person to spend a few minutes alone making a personal list on a sheet of paper.

Then take it in turns to go round the group, with each person calling out an item from his or her private list. Add these to the flip chart, to produce a composite concept map for the group.

Continue until all the ideas have been used up. If someone has contributed all the items from his or her list, then he or she 'passes'. If someone thinks that an idea already on the map is similar to one of his then he needn't bother to call it out. If anyone thinks of new ideas while the composite list is being built up, he should add these to his private hoard, and contribute them when his turn comes.

You will probably find that this process of developing a group list generates quite a lot of discussion about what we mean by problems.

The procedure used is actually a variant of Nominal Group Technique, a widely used planning process.

Concept maps: Eden, Jones and Sims, 1979
                          Eden, Jones and Sims, 1983.
Nominal Group Technique: Delbecq, van de Ven and Gustafson, 1975.

LDI 1.3

Perceptual exchange, Negotiation, Hypermaps

Differences in perceptions often underlie apparently irresolvable conflicts. Consider this example, given by Fisher and Ury (1982), of the contrasting perceptions of a tenant and landlady negotiating renewal of a lease:

Tenant's View	**Landlady's View**
The rent is already too high.	The rent has not been increased for a long time.
The flat needs painting.	He has given that flat heavy wear and tear.
I know people who pay less for a similar flat.	I know people who pay more for a similar flat.
I always pay the rent when she asks for it.	He never pays the rent until I ask for it.
She is cold and distant; she never asks me how things are.	I never intrude on a tenant's privacy.

And so on!

Take an issue that is currently exercising you, either in your employment or in your social or domestic life, and meet with the other party involved.

Each set down in note form, his or her own perceptions of the situation, on the understanding that whatever is written will only be shared with the other person. Stress that the more honest one is, the more useful the exercise will be.

After an agreed interval, exchange lists.

There is no need to comment upon or to discuss them at all, but if you decide to do so, first return the lists to their originators.

As an alternative to this process, work upon an agreed issue in the manner just described, except that this time set down in your notes what you believe to be the other person's perception of the situation.

Negotiation: Fisher and Ury (1982).
Perceptual exchange: Bryant (1987)
                        Pfeiffer and Jones (1973).

LDI 1.4

Frame analysis, Artificial intelligence

Read the following account (Boden, 1977) and then either attempt to provide your own explanation of it, or, better still, invite a friend to uncover the one plausible justification by means of a series of questions to which you answer either 'Yes' or 'No'.

There is a room. In the room is a bed. On the bed is a man. Under the bed is a small pile of sawdust. On the floor by the side of the bed is a piece of wood 99 cm long. The door opens and another man comes in. He sees what is in the room, looks pleased and walks out.

Do not read on unless you want to know the explanation.

The man on the bed is dead. Before his death he was the star of the circus, billed as the shortest man in the world. He was exactly one metre tall and had a metre-long stick (*not* a graduated rule) in his room against which he measured himself on ceremonial occasions. The second man, also a dwarf, persuaded him that he had grown 1 cm, so that he himself (at 1 m 0.5 cm) was now the shortest man. While the first man was absent from his room, the second man sawed 1 cm off the stick and hid the sawdust. When the first man checked his height and found that he had apparently grown 1 cm, he understandably committed suicide, since his supreme place in the world's circus community had seemingly been irredeemably lost to his hated rival.

Footnote:

'A dwarf who brings a standard along with him to measure his own size – take my word, is a dwarf in more articles than one'.
Lawrence Sterne   *The Life and Opinions of Tristram Shandy, Gent.*

Frame analysis: Goffmann (1974).
Artificial intelligence: Boden (1977).

LDI 1.5

Role, role play

Bernard Shaw gives a delightful example of role expectations in his play
Heartbreak House:

Noises are heard upstairs at Captain Shotover's eccentric country house:
a burglar has been apprehended after a brief scuffle, and is brought down to
the company in the main room. Apparently he had put his hands up when
challenged and said it was a 'fair cop'. The burglar urges the company to see
justice done: he must inevitably be consigned to a ten-year prison term.
However, they are unenthusiastic about the publicity accompanying a court
appearance, and rather than gratifying the burglar's moral enthusiasm offer
him the chance to leave free. Disobligingly he demurs. As one of the party
says in exasperation 'The very burglars can't behave naturally in this
house'. Undismayed by their leniency, the burglar threatens to go to the
police station to give himself up: he further threatens to implicate the house
party as accomplices to his crime if they persist in their unwillingness to
charge him. Of course they attempt to buy him off: a sum of twenty pounds
is mentioned. Eventually a suitable bribe is agreed and the burglar makes to
leave.

The rigidities of role labelling can lead to all sorts of problems! More
seriously, it can blind us to the qualities of individuals whom we may
summarily label, perhaps by virtue of their sex, colour or occupation.

Try some of the following role plays with a colleague. In each play there are
two parts, A and B, and an imagined situation (S):

A: Traffic warden
B: Motorist
S: A confronts B that his car is parked at a meter which shows that a penalty
is due

A: Manager
B: Subordinate
S: B has arrived at work late every day this week

A: Pensioner
B: Teenager
S: B's loud late-night music has disturbed neighbour A

Stop after five minutes or so, and switch parts.

Role play for a further five minutes.

Discuss with your partner, what it felt like to be in each of the roles.

You may like to make up your own role plays involving potentially
stereotypied parts and based upon situations with which you coped badly
in the past, or which you are expecting to face in the near future.

Role play: Johnson and Johnson (1975)
            Kolb, Rubin and McIntyre (1974)
            Shaw *et al.* (1980).

LDI 1.6

Transactional analysis

According to Berne's (1964) model of personality each of us is animated by three distinct and coherent sources of behaviour. He termed these 'egostates', and defined them as consistent patterns of feeling and experience which determine actions. The three egostates are colloquially labelled Parent, Adult and Child, to encapsulate their respective characters and origins. They are shown in Figure A.1, which uses the conventions of Berne's structural analysis.

Figure A.1. Egostate structure

The Parent egostate contains the attitudes, values, morals, prejudices and behaviours derived from our parent figures. It finds outward expression in both critical and caring responses to others. Inwardly it is experienced as constraining or supportive messages or commentary on our actions.

The Adult egostate is the determiner of responsible action and the generator of thoughtfully considered judgements. It is manifested in rational behaviour based upon critically examined evidence. Despite its label it is independent of chronological age.

The Child egostate incorporates our archaic natural responses to experiences. Externally it may be reflected in impulsive, manipulative or placatory behaviour; internally, feelings of fear, guilt or aggression may signal that this egostate is active.

Any of the three egostates can be the base for feelings and behaviour at a given time. The corollary is that individual personality represents the balance struck between Parent, Adult and Child.

Following this model, interpersonal relationships can be regarded as involving transactions between the several egostates of the parties concerned. Such transactions may harmoniously complement each other or they may clash in painful miscommunication. The former is illustrated when I complain to my boss about a heavy workload and elicit the hoped-for sympathetic response (Child – Parent and Parent – Child transactions). The latter would occur if in these circumstances the boss ignores my concern and just says, 'You think you've got problems!' (Child – Parent response), or more kindly suggests that I attend a time management course (Adult – Adult reply). Sometimes there is a covert message hidden beneath the overt transaction: this is termed an ulterior transaction. Pursuing the example, I might hide my plea for sympathy under an Adult – Adult transaction; for instance, by saying that I shall be able to handle the workload if I work overtime. Naturally, non-verbal messages play a prominent part in transmitting such hidden communications. The transactions which we have discussed are illustrated in Figure A.2

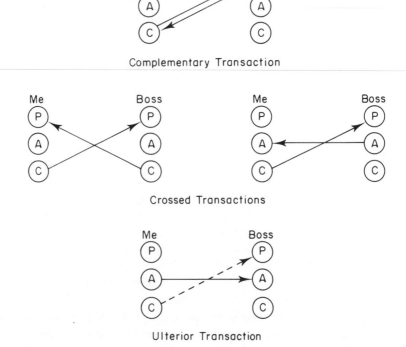

Figure A.2. Analysis of transactions

The lives of most people are played out according to scripts in which particular transactions recur as familiar motifs. This is hardly surprising, but it can be disturbing to others when transactions are regularly played with a hidden agenda: this pernicious habit is called game playing and has a special place in psychotherapeutic analysis.

Imagine yourself to be in each of the situations described below.

What would you do, and what thoughts and feelings are running through your mind?

What are the voices in your head saying?

How would each of your parents deal with this situation?

How would you have reacted as a child, and what would you have felt then?

What would be the most reasonable thing to do?

- You are driving alone along a remote country road at night when a desperate-looking person appears through the rain and attempts to flag you down.
- When the waiter brings you the bill for your meal at an exclusive restaurant, you notice that an item has been omitted.
- You are accosted by a street hawker selling costume jewellery of a type which you have long coveted but never been able to afford. It is obviously stolen.
- You are selling your car privately, but know that the chassis is badly corroded. A purchaser is very keen to buy it, but confesses to being totally naive about cars.
- When you arrive at work you are confronted by the boss. The previous evening you were the last person out and you forgot to lock up. Luckily no harm was done.

Repeat the exercise, this time taking a problematic situation which you currently face, but asking yourself the same questions.

Berne's (1964) ideas have been taken and extended by a number of psychologists who have used them in organizational contexts. As a route into this area, the work of James and Jongeward is useful: they have written variously about the uses of transactional analysis applied to self-discovery (1971, 1975) and also in organizational contexts (1976). A slightly more elaborate model has been developed by Dusay (1977) who provides an alternative view for assessing one's own personality, and for looking at its impact on relationships.

Life games: Berne (1964)

Transactional analysis: James and Jongeward (1971)
                              James and Jongeward (1975)
                              Jongeward (1976)
                              Dusay (1977).

LDI 1.7

Personality

For all their faults, people can rarely resist the opportunity of completing a psychological test.

One of the most respected and widely used is the Myers–Briggs Type Indicator (MBTI) which is accompanied by a Jungian interpretative framework.

If you would like to try this test, it is available in a number of formats, including an abbreviated self-scoring version, and can be obtained from the copyright holders:

> Consulting Psychologists Press, Inc.
> 577 College Avenue (PO Box 66070),
> Palo Alto,
> California CA 94306,
> USA.
> (Telephone: (415)857-1444)

LDI 1.8

Personal construct theory, Repertory grid analysis

The basic elements of a person's system for contrasting his world are what George Kelly (1955) termed 'constructs': these are dichotomous in nature with poles containing psychological (as opposed to logical) opposites. Each construct provides a dimension on which we may place encountered objects or experiences: for example, I may think of people as being mean/generous, friendly/hostile, and so on.

Linkages between constructs amount to theories about the world. Thus, I may believe that people with thin lips tend to be mean. This is, for me, an association between the constructs thin/full lips and mean/generous. A network of such associations or theories may be called 'personality'. We can begin to understand someone if we can access and explore their construction system, and we may be able better to relate to them if we can do this.

Psychiatrists are frequently interested in how patients relate to other people in their lives, especially their immediate family and friends. In order to gain insights into the constructs which individuals use to think about these significant others, a method known as the Repertory Grid Technique (Fransella and Bannister, 1977) has been developed. This method has been extended outside the confines of psychotherapeutic practice and is now widely used: most relevant for our present purposes is the work of Eden and Jones (1984) who applied this technique in examining people's perceptions of messy organizational problems: one intriguing case illustrates its use in probing aspects of organizational politics (Jones and Eden, 1981).

Try this short exercise which will enable you first to access areas of your personal construct system and then to see how you apply the constructs elicited to elements of experience.

You will first need to decide upon an area for investigation. Perhaps you are involved in a major purchase decision in your domestic life (a new house, car, television or toaster, for example); alternatively, you may like to think about some class of items which you regularly encounter (e.g. daily news-papers, television programmes, colleagues at work). The exercise will be more useful if the area is one about which you have some opinions or ideas, though you may be surprised just how rich your construct system actually is.

Select, say, a dozen or so items in the chosen field, and taking the same number of small identical pieces of card or paper, write the name of an item on each card (or draw a picture if your prefer). Shuffle the cards and lay them face down.

Draw three cards randomly from the set. Examine them and ask yourself how any two differ from the third. For instance, if the items were trees, two might be deciduous and the other evergreen. Note down the bipolar distinction: this is a construct. Don't worry if no construct comes to mind. Simply return the cards and take three more. On the other hand, if a triad generates more than one construct, note them all down. Continue in this way until you feel you are running out of ideas: in any case there is no point in producing more than, say, twenty constructs for this example.

Now set out your constructs (in bipolar form) and the elements which you used to generate them, on two edges of a grid, on another piece of paper. There may be over 200 cells in this grid if you've worked at the limits of my suggestions. Within this grid, each row/column intersection corre-sponds to an application of a construct to an element. Tick each cell in which, say, the first pole of the construct applies to the corresponding element; otherwise leave it blank. This will produce a pattern of ticks across the grid.

You may like to review the completed grid to see what patterns emerge. Does it appear that you think about certain elements in a similar way? Do some constructs seem to be applied on the same occasions?

If you are adept with the techniques, you may even decide to attempt some sort of cluster analysis.

The outcome may be a better understanding of how you think about the elements; possibly new insights into your mind! You may even find the grid helpful in differentiating between those seemingly similar products which you've been thinking of buying!

Personal constructs: Kelly (1955)
                    Bannister and Fransella (1980).
Repertory grids: Fransella and Bannister (1977)
                    Eden and Jones (1984).

LDI for Chapter Two

LDI 2.1

Attention

Stop and reflect upon the setting in which you are reading this sentence. Had you noticed the sounds and sights of the world around you? Had you felt the hardness of the seat you are on, or the warmth of the sun through the window? Only now that you have deliberately directed your attention to it are you aware of the sensory richness of your surroundings.

LDI 2.2

Personal psychology

This exercise is a version of McFall's (1965) Mystical Monitor. You will need a tape-recorder and a private room.

Start recording and talk into the microphone about your current problems and preoccupations for about twenty minutes.

Rewind the tape and listen through it all.

Wind back the tape again and record again over the first monologue. Then listen through this.

Repeat this process as many times as you wish.

At the end of the session erase anything remaining on the tape.

I shall refrain from making any clever comments about the possible results.

The process outlined above is described (in little more detail!) in Bannister and Fransella (1980) and in Priestley *et al.* (1978).

LDI 2.3

Patterning

Take a piece of card or paper and cut out shapes based on those in Figure B.1. You may make these any size you like, but keep the proportions the same as shown.

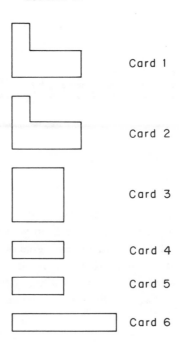

Card 1

Card 2

Card 3

Card 4

Card 5

Card 6

Figure B.1. Patterning

Set the first card down in from of you.

Take card '2' and set it down in such a way that the best possible arrangement is made of the cards on the table.

Take card '3' and repeat the process, if necessary, moving the first two cards.

Continue until all the cards are set down.

Reflect upon your progress, and identify any points at which you became 'stuck'. How did you feel at these points, and what enabled you eventually to proceed?

A similar approach can be used to analyse our thinking in other areas.

Take a current problem of yours and mentally run through the chronology of events which led up to the present situation. As you do so, note on a succession of separate cards, the bits of information which came to your attention: for instance, these might be finding out about some altered plans, hearing someone express his or her opinions, being told the cost of a proposal.

Now imagine yourself at the start of the affair. Shuffle the completed cards and take them one at a time from the pack. How differently would things have turned out if this had been the order of events?

Repeat this process a number of times and seek to identify if any of the pieces of information appear to be critical in all of the different sequences.

 Patterning systems: de Bono (1971).

LDI 2.4

Data filtering

Selective filtering of data about events means that two people may tell very different stories about what happened. This is exemplified when we hear accounts of a meeting from a number of different people. Each will recall different aspects of the episode, each will pick up different signals from participants, each will reach different interpretations of the outcome. You may easily confirm these assertions by seeking independent accounts of a meeting for yourself.

Alternatively, in order to demonstrate just how divergent accounts can be, buy copies of two or three daily newspapers tomorrow, and picking some event, see how differently it is reported in each. You can do the same by tuning in to television news bulletins on different channels.

Whichever the exercise you carry out, when you have completed it, set the different accounts alongside each other. Could you have identified the source from the content, style and character of these accounts alone? What do you learn about each source from the accounts given?

LDI 2.5

Cast list, Hypermap

Every individual is a nexus linking a set of subjective worlds: the varied stages on which he plays parts. Each of these segments of a person's life is peopled by others whom he perceives as being significant, self-determining actors in the relevant ongoing social processes. These others can be enumerated as 'cast lists' for a particular individual and scene (situational segment).

A number of conventions can be used to portray the set of persons or groups whom an individual sees as caught up with him in a specific problem field.

One method, based on systems concepts, has been suggested by Bowen (1983), and a typical diagram based on his conventions is shown in Figure B.2.

Each circle represents an individual role, and each box represents a system of individuals: thus some people can appear more than once in the picture if they occupy multiple roles. Each successive hierarchical level is shown by a box indicating the higher level grouping embracing all subordinate items. Figure B.2, which shows the structure of the academic group in which I currently work, demonstrates these two notational ideas. Bryant (1987) has suggested an alternative notation based upon the Venn convention: set membership is denoted by inclusion within a topographical region. The

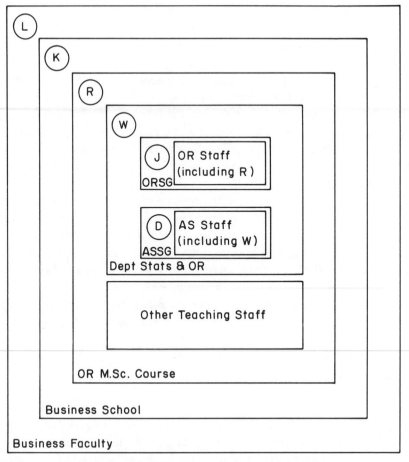

Key: L = Dean of Faculty;   K = Head of Business School
     R = Course Leader;   W = Head of ASOR Department
     J = OR Subject Leader; D = AS Subject Leader

Figure B.2. Management hierarchy for M.Sc. in OR course Bowen's notation

corresponding picture for the same specimen system as before is shown in Figure B.3.

Individuals are represented, as previously by their initials. Regions delimited by a continuous line represent purposeful groupings (as labelled) of the people contained therein. Each individual appears once only in this diagram. When two or more regions overlap around an individual, then that person is active in each of the corresponding systems.

At any time an individual sees himself as involved in a (large) number of distinct scenes. The participation of an individual in different arenas can be represented using the cast list notation by means of overlapping graphic envelopes of the sort shown above, wherein the overlap occurs around the label of the individual concerned. The overall picture can be termed a

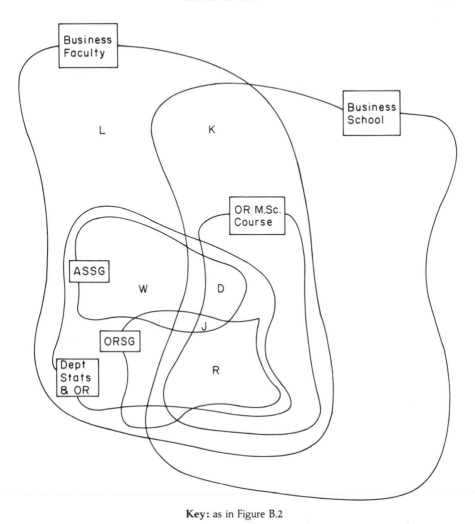

Key: as in Figure B.2

Figure B.3. Cast list of staff related to M.Sc. in OR course Bryant's notation

'synopsis of scenes'. The notion of a current, 'dominant' scene – of focused attention – is also a useful one, and can be shown by a highlighting of the relevant cast list in the synopsis.

Interaction with others requires an individual to make assumptions about how he or she thinks and feels about what is apparently going on. However, we usually appreciate that what others see and what we see may be very different. A hypermap (Bryant, 1983) is a conceptual device which depicts the relationships between these internalized mental models of others' thinking across a group of actors.

For any given individual, scene and associated cast list, we can imagine setting down a representation of each other's perceived thinking about what is happening. That is, taking the point of view of an individual, A, who sees actors B and C as significant in some situation, we can suppose that A will have a mental model of the situation which includes a picture of how B and C see things (whhich may or may not tally with the way in which B and C actually see what is going on). This set of three cognitive pictures belongs to a particular actor: in our example, A is the owner. We can further recognize that each cognitive picture itself can contain cognitive pictures. Thus A's picture of B's thinking in the example, could include (if A is sufficiently far-sighted) B's perception of A's own thinking, of C's view and possibly also the perspective of some other person D. There is in fact an infinite recursion of views of others' views! This whole set of perceptions, and of perceptions of perceptions, can be organized hierarchically, as shown in Figure B.4.

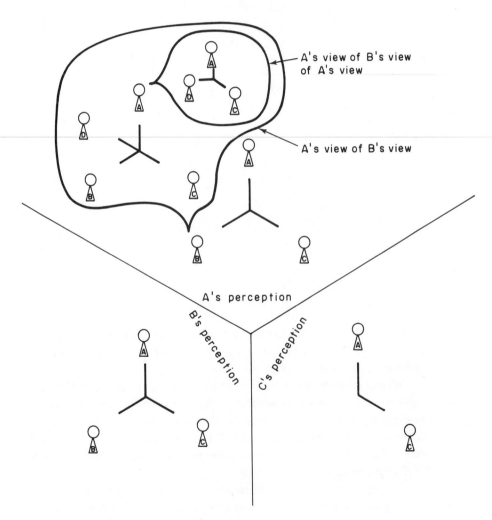

Figure B.4. Excerpts from a hypermap

At the lowest level we have an individual's (say A's) picture of what is happening and of who is involved; at the next level are that person's perceptions of how others see things (say A's views of how B and C view matters); at the next level again are the first person's beliefs about how others see yet others (say A's view of B's view of C); and so on. The whole organizing framework of perceptions is called a hypermap.

First, try applying the two diagramming conventions for showing a list of actors to a problem area in which you are currently active. You may find that one method suits you or the situation better than the other. Examine the pictures generated. Are some individuals involved in many different related arenas, while others are active in only a few? Do the diagrams help you to understand the attitudes and aspirations of those included?

Turning now to the separate actors identified around the problem, attempt to set down in words a position statement describing how what is happening looks from their point of view. It may help to imagine yourself writing a strip cartoon in which these actors feature as characters: you are filling in the speech 'bubbles' coming from their mouths! These statements should include reference to the others whom they see as involved.

Attempt to move to the next stage of recursion, perhaps just for a subset of the more significant actors, and write position statements which cover their views of others' views: in other words, try developing the hypermap. It will probably be apparent if any further recursion is likely to be revealing.

Review the system of statements generated. Do they help you to appreciate or understand any conflicts of opinion around the problem? Do they suggest any exit routes which could be mutually agreable?

Cast lists: Bowen (1983)
           Bryant (1987).
Hypermaps: Bryant (1983).

LDI 2.6

Garbage can model

Cohen, March and Olsen (1976) have suggested that people facing choice opportunities are inconsistent in their preferences, inconstant in their evaluations, uncertain about possible outcomes, and reluctant to commit themselves to specific courses of action. They thus argue for a model of choice which emphasizes the inherent ambiguity of decision relevance.

What matters then is how a situation fits into 'a mosaic of simultaneous performances involving other individuals, other places, other concerns, and the phasing of other events. What happens is often the almost fortuitous result of the intermeshing of loosely coupled processes.' The model which they propose portrays a choice opportunity as a garbage can into which various problems and solutions are dumped by participants.

We can gain a useful insight into our personal difficulties by applying the garbage can model at the level of the individual. Here the participants involved are the distinct elements of our individual psychic make-up (perhaps the egostates of transactional analysis); the problems and solutions are the concerns and products which are simultaneously milling around in our minds.

Make a list of all the problems which you currently face across all areas of your life. For instance, these may concern your family, lifestyle, career, projects, ideology, status or relationships.

Without reference to the list of problems, make a list of the answers or solutions which you currently find attractive. For example, these could include artefacts, methods, approaches, ideas or philosophies.

Now go back to the list of problems and label each one with an initial to identify its originator: e.g. if the Parent egostate is the primary source of concern, label it 'P'. At the same time, write down an estimate of the length of time that the item has been in your personal garbage can. Do the same for the solutions.

Review your lists.

Do the various psychic elements share responsibility for problems and solutions or are there any patterns of dominance? What do these suggest?

If the current contents of your personal garbage can are taken as representative of its usual state, what do you observe about the mix of problems and solutions? How does this mix correlate with the time and nervous energy which you normally expend upon the various items?

Choice under ambiguity: Cohen, March and Olsen (1976).

LDI 2.7

Priority

Although we may face many problems at one time, some may be considered as superordinate or subordinate to others to which they relate. Thus, I may have a problem of tidying up the garden, and subordinate problems of cutting the grass and pruning the bushes; in turn these may contain, respectively, subordinate problems of sharpening the lawnmower and finding the secateurs. Such a set of related issues can be set out in many ways; for example, using a hierarchy tree diagram. My gardening example is set out in this way in Figure B. 5.

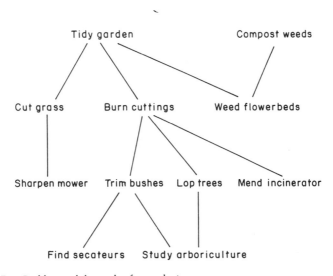

Figure B.5. Problem task hierarchy for gardening

Each link can be read downward as 'depends upon'. This is a ready way of arranging a longer list of problems or tasks, perhaps involving a number of different 'root systems', each corresponding to a different cluster of problems.

Sometimes we have to tackle one problem before we can tackle another: that is, there is a time dimension to be considered in organizing a list of problems. This can be done using network notation as shown in Figure B.6, which depicts some problems I faced in renovating a house.

The arrows show the passage of time. No job can be carried out until all the jobs leading into the node (or intersection) where it begins have been completed. I have found this simple level of description valuable in indicating the prerequisites for tasks in major projects: the added benefits of producing a full network analysis in which times are attached to activities (Battersby, 1967) are not always justified.

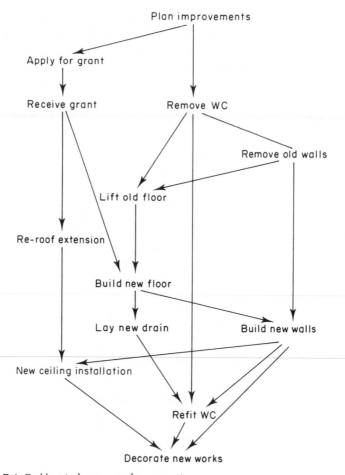

Figure B.6. Problem task sequence for renovation

 Make a list of your current concerns. This will be easier if you have recently done **LDI 2.6** above.

Try using the structuring notations suggested above to organize your lists.

Do the results suggest anything about the way in which you might tackle your problems?

 Network analysis: Battersby (1967).

LDI 2.8

 Time management

 Draw two circles on a sheet of paper.

Divide up the first into portions (like a cake) so that the size of each portion is proportional to the amount of time you spend during a typical month on each of your main activities (work, household, hobbies, holidays, entertainment, eating, etc.).

Divide up the second circle between these activities in proportion to the amount of time which you would like to spend on each of them.

Compare the results. Do they tell you anything?

You may care to repeat this exercise within more limited areas of your life: for instance, dividing a circle between the various tasks you are engaged in at your employment . If you do not have the necessary data to hand, does this suggest a possible exploration?

LDI 2.9

Role focusing

Dearborn and Simon's (1958) study well repays repeating.

Ask individuals holding different positions in an organization to which you belong what they regard as the most important problems currently faced.

If you do not have access to these individuals, or they are unable or unwilling to participate, then you may still get much of value from this exercise by conducting it through role play (see **LDI 1.5**).

Such a process can be strengthened considerably by appropriate preparation of parts, and for this the hypermap framework (see **LDI 2.5**) is useful as a way of systematically forcing examination of a situation from the perspective of the several participants. The approach here would be to develop that portion of the hypermap attaching to each of the chosen individuals, setting out the way that things might appear to them in terms of the actors whom they see, the drama in which they are engaged, and any higher level perceptions which also are believed to moderate action.

Conducted in either way, this experiment can be very revealing, especially in informal organizations or social groupings, as well as in more formal settings. If the various individuals can be got together as a group, then feedback – protecting individual responses if thought necessary – can give a productive basis for subsequent joint problem exploration.

LDI 2.10

Perceptual shift

It is the freshness of view which can make open discussion of a problem with others both refreshing and discomfiting and which can awaken awareness of aspects of a situation which hitherto were unnoticed.

The differential emphasis across participants upon key features of a situation can be readily demonstrated. Imagine that you are in turn:

– A burglar contemplating a break-in at your present place of residence.
– A doctor whom you are consulting for a complete medical checkover.
– Your immediate boss at work carrying out an annual evaluation report on yourself as an employee.
– A guest resident in your household for a short holiday, writing home about the experience to his or her partner.

In each case, think through in detail what you would say or do. Then, as yourself, respond to the challenge presented.

LDI 2.11

Problem

Look back at your response to **LDI 1.1** .
Would you like to alter your definition now?

LDI for Chapter Three

LDI 3.1

Wu-wei

There is a simple aikido demonstration of the principle of *wu-wei*. Extend your arm in front of you and invite an opponent to bend it.

The chances are that you will have held your arm rigidly and that your opponent will have been able to bend it, albeit maybe with some effort.

However, now try the exercise again, this time holding your arm out easily. As you do so, fix your eyes on some distant spot, and imagine your arm to be a flexible conduit through which water or power is streaming to that point. While your opponent struggles to gain advantage, breath out, thinking of your breath too as flowing through the outstretched arm. I will be surprised if this time your arm does not remain unbent.

The aikido master simply assumes that because of the outgoing flow of *ch'i* the arm will remain straight, come what may.

Tao: Watts (1979).

LDI 3.2

·Feelings, Gestalt therapy

An awareness of one's own feelings is a first step to understanding them and to achieving personal change. While many feelings are perfectly genuine, others may be deliberately conjured up *à la recherche du temps perdu*! For example, I may, quite reasonably, feel angry if someone fails to keep an appointment for an important meeting without letting me know that he wouldn't be coming. However, if I in my turn fail to make an appointment because I forget about it, and then vent my anger upon my secretary for not reminding me, I am probably playing the nasty game called 'See what you made me do!': in this, I disclaim any personal responsibility for what happened (as I may have tried to do all my life, whenever the opportunity arose), and indulge myself in the familiar, archaic feelings of self-righteous

237

freedom from blame. Transactional analysts have made an extensive study of such 'rackets' – the manipulation of others to recreate old feelings – and of the way in which these feelings are subsequently used to justify behaviour. These forms of game playing are relevant to problem handling since our very identification of problems arises from feelings which we have about situations. If these feelings themselves are false or exaggerated, then any subsequent treatment of the situation will be ill-founded and possibly quite pointless. Indeed games like 'Why don't you? – Yes but' rely precisely upon the statement of, and frustration of, a solution to a problem.

 In order to get in touch with and to explore feelings which you have when faced with a problem try some of the following experiments:

Exaggerate the problem.
What is the worst thing that could happen?
How would it feel to be in this situation? Imagine yourself in this worst case scenario and become aware of your body's response. What do you notice?
Now turn to consider the best possible outcome.
What would it feel like to be in this ideal scenario?
Tune in to the way your body feels now. Do you get any messages?

When you are faced with a problem ask yourself, 'What do I feel right now?' What *is* the feeling that you have most about this problem? Fear? Helplessness? Depression? Inadequacy? Anger? Guilt? Anxiety? Resentment?

In what kinds of situation do you commonly get this feeling? What do you think are the benefits of feeling this way? When and with whom do you experience it? Why not at other times?

Does it remind you of an earlier situation; perhaps one in childhood? What happened in this earlier scene? Re-enter it and feel how you did then. How would you replay that scene if you had the chance? Imagine yourself doing just that. Experience and note the feelings.

Come back to your present problem and look at it the way you did in your fantasy.

Focus on your *Lebenswelt*: your experience of your external world and of your internal world.

When is your problem: now, or in the past, or in the future?

Ask yourself if there is anything that you can do *now* to deal with it: decide on some action; find something out; determine to wait until something has happened. Is there anything which prevents you from committing yourself to these intentions? Imagine that you have carried out your plan; how does it feel?

 Transactional analysis: James and Jongeward (1971).

LDI 3.3

Patterned response, Assumption surfacing

It is all too easy to treat the routines or rules which we use in certain types of situation as inevitable and ordained.

Make a list of some of the stock responses by which you run your life, or which you make use of to ease decision making in an organizational context: for example, how you customarily decide what dishes to select in a restaurant; which way to travel to the football match; which TV programme to watch; which clothes to wear to work; whom to consult about a lightfingered workmate; which sub-contractor to employ or supplier to use.

Ask yourself, for each situation, upon what critical assumptions your customary behaviour depends. Make a list of these assumptions.

For each assumption formulate a counter-assumption: not necessarily its negation, but rather the opposite pole of the construct (see **LDI 1.8**) which it represents. Write these down alongside the corresponding assumptions.

Now consider what would happen if the counter-assumption were in fact the case. Would it make any difference to your behaviour. If not, then the pair of items can be ignored as irrelevant to your actions.

For those assumptions which remain after this dialectical filtering, assess each in terms of two factors: its importance (how crucial it is to the validity of the pattern of behaviour); and its strength (how confident are you that it is the case). Plot the assumptions on a chart like that in Figure C.1.

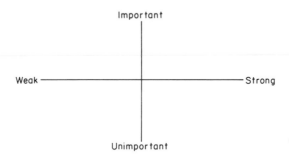

Figure C.1. Assumption plotting graph

Look carefully at those assumptions which lie to the top on the chart. These justify your actions. What could change them? What benefits would there be in this and for whom?

Look at the assumptions which lie in the top-left quadrant. These could be crucial to your behaviour but you are unsure as to their validity. Can you check them out in some way?

Finally, ask yourself the general question as to whether there is any consistent pattern in your routinized behaviour across different areas. Do you strive to avoid risks or deliberately to seek them out? Do you enjoy the experience of novelty or does it worry you? Do you try to minimize physical or mental effort?

 Assumption surfacing: Mason and Mitroff (1981).

LDI 3.4

Expert system, knowledge base

The issue of capturing expert knowledge within a structured framework has come to the fore as one of the principal problems to be addressed in the domain of machine intelligence. Buchanan (1982) gives a useful and readable account of this work. Some appreciation of the way in which expertise may be held can be gleaned from a small example.

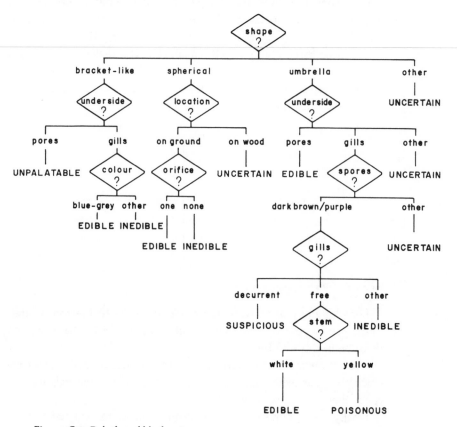

Figure C.2. Rule for edible fungi

Consider a crucial question in gathering wild plants – of taking 'food for free': is it safe to eat? A knowledge base relating to the edibility of, say, wild fungi, might be developed by allowing human experts to tell the computer about the attributes of a broad range of specific fungi. This database would then be scanned by a so-called inference engine, which attempts to extract some workable rules that are consistent with what it has been told. Thus if attributes like shape, spore print colour , form of gill attachment, and so on, as well as edibility are mentioned, the expert system will elucidate apparent rules which will subsequently enable it, through a series of questions, to determine if a newly discovered fungus is likely to be poisonous. This rule base might be represented in the form of a decision tree as shown in Figure C.2.

Once sufficiently validated, the system can then 'stand in' for the human experts in responding to user enquiries about further specimens which are found.

Expert systems: Buchanan (1982).

LDI 3.5

Strategic surprise, Game theory, Hypergame

Failure to recognize the complexity of a situation frequently lies at the root not only of military defeat, but also of competitive disadvantage in other areas. One way in which such episodes can be viewed is through a framework which characterizes the situation in terms of a number of elements, some of which are invisible to some of those taking part: it is therefore unexpected when these hidden elements are exposed.

The hypergame concept provides one framework for representing (*inter alia*) strategic surprise. Formally, the hypergame framework builds upon a game theory foundation, which conceives of any situation as involving a number of distinct players or parties (be they individuals or broad interest groups), whose deliberate actions impinge upon each other. Each player is thought of as having available a number of alternative courses of action. If an action strategy were to be chosen by each of the players, then the resultant outcome of this set of simultaneous strategies would probably be viewed very differently by each party. The hypergame concept recognizes that for practical application, the system that is described by game theory is hopelessly idealized, since there will usually be an imperfect flow of information and so the situation will be seen quite differently by each of those involved. Consequently players may be unsure as to the identity of the other parties concerned, may misperceive their strategies or preferences,

and may have a false idea of the way in which these same matters are seen
by others. All these features can be simply depicted in the notation of
hypergames, which can therefore be used to examine the structure and
dynamics of situations in which players' moves interacts.

 I can think of no better example to illustrate the idea of hypergame analysis
than that referred to in the text: the fall of France in 1940. This spectacular
military disaster (to the French) has been explored in some detail by Bennett
and Dando (1979) using the hypergame framework, and you are referred to
the original paper for full details: what follows is an outline summary.

Essentially, the situation in 1940 was that the Allies believed that a
German attack on France would either come from the North through
Belgium, or else that it would focus on the Maginot line in the East. In the
event of the latter, it was felt that an offensive could be held; if the former
came about, then the situation would be more finely balanced, but might be
sustainable if the French defence were already concentrated in the North.
From the French point of view the 'game' appeared as in Figure C.3.

FRENCH STRATEGIES

		Defend Maginot	Deploy in North
GERMAN STRATEGIES	Attack Maginot	Germany 1 France 4	Germany 2 France 3
	Attack in North	Germany 4 France 1	(Germany 3 France 2)

Figure C.3. 'French' game. 'Scores' denote payoff to each side as preference ratings of each
outcome

Now if this were also the way that the situation was seen by the
Germans, a little thought shows that events would unfold to produce the
ringed outcome, as each side sought to achieve the best result for itself,
while recognizing the effect of counter moves. However, evidence shows
that the Germans saw that a third strategic possibility was open to them: to
attack through the Ardennes. It might be reasonable to assume that this
would be met by the Allies with a counter-attack behind the German
penetration. This 'German game' is shown in Figure C.4.

In this situation, the best option for the Germans is still to attack in the
North, as in the 'French game'. If, however, instead of supposing that the

FRENCH STRATEGIES

	Defend Maginot	Deploy in North	North then Counter
Attack Maginot	Germany 1 France 4	Germany 2 France 3	Germany 2 France 3
Attack in North	Germany 4 France 1	Germany 3 France 2	(Germany 3 France 2)
Ardennes Offensive	Germany 3 France 2	Germany 5 France 0	Germany 2 France 3

(GERMAN STRATEGIES — row label on left side)

Figure C.4. 'German' game

Allies also saw the Ardennes offensive as possible, we now assume that they were oblivious to it (or believed that such an attack was impossible), but that the Germans both recognized the option *and believed that the Allied had not seen it* then the hypergame of Figure C.5 obtains.

FRENCH

	Maginot	North
Maginot	Ger 1 Fr 4	Ger 2 Fr 3
North	Ger 4 Fr 1	(Ger 3 Fr 2)

(GERMAN — row label on left)

FRENCH

	Maginot	North	Counter
Maginot	Ger 1 Fr 4	Ger 2 Fr 3	Ger 2 Fr 3
North	Ger 4 Fr 1	Ger 3 Fr 2	(Ger 3 Fr 2)
Ardennes	Ger 3 Fr 2	Ger 5 Fr 0	Ger 2 Fr 3

(GERMAN — row label on left)

Figure C.5. 'French-German' hypergame. A 'system' of games with restricted information

In this system, it is perfectly rational for the Germans to exploit the Allied blindness to an Ardennes offensive and to drive their forces into France by this route. From a knowledge of the limited French perception of the situation, the Germans were able to exploit the rational French response to their own ends.

The strategic surprise therefore came about not only as a result of one side conceiving a strategy which the other had not recognized, but also by their making a specific assumption about their opponent's view of affairs. The hypergame framework provides a way of encapsulating this combination of circumstances, and an analytical base for exploring it, both in the simple case of this illustration, and in more complex situations involving many more players and outcomes.

 Game theory: von Neumann and Morgenstern (1944)
                                      Jones (1980).
Hypergames: Bennett (1977)
                                      Bennett and Dando (1979).

LDI 3.6

 Complexity, Systems, AIDA, Strategic choice

 Take a sheet of paper and without further ado make a short list down the page of the major problems facing you in one area of your life: perhaps in your employment, in your place of residence, in your family, or in your personal life.

Turn the paper at right angles and write these same items across the page so as to form two sides of a square matrix.

Next consider each possible pair of problems in turn and ask yourself if tackling one would affect the other. At the point within the matrix corresponding to this particular problem pair, place a cross whose size is proportional to the degree of relationship which you see between the problems.

When you have dealt with all pairs, review the resulting matrix and identify any strong clusters of problems.

You may obtain a clearer view of the interconnections between the problems by producing a graphic description of your current 'mess'. To do this, simply arrange the items which you listed above on a sheet of paper, linking related problems with a line to show their relationships. The matrix from the earlier work may help you to arrange the words on the page so that clusters of problems are kept together, and so the resulting diagram looks less like a plate of spaghetti!

This exercise can be done even more easily by making use of self-adhesive notelets. Here you write a problem descriptor upon each notelet and then arrange and rearrange them (on a wall is best) until you have a pattern which reflects the relationships that you perceive.

 Problems have been defined as uncertainty-saturated choice situations. Within any problem there may be a number of decisions facing the problem-owner, and for each of these a number of alternative courses of action may be available. An individual facing a confusion of problems thus faces a profusion of options in many different arenas of action. Were these choices quite independent of each other, then we could, in theory at least, pick them off one at a time and so construct a set of policies for implementation. However, as we have just seen, problems interconnect to form an intractable mess. The only way forward is to recognize and work within this system.

An approach called the Analysis of Interconnected Decision Areas (AIDA) has been developed (Luckman, 1967) to provide a means of structuring problem messes. It is based upon the concept of decision areas, which are defined as identified opportunities for choice in which a number of mutually exclusive options are available. A problem may involve just one or several decision areas, and a mess may contain just a few of them or many dozens. The systemic nature of the mess means that the decision areas are interrelated: these links can be shown graphically in a picture called a decision graph, wherein decision areas are denoted by labelled circles, and the relationships by linking lines. Any decision area may include two or more options and these can also be shown graphically as labelled blobs within the decision circles. The practical meaning of interrelated decisions is that certain combinations of options across different decision areas are incompatible: these too can be shown graphically by linking such infeasible combinations of options by lines called option bars. A route out of a problem consists in a set of mutually compatible options, one from each decision area. The enumeration of all the feasible outcomes in a problem represented as a decision graph is a matter of simple combinatorial analysis. Once this set has been recorded the movement to a committed action about the problem is a matter of evaluation and eventual selection.

A simple example will suffice to demonstrate the principles of AIDA. Consider a group planning the production and distribution of a newsletter about its activities. Facilities exist for it to be printed in-house, though an outside printer could be used (at greater cost) if necessary. However, the in-house print unit could only handle a quarterly issue frequency because of other commitments. It is possible that distribution could take advantage of the regular quarterly mailshot to interested parties. However, if an outside printer is used there can be no guarantee that materials would be ready for mailshot distribution, so that a separate mailing could be required (again at greater cost).

The decision graph for this problem is shown in Figure C.6(a): decisions have to be made about newsletter frequency, printing and distribution.

The account above indicates the options available; there happen to be two in each decision area here, shown in Figure C.6(b). Option bars exist between the in-house print option and monthly production, and between mailshot distribution and both monthly publication and outside printing: these are also shown in Figure C.6(b). There are $2 \times 2 \times 2 = 8$ combinations of options in all, of which four are feasible, as the solution tree in Figure C.6(c) shows. It remains for a selection between these to be made,

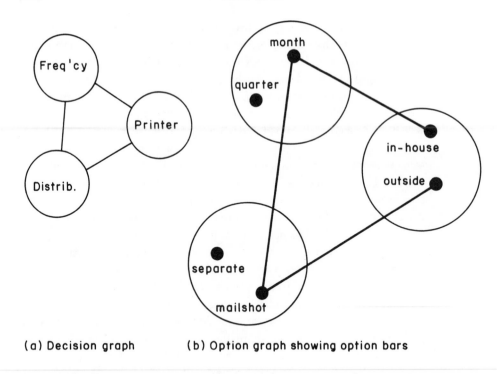

(a) Decision graph   (b) Option graph showing option bars

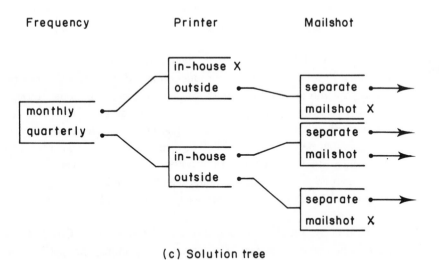

(c) Solution tree

Figure C.6. Specimen of AIDA method

perhaps on the basis of cost (the outside print + separate mailing combinations would fare badly here) or service to recipients (the remaining monthly option would probably score best on this criterion). The eventual choice depends upon deciding the right balance between the various comparison measures.

Try your hand at using the AIDA framework on a problem of your own. To begin with at least, choose something fairly simple with no more than half-a-dozen decision areas: otherwise the solution list can easily become unmanageably long. To deal with larger problems, the best route is to see if they cannot be divided into a number of more-or-less independent foci to be treated separately: alternatively, you may need to have access to one of the available computer packages to generate the list of feasible outcomes from the option graph.

Do not expect simply to work through the steps outlined above just once. The process will usually generate new ideas and suggest reformulations of the various pictures, so that a cyclic treatment is used to work through the system of problems. Frequently the insights gained in this way are just as valuable as any 'solution'.

 AIDA: Luckman (1967)
        Morgan (1971).
Strategic Choice approach: Friend and Hickling (1987).

LDI 3.7

 Organizational script

 It has been suggested that every organization follows a 'script' which determines its nature and development path. The script, which sets out the parameters of change, is itself ultimately derived from the aspirations of its founders. Some organizations play out a tragic script, while for others it resembles a comedy, a melodrama or simply a boring soap opera. Within such a script there are roles to be played by those involved , roles which place demands and pressures upon individuals, and which collectively give the organization its identity and character.

 Take an organization (or a part of an organization) to which you belong and answer the following questions:

What adjectives would you apply to your organization?
Innovative? Exciting? Stable? Sleepy? Stuck? Disciplined? Parochial? Introspective? Busy? Traditional? Fashionable? Shoddy? Elderly? Strong? Flexible? Bungling? Predatory?

Design a crest or coat of arms for your organization which expresses its personality. What would be its motto?

If you had to choose an animal to symbolize your organization, what would you select? What shade would you colour this creature?

What is the code that determines appropriate dress or personal grooming in your organization? What forms of costume or make-up would be regarded as unacceptable?

Why?

How are individual roles symbolized by resource allocation in your organization? How can you tell a person's status? By size of office? By access to clerical help? By flexibility of hours? By company car? Are these privileges appropriate to the jobs being undertaken?

What are the traditions of your organization? Imagining that you were asked to give a newcomer a list of the 'Ten Commandments' of the organization, what would they be? Where did these rules come from? Do you agree with them? Did you agree with them when you joined the organization?

Every organization has its skeletons in the cupboard. What are the untellable tales in your organization? Who were the culprits and what did they do? How do these ghosts affect present policies?

Would your organization make a good basis for a TV series? What sort of stories would you tell? Who would be the stars of the show, and who would you cast to play them?

What would be the flavour of the episodes? Romantic? Dramatic? Nail biting? Hilarious? Farcical?

 Transactional analysis: Jongeward (1976).

LDI 3.8

 Heuristic

 The rules which are elucidated through repetition of experimental trials may be explicitly formulated as heuristics (systematic methods of discovery). These are particularly common as a way of handling extremely complex problems for which exhaustive analysis is impossible. For example, Eilon, Watson-Gandy, and Christofides (1971) give some examples of heuristics used in physical distribution management for depot location and vehicle loading.

 Derive an heuristic which might be used by someone wishing to explore the whole of a labyrinth without the benefit of a plan. Use the layout in Figure C.7 to test your method.

Do not read on until you have tried the exercise.

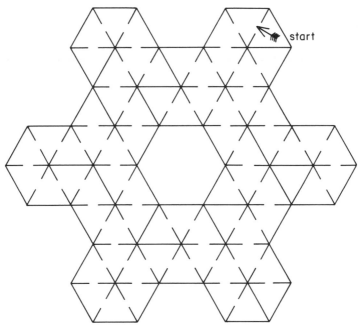

Figure C.7. Labyrinth

One method of exploring a labyrinth involves marking the paths at each node encountered.

Arriving at any node, see if it has been visited before: we can tell this easily for we will have more marked one or more paths on such a previous visit.

If the node is a new one, then mark the path just taken with three crosses. Choose any exit route and as you leave the node make two crosses on this path.

If the node has been visited before, place just one cross on the incoming path. Then see which other routes have already been used. If all other exits have already been marked, then retrace your steps along the incoming path; otherwise, choose one of the other exit routes. As you leave a node, add two more crosses to your exit path if it already bears a single cross.

By following these rules you will eventually cover the whole labyrinth.

An entertaining account of the use of this rule (and much else besides) is given by Eco (1984).

LDI 3.9

Insight, Problem-solving set

Given a balance and eight coins, find in two weighings the single (lighter) counterfeit coin in the set.

If you find this difficult, first try an identical problem with nine coins of which one is counterfeit.

This problem illustrates the importance of not taking things for granted, and how a solution pattern may usually be carried over between situations. The answer is to take triples of coins for the first weighing in either case. This identifies a set of three (or two) coins which contain the counterfeit. For the second weighing use just two coins from the set known to contain the counterfeit.

Given a balance, what is the smallest number of weights needed to weigh objects of any whole number of grams from one to forty inclusive?

This problem illustrates how easy it is to impose unecessary restrictions on a solution. The answer is to use weights of 1, 3, 9 and 27 g, placing them on either side of the balance as necessary.

Given a candle, some drawing pins and a box of matches, provide a makeshift wall lamp for a railway carriage.

This problem illustrates functional fixedness. The answer is to pin the empty matchbox to the wall and stand the lighted candle on top, held in place by melted wax and/or a pin through the box as its base. It is too easy to define the function of the matchbox as simply to hold matches.

 Gestalt experiments: Wason and Johnson-Laird (1968).

LDI 3.10

 Problem space, Solution path

 Three couples come to a river. A boat which can carry two people is available for the crossing. However, none of the women is prepared to be in the boat or to be left ashore with a strange man, unless her own partner is present. How can they all cross the river?

Labelling the women X, Y and Z, and their partners x, y and z respectively, and if → and ← indicate the direction of crossing, then if they start from the left bank a solution is: → YZ; ← Y; → XY; ← X; → yz; ← Yy; → xy; ← Z; → YZ; ← x; → Xx.

The Knight's Tour in chess involves the knight moving from an initial square in such a way as to visit each of the other squares on the board once and only once. Using, for simplicity, a reduced chessboard five squares by five, with a white centre square, how can the Tour be done from this centre square? On a full sized board, can the Tour be arranged to start in one corner and to end in the opposite one?

To find a solution, it helps to number the squares and then to redraw allowed moves in the form of a network as in Figure C.8.

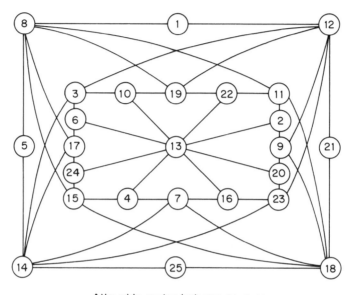

Key to numbering
of squares

Knight's Tour begins
at square 13

Allowable routes between squares

Figure C.8. Solution to Knight's Tour on five by five chessboard

Various solutions can be found.

The answer to the second part of the question is 'No', since 63 moves would be required to cover the board, and as the Knight's move takes the piece to alternate coloured squares it would be impossible to make the Tour from corner to corner as the squares are the same colour. Did you succumb to problem-solving set again?

 Problems of the type which we have just looked at are called 'Move' problems for obvious reasons. The graphical representation used in the Knight's Tour problem is a common way of depicting the problem space: the set of all possible states and the links between them. Solving a problem of this type is equivalent to finding an efficient path through the problem space. Various structured search procedures may be used including variants of hill-climbing methods (continually seeking improved positions, i.e. states closer to the eventual goal) and means–ends analysis (in which transform, reduce and apply subgoals are established towards the eventual solution).

The analytical complexity of deductive processes such as those illustrated above is not the only issue to be handled in everyday affairs: there are

pitfalls awaiting the unwary in this area, just as there are in inductive reasoning. Two tongue-in-cheek examples will show what I mean:

— The story is told of the biology teacher who was taking a class in animal behaviour. Today, he said, he would give a live demonstration using a trained frog. He set the frog down on the bench and told it to jump: the frog jumped. Returning the frog to the starting point he again commanded the frog to jump: once again it did so. Swiftly drawing out a scalpel, the teacher picked up the frog and cut off its legs before setting it down again on the bench. 'Jump!' the teacher commanded. The frog failed to move. 'And that,' the teacher said, turning to the class, 'shows that when you cut off a frog's legs it affects its hearing'.
— William Buckland, first Professor of Geology at Oxford University was visiting a European city with his son. In the cathedral they were shown a patch of floor miraculously stained with the blood of a martyr: each day the red-brown marks would be renewed overnight. Buckland knelt down and touched the marks with his wetted finger. Tasting the deposit he immediately pronounced that it was simply bat's urine.

The points raised by these tales are quite serious ones in practice. I am sure you can bring to mind some examples of your own, and will realize their potential consequences.

 Computer problem solving: Newell and Simon (1972)
Wickelgren (1974).

LDI for Chapter Four

LDI 4.1

Gestalt therapy

One of the most effective ways of making sense of the babble of problems going around in one's head is to make use of the 'hot seat' technique originated by Perls (1969). This method involves drawing out the internal dialogues and gaining emotional and intellectual awareness through exploring it in role play.

Begin by trying to eavesdrop on one of the internal voices or conversations. Who is it talking and what are they talking about? Perhaps the others are people (the boss, a parent, a customer); perhaps they are things (a product, an ailment, an idea). Whatever their identity, they have something to say to you, the problem-owner. Set out a couple of chairs facing each other, and speaking aloud from one, address the other party imagined in the other. I daresay this will seem silly: don't worry, do it all the same! In order to pursue the conversation, switch chairs when appropriate and assume the other role. Continue the dialogue, switching chairs with every change of role, and drawing in additional roles to the discussion if it feels right to do so. Attempt to reach some sort of termination of the discussion.

Role play: Perls (1969).

LDI 4.2

Stress

Are you under stress? The demands which are made of us are often hard to cope with, particularly at times when the whole format of our lives is altering. The following inventory may help you to check up on the pressures to which you are currently exposed.

Life Events Inventory (from Cooper, Cooper and Eaker, 1988)
Place a cross in the 'Yes' column for each event which has taken place in the last

two years. Then circle a number on the scale which best describes how upsetting the event concerned was to you, e.g. 10 for death of husband.

Event	Yes Scale
Bought house	1 2 3 4 5 6 7 8 9 10
Sold house	1 2 3 4 5 6 7 8 9 10
Moved house	1 2 3 4 5 6 7 8 9 10
Major house renovation	1 2 3 4 5 6 7 8 9 10
Separation from loved one	1 2 3 4 5 6 7 8 9 10
End of relationship	1 2 3 4 5 6 7 8 9 10
Got engaged	1 2 3 4 5 6 7 8 9 10
Got married	1 2 3 4 5 6 7 8 9 10
Marital problem	1 2 3 4 5 6 7 8 9 10
Awaiting divorce	1 2 3 4 5 6 7 8 9 10
Divorce	1 2 3 4 5 6 7 8 9 10
Child started school/nursery	1 2 3 4 5 6 7 8 9 10
Increased nursing responsibilities for elderly or sick person	1 2 3 4 5 6 7 8 9 10
Problems with relatives	1 2 3 4 5 6 7 8 9 10
Problems with friends/neighbours	1 2 3 4 5 6 7 8 9 10
Pet-related problems	1 2 3 4 5 6 7 8 9 10
Work-related problems	1 2 3 4 5 6 7 8 9 10
Change in nature of work	1 2 3 4 5 6 7 8 9 10
Threat of redundancy	1 2 3 4 5 6 7 8 9 10
Changed job	1 2 3 4 5 6 7 8 9 10
Made redundant	1 2 3 4 5 6 7 8 9 10
Unemployed	1 2 3 4 5 6 7 8 9 10
Retired	1 2 3 4 5 6 7 8 9 10
Increased or new bank loan/mortgage	1 2 3 4 5 6 7 8 9 10
Financial difficulty	1 2 3 4 5 6 7 8 9 10
Insurance problem	1 2 3 4 5 6 7 8 9 10
Legal problem	1 2 3 4 5 6 7 8 9 10
Emotional or physical illness of close family or relative	1 2 3 4 5 6 7 8 9 10
Serious illness of close family or relative requiring hospitalization	1 2 3 4 5 6 7 8 9 10
Surgical operation experienced by family member or relative	1 2 3 4 5 6 7 8 9 10
Death of husband	1 2 3 4 5 6 7 8 9 10
Death of family member or relative	1 2 3 4 5 6 7 8 9 10
Death of close friend	1 2 3 4 5 6 7 8 9 10
Emotional or physical illness of yourself	1 2 3 4 5 6 7 8 9 10

Serious illness requiring your own hospitalization	1 2 3 4 5 6 7 8 9 10
Surgical operation on yourself	1 2 3 4 5 6 7 8 9 10
Pregnancy	1 2 3 4 5 6 7 8 9 10
Birth of baby	1 2 3 4 5 6 7 8 9 10
Birth of grandchild	1 2 3 4 5 6 7 8 9 10
Family member left home	1 2 3 4 5 6 7 8 9 10
Difficult relationship with children	1 2 3 4 5 6 7 8 9 10
Difficult relationship with parents	1 2 3 4 5 6 7 8 9 10

Plot total score below:

Low stress		High stress
1	50	100

Some people are better able than others to handle these pressures. For example, those who are able to look constructively at the experiences that life throws their way, often manage stressful situations better than those who succumb to recrimination and regret. Frequently, individuals suppress their feelings in stressful situations but these may be cruelly exposed later as physical and mental symptoms take their toll. The following checklist includes many of the most common warnings of stress, and can provide a clue to hidden tensions.

Stress Symptoms (from Cooper, Cooper and Eaker, 1988)

Physical symptoms

Lack of appetite
Craving for food when under pressure
Frequent indigestion or heartburn
Constipation or diarrhoea
Insomnia
Constant tiredness
Tendency to sweat for no good reason
Nervous twitches
Nail biting
Headaches
Cramps and muscle spasms
Nausea
Breathlessness without exertion
Fainting spells
Frequent crying or desire to cry

Impotency or frigidity
Inability to sit still without fidgeting
High blood pressure

Mental symptoms

Constant irritability with people
Feeling unable to cope
Lack of interest in life
Constant or recurrent fear of disease
A feeling of being a failure
A feeling of being bad or self-hatred
Difficulty in making decisions
A feeling of ugliness
Loss of interest in other people
Awareness of suppressed anger
Inability to show true feelings
A feeling of being the target of other people's animosity
Loss of sense of humour
Feeling of neglect
Dread of the future
A feeling of having failed as a person or parent
A feeling of having no one to confide in
Difficulty in concentrating
The inability to finish one task before rushing on to the next
An intense fear of open or enclosed spaces, or of being alone

However, some people may be under stress and yet not show any of these symptoms: they are simply better able to handle it.

These ideas can be widened to investigate the mental state of organizations. I imagine that you can think of groupings that you might call neurotic, tense, humourless, fearful, and so on. Just as with individuals, some organizations are better equipped than others to handle the stresses imposed by a rapidly changing environment.

Using the inventories which have been given above, you might like to build up an inventory of stress-inducing events (and maybe of stress symptoms) which would be appropriate to organized groups in the world in which you live and work. For instance, a company merger might correspond to 'got married'; a new product launch to 'birth of baby', and so on. Then apply your inventory to some of the organizations in which you operate and review the results.

 Stress: Cooper, Cooper and Eaker (1988).

LDI 4.3

Context, Bounded vision, Role view

Consider the following problem:

A farmer went to market with a certain sum of money and 24 sheep. After selling the sheep at 3 guineas each and buying ten cows at £20 each, he had no money left when he went home. How much had he at first?

If we ignore what real farmers do at market, we can easily get an answer. However, we all know that after he sold the sheep, the farmer went into a pub for lunch and a few drinks; that he lost a few pounds with a wager on a horse race; and that he went home without a penny to his name because he was mugged after he'd bought the cows.

The framing of problems which we encounter every day is a good deal more subtle that this none-too-serious example, but I hope it drives home the point.

It is often helpful when addressing problems to 'step outside' oneself, so as to overcome the constraints which may limit one's perception of what is going on and what to do.

Take an issue which is currently exercising you and imagine yourself to be possessed of superhuman physical strength, mental ability and powers of persuasion: what would you do about the problem? Does this suggest anything?

What problems would you like to be involved in, from which you are currently excluded? What prevents you from becoming involved? What sort of problems do you feel that people push your way? Why is this?

If no one knew that it was you who had instigated the action, what would you do to handle the current problem? Why would you seek to remain anonymous?

LDI 4.4

Lateral thinking

It is both the peculiar strength and the especial weakness of the mind that it is so effective at patterning information. The facility enables us to make sense of what is going on; but it also constrains what we perceive and what we do. If we are to be freed, albeit temporarily, from the constraints which we ourselves impose upon our thinking about the handling of problems, then a self-conscious effort must be made to act creatively. This may be achieved through a deliberate search for alternative ways of looking at situations, for instance, through engineering discontinuities in thinking processes. It may be supported by creating environments for working on problems in which it is all right to propose 'silly' ideas.

 Take a problem which you are facing.

Begin by appraising what you currently think you might do about it. You may find it easiest to do this by noting down some *key words* which summarize your present view: these might be issues, criteria or decisions. Then set down the *assumptions* upon which this view depends. For instance, if you are a retailer concerned about store layout, keywords might be 'customer flow', 'ease of shelf replenishment' and 'security'; you may be assuming that 'customers know the store plan', 'stocks are replenished from the central stockroom' and 'customers are responsible for pilferage'.

Now is the time to introduce some discontinuity in your ideas. To begin with take your keywords and assumptions in turn and for a moment pretend that they do not apply; that they have no relevance to the problem. What ideas does this suggest to you? Thus in our store layout example, what would happen if we disregarded 'customer flow'? Perhaps we would move to thinking of a store design in which customers don't move at all, and in which goods are brought to them.

Next try some unreasonable distortions of your present ideas as a provocation which may suggest productive new ways of addressing the issues of concern. One possibility is simply to reverse your current view, or at least grossly to exaggerate or modify it. What ideas are suggested, for example, if in the retailing situation we pretend that all pilferage is from the stockroom by staff, not from the shelves by customers? No matter that this is unlikely; the purpose is to create an outrageous alternative from which new security measures could be devised. Perhaps an 'answer' would be to get rid of the stockroom. This idea could suggest having decentralized stocks (or no stocks at all), which in turn could help with replenishment; and so on.

The use of analogy is a powerful device for introducing discontinuity. At least four distinct sorts of analogy may be recognized (Gordon, 1961): direct, symbolic, fantasy and role play. In our retailing illustration these would be exemplified by: reflecting that the flow of customers round the store resembles the body's circulation of the blood; recalling the phrase 'as busy as a bee' in connection with staff shelf replenishment activity; allowing images stimulated by the situation, such as that of an Eastern souk, to spring to mind; and, pretending to be a tin of beans that is being shoplifted by a customer. Can you generate some ideas for your own situation in this way?

In each of these cases where apparently irrelevant ideas are induced, the key is that they must not be summarily rejected, but retained as stepping stones towards a viable solution. De Bono (1971), terming such thoughts 'intermediate impossibles', has shown their value in a wide range of practical situations. It is essential that you allow yourself the luxury, as the White Queen said, of 'believing as many as six impossible things before breakfast'!

 Lateral thinking: de Bono (1971)
                  Gordon (1961).

LDI 4.5

 Systems impact

 The proliferation of problems is easily demonstrated. Consider in turn the consequences of any or all of the following:

- The discontinuation of the doorstep delivery of milk.
- The prohibition of cigarette smoking in public places.
- The widespread ownership of second homes for holidays.
- The generation of electricity only from nuclear power.
- The writing off of all Third World loan debts.
- The accelerated spread of AIDS through tourism.

You may find it helpful to structure your thoughts by setting down the resultant changes in the form of a 'tree' of consequences, where each consequence spawns a number of new 'branches' corresponding to its effects.

Turn now to a dilemma which you currently face, and taking each of the alternatives open to you think through the chain of consequence which will follow from that choice.

Can you indicate on your picture, points at which the outgoing ripples of your decision fall over into areas which are primarily the concern of other people? Linking such points produces a crude boundary around your perceived field of responsibility. At these points, can you identify to whom you are handing over responsibility? Such individuals are likely to have views about your actions? What will they think?

LDI 4.6

 Storytelling, Rich picture

Take some time out to set down a detailed account of a problem which you are currently facing, as you would tell it with a particular audience in mind.

If your problem was described in sufficient detail for its nuances to be appreciated by someone else, you should have found this a time-consuming exercise. At the same time, a potential reader might well have found it difficult to see 'the wood for the trees', and to appreciate the key issues that you find troublesome. One way around this is to create not a verbal, but a graphic picture of what is going on.

 Checkland (1981) had advocated the use of what he terms a 'rich picture' to summarize the expression of a problem. This is a graphic device which should capture three essential features of a situation: structure, process and climate. The structure is the slow-to-change form of the situation and the systems involved: examples of structural representation are organization charts, plans of physical plant layout, accounting rules and so on. Process covers what is going on in the systems concerned; for instance, flows of information, materials or funds. The climate is the general mood and atmosphere of a situation, and results from interaction between structure and process elements.

The most efficient rich pictures are graphically exciting, as well as being clear in format and comprehensive in coverage. This visual appeal is important if they are to be effective communication media. Both 'hard' (e.g. statistics, numbers) and 'soft' (e.g. hunches, attitudes) information about a problem should be recorded. Although pictures are holistic devices, the most common error in constructing a rich picture is paradoxically that of uncritically including too much in it. Selection of the key features of a situation is a crucial skill in developing a picture, and is a task which in itself can be valuable, especially if it is done as a group exercise, since important arguments will usually be articulated as individuals attempt to justify the inclusion or exclusion of particular things. Figure D.1 illustrates a rich picture developed around some problems in a library.

Having got an overview of a situation, critical complexes of issues can then be teased out. This may be done by identifying pervasive, persistent general themes within the rich picture (for the example, these have also been indicated in Figure D.1). Recognizing themes is usually an iterative process, new themes also being identified later on as the problem fabric is examined. Specific approaches to tackling these problem symptoms can subsequently be addressed.

 Return to your earlier problem and create a rich picture for it, addressing the same audience as before. Note too any apparent themes.

Before you return to the text, it might finally be worth considering why you chose to address this specific audience, and how this choice affected what you said.

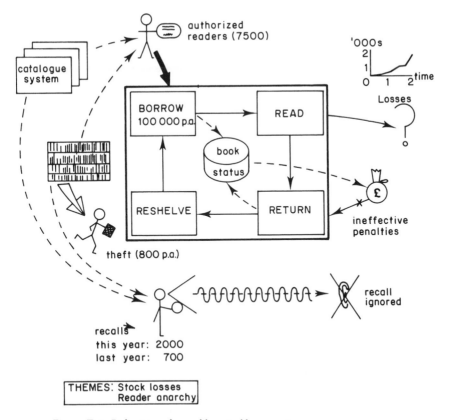

Figure D.1. Rich picture for problematic library system

 Soft systems approach: Checkland (1981)
Wilson (1984).

LDI 4.7

 Scripts

Scripts of the type referred to in the text, involving the concatenation of a set of elemental themes, lie at a far higher level of generality than many of those which we routinely rely upon. It is probably easier to gain an appreciation of the nature of scripts by accessing some of the more specific scripts which we rely upon in everyday social interaction. Consider, for example, a commonplace holiday script (which might well appear in a beginner's language course): the café. This might be formally set out as below, where the element categories are self-explanatory:

Title: Café
Roles: Customer
        Waiter
        Cook
        Barman
Props: Tables and chairs
        Menu
        Food and drink
        Bill
        Money
Transformation: Customer's appetite satisfied.
                 Customer hands over money.
                 Waiter receives tip.
                 Waiter/cook/barman remain employed.

Scene 1: Arrival
    Customer arrives.
    Customer selects table.
    Customer peruses menu.
    Waiter comes to table.
    Waiter takes order.

Scene 2: Action
    Waiter transmits food order to cook.
    Waiter transmits drinks order to barman.
    Barman prepares drinks.
    Cook prepares food.
    Waiter takes drinks to table.
    Cook signals waiter that food is ready.
    Waiter takes food to table.
    Customer consumes order.

Scene 3: Departure
    Customer signals waiter.
    Waiter prepares bill.
    Waiter gives bill to customer.
    Customer pays waiter.
    Waiter gives change to customer.
    Customer gives tip to waiter.
    Customer leaves.
    Waiter clears and resets table.

This script would naturally vary from place to place, but it is probably
recognizable through its variants in most countries: the subtle variations are,

of course, part of what make foreign travel 'foreign'. It is structures like this that, strung together, make up much of our daily routines.

Set down some of the scripts which you make use of employing the format shown above. Good topics might be:

- Buying a newspaper/take-away meal.
- Making a bus/train/plane journey.
- Obtaining a library book.
- Visiting the doctor/dentist.
- Going to the theatre/cinema.

You will probably find this surprisingly easy to do.

Now run through some of the scripts which you make use of in your job or in relationships with others. These may be more difficult to access, but should prove rewarding to produce.

Knowledge structures: Abelson (1973)
                                 Rumelhart and Norman (1985).

LDI 4.8

Stakeholder, Repertory grid analysis, Assumption analysis

The parties whom we see as having some claim on the outcome of a situation have been termed stakeholders (Ackoff, 1974b). It is these individuals or groups who feature in the cast lists which we may implicitly draw up in an account of a problem. It may be crucial to our treatment of a problem to recognize the implications which it and its handling have for those upon whom it impacts. Further, the range of possibilities which we see, may be constrained or modified by consideration of the views or actions of other interested parties.

A range of formalized approaches have been suggested (Mason and Mitroff, 1981) for generating comprehensive lists of stakeholders. These include listing for the chosen situation: those who are sources of reaction or stated discontent to what is going on; those with relevant positional responsibility; those who are generally regarded as 'important' actors by others; those who participate in activities related to the situation; those who shape or influence opinions about the issues involved; those demographic groups who are affected by the problem; and those with clear roles with respect to the situation (e.g. customer, friend, adviser, etc.). Within each category the listing process may be aided by a systematic widening of focus, starting with the situation itself, but expanding to embrace potential stakeholders in the broader system.

 Drawing upon a problematic situation which matters to you now, construct a list of stakeholders using the approaches indicated above.

You may find it helpful to categorize your stakeholders in terms both of the chance of their affecting the situation, and of the impact which they would have if they did so. This categorization can be brought out by plotting each stakeholder on a graph as shown in Figure D.2.

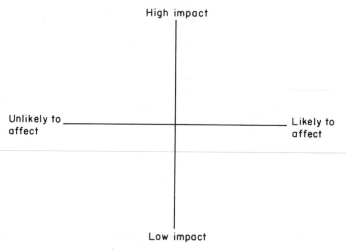

Figure D.2. Stakeholder plotting graph

You should think again about your list if any quadrant is empty. Have you really included everyone?

In order to become more aware of the significance which the various stakeholders have in the situation, the repertory grid method (see **LDI 1.8**) may be useful for exploring your beliefs about them.

Choosing those stakeholders which you earlier plotted as having potentially a major impact upon events, use these as elements in the repertory grid approach, and thereby elucidate the constructs which you use to think about these actors. Look for any clustering of actors or of constructs which appear revealing.

A rather different insight can be obtained by generating for each stakeholder a list of the assumptions which apparently underly his stance. This may best be done using the assumption surfacing technique (see **LDI 3.3**) from the point of view of each identified stakeholder. The result will be a list of robust assumptions (following counter-assumption testing) which can be plotted to highlight those that merit greatest attention.

Those critical assumptions are what tie the situation together. Review them carefully, especially in relation to the stakeholder for whom they have been derived. Does this actor have any special power in the situation? How could this stakeholder be influenced to change his position or course of action?

Stakeholder analysis: Mason and Mitroff (1981).
Repertory grid analysis: Jones and Eden (1981).

LDI 4.9

Cognitive mapping, Argumentation analysis

The plots of the stories which we tell about our personal or organizational lives are based upon theories which we have about the way the world is for us. The exploration and articulation of these theories can be aided by their encoding and representation as causal networks.

Cognitive mapping is a graphic technique which provides a visual language for setting down an individual's system of beliefs about a situation. It is based, like the repertory grid method (see **LDI 1.8**) upon Kelly's (1955) personal construct psychology. Specifically, it enables us to set out explicitly the relationships between the constructs which we use to make sense of our experiences. The result is a directed graph that indicates the nature of the beliefs which we have about a problem, which can be shared or discussed with others, or which simply provides revealing insights in its own right.

As a simple example of the product of cognitive mapping, a tiny fragment of a map based upon some recent work of mine, is shown in Figure D.3.

The map is based upon an account given by a social worker of the women's health problems in her area. To simplify outrageously, one line of argument ran that women in the locality were under unusual stress, which was causing many of them to smoke excessively, and generally leading to a high incidence of heart-related disease; a second line was that heart disease was related to unbalanced dietary intake, itself frustrated by poor shopping facilities, a lack of time for food preparation, and limited incomes. These and other chains of argument are shown in Figure D.3 by the arrows which link the stated constructs together.

Some points about the notation must be made. Each arrow represents a theory about the problem-owner's world: the item at the tail of the arrow is believed to contribute to the item at its head. Note that each item is a psychological construct, so that it contains two contrasting poles: where a

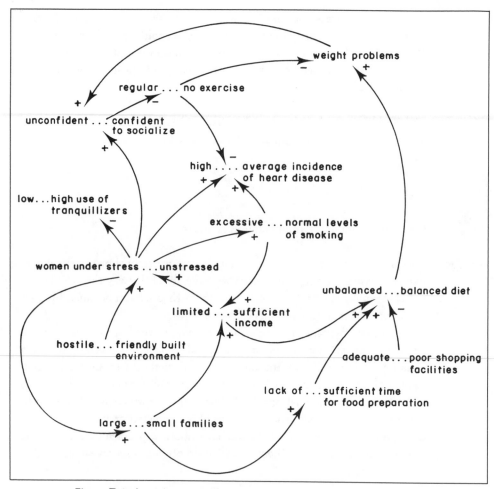

Figure D.3. A specimen cognitive map

second pole is not made explicit, the two poles are by implication 'an increase in . . .' and 'a decrease in . . .' the stated concept. Arrows have signs attached to them. These indicate the nature of the causality: a plus (+) sign indicates that the first pole of the 'tail' construct leads to the first pole of the 'head' construct (and similarly for the second poles); a minus (−) sign indicates that the reverse is the case, and that the first pole of the 'tail' construct leads to the second pole of the 'head' construct (and vice versa). A few minutes' examination of the illustration should serve to demonstrate these ideas.

 Now it is your turn to try your hand at cognitive mapping.

Set down a brief label for a problem that is bothering you. Then set down as its contrast – the second pole of the construct – an alternative 'better' situation. This is the seed from which your cognitive map will grow.

Now ask yourself what you believe this problem (or its contrast) will lead to. There may be a number of implications which you should set down separately as consequential constructs, using the notation I have introduced above. Ask yourself the same question about these in turn, and follow any chains of argument as far as you feel you are able, continuing to use the notation in a rigorous manner.

Perhaps at this point you may feel you have explored enough in this particular direction, and you could then return to the initial construct (or to some intermediate one which seems important to examine further), and ask yourself about its antecedents; or indeed about any further consequences which you have now realized. These can be set down in precisely the same manner as before, the arrows reaching back to add in new causal factors and forward to supplement the impacts already identified. Quite quickly a fairly detailed map can be produced. If you get stuck at any point, try asking the simple questions 'Why?' or 'So what?' about any construct on the map, and you will probably find that you will be able to elaborate further.

After a time, step back to see what you have produced (it can be most productive to produce your maps on big sheets of paper fixed to a wall, so that you can literally step back to review progress). Can you identify any clusters of ideas which appear to be worth considering together? Follow some of the chains of argument through and see if there are any complete loops present: what are their effects? What constructs lie at the heads and tails of open-ended arguments, and what can you do about these? While such analysis can be formalized – indeed this is usually essential in the case of very detailed maps, and computer software can be employed to carry this out – you should learn a lot by simply reviewing your work in this way.

The chains of argument which we have produced in our maps are theories about the world. Each link is an assertion about the way we think things are. While we may often be quite content with these, when challenged by others we may need to scrutinize some of our theories more carefully, to see what underpins them. One framework for doing analysing arguments has been proposed by Toulmin (1958) and developed by Mason and Mitroff (1981). This framework is shown in Figure D.4.

We may regard an argument as a movement from some evidence or data to a conclusion or claim. This movement can be supported by a variety of inferential devices (rules, principles, etc.) which permit the making of the claim on the basis of the evidence. Such permits (or 'warrants') must themselves be founded upon some underlying facts or assumptions, and may be open to challenge, either in general or specific circumstances.

Reverting to the women's health example, one theory advanced in the map shown in Figure D.3 is that cigarette smoking contributes to heart disease.

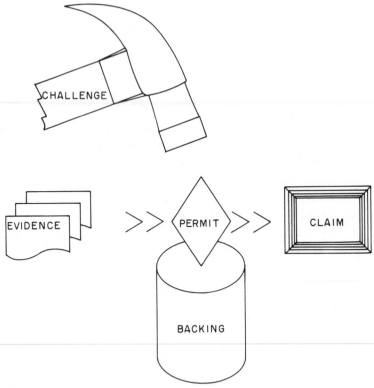

Figure D.4. Toulmin's argumentation framework

This *claim* is one which we may suppose to be based on the *evidence* of medical reports about which the social worker had read. The *permit* in this case was that these reports were felt to be reliable, and the *backing* would refer to the credentials of those producing the reports: a *challenge* to the permit might be offered by pointing out that the social worker had not seen the reports first-hand, and that the conclusions might have been distorted by the secondary reporting.

To take a second, wider example, the *claim* that smoking damages one's health is based on experimental and survey *evidence*. The *permit* is that such limited experiments and surveys represent the whole picture, and has the *backing* of statistical principles; these could be subject to a *challenge* that the systemic effects of other variables need to be considered in any analysis.

 Look back now at the cognitive map you constructed around your problem. Some of the links involved may be more vulnerable to investigation than others. Take these and mercilessly apply the Toulmin framework to the arguments made.

Maybe you feel that the map should be modified?

Cognitive mapping: Eden, Jones and Sims (1979)
Eden, Jones and Sims (1983).
Argumentation analysis: Toulmin (1958)
Mason and Mitroff (1981).

LDI 4.10

Garbage can model

Next time you are in a meeting look at it using the framework of the garbage can model.

See if you can identify the problems, solutions and choices which individuals bring into the meeting, and who carries them away.

Notice which problems and solutions eventually get paired up, and which remain in the can (or on the agenda) for a future occasion.

If you repeat this exercise at successive meetings of a particular group, does any pattern emerge?

Garbage can model: Cohen, March and Olsen (1976).

LDI 4.11

Metagame analysis

Metagame analysis (Howard, 1971) provides a structure to inform policy in multi-party situations where a number of decision-makers (players) interact through negotiation and action. It shares, in game theory (von Neumann and Morgenstern, 1944) a common ancestor with hypergame analysis, but in contrast to the latter has developed more strongly as a tool for investigating the stability of outcomes of a situation, including possible improvements or sanctions which particular actors might like to see.

In the earlier stages of the analysis, the method centres upon the specification of the situation (game) in terms of actors, options and scenarios. First a list of the actors involved is drawn up. This might be generated using various methods [e.g. Nominal Group Technique (**LDI 1.2**); stakeholder analysis (**LDI 4.8**)] and organized using various frameworks [e.g. cast lists (**LDI 2.5**)]. For each of these actors, policy options are then defined. These are each expressed in 'on–off' form: that is, the actor can either take the option or not. What is probably a lengthy list is then trimmed down, first by removing actors (and their options) if they are not fully involved in the interaction; this would be the case if their decisions did not result directly from what went on in the game. Additionally, options which are not part of the present negotiation between the stated actors are removed. We can now take it that the remaining list represents the full range of live options, and that each actor may proceed in the situation by choosing one or more (provided that they are not incompatible) options from his own sub-list of policies. Any set of choices made simultaneously by each of the actors is termed a 'scenario' and is a possible future history of the problem situation. These can be enumerated in various ways. While a scenario list could be produced along the same lines as a solution tree in AIDA (see **LDI 3.6**) it is more usual to use a tabular notation.

Figure D.5 shows an industrial relations conflict in metagame format. Management at a factory have introduced a new roster system, and the union has withdrawn the workforce. Two options are now apparent to management: to reintroduce the old roster system or to call in non-union labour. The unionized members simply have the option of returning to work.

Management								
Revert to old roster	X	✓	X	X	✓	✓	X	✓
Call in non-union labour	X	X	✓	X	✓	X	✓	✓
Union								
Order a return to work	X	X	X	✓	X	✓	✓	✓
OPTION NUMBER:	1	2	3	4	5	6	7	8

Figure D.5. Metagame analysis of industrial relations problem

Each column represents a fresh scenario, the ticks and crosses indicating whether or not an option is taken up. Every feasible combination of policies is shown (it is a simple combinatorial exercise to produce them). The first column (Option 1) represents the *status quo*, while others can easily be interpreted. Not all options are feasible or plausible. Options 7 and 8 involve a simultaneous return by union members and use of non-union labour: this is a non-starter. Option 2 is pointless, as despite the reversion to the old roster, the workers have not returned. Similarly Option 5 is unlikely, since management would presumably like to implement the new roster rather than the old, if freed from union pressures. Option 4 represents capitulation by the union to the new conditions. Most likely alternatives to the *status quo* are Option 3 (switch to non-union workforce) and Option 6 (revert to the old system pending negotiations). Having reached this point, analysis might now continue by investigating what pressure can be brought to bear from either side to achieve a desired result by means of threats and promises: the credibility of these would also need to be considered carefully.

 See if you can make use of metagame analysis in a socially rich problem of your own, involving a number of players. The stages should be easy enough to follow through up to the generation of scenarios – and that should be far enough to yield insights of some benefit.

A final hint: keep it simple!

 Metagame analysis: Howard (1971)
Howard (1987).

LDI 4.12

 Group problem handling

 Another exercise to try when you are meeting with others to explore a problematic situation.

See if you can identify the phases suggested by Eden's (1986) model of the social process of working on problems. Does the model tally with your experience? Can you identify the points when a shift was made from one mode of working to another? If so, who initiated the shift? What was it about the preceding activities that encouraged this development?

 Working on problems: Eden (1986).

LDI for Chapter Five

LDI 5.1

Problem helper, Nominal Group Technique, Open canvass

Consider yourself to be faced in turn by the following situations. Take some time to think yourself into the part outlined and to consider the ramifications of the dilemma posed. Then set down a list of those to whom you might turn for help or advice:

- You are employed as a labourer on a building site, where workers who wish to retain their jobs are expected to ignore safety regulations in the interests of rapid job completion: alternative employment opportunities are negligible.
- You have smoked heavily since your divorce five years ago but now have the opportunity of an exciting promotion at work – provided that you are a non-smoker.
- A friend tells you that it is normal practice in the country to which next week you are travelling on business, to make payments to minor government officials in order to smooth the path of a contract. Your job could depend upon the completion of this particular deal but you are unhappy about the prospect of bribery.
- As an independent elected member of the local council, you have no party affiliation to constrain the way that you vote on a contentious local issue: the refurbishment and public sale of a large estate of council-owned high-rise flats.
- Your company is considering diversification from its historical base in the manufacture of packaging materials, into the highly competitive business of offering a nationwide distribution service for the retail sector.

Now re-examine the lists you have produced for each case and examine the reasons why you have selected these helpers. What is it that they are offering: information, reassurance, advice, encouragement; or something else?

Next take a problem with which you are currently faced and make a similar list of the helpers on whom you might call.

273

Being perfectly honest, it is probable that you will not call upon all of these sources of support. What criteria will guide your eventual selection? Do you customarily use these criteria in choosing helpers, and do you think that this affects the effectiveness with which you deal with problems?

It will be illuminating to carry out either of the above exercises in concert with other people.

An effective way of doing this is to make use of the Nominal Group Technique (see **LDI 1.2**) taking the generation of a list of sources of support as the task involved. The creation of the individual lists involved may be further aided by using a checklist to ensure that the following categories of help have been covered: relevant disciplinary specialists, information sources, resource/funding providers, documentary materials, cognate organizations.

Once a group list has been produced you will probably find it worthwhile producing a rough ranking of the relative perceived values of the varied problem-helpers mentioned.

This can be done quite straightforwardly using a method which I shall term 'open canvass'. Provide each of the people in the group with a number of small, coloured self-adhesive labels (say 15 mm circular 'blobs') with which they can 'vote' for their preferred candidate helpers. As a rough guide, each person may have half-a-dozen or so labels, of which they can affix any number beside any of the items on the flip chart containing the total group list. Voting is done publicly in any order ('tactical' voting is not prohibited!), and an individual can use any number of labels (including none) in total. The result will be a tally of votes cast for the different potential sources of help.

Frequently this product of the process starkly illuminates key areas of support, highlights choices to be made and suggests approaches to be taken.

Nominal Group Technique: Delbecq, Van de Ven and Gustafson, 1975.
Open canvass: Friend and Hickling, 1987
Huxham *et al.*, 1988.

LDI 5.2

Personal constructs, Repertory grid analysis, Content analysis

To draw out the constructs which you use to think about potential problem-helpers, the repertory grid method (see **LDI 1.8**) can be applied to a sample set of occupational descriptors. A suitable set, which has been used extensively in related research (e.g. Coxon and Jones, 1979), is given below:

1. Church of Scotland Minister
2. Comprehensive School Teacher
3. Qualified Actuary
4. Chartered Accountant
5. Male Psychiatric Nurse
6. Ambulance Driver
7. Building Site Labourer
8. Machine Tool Operator
9. Country Solicitor
10. Civil Servant (Executive)
11. Commercial Traveller
12. Policeman
13. Carpenter
14. Lorry Driver
15. Rail Porter
16. Barman

Take these as elements in a standard application of the repertory grid approach, and review any patterns in the results.

Consider how this personal typology of individuals by occupation affects the use which you make of others in helping you with your problems in the various arenas of your life.

The repertory grid approach need not necessarily be – indeed quite commonly it is not – self-administered. It may be easier for you to carry out if someone else leads you through the triadic grouping, and if he or she notes down as you tell him or her the constructs which you are successively employing.

Conversely, you could carry out a series of interviews with different people based on this approach in order to elicit the distinct ways that each perceives occupational groups.

A distinct approach, also based upon interview data, has been used to investigate the images of different occupations. It involves a hierarchical clustering procedure. You can easily try this out for yourself as follows:

Set down the list of occupations above (or any other list if this one is unsuitable), one on each of a pack of separate cards, just as you would do for the repertory grid method.

Ask your interviewee to pick any pair of cards which appear to go naturally together. When these have been chosen, ask why they were put together, and note the reason given.

Next ask the interviewee either to make up another pair from the pool of remaining cards, or to add one to the existing group. Again ask and note the justification provided.

Continue in this way, producing further groups or adding to the existing ones. However, when two or more groups have been formed, there is also the option at any stage of merging two of the existing groups. Elicit an explanation for each 'move'.

Eventually, all the original cards have been placed in a group, and the interviewee must then continue by merging groups together on the same basis as before, until at last all the cards are in just two groups: here the process ends.

An example of the result of such a process is shown in Figure E.1.

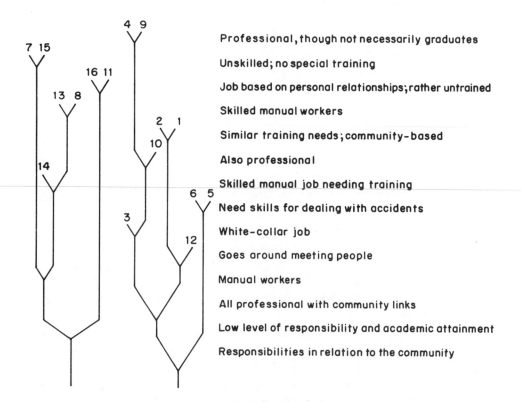

Professional, though not necessarily graduates

Unskilled; no special training

Job based on personal relationships; rather untrained

Skilled manual workers

Similar training needs; community-based

Also professional

Skilled manual job needing training

Need skills for dealing with accidents

White-collar job

Goes around meeting people

Manual workers

All professional with community links

Low level of responsibility and academic attainment

Responsibilities in relation to the community

Figure E.1. Occupational classification hierarchy (Job codes as listed on page 275)

You may find the business of note-taking difficult to handle while you are also prompting your interviewee. In this case, use a tape-recorder to capture what was said in the interview, and carry out an analysis of this afterwards. This can even be extended into a full content analysis of the interview protocol in which the frequency of occurrence of words in the complete transcript is noted. For example, in one study (Coxon and Jones, 1979), the job-related words 'people', 'training', 'group', 'class', 'skill', 'professional', 'public', 'service', 'education' and 'community', all featured strongly in a particular transcript, giving a strong indication of the interviewee's way of thinking about different occupations.

Repertory grids: Eden and Jones (1984).

LDI 5.3

Helping roles, Transactional analysis

Make a list of the major problems with which you have had to contend during the past twelve months.

Turn the paper at right angles and write below one another the labels of the various problem-helping roles which I have introduced in the text. Draw a rectangular grid so that the problem labels are along one edge and the role labels along another.

Now place crosses on the grid to indicate the sort of help which you obtained with each problem.

Are any patterns apparent? For instance, do you tend frequently to use a subset of the role types in handling problems, or to use particular types for particular sorts of problem or in particular arenas? What does this tell you about your use of others in dealing with problems?

If you often work as a helper yourself, can you identify in which roles you predominantly operate? In terms of the personality model used in transactional analysis (see **LDI 1.6**) from which egostate would you say you tend to work? Do those whom you help easily slot into the appropriate role so that the transactions going on in your work on a problem are complementary. Is there any relation between the helping role which you usually adopt and the helping roles which you expect of others when addressing your own problems?

Transactional analysis: James and Jongeward (1971).

LDI for Chapter Six

LDI 6.1

Presentation of self, communication

Imagine yourself in turn in the following sketches, and from the given perspective answer the questions below:

- You are a newly qualified teacher about to start your first lesson with a group of socially disadvantaged teenagers in a remedial class of a secondary school. You know that their last teacher was forced to resign after a nervous breakdown.
- Your business is running through a difficult patch, but a potentially lucrative contract with a new client is in the offing. At his suggestion but your expense, you are meeting this client over lunch at an excessively extravagant restaurant.
- You have just delivered a controversial keynote address at the annual conference of your own professional institution. At a reception shortly afterwards you meet some strong opponents of your views.
- You are a trained repairer of domestic electrical appliances, and are handling a call to mend a washing machine for a housebound and needy pensioner. Quite honestly, the machine isn't worth fixing.
- You were the referee for the national football cup final, that was held today. After the match you must give a press conference, where you can be sure that journalists will question you about the disputed penalty which determined the outcome of the game.
- You are a production line worker in a factory threatened with closure because of a downturn in market demand. The company directors are here on a works visit, but normal manufacturing throughput will certainly not keep you busy as they inspect the line.

What impression would you want to convey to the other person or persons?

How would you give off this impression, other than in the things you actually say (for instance in actions, manner, tone, dress, demeanour, posture, etc.)?

279

Draw up a list of questions which you believe no one would feel proper to ask you in the circumstances.

Draw up a list of possibly relevant statements which you would most certainly not make in this situation.

Now turn to your own occupation, or to a part which you play in some social group, and answer the following questions:

How is authority confirmed and re-acknowledged in this group? Does it have some outward manifestation?

What are the symbols – tangible and otherwise – of your own role? What are the tools of your task?

List a dozen 'tricks of the trade', not generally realized by outsiders. What do they have in common? What is the usual subject matter of jokes told between people in your occupation?

Think of some recent occasions when you have had to be tactful with others. Why have you been protective?

What do your answers tell you about the way in which impressions are managed in your chosen occupation?

 Special communication: Goffmann (1959).

LDI 6.2

 Personality profile

 When you have problems, what do you look for in a helper? And if you help people with problems, what sort of people do you prefer as your clients?

Try to answer these questions honestly, using the list of dimensions below as a prompt:

- Abstract thinking ... Concrete thinking
- Reserved/detached/aloof ... Outgoing/easygoing/involved
- Assertive/competitive ... Accommodating/conforming
- Shrewd/calculating ... Forthright/artless/natural
- Relaxed/tranquil ... Tense/nervous/uptight
- Calm/stable/even-headed ... Sensitive/emotional
- Impulsive/enthusiastic ... Prudent/sober/taciturn
- Socially exact ... Careless of protocol
- Conservative/traditional ... Radical/open minded
- Shy/timid/restrained ... Bold/spontaneous/venturesome
- Trusting/adaptable ... Jealous/suspicious
- Conscientious/staid ... Expedient/rule breaking

– Self-assured/confident ... Apprehensive/worrying
– Self-sufficient/resourceful ... Group led/dependent
– Imaginative/Bohemian ... Practical/proper/careful

It will probably be easier to do this if you think back over some of your specific recent problems.

You may well have recognized that another way into this issue is by carrying out a repertory grid analysis (see **LDI 1.8**), using individual helpers or clients as elements to elicit relevant constructs. (A further alternative would be to use scores from a personality test, but these are unlikely to be available!)

Whichever approach you have used, you might subsequently attempt an assessment of yourself along the same dimensions and look for any relationship between your own personality profile and that of the others with whom you get involved in problems.

Finally, if you and your client (or consultant) in a current problem have the stomach for it, you could both try this personality assessment of other and self: and then exchange the profiles produced, much as in a perceptual exchange (see **LDI 1.3**). This can be a refreshing and cleansing experience when attempted in an appropriately supportive context of mutual learning.

LDI 6.3

Project mix, consultancy life-cycle

The birth, growth, decay and demise of internal consultancy groups is a commonplace of organizational life. The process has been investigated through longitudinal studies of groups by Pettigrew (1975) and transverse studies across groups by Conway (1987). Taking the latter model, a number of distinct stages are seen within a group's life-cycle: these are shown in Figure F.1.

Essentially, beyond the earliest pioneering phase, a group may respond more or less successfully to circumstances; in the former case the work survives, perhaps under a changed title or within another area, while in the latter case the work eventually fizzles out, at least in recognizable form.

Conway (1987) claims – and the evidence seems to support this – that the mix of projects tackled by a group varies according to which stage of the life-cycle it has reached. He suggests that it can conversely be useful for a consultancy group to infer its development position from an analysis of its portfolio of work, and thus have warning of potential future problems.

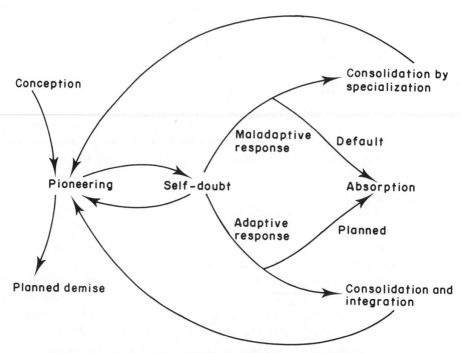

Figure F.1. Consultancy group life-cycle (after Conway, 1987)

 Maybe you work in a consultancy group, or make use of one within your organization? If so, try this exercise.

Look back over the history of the group. How long has it existed? Do you know who started it and what sort of work was carried out?

How large is the group now? Has it stayed at about this size throughout its life?

To whom does it report and for whom has it tended to carry out work? How has this changed over time? On the basis of this review, where would you place the group in its life-cycle?

Apply Conway's classification of projects to the work which the group has tackled during the past year. This involves identifying the source of each project undertaken.

Does the group have a sound core of internal/external linkage work? If so, then it is probably responding adaptively to change, though a high preponderance of internal linkage jobs may presage planned absorption because of over-dependence on a narrow set of sponsors. Otherwise, if closed linkage-derived projects are prominent, then the group is vulnerable and tending to increasing specialization and loss of robustness.

Are the results suggestive of what the group management should plan to do?

 Project process: Conway (1987).

LDI 6.4

Commitment package, Strategic Choice approach

The commitment to working with someone else is perhaps the most important decision that we make in handling a problem. On both sides the choice is crucial, yet it is often reached carelessly and precipitately. Frequently this casualness stems from an unwillingness to face the full ramifications of the decision situation involved, in the desire for a rapid and unambiguous settlement. A valuable way into the treatment of complex problems of this sort is provided by the framework of the Strategic Choice approach (Friend and Hickling, 1987).

The strategic choice model visualizes a process of problem handling in which there are four complementary foci, corresponding to four distinct modes of work: shaping, designing, comparing and choosing. Work on a problem involves a shifting of attention from one focus to another as the problem fabric is progressively unwrapped and explored, and as the problem-owner moves towards a commitment to considered action: this process is shown in Figure F.2.

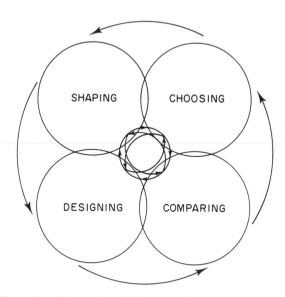

Figure F.2. The modes of the strategic choice approach

The shaping mode is addressed to identifying key issues and to bounding the confusion of problems in an appropriate way. The designing mode is concerned with identifying what can be done, taking account of both opportunities and restrictions. The comparing mode is about the balancing of alternative courses of action against one another, using declared criteria and making relevant evaluations. The choosing mode is formed around the building of a package of commitments to present and future actions and explorations, taking account of acknowledged uncertainties. The overall process is a strongly cyclic one in which attention moves smoothly around and between these foci until the problem-owner feels that the commitment package developed is adequate for the occasion.

The shaping and designing modes of strategic choice are based around the AIDA method (see **LDI 3.6**) and so make use of the concept of decision areas as a means of generating a list of viable solutions. Further elements of technical apparatus are employed to lead through the comparing and choosing modes. In the former mode, the idea of a comparison matrix has been found useful. This is a rectangular table in which criteria (columns) are set against identified solutions (rows); later, overall assessments are made by judging the relative importance of these comparison areas. For a more focused comparison of just two alternative solutions, an advantage balance may be used. This is another graphic device in which the two alternatives (set left and right on a chart) are rated on cardinal scales (typically 5-point) for each criterion (row). In the choosing mode a radial chart is frequently used to plot the uncertainties which remain as the time for a commitment to proceed approaches. This differentiates between uncertainties about the environment (where more information is needed), about values (where clarification of objectives is required), and about related decisions (where more coordination seems to be demanded), and also shows the relative importance of each one plotted. The other device, employed to summarize progress after the choosing mode, is termed a 'commitment package'. This is a summary (usually tabular) of the actions, explorations, deferred choices and contingency plans (all as columns) for each identified decision area (row).

We shall sketch how the remaining aspects of the Strategic Choice approach work by taking up again the example used earlier (see **LDI 3.6**) of newsletter production.

From the option graph analysis, four solutions remained, and these are shown in Figure F.3.

Suppose that to the comparison areas mentioned before (cost and reader service) another is added: the amount of control which management will have of the newsletter production and dispatch process. Then the solutions

SOLUTION	FREQUENCY	PRINTER	DISTRIBUTION	COST	SERVICE	CONTROL
1	Monthly	Outside	Separate	£ £ £ £	* * *	X
2	Quarterly	In-house	Separate	£ £ £	* *	X X X
3	Quarterly	In-house	Mailshot	£	*	X X
4	Quarterly	Outside	Separate	£ £ £	* *	X

Figure F.3. Specimen solution evaluation

could score as shown in Figure F.3, where higher numbers of symbols denote higher ratings on a criterion. It is not hard to see that Solution 4 is dominated by (i.e. is always worse than) Solution 2, and so can be ignored. However, no other clear overall preferences emerge so far. Moving on to the choosing phase of analysis, two further principles can help us: robustness and variety. The former suggests that options should be chosen so as to leave the maximum possible flexibility for the future: in the example, using the mailshot is more robust as it costs nothing and doesn't preclude switching to a separate mailing later, whereas a switch in the opposite direction might have an adverse reader reaction. The latter principle of variety, suggests that options should be chosen so as to leave the greatest choice open: in the example, a choice of monthly mailing leads to less variety (one solution) than a choice of a quarterly mailing (two solutions). On these grounds applied across the three remaining solutions, Solution 3 appears to be the best. All this assumes that the assessments made earlier are reliable. In practice they will usually be uncertain, and these uncertainties would be plotted as shown in Figure F.4.

So what is the final outcome. It cannot be simply to plump for Solution 3, since there is residual uncertainty. Instead a package of commitments would be made: this might look like the example of Figure F.5.

Note that as well as immediate actions, things which need to be explored are noted. So too are actions to be taken later, including some which will depend upon evidence not currently to hand.

And even this is not necessarily the end of the story, for another cycle might have been essayed at any point. For instance, the assumption that the in-house service could not handle a monthly newsletter might be challenged: indeed this could feature in the commitment package as something to be explored.

Try, using the Strategic Choice approach, to help you to identify a suitable partner in a garbage can where you currently find yourself: if you are a problem-owner, use the process to find a helper; if you are a solution-owner, use the process to find a suitable client. And if 'you' is best interpreted here as a group of which you are a member, so much the better, for the process will be doubly worth while.

Begin by asking yourself why the choice of partner is problematic. Make a list of all the thoughts which come to mind. Don't worry if they are an odd mixture as we shall sort them out directly.

Next review your list and see if you can identify within it items which fall into the following categories:

Decisions
Criteria
Uncertainties
Miscellanea

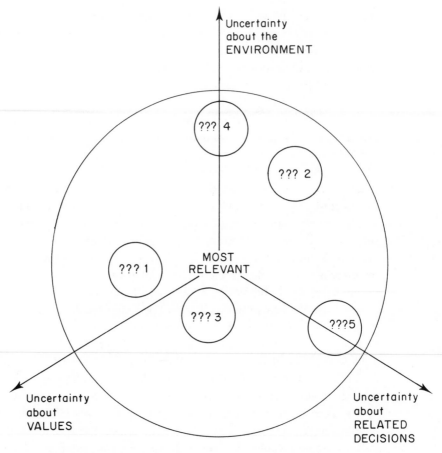

Key to uncertainties:
1   Importance readers attach to up-to-the minute news.
2   Printing delays possible because of other in-house work.
3   Priority which in-house unit would give to the Newsletter.
4   Actual cost of outside printing.
5   Mailshot planned distribution dates

Figure F.4. Specimen radial uncertainty chart

Split your original list on to four separate sheets of paper, one for each category.

Imbalance across these lists may cause you after reflection to add further items in one or other area. Do so by all means: and subsequently at any stage!

Start by looking at the 'Decisions'.

Are any of these genuinely independent of all the others? Mark them. Transfer the rest to a new sheet of paper and draw them as separate decision areas.

Now indicate the mutually exclusive options within each decision area.

SOONER		LATER	
DO	FIND OUT	DECIDE	IFs and BUTs
First issue on quarterly basis		In 3 months Basis of subsequent issues	
Print first issue in-house	Likelihood of delay for in-house work		
Distribute first issue with mailshot	Reader perceptions of mailshot mode of distribution		If readers prefer separate mode then switch

Figure F.5. Specimen commitment package

Considering every pair of options draw in option bars to denote infeasible choice combinations.

From the resulting option graph, you will be able to produce a solution list.

Next set out a solution table and assess each solution on each of the 'Criteria' on your sheet.

Now review the feasible solutions, applying the principles of dominance, robustness and variety to see if any can be discarded and if any favourites emerge.

Looking at your list of 'Uncertainties' and at the front runners for the 'winning' solution, see what impact the former have upon the candidacy of the latter, using a radial chart to clarify matters.

Finally, draw up a commitment package which takes account of all that you have learnt from the process; and to which you are willing to be committed!

 Strategic Choice: Friend and Hickling (1987).

LDI 6.5

 Terms of reference

 Since terms of reference are such a common source of misunderstanding, it may be worth while running through this short process with your intervention partner so as to expose possible ambiguities of expectation. If the exercise can be done with candour on both sides it should also help to cement relationships and will augur well for a fruitful and open partnership in action.

The *problem-owner* should answer these questions:

- Who is the helper (/helping team)?
- What personnel can the helper call upon?
- What relevant skills does the helper offer?
- What total time input can the helper provide?
- Over what elapsed time will the helper be available?
- How could the helper's involvement be extended?
- What technical resources are available via the helper?
- To what information sources has the helper access?

The *problem-helper* should answer these questions:

- Who is the problem-owner?
- What does the client wish to achieve?
- Why does the problem-owner want the problem addressed?
- What resources can the problem-owner provide?
- How can the problem-owner be accessed?
- How will the problem-owner be involved in the process?
- How could the problem-owner extend the intervention?
- When will the problem be finished?

When you have completed the answers, exchange them with your partner and then discuss the results, just as in a perceptual exchange (see **LDI 1.3**).

If the exercise is not possible in this form, ask yourself the obvious question as to why it is infeasible, and whether you are prepared to be involved in the problem-handling process on this basis.

In this case too, review the areas in which you are unable to answer the questions. How much do these particular answers matter? What are the implications of proceeding in ignorance?

Since you were presumably intending to proceed with the intervention despite these gaps in your knowledge, it would have been necessary for you to make assumptions about your partner's views and behaviour. Seek to uncover and analyse these assumptions using the surfacing technique (see **LDI 3.3**). Does it now seem worth while to research any of these untested beliefs?

LDI 6.6

PPS diagram, Metagame, Hypergame,
Hypermap, Role-play workshop

When there are a large number of participants (greater than two!) caught up
in a problem or impacted by its effects, there will normally be a variety of
diversely related issues over which they interact. These may be clearly
represented using a so-called PPS (Preliminary Problem Structuring) diagram
(Bennett and Huxham, 1982). An example, given in Figure F.6, will both
introduce the concept and explain the notation used.

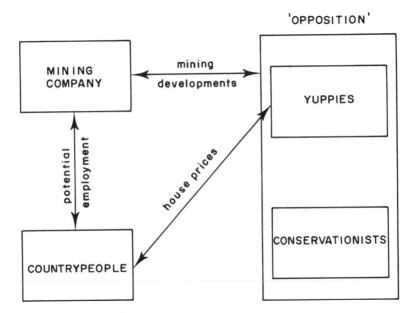

Figure F.6. Specimen preliminary problem structuring diagram

The illustration (Figure F.6) shows some issues that arise in connection
with an open-cast mining operation. The mining company, which has just
applied for planning permission to extend its operations, is in conflict with a
variety of local objectors. These include 'yuppies' (who moved to the area
because they see it a a tranquil rural haven, yet still commutable to London)
and conservationists (who are opposed to the development because of its
ecological impact). However, native countrypeople support the development, since it offers employment and will help to subsidize the local taxes.
The countrypeople also resent the yuppies, since the latter's coming has
pushed house prices far beyond the reach of the former. These interactions
are captured in Figure F.4 as labelled lines linking the boxes which represent
the various parties. The picture illustrates the potential for the formation of

coalitions over issues, and the factors which may also undermine trust in such cooperation.

 Turn now to a significant problem which you face.

Begin by identifying the others whom you see as also involved or needing to be involved in its management, or who are affected by its outcome: that is, those who would occupy roles around any intervention. You could use the notion of a cast list (see **LDI 2.5**) to organize these data.

Next construct a PPS diagram about the problem, following the example given above for guidance. This provides a number of foci for subsequent analysis.

Choosing what appears to be a key issue in the problem complex as shown in the PPS diagram, a number of routes forward present themselves.

One possibility is to proceed directly towards a modelling of the situation using a strongly game-theoretically driven framework. For example the metagame approach (see **LDI 4.11**) could be drawn upon. This would involve identifying the options apparently open to each actor over the chosen issue, and subsequently analysing the stability conditions of the possible outcomes. Alternatively, the hypergame model (see **LDI 3.5**) might be applied to some of the elemental two-person conflicts present. While apparently involving a *reductio ad absurdum* such consideration of highly simplified, idealistic game models, when set in the explicitly developed and richer context of the PPS diagram, can be invaluable in forcing reflection and debate through comparison with the 'real' system of interactions.

A rather different path forward from the initial PPS diagram is provided by using the hypermap concept. Quite simply, the intention here is to construct relevant fragments of the hypermap (see **LDI 2.5**) corresponding to the chosen issue as it appears to you. This involves stepping imaginatively into the shoes of the various actors taking parts about the issue, and working to develop a picture of the situation as seen from each other's perspective; it may or may not include higher order perceptions of other actors. The cognitive mapping notation (see **LDI 4.9**) could be used to express these pictures in a strong verbal structure; alternatively, a set of rich pictures (see **LDI 4.5**) or other looser conventions could be used. The resulting insight into each actor is far deeper than that produced by mere consideration of options or strategies as in the earlier approaches suggested, but less amenable to direct analysis. However, there are some more intuitive methods available to take the investigation further. One is to bring the 'portraits' of the various actors together in 'art gallery' format, wherein each subjective picture, displayed on a separate sheet of paper, is set alongside others to provide a 'rogues gallery' of issue participants. Alternatively, if a group is carrying out the exercise, the portraits can be used as the basis of a full role play (see **LDI 1.5**) of the issue, with different parts being taken by different individuals. Either of these two methods will generate insights into the positions of the various actors, and, importantly, may be suggestive of directions in which the issue will, or could be encouraged to develop through time.

PPS diagram: Bennett and Huxham (1982).
Role-play workshop: Bryant (1987)
                              Eden and Huxham (1988).

LDI 6.7

Hidden agenda

Straightforwardly, apply the typology of roles within an intervention presented in the text to some recent problem-handling processes in which you have been involved. Seek to set names of individuals or groups against each of the identified parts, reconsidering carefully if any role at first appears to be vacant.

For each actor in the developed list of those taking roles in the intervention, set down a statement of their overt and covert reasons for being there: their public and hidden agendas for the event. You may find it helpful to slip as firmly as possible into their place, using the notion of role focusing (see **LDI 2.9**) as justification.

Reflect on the success of the intervention (or its likely success if this is a prospective rather than a retrospective study) in the light of these aspirations. How could affairs have been arranged to produce a more auspicious outcome?

LDI 6.8

Situational scripts, Group insignia

Think of a group facing problems and of which you have recently been a member, either as problem-owner or helper. Answer these questions:

– How is a meeting agenda determined?
– How does the group resolve differences of opinion?

- How are personality clashes handled?
- How is specific expertise drawn in?
- How does a *quid pro quo* work in the group?
- How are 'natural' breaks/absences arranged?
- How are new ideas processed through the group?
- How is the time of the next meeting fixed?
- How is the sense of a meeting recorded?

On reflection, how much of the group's work would you say could loosely be described as situationally scripted? Can you set down any of these scripts in the form of a libretto or perhaps just sketch their dramatic outlines (see **LDI 4.7**)?

The style and tenor of a group's approach to problems and of its internal processes can usefully, and often revealingly, be summarized by means of a succinct slogan or aphorism (e.g. 'We work hard and play hard'; 'We're bad losers'; We enjoy chatting').

Can you think of some slogans for your group?

Usually there are also hidden, inadmissible slogans, which may provide a bitter side to the more public face of the group. These have been likened (James and Jongeward, 1971) to sweatshirt messages, with the overt message printed on the front, and the twist in the tail emblazoned on the back (e.g. 'We share out our work fairly' on the front; 'Except for the nasty jobs!' on the back). Further, individuals may carry additional messages on their vests beneath the sweatshirt (e.g. ' . . .and I do as little work as I can').

Can you identify these hidden messages for your group and its members?

What would be a good epitaph for your group? Perhaps 'They did a good job', 'They ran out of time', 'They tried hard'? Seeing what is written on the tombstone of your endeavours can be a salutary experience!

  Game playing: James and Jongeward (1971).

LDI 6.9

  Cognitive mapping, Root definition

  Maintaining the momentum of a group process in which people are addressing problems is a crucial determinant of eventual success. It usually relates to such factors as the motivation of individual members, the management of time within the working context, the logging of progress on the problem, and many other issues.

Develop a cognitive map (see **LDI 4.9**) around the issue of maintaining momentum.

You may wish to tackle this alone, or perhaps within the context of the problem-handling group itself.

In the former case, perhaps you could begin with the simple construct 'Maintaining momentum . . .' and elaborate your map from there.

In the latter case, someone will need to act as dialectician for a more complex process. This role requires a sensitive awareness of individual views, and a preparedness to withold one's own views from the group product: facilitation and content involvement tend to be uneasy bedfellows.

The business of producing a 'map' in a team setting – strictly speaking the product is not a cognitive map, since maps belong idiosyncratically to individuals – is often eased by starting with a nominal group exercise (see **LDI 1.2**) to produce a concept map. This will help to identify clusters of ideas any one of which might be a worthwhile starting point for the next stage. Choose as your 'seed construct' one which seems to attract a good degree of interest from participants.

Map building should then continue 'on the hoof' with chains of argument being publicly recorded on flip charts on the wall as they are offered. The map should include everyone's views, so when disagreements arise, do not feel that they must be resolved; simply record both views using the mapping notation. If map development gets bogged down, it can usually be prompted by asking for elaboration of the producers or products of specific constructs already included.

In either map-building setting, whether individual or team focused, you will run out of steam eventually. Much of value will already have been achieved through the articulation of ideas as the map was constructed. However, you may find it worthwhile also carrying out some analysis of the overall picture produced.

This could begin by an identification of the major 'clumps' of constructs, since these indicate the main areas of concern. Within these there may be specific chains of argument which form loops – perhaps 'vicious circles' – which could have implications for handling the central issue. Further, it can be helpful to identify constructs which correspond to potential policy actions, and to trace through their ramifications.

Whichever route you chose, the map-based process should have suggested some of the factors which lend movement to group problem-handling processes, and may suggest to your own group ways in which this can be sustained.

 An effective way of stimulating ideas for beneficial change in problem situations is offered by Checkland's (1981) concept of 'human activity systems'. Essentially, these are intellectual constructs which are intended to be contrasted with the world as seen to generate a debate about potential change. They are built up from 'root definitions' which provide full specifications of their characteristics. A well-constructed root definition will indicate the system's:

- *owner*, who has the power to terminate the system's existence;
- *environment*, taken as given, which constrains it;
- *transformation*, by which inputs are turned into outputs;
- *actors*, who work within it to bring about the transformation;
- *customers*, who are the victims and beneficiaries of its activities;
- *Weltanschauung*, or world image, which makes the transformation meaningful.

A root definition will have action implications that can be organized in the form of a 'conceptual model'. It is these latter models of human activity systems, which, when juxtaposed with the 'real world', provide the stimulus to thought and considered policy.

Suppose that the general theme of monitoring progress emerged as important in relation to maintaining momentum in a working party looking at some organizational issue. Then a system relevant to this theme would be 'a progress monitoring system'. A root definition (in which the key elements are indicated by their initial letters) might be written out more fully as: 'A working-party-owned (O) system which, given the need to meet infrequently (E), monitors (T) the progress made on each occasion, through a recording function (A), so as to benefit the whole group (C). The assumption (W) is that a meaningful record can be produced.'

This definition leads logically to a conceptual model containing as minimally necessary such activities as: identifying significant meeting outputs; representing what is said and done in meetings; distributing meeting records to participants; and reviewing progress against some aspirations. This can then be compared with the system actually in place – perhaps one in which the members just keep their own informal notes – to suggest changes: or at least to stimulate discussion.

Having seen one illustration of the systems approach applied to the issue of maintaining momentum in group work, try it out on the issues which appear in your own cognitive map around the same subject.

Mapping in teams: Eden, Jones and Sims (1983).
Soft systems approach: Checkland (1981).

LDI 6.10

 Interpersonal interaction

You have read about Fry and Pasmore's typology (1983) of working interaction. Now spend some time making it real through an analysis of your own experience of group processes.

Most beneficially, take some groups within which you are regularly involved in meetings and other social interactions: these could be in your professional or in your private life, and range from organizational project groups to sport societies to family units.

For each group think through the recent sequence of meetings and attempt a categorization of each one along the lines suggested by Fry and Pasmore. Naturally any given meeting may contain examples of any or all modes of interaction: simply think here about which predominates.

Look then at the results to see what patterns emerge. Do certain sorts of interaction tend to occur in certain sorts of group? Do groups tend to stick to one or other mode of interaction or do they flip between them? Is there any sense of a development from one mode to the next by a group, perhaps as people get to know each other better? When switches occur, can you identify what made them happen, or made them possible?

Finally, are there any lessons here for the way that each group might conduct itself in future?

 Effective group working: Fry and Pasmore (1983).

LDI 6.11

 Activity record, Interpersonal dynamics

Most people have a rough idea of the chronology of their own past. One way of externalizing this is to set the dates of critical events along an arrow representing the passage of time. However, this tends to limit attention to such turning points, and to de-emphasize the ongoing flow of activity between and through them, which constitutes most of our experience. Further, since social life consists in relationships with others, these too need to be depicted in any record. For a complete picture we must state both what we did and with whom we did it as a function of time. Because of this triple dimensionality, graphically representing the process of working with others, is difficult in two dimensions. A Gantt chart, for example, shows the time sequence of activities within a particular project, but cannot easily also capture who is involved at different stages. I have no bright ideas for getting over this problem, but simply point it out here as something to be guarded against.

I suggest now that you carry out a short audit of your own participation in problem-centred interventions over the past year, noting the identities of the other participants, and the duration of their involvements. If you can find a suitable way of doing so, produce a graphical representation of these processes. Attend to the presence of particular individuals in different arenas; to the development of relationships with specific others through a variety of common experiences; to the spawning of certain activities by earlier events; and to the time pattern of occurrence of different sorts of interventions.

LDI for Chapter Seven

LDI 7.1

Success

A clearer insight into the purpose of an intervention can be gained by reflecting upon the meaning of the terms 'success' and 'failure' in this context.

In common with most professionals, those who operate as consultants to people facing problems are reticent about their failures, although there are noble exceptions (Corner, 1979). Nevertheless, given the precarious nature of assisted problem management, it is inevitable that many interventions will go awry. Majone and Quade (1980) have identified a large number of pitfalls for those engaged in the craft of policy analysis. These can be grouped into dangers faced at each stage of some typical intervention process (for example, in Eden's model of Figure 4.2 or the strategic choice approach of Figure F.2). The following list indicates just a few of the factors that can cause things to go wrong:

- unquestioningly accepting a preselected problem;
- inappropriately bounding the problem focus;
- being impatient to begin analysis or find solutions;
- misinterpreting data into information;
- ignoring uncertainty;
- carrying solutions in search of problems;
- losing ownership of the products of the process;
- assuming that rational argument is persuasive;
- ignoring the organizational and political context.

However, it is also as well to remember Vickers's (1970) words: 'A trap is only a trap for creatures which cannot solve the problems which it sets. Man-traps are dangerous only in relation to the limitations on what men can see and value and do. The nature of the trap is a function of the trapped. To describe either is to imply the other.'

I have said a little about failure above. Can you now consider what constitutes success in an intervention?

First draw up a list of the concepts which for you, either as helper or as problem-owner, would connote success in a problem-handling intervention. See if you can identify any clusters of ideas in your list: that is, any pervasive themes. For each of these then try to develop a cognitive map (see **LDI 4.9**) around the area concerned.

What actions or approaches does the argument of your map suggest?

You may like to carry out this same exercise with a specific focus upon a problem of current concern, so as to establish what it is you are seeking there.

If others are involved, you could follow a similar process to that outlined above, but in a group format. In this case, the first stage of identifying important themes is probably best approached through a nominal group exercise (see **LDI 1.2**) so that the widest possible range of relevant ideas can be captured.

Pitfalls in systems analysis: Majone and Quade (1980)
Corner (1979).

LDI 7.2

Mental map, Perceptual exchange

Set down, in whatever seems to you the most appropriate format, a picture which portrays the antecedents and context of one of your own fields of activity. For instance, such a map might depict the development of a functional specialism in which you are employed; the influences over time on a subject in which you have a leisure interest; the evolution of a social group of which you are a member, indicating individuals who had a significant impact on this process; and so on.

Review your map. Better still, compare it with others who are active in the same area and discuss the differences.

LDI 7.3

Classification of methodologies

Two distinct methods for the classification of approaches in problem management have been indicated in the text. If this is an area of which you have knowledge, try to overlay these typologies in turn upon my systems map in Figure 7.1.

Does the development process appear to track through the taxonomies in any particular pattern?

LDI 7.4

Repertory grid analysis

Apply the method of repertory grid analysis (see **LDI 1.8**) to the investigation of an area with which you are especially familiar: the map from **LDI 7.2** could be useful as a prompt here. You might take as elements for the repertory grid process, significant individuals, organizations or approaches, and thereby generate a list of the constructs which you use to think about them.

The grid which you construct might be compared with that produced by others who have an interest in the same field.

LDI for Chapter Eight

LDI 8.1

Intervention design, Practice

The bulk of Chapter Eight makes use of a dramaturgical analogy systematically to review key aspects of intervention practice. The structure of this analysis can be appreciated from a review of the Contents pages.

I assume that you have some interest in the business of intervention design, whether as an intending dialectician, as a potential participant, as an educator in problem management methods, or simply as an interested party in the constituency of some problem. In this case, I suggest that as you read through the remainder of the chapter, perhaps after a cursory prior review, you stop to consider at each stage the way in which you might proceed in designing an intervention for managing a problem that is currently exercising you. Treat this initially as an assignment in idealized design: that is, set down how you would ideally like the intervention to be. Subsequently, realistically assess and critically appraise the factors which constrain your ambitions, and from the dialectic between what might be done and what seems to be possible, develop a practical proposal.

To provide some illustration of the application of structured interventions, I have set down below a number of short cases. I have chosen these to demonstrate the range of intervention processes which may be used, and the range of subject content which may be addressed using such methodologies. I have also intentionally focused upon examples from the informal or educational sectors since these are likely to strike a chord with most readers, regardless of their occupation. Thus, although the substantive content may not always appear directly relevant to your own situation this should seldom be important; do read through them actively rather than passively, looking at their principal features and asking how these might apply to your own situation. The cases are most certainly not intended to be in any way prescriptive – quite possibly alternative, equally effective approaches could have been used in each one – but they should show how the pragmatic business of intervention design may work out in practice. The stories which I tell are in every case highly selective. I have chosen to focus on specific aspects of each situation rather than to provide a more rounded case history; some describe single episodes within a much more extended intervention process. I hope that they will help to make the design of interventions real for you , and will encourage you to try it for yourself.

Distance learning has deservedly become a popular mode of study for courses at all levels. I am involved in one such course leading to a Master's degree in OR. The course begins with a residential period when all new students attend at the polytechnic. During this week, introductory course material is covered; more importantly the general ethos of the course is inculcated and the social cohesion of the group of students and staff is encouraged. Students embarking on any extended course of study in their own time, probably while also in full-time employment, are taking on a big commitment; this can understandably be quite a worry, especially at the start. For this reason, I have opened the residential period each year with a short process intended to allow newly enrolled students to express and explore their concerns about the venture that they are taking on, and to find ways in which they can sustain themselves, with the support of others, during the years ahead.

I have begun with a short Nominal Group process (see **LDI 1.2**) to generate a list (not a concept map) of the students' concerns about embarking on the course. I have built up this list on flip charts on a wall of the room until there were no more items to be added. Working with a group of about a dozen students, there has been no difficulty in producing a list of 30–40 items: some extracts are shown in Figure H.1.

We have then looked to whether there were any obvious clusters of concerns in the list. Usually about six to eight broad areas can be found (see Figure H.1).

Since not all of these issues worry each member of the group we have then formed subgroups to examine selected clusters in more detail. I have done this, for example, by using the open canvass idea (see **LDI 5.1**) to choose 'important' issues, and then forming subgroups around these on the basis of individual interest. Each subgroup has been asked to report back to a later plenary session, indicating the outcomes of its investigations.

I have generally given guidance to each subgroup on the exploration of its topic area. For instance, I have suggested that individuals set down their own ideas about the issue on 'Post-its', and then add them to a group collage on the wall in a way which makes sense to them. As each item is added, theories are articulated to justify its positioning on the composite picture; this helps all of the subgroup to understand others' points of view. From there it has frequently been an easy step to suggesting ways of handling the situation, for report to and discussion with the rest of the class.

This whole approach is so apparently generalizable that it seems superfluous to cite additional examples. However, it can obviously be used as an entrée in executive workshops, as well as in educational settings.

making time to do work	T
what to do about course/work clashes?	T E
uncertainty about time needed for course	T
finding a quiet place	D
effectiveness of interaction with course tutors	R D
travelling up to examinations on Saturdays	D
effectiveness of interaction with other course members	R D
effect of changing jobs	P E F
having to write essays	C
loss of holiday	T
loss of earnings	F
inexperience in distance-learning	D
scheduling first residential period	R
maintaining enthusiasm for 3 years	D
chance to apply the skills	E
employer's reaction to my doing the course	E
scared of projects	C P
course balance: application/theory	C
does employment give suitable material for project?	E P
isolation	D
having to sit exams after such a long time	C
value of course to future employers	E
consequences of failure	C E F
will I be able to keep up with the pace (content)?	D C
arrangements with employers for project	E P
effect of moving house on doing course	T
working in teams ... by oneself	R
lead time for receipt/submission of materials	D T
lack of OR problems	E
colleagues' reactions	E
meeting assessment deadlines	T
availability of 'tools' for project (e.g. computer)	D P
availability of reference material	D
evening sessions at residential	R
the pace (time)	T

Key to agreed categories and 'votes' cast:

Time	24
Finance	5
Project	11
Distance-learning	5
Employer-related	4
Course (content)	13
Residential	2

Figure H.1. Specimen results of nominal group process

Probably, like me, you belong to a number of occupational or leisure societies. Such associations can face problems which are every bit as knotty as those encountered in business organizations. Frequently, these problem messes centre upon the topics of group membership and commitment, and are the subject of discussion by the core of individuals – perhaps a committee – which keeps the whole enterprise alive. I shall here take just one example of this type to illustrate an approach to such concerns. This happens to concern a local professional association, though I have applied similar ideas to look at the problems facing an amateur drama society and an academic teaching group.

The situation was opened up in the familiar way: through discussion, at a routine meeting, of the issues facing the group, and a depressingly familiar 'whirling' around (Friend, 1987) the complex of interconnected problems identified. During this process I took notes of the distinct issues that were raised by individuals, as well as recording some fragmentary theories which were simultaneously advanced in connection with them. As frustration built up, I proposed that it could be helpful to carry out an 'audit' of individual perceptions of the problems facing the group, and feeding this back to a later meeting for discussion. This was accepted.

I give an example in Figure H.2 of a picture that summarized one person's view of what was the matter with the group.

It was produced using a conventional cognitive mapping process (see **LDI 4.9**) to record the views expressed. This is obviously not a highly developed map, but it still contains a lot of ideas, most notably around the issue of student involvement in the association (the respondent was an academic). From this and other discussions, a later meeting of the committee was able to home in fairly rapidly upon some related actions which the group could take to regenerate itself. These were agreed and passed to a subgroup for implementation.

There are no startling methodological ideas here: this is a quite routine application of mapping. Nevertheless, I trust that it shows how such methods can be used by groups in quite 'ordinary' circumstances to develop understanding and considered action. As a variant on this, for example, I have had student groups self-administer a mapping process – on 'the problems of doing group work' (!) – with pleasing and worthwhile results.

 Something that concerns anyone involved in training novice consultants is that they should develop as full an awareness as possible of the situations which they are entering, as they commence work with a client. To this end I have used the following short process to produce a worthwhile summary, as well as employing it as an *aide-mémoire* myself in similar situations.

I have begun by asking the members of the consulting group – usually a small project team is involved – individually to list the others whom they see as significant to the project. When this has been done, a group list is then collected on a round-robin basis to produce a composite list of actors. The group is then asked to trim this list down by identifying whom they see as the key actors in the situation. Discussion within the group at this stage can be very revealing by exposing contrasting perceptions of those who appear

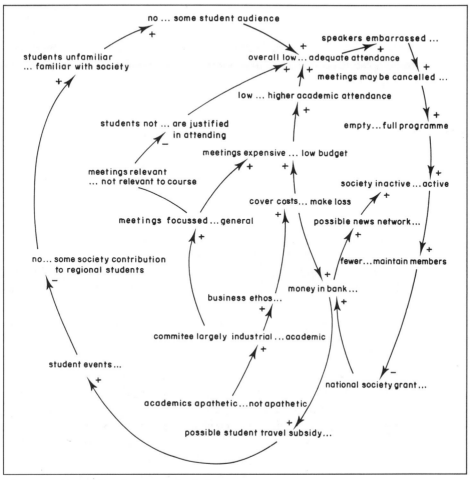

Figure H.2. Specimen individual cognitive picture

to be active in the problem arena. Eventually a cast list (see **LDI 2.5**) can be produced.

The consultancy team is next asked to view the project in turn from the perspective of each of the three or four main protagonists. In each case I ask them to consider of this actor: How do they see the project? How would they like it to run/end? What are their aspirations for the project? How they see the consultancy team? What sanctions/power they have with respect to the project? The group has then to produce answers to these same questions from its own position. The final stage involves juxtaposing these contrasting visions of the work and using the contrast to anticipate any potential difficulties that may be faced in the work. I have sometimes made use of a short role-playing exercise to dramatize the usual differences in view of what is expected from the project: this can be most effective in bringing home to the inexperienced practitioner the dangers of a mismatch of expectations.

Transparently this process is based on the hypermap concept (see **LDI 6.6**), and could be used in a variety of other situations. For example, a contrasting application has been to aid a closed research group which was contemplating drawing in new members: here the 'other actors' were potential nominees.

 Consultants frequently work in partnership with a specific client group through a succession of problems. I shall take here just one brief episode from a longer programme of work with a community group. My focus will not be upon the substantive content of the work, but rather upon the behind-the-scenes process management activity.

In the immediately preceding workshop with the group, we had used the Strategic Choice approach (see **LDI 6.4**) to explore some issues around the management of resources for which the group were collectively responsible. It was agreed that a further workshop would be needed to develop further and critically examine a small number of alternative management policies open to the group.

A review meeting of the consultancy team was held to assess the last workshop and to make plans for the forthcoming one. This was greatly aided by a comprehensive memoir of the earlier event produced by one of the team. During a general discussion of possible formats for the next workshop, the idea was floated of using a synthesis of the Strategic Choice and SAST (see **LDI 4.8**) methodologies. Plans hardened around this broad concept, though with different emphases being placed by individuals according to their particular predilections. It was agreed that a one-day workshop should be arranged with the group. Meantime an outline programme for the event was developed. This involved, in the morning, a reappraisal of the previous workshop with the group and a definition of alternative policies: in the afternoon a generation of the assumptions underlying these policies – through the SAST device of stakeholders – and the drawing up of a suitable commitment package.

The negotiation of the timing of the proposed workshop had an unexpected outcome: a further half-day session was possible. Plans were recast and refined. The SAST process and its follow-up were now to occupy a whole day, with policy generation taking place the previous afternoon. These SAST elements involved splitting the group into two subgroups, one to examine each of two 'extreme' management policies. This idea caused some unease within the consultancy team – it was felt that dividing the group into competing advocacy subgroups might be misinterpreted and prove to be detrimental to overall group dynamics – but it was agreed on balance to be worth attempting. This structure was also made possible by the availability of a third member to join the consultancy team for the full day session only, since each subgroup could be facilitated by one member, with the third 'floating' between them. The final part of the second day was seen as an opportunity to agree on a way forward and to draw out the timing implications of the package of proposals.

The opening half-day session came and was attended by a rather smaller group than had been anticipated. Nevertheless, it provided a useful recapitulation and resulted in (perhaps rather lukewarm) agreement to proceed with the next day broadly as planned. At least the passage of time since the earlier workshop had not significantly altered the salience of the issues involved. However, the consultancy team had misgivings about the more openly confrontational elements of SAST and, that evening, rethought plans for the coming day. The revised agenda – which was agreed with the client group the next day – brought in a community worker, whom the group valued as an adviser, to act as advocate for one of the extreme management schemes, with the community group itself as the 'expert' on the other extreme (which simply meant a prolongation of the *status quo*): no subgroup working was firmly scheduled, though it remained as a possibility, if additional options were generated during the day.

We were able to proceed broadly as planned – thankfully the community worker agreed to take our designated role – and with one of the consulting team acting as interrogator and another as scribe, a list of stakeholders and assumptions around the first policy was produced. The client group engaged actively in this process, discussing the assumptions as they were set down. However, time passed more quickly than we had anticipated, so that the corresponding work on the *status quo* solution was more sketchy than we had wished. Disconcertingly, no intermediate solutions were considered. Following the exposure of assumptions, the action implications, first of one policy, then of the other, were drawn out with the group: these included initiating actions, obtaining information, and making provision for later decisions and eventualities. It was now lunchtime.

Some rapid rearrangements were made by the facilitators over the lunch break as only one hour was now left. The contrasting policies were set against each other to the left and right of the wall display with a central space to create the action programme. Implied actions were written on to 'Post-its' in preparation for the afternoon when they would be affixed to a preprepared time chart.

Despite these arrangements, the afternoon turned out quite unexpectedly. An additional person joined the client group, strongly altering the group dynamics, and causing a need to restate much of what had been covered in the morning: this quite destroyed the intended timing. Additionally, it was recognized that many of the implied actions had to be taken within weeks rather than months and this led to a rapid redesign of the group's prospective programme. Eventually, much later than intended, a schedule of actions corresponding to the chosen policy was agreed, and the meeting concluded on a very positive note.

A footnote. In the car on the way back after the workshop, one of the consulting group suggested that we could 'Do a Checkland' (use the idea of root definitions of relevant systems as described in **LDI 6.9**) to take forward the identified actions. But that is another story . . .

It is a commonplace experience for a consultant to be called upon to help a group to grapple with a complex problem which they see themselves as collectively to be facing, only to find that the focus of the intervention turns imperceptibly to an examination of the social process going on within the group itself. That is what happened in this case.

I was called upon by the clients in this study, following earlier discussions which they had had with a statistician colleague of mine about the possibility of his designing a survey for them. Some months earlier a report had been published which had indicated an abnormally high level of heart disease among women in a local community. Concerned about this problem, the *ad hoc* group of community workers had come together with the aim of establishing the health service needs of the community (hence the interest in a survey) and making appropriate recommendations. They had been meeting as a group during lunch hours at approximately monthly intervals. I arranged to go to their next meeting.

Four of the group were at the meeting. Apparently attendance varied widely from month to month, since all those involved (a community worker, an adult education worker, two doctors, a recreation services manager and a nursery school teacher) had hectic personal schedules. The group presented their predicament to me. As their discussions had continued over the year, the more complexity became apparent to them around the problem of heart disease: it seemed to be linked to a host of social as well as clinical factors, and it was proving impossible to find a suitable point of leverage on the mess.

The variety of personal perceptions and the need to produce a set of agreed proposals suggested a possible process design: this would involve me in a round of individual interviews with group members, followed by a group session to bring these views together and (possibly at a further session in view of the enforced brevity of each meeting) then to develop a commitment package. This format was agreed by the group. To be honest I had naively expected that the overall intervention would have involved 'cognitive mapping-type work' drawing out the specialists' views of the 'heart problem', followed by 'strategic choice-type work' to obtain a group-owned product. The outcome I suspected might include some firm proposals for funded action research into specific local health issues, coupled with some initiatives to introduce positive change into the community (e.g. fitness classes, education programmes). I was wrong, at least as far as this first intervention was concerned.

The interviews took place over a period of a fortnight. Each began with the same question – 'Why are you concerned about "the problem"' – and through subsequent dialogue was intended to clarify the individual's focus of concern, and preferred level and type of attack upon it. I also decided to ask each person about the role that he or she saw for his or her *ad hoc* group and, incidentally, about any problems which were being experienced in working together. As the programme of interviews proceeded, a pattern emerged: although personal prescriptions for dealing with the health issues were advanced, and individual values and beliefs were aired, a substantial majority of the issues raised were to do with the group process itself. This was confirmed when later I reviewed the complete set of transcripts (recorded as ideographs – see **LDI 0.2**).

I felt that the best approach for the next group meeting, at which I was to report back on the interviews, was to share with them in unattributed form the issues which they had raised. However, to stress their apparent concerns I did this in a structured way. To this end I wrote out on 'Post-its' the matters that they had raised, and then during the meeting affixed these to sheets of paper on the wall. First I took the items which related to group process, for which there were many labels (see Figure H.3) and later those to do with the substantive problem content. Within each set a division into theories, choices and criteria was made.

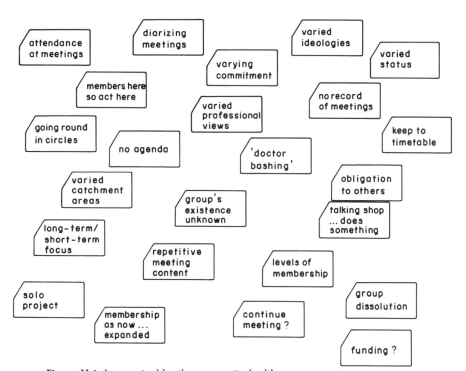

Figure H.3. Issues raised by the community health group

Little further debate was necessary. The group turned quite naturally and easily to a discussion of group membership and commitment, a topic which they had tended previously to avoid within the meeting context. A number of actions were agreed that led to a redefinition of the group's structure and way of working, and paved the way for proposals to be developed towards a more specific and realistically limited target. Essentially, this was achieved by the definition of two levels of participation, freeing a core group to proceed with actions and legitimizing the inability of others to be fully involved in all group work, while still permitting them to affirm their commitment to group aims.

Since achieving appropriate working relationships is frequently a major issue in group work (see also, for instance Huxham *et al.*, 1988), I would be surprised if you do not encounter your own problems of this type.

 More applications of structured approaches in group decision support are now being reported. Some suggested readings are as follows: Bennett and Cropper (1987); Bowen (1983); Checkland (1985); Cropper and Bennett (1985); Eden (1985c); Eden and Huxham (1988); Eden and Jones (1980); Huxham and Bennett (1985); Huxham *et al.* (1988); Jones and Eden (1981); Matthews and Bennett (1986); Phillips (1982); Rosenhead (1980).

Most recently, Rosenhead (1989) has published an ideal companion volume to the present text by providing succinct and accessible discussion of the theory and practice of six distinct problem structuring methodologies.

CODA

Reader's digest

Part 1: Problems

Chapter One

- The verbal tag 'problem' is used in many ways, some of which seriously diminish its range of convenience.
- Rather than attempting a definition, it is more productive to consider when a problem is said to exist.
- Immediately we recognize that there are no ground rules for this: an individual can label any situation as a problem.
- The motivation for doing so lies in the basic human instinct to categorize experience to make sense of things.
- An enquiry into problem identification must therefore start with an understanding of the mind of the problem-owner.
- Central to this study is the way in which individuals construct their reality and ascribe meaning to events.
- We can suppose that the raw data of experience are mediated to us through so-called personal construct frameworks.
- Such frameworks are in part the outcome of social factors, in part the result of individual historicity.
- However, we cannot access individual meaning by working on problem-owners as objects; we must work with them as people.

Chapter Two

- People necessarily have to be selective in paying attention to the confusion of events which they encounter.
- The filtering and subsequent interpretation of experience is shaped by the ever-changing personal construct system.

- Among the things encountered, some will be puzzling, others unexpected, possibly threatening: these are problem signs.
- Faced with anomalies, the first instinct is to frame them: if this fails despite repeated attempts, a problem exists.
- It is easy to overlook two crucial features of real problem recognition: multiple problems and the social context.
- Juggling with a confusion of problems is achieved by a switching of energy between competing arenas.
- Both personal and organizational forces determine the effort put into different current issues.
- The way in which we construct and treat a problem may also be influenced by concurrent concerns elsewhere.
- The social context of a perceived problem also moderates the way in which it is seen and handled.
- The act of construal is therefore a complex one, only fully understood through the problem-owner's eyes.

Part 2: Handling Problems

Chapter Three

- In the modern world, problems tend to be addressed through external action rather than through internal adjustment.
- We may face problems with equanimity or calmness: our state of mind will affect what happens next.
- The usual response to a problem is to call up a time proven strategy: this often works even when it shouldn't.
- However, novel elements in a situation may force some reappraisal: the familiar recipe may need trimming.
- More dangerously, the problem itself may be recast to fit the intended approach.
- Wherever possible we try to retain fragments of historical performances, even in new or improvized routines.
- People's observed problem-handling tactics can be compared with the psychological theory of problem solving.
- Behaviourists suggest that individuals learn how to deal with problems by repeated experimentation.
- Gestaltists suggest that problem solving is about the rearrangement and patterning of experiences.
- Both views find some corroboration in practical studies, as do those relating to deductive reasoning.

- However, problem handling in an organizational context provides many confounding features.
- The two common simplifications of problem recognition–singularity and context freedom – have implications here.

Chapter Four

- Dealing with a portfolio of problems requires attention management and imposes stress on the problem-owner.
- The context in which we deal with problems moderates what we do and how we do it.
- One of the most common desires is to solve problems, rather than to work on them with others or to dissolve them.
- This works against one of the two further complications in problem handling: problem wickedness.
- The crucial question becomes not 'What is the solution?'
  but 'What is the problem?'
- The second complication is that we usually share problems with other people.
- To do so we artfully present them to our audience, possibly just seeking reassurance for our intended actions.
- At other times, we wish to draw people into the problem-handling process, and work with them on the problems.
- This conjoint action is commonplace in organizations but may conceal all sorts of political manoeuverings.
- Collaborative problem management instead is best managed with external expert support.

Part 3: Help with Problems

Chapter Five

- Consultation with others is a commonplace aspect of handling the problems which we individually face.
- In order to choose an appropriate helper we must categorize both the problem and the potential sources of help.
- Within a broad category the location of a suitable individual helper may be achieved in various ways.
- There is a range of roles which can be filled by someone whom we ask to work *for* us on a problem.

- The 'superhero', takes over the whole matter on our behalf; other roles involve handling just one aspect of it.
- Each role has its strengths and weaknesses for the problem-owner.
- Each role also has an interpretation in the context of managerial problem solving in organizations.
- All these roles share the shortcoming that the problem must be successfully predefined by the owner.
- A more productive range of roles exists based on a paradigm of the helper working *with* the problem-owner.
- These include the parts of jester, expert conceptualizer, facilitator and dialectician.

Chapter Six

- Cooperative work between problem-owner and helper has as a prerequisite agreement on a suitable script for the task.
- A willingness to become involved with the other on each side is contingent upon many factors.
- When a working consensus is achieved, this is usually formalized in terms of reference for the work.
- The actual intervention process draws in people beyond the problem-owner and helper.
- These others include the commissioner, determiner, executor and constituency for the problem handling.
- When work commences, further roles must be filled in relation to the content, process and context of work.
- The players will then usually slip into a suitable situational script to work through the interaction.
- However, this is not to deny the possibility of personal interpretation.
- The resulting performance will thus be unique in its pace, tensions, mood and eventual success.
- Skilful work by key performers can alter the outcome of the intervention by aiming at different levels of interaction.
- In turn the interaction will reflect back upon the individuals modifying the meaning of events for them.
- Eventually there will be a sense that the problem is finished and the intervention ends.
- This may, however, also be seen as simply one manifestation of a dynamic ongoing relationship between the participants.
- In fact this personal growth is in many ways the true outcome of the process.
- As a result those involved are supported in acting more thinkingly in their lives.

Part 4: Practising Problem Management

Chapter Seven

- Most modern professional problem-managers draw on a tradition rooted in the application of scientific method.
- The twin weaknesses of this approach are the assumptions of technical rationality and of managerial authority.
- Practical problem management must further be founded on a recognition of the plurality of relevant *Weltangschauungen*.
- A shift from the 'external' problem focus of OR to a focus on the 'internal' client group process is essential.
- Assistance can be offered by a helper in providing a framework for thinking about the group process.
- Alternatively, or additionally, a framework for structuring the substantive problem content can be given.
- In each of these areas, the helper can be more or less doctrinaire in imposing his own language on the group.
- A considerable range of developed methodologies, closely linked historically, appear as likely candidates.

Chapter Eight

- Problem management methodologies can be characterized in terms of their underlying theoretical bases.
- Each methodology provides a way of thinking about context (people and setting) and craftwork (process and content).
- An intervention can be handled so as to draw in a variety of individuals as participants.
- Its development will be affected by these individuals' relationships both within and outside the problem arena.
- The setting of interventions often involves planning 'time out' from day-to-day concerns.
- Within an intervention people can signal their desired role and intentions by their dress and manner.
- The location for an intervention affects what goes on, since it may inhibit or encourage certain behaviours.
- Similarly, the materials and equipment available can be so planned as to assist processes of different types.
- The production of an intervention requires many skills of the facilitator.

- These depend on choices made about the use of backstage work, time scheduling and subgroup formation.
- It is common for deliberate emphasis to be placed on evaluation as the process unfolds.
- The text of an intervention can be set down in many ways and depends upon the saliences for a particular methodology.
- Nevertheless there is a common aim of energizing a debate within the client group.
- This may be done through discussion of a joint product, or by deliberate exploration of contrasting problem views.
- Data for debate are captured by asking about agents or alternatives, the rules of evidence varying widely.
- Throughout, ownership of the products by the group, and some understanding of the models used can be critical.
- There can be yet no definitive practice guide to using structured approaches either singly or in combination.

It must be hellishly ticklish to work out a plot in a detective story, I should think. I suppose you have to scatter clues all over the place.

Dennis Potter   *The Singing Detective*

References

Abelson, R.P. (1973). 'The structure of belief systems', in *Computer Models of Thought and Language* (Eds. R.C. Schank and K.M. Colby), W.H. Freeman & Co., San Francisco, California.

Ackoff, R.L. (1971). 'Towards a system of systems concepts', *Management Science*, **17**, 661–671.

Ackoff, R.L. (1974a). 'The social responsibility of operational research', *Journal of the Operational Research Society*, **25**, 361–371.

Ackoff, R.L. (1974b). *Redesigning the Future: a systems approach to societal planning*, Wiley, New York.

Ackoff, R.L. (1979). 'The future of operational research is past', *Journal of the Operational Research Society*, **30**, 93–104.

Ackoff, R.L., and Emery, F. (1972). *On Purposeful Systems*, Tavistock Press, London.

Amstutz, A.E. (1967). *Computer Simulation of Competitive Market Response*, MIT Press, Cambridge, Massachussetts.

Argyris, C. (1970). *Intervention Theory and Method: a behavioural science view*, Addison-Wesley, Reading, Massachussetts.

Argyris, C. (1983). 'Productive and counterproductive reasoning processes', in *The Executive Mind* (Ed. S. Srivastva), Jossey-Bass, San Francisco, California.

Austin, N. (1985). 'The Pod: a unique environment', International Computers Ltd, Reading, Berkshire.

Bannister, D., and Fransella, F. (1980). *Inquiring Man*, 2nd edn, Penguin Books, Harmondsworth, Middlesex.

Bartlett, F.C. (1932). *Remembering: a study in experimental and social psychology*, Cambridge University Press, Cambridge.

Battersby, A. (1967). *Network Analysis: for planning and scheduling*, Macmillan, London.

Baum, H.S. (1982). 'The advisor as invited intruder', *PA Review*, **42**, 546–552.

de Beaugrande, R. (1985). 'General constraints on process models of language comprehension', in *Issues in Cognitive Modelling* (Eds. A.M. Aitkenhead and J.M. Stark), Lawrence Erlbaum Associates, London.

Beer, S. (1966). *Decision and Control*, Wiley, London.

Beer, S. (1972). *Brain of the Firm*, Allen Lane, London.

Beer, S. (1975). *Platform for Change*, Wiley, London.

Bennett, P.G. (1977). 'Towards a theory of hypergames', *Omega*, **5**, 749–751.

Bennett, P.G. (1985). 'On linking approaches to decision-aiding: issues and prospects', *Journal of the Operational Research Society*, **36**, 659–669.

Bennett, P.G., and Cropper, S.A. (1986). 'Helping people choose: conflict and other perspectives', in *Recent Developments in Operational Research* (Eds. V. Belton and R. O'Keefe), Pergamon Press, Oxford.

Bennett, P.G., and Cropper, S. (1987). 'Maps, games and things in-between', *European Journal of Operational Research*, **36**, 33–46.

Bennett, P.G., and Dando, M.R. (1979). 'Complex strategic analysis: a hypergame study of the fall of France', *Journal of the Operational Research Society* , **30**, 23–32.

Bennett, P.G., and Huxham, C.S. (1982). 'Hypergames and what they do: a "soft" O.R. approach', *Journal of the Operational Research Society*, **33**, 41–50.

Bennis, W. (1969). *Organisation Development: its nature, origins and prospects*, Addison-Wesley, Reading, Massachussetts.

Berger, P. (1966). *Invitation to Sociology: a humanistic perspective*, Pelican Books, Harmondsworth, Middlesex.

Berger, P., and Luckmann, T. (1967). *The Social Construction of Reality*, Penguin Books, Harmondsworth, Middlesex.

Berne, E. (1964). *Games People Play*, Grove Press, New York.

Berresford, A., and Dando, M.R. (1978). 'O.R. for strategic decision-making: the role of world view', *Journal of the Operational Research Society*, **29**, 137–146.

von Bertalanffy, L. (1968). *General System Theory: foundations, development, applications*, Penguin Books, Harmondsworth, Middlesex.

Bignell, V., and Fortune, J. (1984). *Understanding Systems Failures*, Manchester University Press, Manchester, Lancashire.

Bignell, V., Peters, G., and Pym, C. (1977). *Catastrophic Failures*, Open University Press, Milton Keynes, Bedfordshire.

Boden, M. (1977). *Artificial Intelligence and Natural Man*, The Harvester Press, Brighton, Sussex.

de Bono, E. (1971). *Lateral Thinking for Managers*, McGraw-Hill, London.

de Bono, E. (1978). *Teaching Thinking*, Penguin Books, Harmondsworth, Middlesex.

Boothroyd, H. (1978). *Articulate Intervention: the interface of science, mathematics and administration*, Taylor and Francis, London

Bowen, K. (1983). 'An experiment in problem formulation', *Journal of the Operational Research Society*, **34**, 685–694.

Bradbury, M. (1984). 'Terminal sex', *Observer*, 1 April 1984, London.

Broadbent, D.E. (1958). *Perception and Communication*, Pergamon Press, Oxford.

Bryant, J.W. (1983). 'Hypermaps: a representation of perceptions in conflicts', *Omega*, **11**, 575–586.

Bryant, J. (1987). 'Systems of perceptions: developments in hypermapping', presented at *International Symposium on Decision Management*, Toronto, August 1987.

Bryant, J. (1988a). 'Frameworks of inquiry: O.R. practice across the hard – soft divide', *Journal of the Operational Research Society*, **39**, 423–435.

Bryant, J. (1988b). 'Challenges in the process of community O.R.', presented at *Operational Research Society National Conference*, Sheffield, September 1988.

Buchanan, B.G. (1982). 'New research on expert systems', in *Machine Intelligence 10* (Eds. J.E. Hayes, D. Michie, and Y-H. Pao), Ellis Horwood, Chichester, Sussex.

Buzan, T. (1982). *Use your Head*, Ariel Books, London.

Carlisle, E. (1985). *'Mac': managers talk about managing people*, Penguin Books, Harmondsworth, Middlesex.

Carter, C., Martin, J., Mayblin, B., and Munday, M. (1984). *Systems, Management and Change: a graphic guide*, Harper & Row, London.

Checkland, P.B. (1981). *Systems Thinking, Systems Practice*, Wiley, Chichester, Sussex.

Checkland, P. (1983). 'O.R. and the systems movement: mappings and conflicts', *Journal of the Operational Research Society*, **34**, 661–675.

Checkland, P. (1985). 'Achieving "desirable and feasible" change: an application of soft systems methodology', *Journal of the Operational Research Society*, **36**, 821–833.

Checkland, P. (1987). 'Demonstration of soft systems methodology' at *Operational Research Society National Conference*, Edinburgh, September 1987.

Churchman, C.W. (1968). *The Systems Approach*, Dell Publishing, New York.

Churchman, C.W. (1971). *The Design of Inquiring Systems*, Basic Books, New York.

Churchman, C.W., and Verhulst, M. (Eds.) (1960). *Management Science Models and Techniques*, Pergamon Press, Oxford.

Cohen, G. (1983). *Psychology of Cognition*, 2nd edn, Academic Press, London.

Cohen, M.D., March, J.G., and Olsen, J.P. (1976). 'People, problems, solutions and the ambiguity of relevance', in *Ambiguity and Choice in Organisations* (Eds. J.G. March and J.P. Olsen), Universiteitsforlaget, Bergen.

Conway, D. (1977). 'The O.R. project process', in *The King is Dead: Long Live the King?* (Ed. K.C. Bowen), Operational Research Society, Birmingham, West Midlands.

Conway, D. (1987). 'Planning the project mix: a practical application of methodology', presented at *EURO VI Conference*, Vienna, July 1983. (Revised July 1987.)

Cooper, C.L., Cooper, R.D., and Eaker, L.H. (1988). *Living with Stress*, Penguin Books, Harmondsworth, Middlesex.

Corner, L.J. (1979). 'Linear programming: some unsuccessful applications', *Omega*, **7**, 257–262.

Coxon, A.M.P., and Jones, C.L. (1979). *Measurement and Meanings: techniques and methods of studying occupational cognition*, Macmillan, London.

Cropper, S.A. (1983). 'Aspects of problem formulation and treatment: a research memo and agenda', University of Sussex, Brighton.

Cropper, S.A. (1984). 'Ways of working: fine-tuning our ideas about O.R. methodology', University of Sussex, Brighton.

Cropper, S.A. (1985). 'Style and the transferability of O.R. methodologies', University of Sussex, Brighton.

Cropper, S.A. (1987a). 'Perspectives on decision management facilitation and methods: emerging concepts', presented at *International Symposium on Decision Management*, Toronto, August 1987.

Cropper, S.A. (1987b). 'Practice guide', University of Sussex, Brighton.

Cropper, S.A., and Bennett, P.G. (1985) 'Testing times: dilemmas in an action research project', *Interfaces*, **15**, 71–80.

Cross, N. (1978). *Control of Technology: Unit 8 – Methods guide*, Open University Press, Milton Keynes, Bedfordshire.

Crowther, J.G., and Whiddington, R. (1947). *Science at War*, HMSO, London.

Cruickshank, C. (1979). *Deception in World War II*, Oxford University Press, Oxford.

Cyert, R.M., and March, J.G. (1963). *A Behavioural Theory of the Firm*, Prentice-Hall, Englewood Cliffs, New Jersey.

Dando, M.R., and Bennett, P.G. (1981). 'A Kuhnian crisis in management science?' *Journal of the Operational Research Society*, **32**, 91–103.

Dando, M.R., and Sharp, R.G. (1978). 'Operational research in the U.K. in 1977: the causes and consequences of a myth?' *Journal of the Operational Research Society*, **29**, 939–949.

Dearborn, D.C., and Simon, H. (1958). 'Selective perception: a note on the departmental identifications of executives', *Sociometry*, **21**, 140–144.

Delbecq, A.L., van de Ven, A.H., and Gustafson, D.H. (1975). *Group Techniques for Program Planning: a guide to nominal group and Delphi processes*, Scott, Foresman & Co., Glenview, Illinois.

Dember, W.N., and Warm, J.S . (1979). *Psychology of Perception*, 2nd edn, Holt, Rinehart & Winston, New York.

deSanctis, G. and Gallupe, B. (1986). 'Group decision support systems: a new frontier', in *Decision Support Systems: putting theory into practice* (Eds. R.H. Sprague and H.J. Watson), Prentice-Hall, Englewood Cliffs, New Jersey.

Deutsch, J.A., and Deutsch, D. (1963). 'Attention: some theoretical considerations', *Pyschological Review*, **70**, 80–90.

Dewey, J. (1933). *How We Think*, Heath, New York.

Duncker, K. (1945). 'On problem solving', *Psychological Monographs*, **58**: 5, No.270.

Dusay, J.M. (1977). *Egograms: how I see you and you see me*, Bantam Books, New York.

Easterfield, T.E. (1987) 'Reminiscences of O.R. in World War II', presented at *Operational Research Society National Conference*, Edinburgh, September 1987.

Eco, U. (1984). *The Name of the Rose*, Pan Books, London.

Eden, C. (1982). 'Problem construction and the influence of O.R.', *Interfaces*, **12**, 50–60.

Eden, C. (1985a). 'Perishing thoughts about systems thinking in action', *Journal of the Operational Research Society*, **36**, 860–861.

Eden, C. (1985b). 'The future consultant: finding the multiplier', University of Bath, Avon.

Eden, C. (1985c). 'Perish the thought', *Journal of the Operational Research Society*, **36**, 809–819.

Eden, C. (1986). 'Problem solving or problem finishing?' in *New Directions in Management Science* (Eds. M.C. Jackson and P. Keys), Gower Press, Aldershot, Hampshire.

Eden, C. (1988). 'Working dialogues: personal reflections', at *Operational Research Society National Conference*, Sheffield, September 1988.

Eden, C., Bennett, P.G., and Huxham, C.S. (1986). 'Colin, Peter and Chris try to write a paper' (mimeo).

Eden, C., and Huxham, C.S. (1988). 'Action-oriented strategic management', *Journal of the Operational Research Society*, **39**, 889–899.

Eden, C., and Jones, S. (1980) 'Publish or perish', *Journal of the Operational Research Society*, **31**, 131–139.

Eden, C., and Jones, S. (1984). 'Using repertory grids for problem construction', *Journal of the Operational Research Society*, **34**, 779–790.

Eden, C., Jones, S., and Sims, D. (1979). *Thinking in Organisations*, Macmillan, London.

Eden, C., Jones, S., and Sims, D. (1983). *Messing about in Problems: an informal structured approach to their identification and management*, Pergamon Press, Oxford.

Eden, C., and Sims, D. (1979). 'On the nature of problems in consulting practice', *Omega*, **7**, 119–127.

Eilon, S. (1975). 'Seven faces of research', *Operational Research Quarterly*, **26**, 359–367.

Eilon, S. (1980). 'The non-executive director', *Omega*, **8**, 399–407.

Eilon, S., Watson-Gandy, C.D.T., and Christofides, N. (1971). *Distribution Management: mathematical modelling and practical analysis*, Griffin, London.

Evans, E.P. (1986). *The Criminal Prosecution and Capital Punishment of Animals*, Faber, London.

Feldman, J. (1986). 'On the difficulty of learning from experience', in *The Thinking Organization* (Eds. H.P. Sims Jr and D.A. Gioia), Jossey-Bass, San Francisco, California.

Filley, A.C. (1975). *Interpersonal Conflict Resolution*, Scott, Foresman & Co., Glenview, Illinois.

Fisher, R., and Ury, W. (1982). *Getting to Yes: negotiating agreement without giving in*, Hutchinson, London.

Fransella, F., and Bannister, D. (1977). *A Manual for Repertory Grid Technique*, Academic Press, London.

Freire, P. (1976). *Education: the practice of freedom*, Writers and Readers Publishing Cooperative, London.

French, W.L., and Bell, C.H. (1984). *Organization Developoment: behavioural science interventions for organization improvement*, 3rd edn, Prentice-Hall, Englewood Cliffs, New Jersey.

Freud, S. (1962). 'The question of lay analysis', in *Two Short Accounts of Psycho-Analysis* (Trans. J. Strachey), Pelican Books, Harmondsworth, Middlesex.

Friend, J.K. (1987). 'Making progress in groups: the whirling process' (mimeo.).

Friend, J., and Hickling, A. (1987). *Planning Under Pressure: the strategic choice approach*, Pergamon Press, Oxford.

Friend, J.K., and Jessop, W.N. (1969). *Local Government and Strategic Choice: an operational research approach to the processes of public planning*, Tavistock Publications, London.

Friend, J.K., Norris, M.E., and Stringer, J. (1988). 'The Institute for Operational Research: an initiative to extend the scope of O.R.', *Journal of the Operational Research Society*, **39**, 705–713.

Friend, J.K., and Wedgwood-Oppenheim, F. (1970). 'The LOGIMP experiment: a collaborative exercise in the application of a new approach to local planning problems', *Centre for Environmental Studies*, London.

Fry, R.E., and Pasmore, W.A. (1983). 'Strengthening management education', in *The Executive Mind* (Ed. S. Srivastva), Jossey-Bass, San Francisco, California.

Gill, J. (1975) 'Action research: a critical examination of its use in organisational improvement', *Industrial and Commercial Training*, **7**, 286–290.

Goffmann, E. (1959). *The Presentation of Self in Everyday Life*, Anchor Books, Garden City, New York.

Goffmann, E. (1961). *Asylums: essays on the social situation of mental patients and other inmates*, Anchor Books, Garden City, New York.

Goffmann, E. (1974). *Frame Analysis*, Penguin Books, Harmondsworth, Middlesex.

Gordon, W.J.J. (1961). *Synectics: the development of creative capacity*, Harper and Row, New York.

Gould, P., and White, R. (1974). *Mental Maps*, Penguin Books, Harmondsworth, Middlesex.

Greene, J. (1975). *Thinking and Language*, Methuen, London.

Greenwald, A.G. (1980). 'The totalitarian ego: fabrication and revision of personal history', *American Psychologist*, **335**, 603–618.

Hall, A.D. (1962). *A Methodology for Systems Engineering*, Van Nostrand, Princeton, New Jersey.

Hall, P. (1988). 'Managing change and gaining commitment', presented at *EURO IX / TIMS XXVIII Conference*, Paris, July 1988.

Hawkes, T. (1977). *Structuralism and Semiotics*, Methuen, London.

Hayes, J.R. (1965). 'Problem typology and the solution process', *Journal of Verbal Learning and Behaviour*, **4**, 371–379.

Hemmer, H.D. (1983). 'Pioneering O.R.', *Journal of the Operational Research Society*, **34**, 111–117.

Hickling, A. (1987). 'Putting decision management into context', presented at *International Symposium on Decision Management*, Toronto, August 1987.

Hickling, A., and Friend, J.K. (1987) 'Demonstration of the strategic choice approach', at *Operational Research Society National Conference*, Edinburgh, September 1987.

Holsti, O. (1976). 'Foreign policy formation viewed cognitively', in *Structure of Decision: the cognitive maps of political élites* (Ed. R. Axelrod), Princeton University Press, Princeton, New Jersey.

Houlden, B. (1979). 'Some aspects of managing O.R. projects', *Journal of the Operational Research Society*, **30**, 681–690.

Howard, N. (1971). *Paradoxes of Rationality: theory of metagames and political behaviour*, MIT Press, Cambridge, Massachussetts.

Howard, N. (1987). 'The present and future of metagame analysis', *European Journal of Operational Research*, **32**, 1–25.

Huxham, C.S., and Bennett, P.G. (1985). 'Floating ideas: an experiment in enhancing hypergames with maps', *Omega*, **13**, 331–348.

Huxham, C., Eden, C., Cropper, S., and Bryant, J. (1988). 'Facilitating facilitators: a story about group decision-making', *O.R. Insight*, **1**, 13–17.

Isenberg, D.J. (1986). 'The structure and process of understanding: implications for managerial action', in *The Thinking Organization* (Eds. H.P. Sims Jr and D.A. Gioia), Jossey-Bass, San Francisco, California.

Jackson, M.C., and Keys, P. (1984). 'Towards a system of systems methodologies', *Journal of the Operational Research Society*, **35**, 473–486.

James, M., and Jongeward, D. (1971). *Born to Win: transactional analysis with Gestalt experiments*, Addison-Wesley, Reading, Massachussetts.

James, M., and Jongeward, D. (1975). *The People Book: transactional analysis for students*, Addison-Wesley, Reading, Massachussetts.

James, W. (1890). *Principles of Psychology*, Holt, Rinehart and Winston, New York.

Janis, I.L. (1971). *Stress and Frustration*, Harcourt Brace Jovanovich, New York.

Janis, I.L. (1972). *Victims of Groupthink*, Houghton Mifflin, Boston, Massachussetts.

Jenkins, G.M. (1969). 'The systems approach', *Journal of Systems Engineering*, **1**, 1–49.

Johnson, D.W., and Johnson, F.P. (1975). *Joining Together: group theory and group skills*, Prentice-Hall, Englewood Cliffs, New Jersey.

Jones, A.J. (1980). *Game Theory: mathematical models of conflict*, Ellis Horwood, Chichester, Sussex.

Jones, G.C. (1988a) 'On describing O.R. consultancy practice', presented at *Young O.R. Conference*, Warwick, March 1988.

Jones, G.C. (1988b). 'On role types' (ms.).

Jones, S., and Eden, C. (1981). 'O.R. in the community', *Journal of the Operational Research Society*, **32**, 335–345.

Jongeward, D. (1976). *Everybody Wins: transactional analysis applied to organizations*, Addison-Wesley, Reading, Massachussetts.

Jung, C.G. (1923). *Psychological Types*, Routledge & Kegan Paul, London.

Kelly, G. (1955). *The Psychology of Personal Constructs*, Norton, New York.

Kohler, W. (1969). *The Task of Gestalt Psychology*, Princeton University Press, Princeton, New Jersey.

Kolb, D.A. (1983). 'Problem management: learning from experience', in *The Executive Mind* (Ed. S. Srivastva), Jossey-Bass, San Francisco, California.

Kolb, D.A., Rubin, I.M., and McIntyre, J. (1974). *Organizational Psychology: an experiential approach*, Prentice-Hall, Englewood Cliffs, New Jersey.

Lardner, H. (1943). 'O.R.S. Reports: Appendix 2', in *The Origins and Development of Operational Research in the Royal Air Force: AP3368 (Air Ministry)*, HMSO, London.

Levi-Strauss, C. (1972). *Structural Anthropology*, Penguin Books, Harmondsworth, Middlesex.

Lewin, K. (1951). *Field Theory in Social Science*, Harper & Row, New York.

Luchins, A.S. (1942). 'Mechanisation in problem solving', *Psychological Monographs*, **54**: 6, No.248.

Luckman, J. (1967). 'An approach to the management of design', *Operational Research Quarterly*, **18**, 345–358.

Lynn, R. (1966). *Attention, Arousal and the Orientation Reaction*, Pergamon Press, New York.

Majone, G., and Quade, E.S. (Eds.) (1980). *Pitfalls of Analysis*, Wiley, Chichester, Sussex.

Maltzman, I. (1955). 'Thinking: from a behaviouralist point of view', *Psychological Review*, **62**, 275–286.

Mangham, I.L. (1978). *Interactions and Interventions in Organizations*, Wiley, Chichester, Sussex.

Mangham, I.L., and Overington, M.A. (1987). *Organizations as Theatre: a social psychology of dramatic appearances*, Wiley, Chichester, Sussex.

Mann, J.R. (1981). 'O.R. in 2001 – the individual', *Operational Research Newsletter*, **11** (11), 4–5.

March, J.G., and Olsen, J.P. (1976a). 'Organisational choice under ambiguity', in *Ambiguity and Choice in Organisations* (Eds. J.G. March and J.P. Olsen), Universiteitsforlaget, Bergen.

March, J.G., and Olsen, J.P. (1976b). 'Attention and the ambiguity of self-interest', in *Ambiguity and Choice in Organisations* (Eds. J.G. March and J.P. Olsen), Universiteitsforlaget, Bergen.

March, J.G., and Olsen, J.P. (1976c). 'Organisational learning and the ambiguity of the past', in *Ambiguity and Choice in Organisations* (Eds. J.G. March and J.P. Olsen), Universiteitsforlaget, Bergen.

Mason, R.O., and Mitroff, I.I. (1981). *Challenging Strategic Planning Assumptions*, Wiley, New York.

Massarik, F. (1983). 'Searching for essence in executive experience', in *The Executive Mind* (Ed. S. Srivastva), Jossey-Bass, San Francisco, California.

Matthews, L.R., and Bennett, P.G. (1986). 'The art of course planning: soft O.R. in action', *Journal of the Operational Research Society*, **37**, 579–590.

Mayer, R.E. (1983). *Thinking, Problem Solving, Cognition*, W.H. Freeman & Co., New York.

Mayon-White, W.M. (1986). *Planning and Managing Change: Block 3 – Systems concepts and intervention strategy*, Open University Press, Milton Keynes, Bedfordshire.

Mayzner, M.S., and Tresselt, M.E. (1959). 'Anagram solution times: a function of transition probabilities', *Journal of Psychology*, **47**, 117–125.

Mead, G.H. (1966). *The Social Psychology of George Herbert Mead*, University of Chicago Press, Chicago, Illinois.

Mercer, A. (1981). 'A consultant's reflections on client management', *Journal of the Operational Research Society*, **32**, 105–111.

Miles, I. (1984). 'Scenario analysis: contrasting visions of the future', University of Sussex, Brighton.

Milne, A.A. (1926). *Winnie-the-Pooh*, Methuen, London.

Minsky, M.L. (1975). 'A framework for representing knowledge', in *The Psychology of Computer Vision* (Ed. P.H. Winston), McGraw-Hill, New York.

Minzberg, H., and Waters, J.A. (1983). 'Researching the formation of strategies: the history of Canadian Lady', in *Strategic Management* (Ed. R. Lamb), Prentice-Hall, Englewood Cliffs, New Jersey.

Mitchell, C.R. (1981). *The Structure of International Conflict*, Macmillan, London.

Mitchell, G.H. (1980). 'Images of operational research', *Journal of the Operational Research Society*, **31**, 459–466.

Mitroff, I.I. (1983). *Stakeholders of the Organizational Mind*, Jossey-Bass, San Francisco, California.

Morgan, J.R. (1971). *AIDA: a technique for the management of design*, Tavistock Institute of Human Relations, London.

Moss, P., with Keaton, J. (1979). *Encounters with the Past: how man can experience and relive history*, Sidgwick & Jackson, London.

von Neumann, J., and Morgenstern, O. (1944). *Theory of Games and Economic Behaviour*, Princeton University Press, Princeton, New Jersey.

Newell, A., Shaw, J.C., and Simon, H.A. (1958). 'Elements of a theory of human problem solving', *Psychological Review*, **65**, 151–166.

Newell, A., and Simon, H.A. (1972). *Human Problem Solving*, Prentice-Hall, Englewood Cliffs, New Jersey.

Nisbett, R.E., and Ross, L. (1980). *Human Inference: strategies and shortcomings*, Prentice-Hall, Englewood Cliffs, New Jersey.

Norman, M. (1988). 'Managing O.R. in a consultancy', *O.R. Insight*, **1** (1), 10–12.

Optner, S.L. (1965). *Systems Analysis for Business and Industrial Problem-solving*, Prentice-Hall, Englewood Cliffs, New Jersey.

Parsons, T. (1951). *The Social System*, Free Press, Glencoe, Illinois.

Pearson, F.S., and Doerga, R.E. (1978). 'The Netherlands and the 1940 Nazi invasion', in *Studies in Crisis Behaviour*, (Ed. M. Brecher), Transaction Books, New Brunswick, New Jersey.

Perls, F.S. (1969). *Gestalt Therapy Verbatim*, Real People Press, Lafayette, California.

Pettigrew, A.M. (1975). 'Strategic aspects of the management of specialist activity', *Personell Review*, **4**, 5–13.

Pettigrew, A.M. (1983). 'Culture and politics in strategic decision-making and change', presented at *Symposium on Strategic Decision-making in Complex Organizations*, Arden House, Columbia University, New York, November 1983.

Pfeiffer, J.W., and Jones, J.E. (1973). *Handbook of Structured Experiences for Human Relations Training*, University Associates, La Jolla, California.

Phillips, L.D. (1982). 'Requisite decision modelling', *Journal of the Operational Research Society*, **33**, 303–311.

Phillips, L.D. (1984). 'A theory of requisite decision models', *Acta Psychologica*, **56**, 29– 48.

Phillips, L.D. (1987a). 'Demonstration of decision analysis', at *Operational Research Society National Conference*, Edinburgh, September 1987.

Phillips, L.D. (1987b). 'Decision analysis for group decision support', presented at *International Symposium on Decision Management*, Toronto, August 1987.

Pidd, M., and Woolley, R.N. (1980). 'A pilot study of problem structuring', *Journal of the Operational Research Society*, **31**, 1063–1068.

Popper, K. (1963). *Conjectures and Refutations*, Routledge & Kegan Paul, London.

Popper, K. (1976). *Unended Quest*, Fontana/Collins, Glasgow.

Preedy, D.K., and Bittlestone, R.G.A. (1985). 'O.R. and the boardroom for the 90s', *Journal of the Operational Research Society*, **36**, 787–794.

Priestley, P., McGuire, J., Flegg, D., Hemsley, V., and Welham, D. (1978). *Social Skills and Personal Problem-solving: a handbook of methods*, Tavistock Publications, London.

Radford, K.J. (1984). 'Simulating involvement in complex decision situations', *Omega*, **12**, 125–130.

Radford, K.J. (1986). *Strategic and Tactical Decisions*, Holt McTavish, Toronto.

Reed, G. (1972). *The Psychology of Anomalous Experience*, Hutchinson, London.

Reitman, W.R. (1965). *Cognition and Thought*, Wiley, New York.

Restle, F., and Greeno, J.G. (1970). *Introduction to Mathematical Psychology*, Addison-Wesley, Reading, Massachussetts.

Rittel, H.W.J., and Webber, M.M. (1973). 'Dilemmas in a general theory of planning', *Policy Sciences*, **4**, 155–169.

Rivett, P. (1968). *Concepts of Operational Research*, Watts, London.

Rivett, P., and Ackoff, R.L. (1963). *A Manager's Guide to Operational Research*, Wiley, London.

Rosenhead, J. (1976). 'On "The social responsibility of operational research"', *Operational Research Quarterly*, **27**, 266–272.

Rosenhead, J. (1980). 'Planning under uncertainty: II A methodology for robustness analysis', *Journal of the Operational Research Society*, **31**, 331–342.

Rosenhead, J. (1986). 'Custom and practice', *Journal of the Operational Research Society*, **37**, 335–343.

Rosenhead, J. (1989). *Rational Analysis for a Problematic World: problem structuring methods for complexity, uncertainty and conflict*, Wiley, Chichester, Sussex.

Rosenhead, J., and Thunhurst, C. (1982). 'A materialist analysis of operational research', *Journal of the Operational Research Society*, **33**, 111–122.

Rumelhart, D.E., and Norman, D.A. (1985). 'Representation of knowledge', in *Issues in Cognitive Modelling* (Eds. A.M. Aitkenhead and J.M. Slack), Lawrence Erlbaum Associates, London.

Sanderson, M. (1979). *Successful Problem Management*, Wiley, New York.

Sanoff, H., and Barbour, G. (1974). 'An alternative strategy for planning an alternative school', in *Alternative Learning Environments*, Dowden, Hutchinson & Ross, Stroudsburg, Pennsylvania.

Schank, R., and Abelson, R. (1977). *Scripts, Plans, Goals and Understanding*, Lawrence Erlbaum Associates, Hillside, New Jersey.

Schein, E.H. (1969). *Process Consultation: its role in organizational development*, Addison-Wesley, Reading, Massachussetts.

Schön, D.A. (1966). *Technology and Change*, Delacorte Press, New York.

Schön, D.A. (1983). *The Reflective Practitioner: how professionals think in action*, Temple Smith, London.

Shannon, C.E., and Weaver, W. (1949). *The Mathematical Theory of Communication*, University of Illinois Press, Urbana, Illinois.

Shaw, M.E., Cursini, R.J., Blake, R.R., and Mouton, J.S. (1980). *Role Playing: a practical maual for group facilitators*, University Associates, San Diego, California.

Silverman, D. (1970). *The Theory of Organizations*, Heinemann, London.

Simon, H.A. (1985). 'Information processing theory of human problem-solving', in *Issues in Cognitive Modelling* (Eds. A.M. Aitkenhead and J.M. Stark), Lawrence Erlbaum Associates, London.

Sims, D., and Smithin, T. (1982). 'Voluntary operational research', *Journal of the Operational Research Society*, **33**, 21–28.

Smith, D.G. (1978). 'On the role of operational research', *Omega*, **6**, 208–209.

Spiegelberg, H. (1982). *The Phenomenological Movement*, 3rd edn, Martinus Nijhoff, The Hague.

Stansfield, R.G. (1981). 'Operational research and sociology: a case study of cross-fertilisations in the growth of useful science', *Science and Public Policy*, August, 262–279.

Thorndike, E.L. (1898). 'Animal intelligence: an experimental study of the associative processes in animals', *Psychological Monographs*, **2**, No.8.

Toulmin, S.E. (1958). *The Uses of Argument*, Cambridge University Press, Cambridge.

Treisman, A.M. (1960). 'Contextual cues in selective listening', *Quarterly Journal of Experimental Psychology*, **12**, 242–248.

van de Ven, A.H. (1974). *Group Decision-making Effectiveness*, Center for Business and Economic Research Press, Kent State University.

Vickers, G. (1970). *Freedom in a Rocking Boat*, Penguin Books, Harmondsworth, Middlesex.

Wason, P.C., and Johnson-Laird, P.N. (1968). *Thinking and Reasoning*, Penguin Books, Baltimore, Maryland.

Wason, P.C., and Johnson-Laird, P.N. (1972). *Psychology of Reasoning: structure and content*, Harvard University Press, Cambridge, Massachussetts.

Watts, A., with Al. Chung-Liang Huang (1979). *Tao: the watercourse way*, Penguin Books, Harmondsworth, Middlesex.

Weick, K.E. (1983). 'Managerial thought in the context of action', in *The Executive Mind* (Ed. S. Srivastva), Jossey-Bass, San Francisco, California.

Weiner, S.S. (1976). 'Participation, deadlines and choice', in *Ambiguity and Choice in Organisations* (Eds. J.G. March and J.P. Olsen), Universiteitsforlaget, Bergen.

Weiss, C.H. (1980). 'Knowledge creep and decision accretion', *Knowledge*, **1**, 381–404.

Wicklegren, W.A. (1974). *How to Solve Problems: elements of a theory of problems and problem-solving*, W.H. Freeman & Co., San Francisco, California.

Wiener, N. (1948). *Cybernetics*, MIT Press, Cambridge, Massachussetts.

Wilson, B. (1984). *Systems: concepts, methodologies and applications*, Wiley, Chichester, Sussex.

Woolley, R.N. and Pidd, M. (1981). 'Problem structuring: a literature review', *Journal of the Operational Research Society*, **32**, 197–206.

Permissions

I gratefully acknowledge the following for permission to reproduce extracts from the copyright material indicated:

Excerpts from *The Singing Detective* by Dennis Potter
  © 1986 by Dennis Potter
  reproduced by permission of Faber & Faber Ltd, London

Excerpt from *Invitation to Sociology: a humanistic perspective* by Peter L. Berger
  © 1963 by Peter L. Berger
  reproduced by permission of Penguin Books Ltd, London, and Doubleday, New York

Excerpt from *The After Dinner Game* by Malcolm Bradbury with Christopher Bigsby
  © 1982 by Malcolm Bradbury
  reproduced by permission of Century Hutchinson Publishing Group Ltd, London

Excerpt from *The History Man* by Malcolm Bradbury
  © 1975 by Malcolm Bradbury
  reproduced by permission of Martin Secker & Warburg, London

Excerpt from *Passages: predictable crises of adult life* by Gail Sheehy
  © 1974, 1976 by Gail Sheehy
  reproduced by permission of E. P. Dutton Inc, New York

Excerpt from *Winnie-the-Pooh* by A. A. Milne
  © 1926 by A. A. Milne
  reproduced by permission of Methuen Children's Books, London, and E. P. Dutton Inc, New York, and McClelland & Stewart Ltd, Toronto

Excerpt from *Encounters with the Past* by Peter Moss with Joe Keeton
  © 1979 by Peter Moss
  reproduced by permission of Sidgwick & Jackson Ltd, London

Excerpt from *A Private Function* by Alan Bennett
  © 1984 by Handmade Films (Productions) Ltd
  reproduced by permission of Faber & Faber Ltd, London

Author Index

Abelson, R. P., 86, 144, 263
Ackoff, R. L. 10, 79, 105, 117, 131, 137, 140,
    150, 155, 167, 168, 177, 202, 263
Amstutz, A. E., 71
Argyris, C., 134, 147, 150, 159, 199
Austin, N., 188

Bannister, D., 26, 30, 66, 171, 222, 223, 225
Barbour, G., 201
Bartlett, F. C., 66
Battersby, A., 233, 234
Baum, H. S., 114
de Beaugrande, R., 41
Beer, S., 169, 170, 188
Bell, C. H., 126, 134, 149, 168, 189
Bennett, P. G., 117–119, 131, 134, 158, 169,
    170, 173, 174, 194, 197, 202, 203, 207,
    208, 242, 244, 289, 291, 310
Bennis, W., 179
Berger, P., 19, 20, 61, 160
Berne, E., 25, 78, 91, 219, 221
Berresford, A., 37
von Bertalanffy, L. 169
Bignell, V., 48, 169
Bittlestone, R. G. A., 186, 188
Blake, R. R., 186, 187, 199, 218
Boden, M., 217
de Bono, E., 32, 62, 114, 226, 259
Boothroyd, H., 150, 168, 206
Bowen, K., 169, 198, 203, 227, 231, 310
Bradbury, M., 17
Broadbent, D. E., 29
Bryant, J. W., 118, 128, 149, 164, 170, 191,
    192, 197, 201–205, 217, 227, 229, 231,
    274, 291, 310
Buchanan, B. G., 59, 240, 241
Buzan, T., 205, 213

Carlisle, E., 132
Carter, C., 134, 136

Checkland, P. B., 13, 15, 16, 133, 136, 137,
    156, 164, 166, 169, 170, 190, 197, 201,
    204, 260, 261, 293, 294, 310
Churchman, C. W., 137, 168, 202
Christofides, N., 248
Cohen, G., 10
Cohen, M. D., 44, 91, 92, 123, 128, 231,
    232, 269
Conway, D., 106, 129, 281, 282
Cooper, C. L., 253, 255, 256
Cooper, R. D., 253, 255, 256
Corner, L. J., 297, 298
Coxon, A. M. P., 274, 276
Cropper, S. A., 117–119, 128, 134, 160, 161,
    164, 165, 170, 171, 191, 192, 197, 199,
    207, 274, 310
Cross, N., 204
Crowther, J. G., 156
Cruickshank, C., 38
Cursini, R. J., 186, 187, 199, 218
Cyert, R. M., 57

Dando, M. R., 37, 157, 158, 242, 244
Dearborn, D. C., 47, 235
Delbecq, A. L., 119, 180, 186, 190, 197, 204,
    216, 274
Dember, W. N., 30
deSanctis, G., 186, 188
Deutsch, D., 30
Deutsch, J. A., 30
Dewey, J., 168
Doerga, R. E., 37
Duncker, K., 66
Dusay, J. M., 221

Eaker, L. H., 253, 255, 256
Easterfield, T. E., 156
Eco, U., 249

Eden, C., 80, 97, 104, 105, 108, 112, 118, 120, 127, 133, 148, 164, 165, 169, 176, 179, 182, 186, 191, 192, 194, 197, 198, 201, 202, 204, 205, 214, 216, 222, 223, 265, 269, 271, 274, 277, 291, 294, 310
Eilon, S., 112, 113, 116, 117, 248
Emery, F., 10, 79, 168
Evans, E, P., 14

Feldman, J., 70
Filley, 184, 186, 187
Fisher, R., 119, 169, 216, 217
Flegg, D., 198, 225
Fortune, J., 169
Fransella, F., 26, 30, 66, 171, 222, 223, 225
Freire, P., 163
French, W. L., 126, 134, 149, 168, 189
Freud, S., 25
Friend, J. K., 109, 137, 141, 145, 164, 168, 177, 179–182, 184, 185, 190, 192, 194, 197, 198, 203–206, 247, 274, 283, 287, 304
Fry, R. E., 146, 147, 163, 164, 184, 295

Gallupe, B., 186, 188
Gill, J., 168
Goffmann, E., 18, 24, 88, 125, 126, 127, 131, 179, 194, 199, 217, 280
Gordon, W. J. J., 258, 259
Gould, P., 165
Greene, J., 69
Greeno, J. G., 66
Greenwald, A. G., 38
Gustafson, D. H., 119, 180, 186, 190, 197, 204, 216, 274

Hall, A. D., 168
Hall, P., 177, 182
Hawkes, T., 22
Hayes, J. R., 67
Hemmer, H. D., 129
Hemsley, V., 198, 225
Hickling, A., 109, 137, 141, 164, 168, 177, 179, 180–182, 184–186, 190, 192, 194, 197, 198, 203–206, 247, 274, 283, 287
Holsti, O., 89
Houlden, B., 129
Howard, N., 169, 202, 204, 205, 269, 271

Huxham, C. S., 118, 131, 164, 169, 170, 191, 192, 194, 197, 202, 203, 274, 289, 291, 310

Isenberg, D. J., 72

Jackson, M. C., 170, 206
James, M., 221, 238, 277, 292
James, W., 29
Janis, I. L., 43, 48, 56, 180
Jenkins, G. M., 169
Jessop, W. N., 168
Johnson, D. W., 218
Johnson, F. P., 218
Johnson-Laird, P. N., 68, 250
Jones, A. J., 244
Jones, C. L., 274, 276
Jones, G. C., 112, 117
Jones, J. E., 217
Jones, S., 104, 108, 127, 165, 169, 176, 191, 197, 198, 201, 204, 205, 214, 216, 222, 223, 265, 269, 277, 294, 310
Jongeward, D., 61, 221, 238, 248, 277, 292
Jung, C. G., 25

Kelly, G., 26, 27, 30, 33, 62, 69, 169, 222, 223, 265
Keys, P., 170, 206
Kohler, W., 66
Kolb, D. A., 43, 63, 218

Lardner, H., 156
Levi-Strauss, C., 20
Lewin, K., 15, 35
Luchins, A. S., 66
Luckman, J., 245, 247
Luckmann, T., 19, 20, 61, 160
Lynn, R., 30

McGuire, J., 198, 225
McIntyre, J., 218
Majone, G., 297, 298
Maltzman, I., 65
Mangham, I. L., 46, 47, 89, 94, 125, 143, 169, 173, 175, 177, 182, 200
Mann, J. R., 117
March, J. G., 44, 45, 47, 57, 58, 70, 91, 92, 123, 128, 137, 231, 232, 269
Martin, J., 134, 136

Mason, R. O., 13, 82, 120, 137, 164, 168, 170, 176, 178, 181, 182, 196, 202, 204, 205, 240, 263, 265, 267, 269
Massarik, F., 15, 162
Matthews, L. R., 170, 208, 310
Mayblin, B., 134, 136
Mayon-White, W. M., 166
Mayzner, M. S., 66
Mead, G. H., 88
Mercer, A., 131
Miles, I., 202
Minsky, M. L., 37
Minzberg, H., 35
Mitchell, C. R., 44
Mitchell, G. H., 105
Mitroff, I. I., 13, 82, 86, 120, 137, 164, 170, 176, 178, 181, 182, 196, 202, 204, 205, 240, 263, 265, 267, 269
Morgan, J. R., 247
Morgenstern, O., 169, 244, 269
Moss, P., 36
Mouton, J. S., 186, 187, 199, 218
Munday, M., 134, 136

von Neumann, J., 169, 244, 269
Newell, A., 9, 68, 252
Nisbett, R. E., 38
Norman, D. A., 263
Norman, M., 129
Norris, M. E., 168

Olsen, J. P., 44, 45, 47, 58, 70, 91, 92, 123, 128, 137, 231, 232, 269
Optner, S. L., 168, 194
Overington, M. A., 173, 175, 177, 182, 200

Parsons, T., 22
Pasmore, W. A., 146, 147, 163, 164, 184, 295
Pearson, F. S., 37
Perls, F. S., 253
Peters, G., 48
Pettigrew, A. M., 95, 281
Pfeiffer, J. W., 217
Phillips, L. D., 118, 164, 170, 179, 192, 201, 204, 205, 310
Pidd, M., 168, 170
Popper, K., 30, 32, 39, 81
Preedy, D. K., 186, 188

Priestley, P., 198, 225
Pym, C., 48

Quade, E. S., 297, 298

Radford, K. J., 169, 202
Reed, G., 38
Reitman, W. R., 9
Restle, F., 66
Rittel, H. W. J., 10, 81
Rivett, P., 117, 155, 156
Rosenhead, J., 131, 155, 160, 168, 202, 310
Ross, L., 38
Rubin, I. M., 218
Rumelhart, D. E., 263

Sanderson, M., 63
Sanoff, H., 201
Schank, R., 144
Schein, E. H., 107, 116, 131, 133
Schon, D. A., 150, 155, 156, 158, 198, 199
Shannon, C. E., 169
Sharp, R. G., 157
Shaw, J. C., 9
Shaw, M. E., 186, 187, 199, 218
Silverman, D., 20, 95
Simon, H. A., 9, 41, 47, 68, 235, 252
Sims, D., 104, 105, 108, 127, 164, 165, 169, 176, 191, 197, 198, 201, 204, 205, 214, 216, 269, 294
Smith, D. G., 117
Smithin, T., 127
Spiegelberg, H., 15
Stansfield, R. G., 156
Stringer, J., 168

Thorndike, E. L., 65
Thunhurst, C., 131, 155, 160
Toulmin, S. E., 204, 267, 269
Tresselt, M. E., 66
Treisman, A. M., 30

Ury, W., 119, 169, 216, 217

van de Ven, A. H., 119, 178, 180, 186, 190, 197, 204, 216, 274
Verhulst, M., 168
Vickers, G., 14, 168, 297

Warm, J. S., 30
Wason, P. C., 68, 250
Waters, J. A., 35
Watson-Gandy, C. D. T., 248
Watts, A., 237
Weaver, W., 169
Webber, M. M., 10, 81
Wedgewood-Oppenheim, F., 198
Weick, K. E., 57, 63, 72, 150

Weiner, S. S., 91
Weiss, C. H., 63
Welham, D., 198, 225
Whiddington, R., 156
White, R., 165
Wickelgren, W. A., 252
Wiener, N., 169
Wilson, B., 261
Woolley, R. N., 168, 170

Subject Index

Action research, 168
Agent for intervention, 141
AIDA (Analysis of Interconnected Decision
    Areas), 244–247, 270, 283–284
    see also Strategic Choice Approach
Altercasting, 88, 125
Anomalies, 35, 36, 70
Appreciative systems, 168
Argumentation analysis, 204, 267–269
Associationalism, 65, 66
    relevance to problem-solving, 71
Attention, 29, 41, 49
    channelling of, 47, 48, 75
    distribution of, 45

Behaviouralism, 70
Bracketing, 15
    double, 15, 162

Cast list, 227–229, 269, 305
Chronicler role, 113
Cognitive control, 14
Cognitive mapping, 214, 265–269, 292, 293,
    304, 305
    see also SODA
Commissioner of intervention, 136
Commitment package, 283
Complications, Two, 94
Computer problem-solving, 8
Concept map, 10, 11, 215, 293
Conceptual set, 45
Conceptualizer role, 118, 163
Confusion of problems, 41, 75, 283
Constituency of intervention, 137, 138
Consultant,
    choice of work, 129
    external, 106, 129, 131
    internal, 106, 129, 130, 281
    personal code, 131
    portfolio of work, 129, 131, 281, 282
    roles for, 115, 126, 107–120

Consultancy intervention, 134
    loss of control by client, 127
    parts in, 139–142
    researching the client/consultant, 127, 128
    roles around, 135–138
    terms of reference, 133, 134, 287, 288
Content in intervention, 174, 200–205
Context of intervention, 174
Coordinator for intervention, 141
Core group for intervention, 141, 176
Craftwork in intervention, 174
Critic role, 113

Decision-aiding rationales, 173, 174, 194
Decision analysis, 170
    decision conferencing design, 177, 182,
    201
    content management, 205
Design of intervention, 197, 207, 301, 302
Determiner of intervention, 136, 137
Dialectic, creation of, 200, 201
Dialectician role, 119, 120, 163, 165
Doctor role, 112, 113
Dress in intervention, 182, 183

Egostates, 25, 78, 219, 232
Environmental scanning, 35
Environments for decision support, 187–189,
    192
Executor of intervention, 137
Expert systems, 240, 241

Facilitator for intervention, 140
Facilitator role, 119, 163, 195, 199
Filtering, perceptual, 13, 38, 227
Finisher for intervention, 141
Flip charts, 189, 190
Fool role, 116, 117, 156
Frame analysis, 18

Frames in interpersonal interaction, 147, 163, 164
  frame-breaking, 147, 164
  frame-linking, 147, 163, 164
  frame-sharing, 147, 163
  single-frame and multiple-frame, 147
Frameworks of inquiry, 118, 159
  classification of, 170, 171, 173, 206, 298
  design of, 164
  ownership of, 164, 165
Framing,
  experiences, 35, 37, 45, 46, 217
  intervention processes, 163, 164
  substantive problem content, 163–165

Game theory, 169, 173, 241
Garbage can, 91, 123, 231, 269
Genie role, 110, 111
Gestalt, 66, 67
  relevance to problem-solving, 72
  therapy, 237, 238, 253
Group member for intervention, 140
Groupthink, 48, 180

Hermeneutic circle, 15
Hidden agenda, 291
Human problem-solving, 9
Hypergame, 169, 241–244
  intervention design, 194
  content management, 202, 203, 289–291
Hypermap, 227–231
  intervention design, 196
  process technology, 191
  content management, 202–205, 290, 291, 305, 306

Ideograph, 213, 309
Impresario for intervention, 141
Impression management, 125, 126, 179, 194, 195, 279, 280
Improvisation, 62, 63
Interpersonal interaction, 147, 163, 179, 295, 310
  frame typology, 147, 163, 164
Intervention,
  as development of relationship, 149, 177
  content management, 174, 200–205

context, 174
craftwork, 174
design, 197, 207, 301, 302
dress in, 182, 183
mood of, 146, 184
pace of, 145, 181, 195, 293, 294
parts in, 139–142
people involved, 174, 176–180, 182
personalities in, 178, 280, 281
process of, 174, 193–199
roles around, 135–138
roles for problem-helpers, 107–120
setting for, 174, 180–192
time management, 197, 198, 234, 295, 296
venue of, 183–188
Inventor role, 114
Invisible products, 198

Lateral thinking, 257–259
Learning, single-loop and double-loop, 150, 199
Learning cycle, breakpoints in, 70, 71
Lebenswelt, 15
  influence of, 30, 238
Linker for intervention, 141

Management sciences, 155
McFall's Mystical Monitor, 225
Metagame, 169
  content management, 202, 269–271
  process technology, 205
Monitor for intervention, 141
Mood of intervention, 146, 187
Mystic role, 110, 111

Nominal Group Technique (NGT), 180
  content management, 204, 215, 269, 274, 302, 303
  intervention design, 186, 197
  process technology, 190

Open canvass, 274, 302, 303
Operational Research (OR), 156–159, 167, 168
Organizational Development (OD), 164, 168, 169, 189
Orientation response, 30
Outcomes, overdetermined, 57
Ownership of problems, 11

Pace of intervention, 145, 181, 195, 293, 294
Parent, Adult, and Child egostates, 25, 78,
   219, 232
Patterning data, 32, 225, 226
People in intervention, 174, 176–180, 182
Perceptual exchange, 216, 281, 298
Perceptual filter, 29, 30
Perceptual unfreezing, 35
Personal construct psychology, 26, 27, 67,
   169, 222
   C—P—C cycle, 69
Personal construct system, 26, 27, 69, 70
   elaboration of, 27, 30, 31, 62, 69
   influence of, 59
   threatened, 33
Personal constructs, 26, 222, 223
Personal meaning 14, 15
Personality, 25
   tests, 222
   types, 32
Phenomenology, 15
PPS (Preliminary Problem Structuring)
   diagram, 289–291
Prescriptive fragments, 206
Prioritization of problems, 43, 44, 76,
   232–234
Problem, 8, 215, 235
   insoluble, 58
   label, 8, 13, 14, 31
   tame, 10, 81
   wicked, 10, 81–83
Problem diagnosis, 116
Problem dissolution, 79, 93
Problem-finishing, 64, 148, 149
Problem focus, 42
Problem-handling, as social process, 84, 91,
   94, 95, 271
Problem-helper, 103
   choice of, 105–107, 127, 128, 132, 273,
   274, 285–287
   roles for, 107–120, 277
Problem identification and organizational
   power, 160
Problem negotiation, 92, 93, 96, 97, 119, 161
Problem-owner, 11, 13
   plural, 160
   problem portfolio, 43, 79, 128
Problem presentation, 85, 165
   in groups, 95, 104

Problem resolution, 79
Problem solving, 8, 9, 79, 248–250
Problems,
   classification of, 104
   simultaneous, 40, 41, 75
Process in intervention, 174, 193–199

Reactive response, 56, 57, 59, 239
Reasoning, deductive, 64, 68
   relevance to problem-solving, 72
Reasoning, inductive, 64–67
Recorder for intervention, 140
Reflection-in-action, 198
Relationships in intervention, 149, 177
Repertory grid analysis, 222–223, 264,
   274–277, 299
Rich picture, 260–261
Robustness, 202, 285
Role focussing, 47, 77, 178, 235, 257
Role labelling, 218
Role playing,
   intervention design, 187, 202, 290, 291
Root definition, 293, 294, 308

SAST (Strategic Assumption Surfacing and
   Testing), 168
   content management, 204, 239, 240, 306,
   307
   intervention design, 176, 178, 181, 182,
   196, 202
Scientific analyst role, 112, 158
Scripts, 89
   negotiation of, 124, 125, 163
   organizational, 247, 248
   situational, 143, 144, 261–263, 291, 292
Set designer for intervention, 142
Setting an intervention, 174, 180–192
Shaper for intervention, 140
Simplification of problem situation, 60, 61
Simplifications, Two, 40, 94
Social interaction, 47
Social interactionism, 169, 174
Social meaning, 20, 21, 159, 160
SODA (Strategic Options Development and
   Analysis), 169
   content management, 204, 205, 292, 293,
   265–269, 304, 305
   intervention design, 176, 179, 182, 201
   process technology, 191, 197, 205

Soft Systems Methodology (SSM), 169, 197, 201
  content management, 260, 261, 293, 294, 308
  process technology, 190
Software for group decision support, 205
  CONAN, 205
  COPE, 205
Solution, extorting, 80, 81
Solution space, 68, 250, 251
Stakeholder, 263, 264
Stories,
  actors, 87
  plot, 89
  themes, 86
Storytelling, 86, 259, 260
  as a game, 91
Strategic Choice Approach, 168
  content management, 203–205, 244–247, 263–265, 283–287, 306
  intervention design, 177, 181, 182, 186, 194, 197, 198, 206
  process technology, 180, 190
Stress, 43, 76, 253–256
  effect of, 54–56, 60, 76
  handling, 77
Structuralism, 17
Superhero role, 107–109

Systems analysis, 168, 194
Systems methodology,
  'hard', 169, 259
  'soft', 169, 197, 201
Systems planning, 167, 168
  intervention design, 177, 202

Tame problems, 10, 81
Team manager for intervention, 141
Time management of intervention, 197, 198, 234, 295, 296
Transactional analysis, 25, 219, 220, 238, 277
Tunnel vision, 44

Validation, extorting, 38, 39
Venue of intervention, 183–188
Verstehen, 15
Viewpoint,
  relevance for problem definition, 11–13, 237

Weltanschauung, 16
  influence of, 37
  implications of varied, 159, 161
Wicked problems, 10, 81–83
Wise old man role, 109, 110
Working group for intervention, 139, 176
Wu-wei, 53, 237